## Ben Butler

MAJOR GENERAL BENJAMIN F. BUTLER
Engraved from photograph for *Rebellion Record*

# BEN BUTLER

## The South Called Him BEAST!

by
Hans L. Trefousse

TWAYNE PUBLISHERS
New York

Copyright 1957, by Hans L. Trefousse

MANUFACTURED IN THE UNITED STATES OF AMERICA BY
UNITED PRINTING SERVICES, INC.
NEW HAVEN, CONN.

To Arthur C. Cole

SCHOLAR — LIBERTARIAN — HUMAN BEING

# Preface

It was winter. A cold wave had plagued the nation for days, but in spite of the weather, dense crowds were making their way toward the Capitol in Washington, where a great drama was taking place: a final effort of the defeated Republican party to protect the civil liberties of Negroes in the South. Although the Democrats had captured the House in the previous fall, the Republicans would still be in control of Congress until March, 1875. They were determined to take advantage of their period of grace.

The spectators, however, were drawn by more than their interest in the problem of the Negro. They were coming to watch one of the most controversial men in Congress, General Benjamin F. Butler, Federal commander of New Orleans during the Civil War and radical of radicals since. Known for his biting sarcasm, his innumerable rows with opponents in and out of Congress, the bulky, balding representative, easily recognizable by the drooping eyelid which had disfigured him since birth, could always be relied upon to entertain the galleries. Now that he had become the chief champion of the Civil Rights Bill which Charles Sumner had advocated in vain until the day of his death, Butler was sure to put on a show.

The galleries were not disappointed. On February 3, 1875, the General took the floor. He was in no mood to spare Southern sensibilities. Vigorously condemning the prejudices of his opponents, he called for Federal protection of civil rights. "If bad men are in the majority," he shouted, if murderers, lawless men, banditti, if horse thieves are in the majority — men who ride at night in uniform and murder negroes — I think that if the State courts are powerless to punish, jurisdiction should be given to the Federal courts.

Southern members reacted quickly. Was the General implying that the majority of the inhabitants of Dixie were banditti? William McLean, a representative from Texas, demanded angrily. Butler replied he had meant no such thing, but the Texan exclaimed with a profane oath, "You are the only murderer I know of on this floor. You murdered a man in New Orleans."

Pandemonium broke out. The representatives excitedly left their seats, and while Butler and McLean angrily faced each other across the Speaker's desk, members rushed down the aisles to join the fray. Only with great difficulty was the Speaker able to restore order, and the General managed to have the last word. "If the gentleman said I was a murderer because I hanged a man at New Orleans," he retorted, "so far from taking offense, I glory in it, and the trouble has been that I did not hang more than I did." The galleries rang with applause. The crowd was seeing Ben in action, a sample of things to come.

The next day, Representative John Young Brown of Kentucky obtained the floor. Accusations had been levied against the South before, he said, charges which were totally unjust, only now again they had come from one

> who is outlawed in his own home from respectable society, whose name is synonymous with falsehood, who is the champion and has been on all occasions, of fraud; who is the apologist of thieves, who is such a prodigy of vice and meanness that to describe him would sicken the imagination and exhaust invective.

Violent as these attacks were, the Kentuckian had not finished. "In Scotland years ago," he continued,

> there was a man whose trade was murder, and he earned his livelihood by selling the bodies of his victims for gold. He

linked his name to the crime, and today it is known throughout the world as "Burking."

The Speaker interrupted. Was the gentleman referring to a member of the House? he inquired. Brown gave an equivocal answer. Then he concluded:

This man's name was linked to his crime, and today throughout the world [it] is known as "Burking." If I wished to describe all that was pusillanimous in war, inhuman in peace, forbidden in morals, and infamous in politics, I should call it Butlerizing.

By this time, members were on their feet. Supported by noisy demonstrations in the galleries, Republican congressmen violently demanded Brown's expulsion. Amid great excitement, the House debated the question, and although the Kentuckian was not expelled, he was severely censured by a vote of his colleagues. But nothing decisive was heard from Ben Butler. His reply was yet to come.

On the last day of the debates on the bill, the galleries were again crowded to overflowing. The spectators were waiting for Butler's reply, and they did not have to wait long. At 12 o'clock, he took the floor for a final appeal for the measure. Once again he pleaded for equal civil rights for all citizens as an indispensable prerequisite for democracy. Then he turned upon his foes. "What are the objections made to this bill?" he asked, proceeding to answer his own question.

The first objection stated on the other side is that this bill establishes social equality. By no means, by no means. . . . I am inclined to think that the only equality the blacks ever have in the South is social equality; for I understand the highest exhibition of social equality is communication between the sexes. . .

The Southerners were outraged. They protested instantly, but Butler refused to yield. He still had a score to settle with John Young Brown, and without further ado, he went on to contrast his antagonist with the hero of Harper's Ferry. Charles Sumner, he said, was not the real father of the Civil Rights Bill. Its originator was another, a sainted, truthful martyr,

> now in the realms of bliss into which no liar shall ever go. His name was John Brown the elder, not the younger by that name.

It was a telling blow, a deliberately planned setting for the attack which followed. Butler continued:

> I dare not trust myself to be a eulogist of that John Brown, the younger of that name. Therefore I pray the clerk to read it from the report of the Committee on Elections of this House, where it is set down in language that must be parliamentary, however severe.

Attempts of the opposition to prevent the reading of the document were in vain, for Butler could not be stopped. The report was read, and it showed that, in 1861, John Young Brown had not only been a violent secessionist, but that he had made statements calling for the immediate assassination of all volunteers for Lincoln's army. Such were the sentiments of the gentleman from Kentucky, Butler shouted, sentiments which showed conclusively that there were murderers in the South. He deemed the report proof positive that the Negro needed protection. Stormy applause came from the Republican benches and the galleries, and the Civil Rights Bill was passed that afternoon. Once again Ben Butler had repaid his enemies in kind; once again he had lived up to his reputation. No wonder visitors to the Capitol were in the habit of asking to have him pointed out.

Well might they ask. Beast, assassin, thief, he was to his enemies; man of action, courageous champion of the poor and the oppressed, he seemed to his friends. But whatever people's attitude toward Butler, they were never bored by him. They could not fail to look with amazement at a man who professed his preference for Jefferson Davis as President of the United States in 1860 only to be outlawed by that same Jefferson Davis in 1862; an apologist for slavery in 1860 who freed runaways by declaring them contraband in 1861; a lawyer turned general who proposed to blow up fortifications by means of boats filled with powder. The man who knew how to humble the spirited Confederate ladies of New Orleans — he threatened to treat them as common prostitutes — the General who dared execute a "rebel" for tearing down the American flag, the military leader who was one of the first to enlist Negro soldiers during the Civil War, the Congressman who became chief advocate of the impeachment of Andrew Johnson, such a figure was never dull. Alternately delighting and disgusting the country by his antics, his feuds, his rows, his clever explanations of all irregularities charged to him, Butler remained in the public limelight throughout his long life. That he finally fulfilled his ambition to become Governor of Massachusetts only to be defeated after one sensational term, that he made one final attempt at the Presidency as the candidate of a hopeless minority, was in perfect keeping with his stormy career. Although his enemies accused him of demagoguery, it was because of his flair for publicity that he was able to fight for reform and to sustain the causes of intrinsic merit which he often advocated. He entertained the country. He added color to its history. He deserves to be remembered.

# Acknowledgments

My thanks are due in the first place to my colleagues, Professors Arthur C. Cole and Meta E. Schutz. They read the entire manuscript and made many valuable suggestions. I should also like to express my gratitude to Professor David Donald of Columbia University. In spite of his busy schedule, he went over the manuscript and offered much constructive criticism. Many friends were kind enough to allow me to use private letters and manuscripts, among them Professor Henry F. Graf of Columbia University, Professor Robert Ernst of Adelphi College, and Dr. Murray Horowitz of Brooklyn College. The librarians and staff of the Manuscript Division of the Library of Congress, the American History, Genealogy, Manuscript, and Microfilm Divisions of the New York Public Library, the Manuscript Divisions of Harvard University and the University of Chicago, the New York Historical Society, the Massachusetts Historical Society, the Lowell Public Library, and the Library of Brooklyn College, and Miss Jacqueline Bregoff were most helpful. Last but not least I should like to express my appreciation to Mrs. Jessie Ames Marshall, General Butler's granddaughter, whose readiness to help deserves high praise.

# Contents

| Chapter | | Page |
|---|---|---|
| | Preface | 7 |
| 1. | Youth | 17 |
| 2. | Young Lowell Lawyer | 25 |
| 3. | Coalitionist | 34 |
| 4. | A Hunker's Tribulations | 42 |
| 5. | The Great Decision | 52 |
| 6. | Washington and Baltimore | 65 |
| 7. | Fickle Fortunes of War | 77 |
| 8. | Preparing for the Great Expedition | 88 |
| 9. | Off for the Father of Waters | 98 |
| 10. | "Picayune Butler's Come to Town" | 107 |
| 11. | "Butler Must Go" | 122 |
| 12. | From the Mississippi to the James | 135 |
| 13. | "Bottled Up" | 146 |
| 14. | The Election of 1864 | 158 |
| 15. | The Downfall of a Political General | 166 |
| 16. | Return to Active Politics | 178 |
| 17. | Radical of Radicals | 189 |
| 18. | Grant's Lieutenant | 205 |
| 19. | *Enfant Terrible* of the Republican Party | 217 |
| 20. | Return to the Democrats | 234 |
| 21. | Climax and Anticlimax | 244 |
| | Notes | 257 |
| | Bibliography | 326 |
| | Index | 345 |

Table of Illustrations (over)

# List of Illustrations

Frontispiece   Major General Benjamin F. Butler.

(1) Thomas Nast castigates *Widow Butler* in 1876, Daily *Graphic*, September 5, 1876.

(2) Impeachment of Johnson—Butler addressing the Senate.

(3) Anti-Butler cartoon in 1884, New York Evening *Telegram*, October 18, 1884.

(4) Richmond—Petersburg area in 1864.

(5) The Federal Fleet Before New Orleans in 1862.

(6) Origin of the Term *Contraband*.

(7) Approaches to New Orleans.

(8) Benjamin F. Butler, politician.

CHAPTER ONE

# Youth

The winter of 1818-1819 was a very difficult period for Charlotte Ellison Butler. Her husband, John, was away privateering for some fledgling Latin American republic, and she had just given birth to a sickly, unattractive little boy whom she named Benjamin Franklin.[1] A severe panic had hit the country, and while the farmers in Deerfield, New Hampshire, were complaining about the hard times, she received news of John's death. Yellow fever had carried him away in the Caribbean, although nasty neighbors spread the rumor that he had been hanged for piracy.[2] It was a blow which was hard to bear; yet Charlotte was a devout woman. Her Calvinist rigidity enabled her to meet adversity and slander. She boarded her oldest boy, Andrew Jackson, with a relative; her daughter and the baby she took with her to her husband's family's farm in nearby Nottingham.[3]

The Butlers were strict Irish Presbyterians who had come from Woodbury, Connecticut. Zephaniah, Benjamin's grandfather, was a man of great intellect who had settled in Nottingham in 1756, where he taught school for many years. "The schoolmaster," as he was known locally, served with General Wolfe at Quebec and surprised his neighbors by marrying Abigail Cilley, a member of one of New Hampshire's most prominent families.[4] Abigail was a general's daughter, and never once did she permit anyone to forget it. Their son John, a captain of Dragoons in the War of 1812, had carried dispatches for Andrew Jackson at New Orleans. He eventually became a seaman, serving sometimes as a supercargo, sometimes as a privateer. Charlotte Ellison was his second wife;

Scots-Irish like John, she could boast of a grandfather who had fought at the Battle of the Boyne.[5]

Little Ben was a sickly, puny child, his face marred by a drooping eyelid and a severe case of strabism. But he had a good memory, a priceless gift in an age when education consisted of endless learning by rote. He had little trouble with his studies at the village schools of Deerfield and Nottingham. Reading came to him easily, so much so that he soon preferred books to his chores. His mother frowned upon secular literature, but in return for his promise to memorize passages in the New Testament, she helped him with his *Robinson Crusoe*. He studied and made progress, impressing his teachers and family so favorably that they decided to send him to Exeter Academy to prepare for college.[6]

At the age of nine, Ben did not find it easy to be away from home. He was terribly disappointed when other boys, all older, would not let him join "Golden Branch," the popular school society. He managed to learn some Latin and the rudiments of Greek, but his stay at the Academy was anything but pleasant.[7] Fortunately, it did not last long. After one term, his mother moved to Lowell to preside over a boardinghouse. Ben left to join her, and early one spring afternoon in 1828, with a fox skin cap drawn tightly over his ears, linsey-woolsey jacket tightly buttoned, he trudged through the melting snow along the road from New Hampshire to his new home.[8]

Lowell, where the country-born and bred Ben found himself, was not an ordinary city. Not yet five years old, it was rapidly becoming the showplace of America's rising industrialism. The mills dominated it completely, especially the Merrimack Manufacturing Company which was housed in a large building at the water's edge with a typically New England spire as its ornament. Kirk Boott, its President, ruled mill and town with an iron hand,[9] supervising not only his operatives' employment, but also their morals. Every night by ten o'clock sharp the factory girls had to be in the boardinghouses — establishments supervised by respectable matrons who were supposed to take an interest in their charges.[10] Yet in spite of restrictions, in spite of long hours, the girls seemed happy. Generally daughters of neighborhood farmers, they regarded their employment as a temporary interlude before marriage. To the amazement of European visitors who came from afar to see this industrial Mecca, the girls played the piano, attended lectures, and contributed to their own literary magazine.[11] They were clean and prim, and, as a matter of fact, the entire city of Lowell, because of its plentiful supply of water power, looked neat, an unusual thing for a factory town.[12]

Charlotte Butler's boardinghouse was located near the First Calvinist Baptist Church, a great convenience for such a devout woman. Her job was not easy, but she handled it efficiently, and her industry and dignity earned her the esteem of her neighbors.[13]

Little Ben found his new home most interesting. The girls who boarded there were friendly, and they had fascinating stories to tell. He became so familiar with factory workers' problems that he gained a sympathy for the laborer which stayed with him throughout his life. However, there were other boarders, not as well-behaved as the operatives. The Reverend Enoch W. Freeman, pastor of the First Baptist Church, who had scandalized the town by marrying a divorced woman, lived in the Butlers' house with his wife for a while. Tongues wagged; he left town, and eventually his wife was accused of murdering him. Young Ben had a lot to think about.[14]

The thriving new city growing up all around him was even more interesting than his home. He found Lowell fascinating, as he wandered along its ever more complex canal system, marveled at the complicated locks, and watched new mills going up. Steamships abounded on the river and, by 1835, a new railroad to Boston had been built. It was a stimulating environment for an eager young boy.[15]

Ben's formal education was not neglected. At first, he studied Latin at home, amusing neighboring lawyers by scanning Virgil aloud,[16] but before long, he was attending regular classes at the Edson School, conducted by one Joshua Merrill, known as a "faithful knight of the birch."[17] By 1831, the Lowell High School had opened its doors. It was presided over by Thomas N. Clark, later Episcopal Bishop of Rhode Island, and could boast of scholars who would one day make a name for themselves. Young Gustavus Vasa Fox would rise to become Lincoln's Assistant Secretary of the Navy; George Balcolm and Ezekiel A. Straw would eventually play important roles in the political and economic life of New Hampshire; James C. Ayer was to become a physician of wealth and renown.[18] Last but not least, there was young Ben Butler, already a good speaker and writer of themes on topics of the day.[19]

Politics interested Butler even then. He attended lyceum lectures,[20] discussed current events with his chums,[21] and listened attentively to conversations in his home. What he heard there was not orthodox in staid Whig Lowell. The elder Butler had been a passionate admirer of Andrew Jackson, an enthusiasm he had transmitted to his family. When the old hero, now President, came to Lowell in 1833, it was with great pride that the Butlers watched him review the factory girls, four abreast, marching by in spotless white dresses.[22] Jacksonian Democracy was the Butlers' creed and passionate hatred of Whigs, aristocrats, and all things English its natural supplement. Young Ben had often listened to his grandmother's stories of American heroism and British villainy — stories which had frequently been repeated by battle-scarred veterans.[23] Ben eagerly imbibed their prejudices, and he remained an Anglophobe for the rest of his life.

However, he was young, and Ben thought of other things besides politics. He often whiled away the evening with his friend George Balcolm or went calling on the fair Fisher twins, daughters of a machinist at Massic Falls.[24] Nor did he neglect his reading, a pastime made easier by a part-time job at the Franklin Book Store.[25]

Ben had a good youth, and by 1834, he was ready for college. West Point was his first choice, but it was difficult to procure an appointment to the Academy. The Baptist minister did not cherish the Army's alleged free thinking, so he suggested that Ben go to Waterville College. Since Charlotte hoped that her son might become a minister, she consented.[26] For two years more, however, Ben tried to enter the military academy. He obtained letters of recommendation,[27] and his mother even approached the powerful Isaac Hill, Jackson's New Hampshire lieutenant, but her efforts were to no avail. Hill referred her to Caleb Cushing, then Congressman from Massachusetts, and Cushing wrote that he could not help. People with influence had received the Massachusetts appointments, he said.[28] Ben must have been deeply disappointed for not only did he conceive a violent hatred for West Point, but his Democratic prejudices against the leaders of society became more pronounced. Lacking family connections himself, he developed an increasing dislike for men who were well-established, a bias which stayed with him for life.

The College at Waterville, not yet called Colby, was a Calvinist institution of the most rigid type. Compulsory daily prayers at daybreak, mandatory church attendance twice every Sunday, orthodox sermons and rigid discipline were expected to inculcate Christian piety. Yet the institution was far from stagnant. In 1834, a new President, the Reverend Rufus Babcock, Jr., managed to attract over one hundred students whose tuition fees enabled him to clear the college from debt, and, two years later, to erect a large brick building. At the same time, the library was enriched by a gift of fifteen hundred books, and the President was able to hand over a flourishing school to his successor.[29]

Ben did not find the atmosphere at Waterville to his liking. He hated the excessive emphasis on religion, he detested the monetary fines and deductions from academic standing exacted for failure to attend chapel, and he particularly disliked the interminable sermons, which, though preached by the Reverend Samuel F. Smith, author of "My Country, 'Tis of Thee," seemed unreasonable to young Ben. Years later, Butler still remembered with considerable pride the manner in which he had petitioned the President to excuse him from attending chapel. His teachers, he pointed out in his letter to the school authorities, had taught him that according to Calvin's dread decree, the number of the elect was extremely small, and surely he was not among them. Consequently, he reasoned, further attendance at chapel would tend to increase the torments of hell fire in store for him, since the sermons would only make him more familiar with the ways of grace without enabling him to alter his sad fate. Needless to say, Ben was almost expelled for this impudence. His academic standing suffered, and he gave up his plans for the ministry.[30]

Laboratory and library were much more to his taste. Chemistry and physics fascinated him. He relished the opportunity to report the results of scientific experiments to his fellow boarders at Mrs. Eaton's boardinghouse, much to the disgust of the squeamish who did not enjoy talk of "sulphurated hydrogen and anatomy mixed with plum pudding."[31] On current issues, he would argue passionately with fellow members of the college literary society, taking firm stands on educational and religious matters, and he could always be counted on fervently to condemn the wicked abolitionists.[32] Even as a youth, Ben enjoyed a row.

In one respect, Waterville College was up to date. Realizing the value of gainful employment, the administration established a manual labor department as early as 1831 to enable the boys to earn part of their expenses by carpentry. Moreover, winter vacations were arranged to coincide with the local grammar school term, and many a college student doubled as schoolmaster in town. Butler took advantage of both of these opportunities.[33]

Graduation was scheduled for August 8, 1838. Released from chapel attendance at long last, Ben appeared, clad in a suit so extravagant as to cause comment. He complained once more about the injustice of deducting from his standing for his delinquencies, accepted his diploma, and took his leave,[34] a saucy, cross-eyed youth of barely twenty, with a strongly receding forehead and shock of reddish hair.[35]

When he came home, his mother was appalled by his appearance. He was so thin that she feared for his health. The foolish boy had gone swimming in the Kennebec River immediately after the spring thaw and had contracted a severe cold that caused him to cough constantly. Since the family physician suggested a sea voyage to allow him to recuperate, Ben was sent to Labrador, on a fishing boat which belonged to a friend of his father. His health improved, and he learned many things about the sea on that trip which made him a lifelong sailing enthusiast.[36]

Having given up all plans for the ministry, Ben's first task on returning from Labrador was to decide on a career. The decision was not difficult to make. During his last two years at college, he had had occasion to see New England's most celebrated trial lawyer, Jeremiah Mason, conduct a case. A crusty old Federalist who had been in the United States Senate during the War of 1812, Mason had a courtroom demeanor which was arresting. Bitter wit and sarcasm characterized his brilliant cross-examinations which were conducted in a deliberately affected Yankee twang for the

benefit of local juries. Many times he had matched wits with
Daniel Webster, and he had won most of his cases. Greatly impressed by Mason who was much more effective than the ministers
he had heard at school, Ben decided to become a lawyer.[37]

The study of law was not very onerous in the 1830's. After
a young man had clerked in an attorney's office for three years,
his employer could certify to his fitness. Ben became a clerk in
the law offices of William Smith, Esquire, a Lowell attorney who
had a large library and often doubled as a real estate agent. Con-
temptuous even then of society's opinion of him, Ben stayed with
Smith, where he absorbed Blackstone, Kent, the Constitution, and
the usual treatises on pleading. In addition, he familiarized himself with real estate by serving processes on his employer's default-
ing tenants.[38] Attending the courts faithfully to observe some of
the practical aspects of the law, Ben had the good fortune to obtain
help from Judge Joseph Locke, the distinguished presiding officer
of the Lowell Police Court. The Judge had held high positions in
the state government and took a fatherly interest in young law
students.[39] As usual, Ben learned rapidly, and it was not long
before he came to love his new profession.

It was only natural that a young man in the late 1830's would
find it hard to resist the lure of the Great West. Both his brother
Andrew Jackson and his sister Charlotte had left New England,
and for a time, Ben seriously considered joining "Jackson" in
Missouri. But he decided to stay. Whether this decision was due
to concern for his mother, as he claimed in later years,[40] or whether
the thriving industrial community of Lowell really suited him,
cannot be ascertained. Yet once having cast his lot in Lowell, he
made it his permanent home. He soon found a teaching position
across the river in Dracut, and although his students were an
unruly lot, the future taskmaster of New Orleans knew how to
handle them. Moreover, he did not disdain his small teaching
salary.[41]

Dracut, however, had attractions more alluring than a poorly
paid teaching job. It was the home of Dr. Israel Hildreth, a
physician of considerable means and of far-flung intellectual interests,[42] whose daughter Sarah was as fascinating as she was

pretty. When her brother Fisher[43] introduced Ben to her, the fledgling lawyer looked no further. Sarah was the girl for him.

Miss Hildreth was a girl of considerable beauty with long braids that fell over her shoulders. From her father, she had inherited a love for drama, especially Shakespeare, whose plays she declaimed with great gusto. Too spirited to let herself be restricted by convention, she had become an actress and appeared with some success in various cities. She was romantic to the core — very different from Ben — but eventually she reciprocated his affections.[44] Ben was head over heels in love; the young actress was much more fascinating than his friend Eliza Dexter whose rigid Calvinism made him fear that she would force him to attend evening conference meetings if he married her.[45] Since Sarah insisted that he finish his education before getting married, he waited until he had established himself. Then he went to Cincinnati, where Sarah was appearing on the stage, and they announced their engagement.[46] Back home in Lowell, Dr. Theodore Edson, the city's distinguished Episcopal minister, married them one day in May, 1844, at St. Anne's Church.[47] Ben had found his helpmate for life. Even his enemies conceded that his domestic life was happy.[48]

Neither courtship nor teaching hindered Ben's law studies. Even before he had finished the customary three years' apprenticeship, his employer agreed to certify to his readiness for admission to the bar. Ben impressed Charles Warren, Judge of the Court of Common Pleas, by a correct analysis of the points at issue in a difficult case then pending, and so, on September 3, 1840, young Ben Butler was admitted to the bar.[49] A new lawyer had made his appearance in Lowell.

CHAPTER TWO

# Young Lowell Lawyer

For a young lawyer just starting to practice, Lowell offered great opportunities. With a population of almost thirty thousand in the 1840's, the town was growing rapidly. It was still dominated by the mills which employed one third of the inhabitants and owned more than five hundred houses.[1] But there was money to be made in Lowell, independently of the large corporations, and Ben was determined to be rich.

He lost no time in establishing himself. Not too particular about the type of case he accepted, he soon made a name for himself in the criminal law, where he found he could make full use of his dramatic talents. In the manner of his model, Jeremiah Mason, Ben relied on audacity almost as much as on solid law. Quick to detect technical flaws in an indictment, he knew how to get a respite for a counterfeiter because no venue had been laid in the warrant,[2] or how to get an acquittal for a burglar because the key he had stolen was part of the real, not the personal, property of the victim.[3] People said he was a sharp practitioner,[4] but he did not mind. The criminal law entails contact with unsavory characters; thieves need counsel, and Butler learned at an early age that an attorney could profit from crime without being involved in it. To Ben, his practice was a business like any other, and if the neighbors disapproved — well, he always enjoyed shocking people.

Nonetheless, his critics were sometimes irritating. In the summer of 1842, when a favorable verdict which Ben had obtained was reported in Lowell's Whig *Courier* in unflattering terms, the fiery young attorney was outraged. He stormed into the offices of the offending journal, and demanded to see the editor, William Schouler, who later became the state's adjutant general. Schouler's young assistant, William S. Robinson, soon to become famous under the pen name of "Warrington," was there, too. In the brief scuffle that ensued, Robinson lost his glasses, Ben was thrown out of the building,[5] and a lasting enmity resulted between the contestants. But the incident failed to discourage young Butler.

Uproar and disorder were his stock in trade. Muster day was always an occasion of considerable hilarity in Lowell, with many a participant ending up in jail for violation of the liquor law. One such was Daniel Gould who was brought before Judge Locke in 1845. Butler demanded his discharge on the ground that the indictment did not mention the county. When the Judge wanted to wait until a new warrant could be drawn up, Ben protested the delay as "a most miserable quibble." The marshal offered to produce a new warrant; Butler threatened to knock him down, and the heated exchange that followed was not very dignified. In the end, the defendent was fined eight dollars, but Butler's name had appeared prominently in the newspapers.[6] Such advertising was not to be disdained.

The uproar in Judge Locke's court was repeated two years later in that of his successor, Nathan Crosby. After a particularly heated argument in September, 1847, the Judge was about to adjourn court. Butler objected violently. "Is the court adjourned, is the court adjourned?" he shouted, and, turning to Crosby, added, "I'll let you know what I want when you come down from that bench, damn you. . ." The Judge had Ben arrested for contempt, and he was not released until he solemnly asserted that only zeal for his client had motivated him, no insult having been intended.[7]

Saucy behavior and notoriety alone of course could not assure a successful practice. Ben had always had a flair for science; the law gave him an opportunity to turn this interest to good use. He handled many patent suits and often accepted technical cases. Because of his phenomenal memory, he was able to surprise the experts with his extensive knowledge of their special fields, whether medicine, or navigation, or general science, although it is by no means certain that he did anything more than commit whole passages of textbooks to memory in order to impress juries.[8] He also familiarized himself with the new bankruptcy laws and advertised as a specialist in bankruptcy cases.[9]

Although his enemies did not consider him a good or even effective lawyer,[10] his practice flourished. By 1842, he had become a justice of the peace, and before long, he was admitted to the bar of the higher courts.[11] He went into partnership with A. W. Farr, lawyer, printer, and active Democrat, and although the association did not last long, an ever-increasing number of clients came to the offices of Butler & Farr in the Wyman Building.[12]

Many of the petty cases in Lowell involved the factory girls' wages. Since the corporations paid their employees once a month, workers who left their jobs in the interval had considerable trouble collecting their pay. Butler had an arrangement with the mills whereby he would advance the money to his clients and settle with the companies afterward. One day a middle-aged Yankee spinster indignantly told him that she had to return to Vermont to take care of her sick mother. The company owed her money, and she insisted that Butler bring suit. Despite efforts to dissuade her, she persisted. Let him attach the great wheel to satisfy her claim! Ben laughed. He knew that the woman was suggesting a legal impossibility, but he thought the idea amusing and told her to come back. He obtained the money in the usual way, to the delight of the spinster, who was convinced that he had followed her advice. The story spread, and Ben did little to counteract the popular anecdote.[13]

Butler's legal practice accounted for only part of his income. Real estate, business ventures, the Lowell Museum and theater, all contributed to his wealth, and by 1853, he had a bank account of $140,002.57[14] — a tidy sum in those days. Although it is probable that he did not acquire his wealth entirely through his own efforts, he liked people to believe that he had risen from poverty. It is true that his mother had had to work hard in the boardinghouse and was certainly not a woman of great means, but she had been able to send him to Exeter and Waterville. Moreover, the Hildreths were quite wealthy,[15] and Sarah had undoubtedly brought a dowry with her. At any rate, the Butlers prospered and acquired one of the most beautiful mansions in town.[16] To this day their villa, Belvedere, stands on an eminence overlooking a bend in the river.

With an office in downtown Lowell, soon to be supplemented by another in Boston, and a practice which carried him throughout the northeastern states, Ben had little time for relaxation. While still a law student, he had joined the Lowell City Guard, and the annual encampments of his regiment became his vacation. With his love of military life, his abilities and his influence, he advanced rapidly. By 1850, he was a full colonel.[17] Whether the Massachusetts militia received valuable training is doubtful, but it constituted a nucleus for an emergency.

While her husband was making a name for himself in his profession, Sarah was busy too. She no longer appeared on the stage, but now she had to care for a family. Paul, the oldest, was born in June, 1845. Not quite two years later, Blanche, who later became a girl of great beauty, arrived. Paul died in 1850, but by 1852, there was another little Paul, followed by Benjamin Israel two years later. These three children survived and became their parents' pride and joy.[18] The family meant a great deal to Ben — not only his own children, but his nephews, nieces, brothers, and sisters. There were many of these, and his family obligations were to cause him much trouble in later years.

While the Butlers were prospering, great changes were taking place in Lowell. At the mills, production increased rapidly, but wages did not keep pace with prices. The operatives' standard of living remained low. Newer, more intricate machinery tended to put a greater strain on the workers, especially as they still averaged more than twelve hours of labor a day.[19] Nor was it easy to obtain redress; the companies kept black lists, and unionization, not to mention striking, was dangerous.[20] Effective labor legislation was practically non-existent. It was not until 1842 that Chief Justice Shaw exempted unions from conspiracy laws,[21] and not until that same year did the legislature limit to ten the number of hours children under twelve could work each day.[22] The Lowell idyll was drawing to a close. Irish immigrants were replacing the literary, prim Yankee farm girls.[23] Huddled together in their miserable huts on the "Acre," as Lowell's shanty town was called, the newcomers could not be expected to conform to the strict regulations of the boardinghouses. Before Ben had turned thirty, the former industrial showplace of the nation had become another dirty manufacturing town.

Reform was a crying necessity, but as the mill owners were almost exclusively Whigs, and the voting not by secret ballot, they usually succeeded in electing their candidates for office. To them, the protective tariff was a cure for all ills, and many of their employees believed them.[24] What was true of Lowell was also generally true of the rest of the state. Long loyal to the Federalists, Massachusetts naturally turned to John Quincy Adams and Henry Clay after the demise of the old party. After 1833, the Bay State became a stronghold of the Whigs.

Under such circumstances, advocates of reform often turned to the Democrats. The leaders of the Democratic party did not differ markedly from their rivals — the Rantouls, the Bancrofts, the Henshaws, and the Mortons were as comfortably situated as the Adamses, the Hoars, and the Lawrences. Yet they generally tried to appeal to a different class of citizen. Underprivileged city folk, farmers distrustful of the commercial oligarchy of Boston, Irish immigrants suspicious of nativism, could frequently be interested in the doctrines of Andrew Jackson, and as the Whigs were unable to elect more than two presidents within the quarter century of their existence, the Democrats were often in a position to reward the faithful with Federal patronage.[25] This circumstance kept many of them from becoming too radical — the conservative Democrats were distrustful of local issues and were not averse to an alliance with Southern slave holders — but as the Whigs were committed to the policies of the mill owners, the radical wing of the opposition — the loco-focos — were in a good position to take up the causes of the employees.[26]

It was natural that a dramatic young lawyer like Butler would gravitate into politics. He was ambitious, and in politics his talents would be as valuable as they were in criminal law. Nor was there any question where his political sympathies lay. The Whigs, to him, represented the hated aristocracy. Not only his own family, but his wife's, too, were Democratic.[27] For the principles of Old Hickory he would take the field, and as early as 1840 he took part in the presidential campaign. He stumped vigorously for Martin Van Buren,[28] although he could not overcome the bunkum and the liberal potions of hard cider doled out from the Whigs' log cabin headquarters. Amid shouts of "Tippecanoe and Tyler too" the Whigs, with General Harrison at the helm, rode to victory. "Van," they asserted, was "a used up man."

The Democrats thought otherwise. They were sure the defeated President would make a come-back, and there was much work for the loyal party workers. Ben had had his first taste of campaigning, and found that he liked its rough-and-tumble. Although he maintained in his autobiography that he withdrew temporarily from politics after 1840,[29] the records of the time fail to support his recollections. In February, 1841, he was a delegate to the Democratic county convention.[30] One month later, he lent his influence and ability to the establishment of a new radical newspaper, the *Vox Populi*.[31] That journal boasted that it was "edited by the people;"[32] yet the people in this case were Democrats who disliked the Reverend Eliphalet Case, long a power in their party and editor of the Lowell *Advertiser*.[33] With unceasing efforts and racy articles, the *Vox* attacked the *Advertiser*, the Whigs, and the deplorable condition of the workers.[34] No matter how desperately the rival sheet tried to ridicule what it called "a channel of low black-guardism and childish vulgarity,"[35] the *Vox* continued to be printed — a journal of hard-hitting vigor, though of somewhat dubious reputation.[36] Ben did not stay with it long,[37] but the first few numbers bear the unmistakable imprint of his style.

For the next twenty years, he lent his talents to his party. In campaign after campaign he delivered stump speeches and represented his district in one convention after another. He knew well how to berate the Whigs at election time, how to call convincingly for the secret ballot, and how to agitate effectively for shorter hours. Not even the Whig tariff frightened him. A boon for the rich, but a curse for the poor, he called it.[38] He also flattered the Catholics,[39] and even though a ten-hour day petition presented to the legislature by the Democrats in 1842 did not get very far,[40] he became popular with Lowell's working population.[41] To his enemies, his advocacy of measures to relieve labor seemed merely the hypocrisy of a self-seeking demagogue. However, they forgot that he was animated by a cordial dislike for the leaders of New

England society quite as much as by mercenary motives. Nor had he forgotten his mother's boarders.

As Martin Van Buren could not obtain renomination in 1844, Butler supported James K. Polk, his party's dark horse standard bearer. With irony and sarcasm he attacked Henry Clay, and his orations were generally received with hearty cheers by the audience.[42] While it is true that Massachusetts returned the customary Whig majorities, Polk was elected and Butler was able to enjoy the good will of a friendly administration in Washington. He had made the acquaintance of Josiah G. Abbott, lifelong Democrat and distinguished leader of the Massachusetts bar,[43] and when he came to the national capital in the summer of 1845, he carried with him Abbott's letter of introduction to George Bancroft, the historian who was then serving as Secretary of the Navy. Abbott asked the Secretary to introduce Butler to the President and to extend every facility to him in Washington, because, he wrote,

> Mr. Butler is a member of the legal profession and has one of the most extensive practices in the city. As a Democrat, he has always been exceedingly active and has done good service to the party.[44]

Bancroft complied, and later that year, the Lowell attorney was admitted to the bar of the Supreme Court.[45]

At home things also looked well. Butler might not yet be able to secure the postmastership for his faction in Lowell,[46] but his brother-in-law, Fisher Hildreth, had acquired the *Advertiser* and publicity was assured.[47] Ben now occupied a position of prominence in the city, as a lawyer, as a man of affairs, and as a politician.

However there were troubles ahead. The Democrats of Massachusetts were running into serious difficulty. In a state where many citizens disliked what they called the expansionist policies of the slavocracy, the war with Mexico was not popular. Even Ben's own mother had no use for the conflict,[48] and no matter how much he might sound the tocsin of patriotism, no matter how often he might charge his opponents with lack of national feeling, he could not convince his fellow citizens to vote for his good friend Caleb Cushing, a hero of the Democratic party and candidate for governor.⁴⁹ An ordinary defeat would not have been so bad, but it was obvious that the slavery issue would be difficult to avoid in the future.

Ben, eager for political advancement, was not especially interested in that question. He liked the Southerners he met at the National Convention in Baltimore in 1848. If they were willing to accept Lewis Cass of Michigan with his doctrine of popular sovereignty — the right of local settlers to decide whether their territories were to be free or slave — that was all right with Ben, although he had originally advocated the nomination of a fellow Yankee, Supreme Court Justice Levi Woodbury.⁵⁰ Not for him the folly of the Barnburners, the radicals who had followed Van Buren out of the party to fuse with discontented Whigs in a new Free Soil organization. Such a course would only help Zach Taylor, the Whig candidate, he explained to his fellow townsmen. If they disliked slavery, let them remember that Old Rough-and-Ready owned two hundred Negroes himself. Cass had no such property. Moreover, Butler assured his listeners that popular sovereignty was very similar to Free Soilism.⁵¹

At any rate, why should New England bother about the "peculiar institution?" Were there not more immediate issues at hand? These Butler never ceased to agitate. For hours, he harped on the outrages committed by the lords of the loom. Thanks to the Democratic tariff of 1846, he asserted, the mills were in a flourishing condition. Yet their owners wanted to reduce wages. They ought to know that labor, which created all wealth, was oppressed, ground down by absentee owners who had little in common with the founders of what was once an industrial paradise. Not that Butler was in favor of strikes; such desperate measures befitted only oppressed Europeans. In free America, the answer was the ballot. If only the workers voted the Democratic ticket, enlightened legislation would soon stop the abuses of the corporations.⁵² As many of his charges were justified, labor appreciated his efforts. At least Ben knew how to call its grievances to the attention of the public.

But in spite of Ben and his fellow party workers' oratory, not only in Massachusetts but throughout the country, the Democrats lost the election. Whether they could make a come-back the next four years would show. Butler, for one, was determined that they should.

CHAPTER THREE

# Coalitionist

In politics as in the law, Ben Butler was ambitious. He could not help it. Something within him drove him — gave him no peace. His external appearance belied his restlessness, for, still disfigured by his drooping eyelid, he was rapidly losing his hair and putting on too much weight. His energy, however, was astounding. Every morning at seven, he would be at the depot to catch the train to Boston, where he had opened a second office. He would spend the day in town, return late for supper, only to devote the rest of the evening, often until midnight, to his local practice.[1] His cases were more interesting now — murder trials to tax his ingenuity, rape cases which brought welcome publicity, and civil suits bringing fat fees.[2] For an ordinary man, such a strenuous schedule would have been more than sufficient. But he was no ordinary man. He loved the rough-and-tumble of campaigns, and he was determined to play a role in politics.

It was not easy to satisfy this ambition in the Democratic party of Massachusetts. Butler's services in the 1840's had brought him to the attention of party leaders, but the organization was rent with factionalism. As a young politician, Ben could not tell from one day to the next which faction would emerge triumphant. And the slavery issue had become so explosive that it was not certain whether the old party structure would survive at all. But neither Ben nor his associates could be expected to relish continual defeat at the polls, especially after national Whig victories had deprived the Democrats of the hope of Federal patronage. The minority party had to look for some way to secure tangible rewards for its labors.

By 1848, it was evident that new opportunities existed. The appearance of the Free Soilers had added a third force to Massachusetts politics. Allied with the new party, the Democrats might outvote the Whigs. Coalition seemed the logical course, especially since the state constitution still required election by absolute majorities.[3] If only the Democratic National Committee were not so suspicious of the Free Soilers![4] This suspicion was an obstacle that Ben could not afford to overlook, but he knew how to play down the slavery issue and still cooperate with men considered little better than abolitionists by Caleb Cushing and his associates.

Butler seriously considered the possibilities of coalition. Tentative local combinations between Democrats and Free Soilers had pointed the way in 1849.[5] In 1850, with the Whigs weakened by Webster's Seventh of March Speech, the experiment was tried on a state-wide basis. Free Soilers like Charles Sumner and Henry Wilson collaborated with such Democrats as George Boutwell and Nathaniel Banks,[6] and Butler saw no reason why he should remain aloof from a coalition which held such promise for the future.[7] At long last he might campaign with some chance of success — an expectation which proved correct in November. Victory at the polls enabled the Democrats to obtain the principal state offices and the short term in the United States Senate. In accordance with prior arrangements, the Free Soilers were allowed to elect Charles Sumner for the long term.[8] In addition, the new state legislature was finally able to pass a secret ballot act — a boon for radicals like Butler.[9]

Ben made the most of this windfall. The issues which he raised at election time were still the same: the impudence of the corporations, the woes of labor, and, above all, the long working day. But under the new law, the lords of the loom would find it more difficult to intimidate their employees. So strenuously did Ben campaign against the Whigs in 1851 that the slate he supported became known as the "Ben Butler Ten Hour Ticket" — a platform which realized success on election day.[10]

The Whigs suffered defeat with ill grace. Taking advantage of a mistake in reporting the returns of one ward, they refused to recognize the result.[11] Prior to the subsequent run-off election, rumors were rife that the corporations were threatening to discharge all supporters of the coalition. It was said that a notice had appeared at the Hamilton Corporation's gate, announcing that

> Whoever votes the Butler Ten Hour Ticket on Monday next will be discharged.[12]

And the *Advertiser* reported that Linus Child, head of the Boott Corporation, had vowed that none of the ten-hour men would be employed in his mill.[13]

The preliminaries of the second election kept the town in an uproar. Butler refused to submit tamely. The workers were not going to allow the aldermen to "cheat the people out of their rights," as the *Advertiser* put it.[14] At a mass meeting at City Hall, Ben told his listeners what was on his mind. Linus Child had shown his true colors. The cloven foot was out, and if the mills did not abandon their practices, Ben would see to it that their charters were taken away. Let the employers beware. Butler was willing to see the stocks of the corporations reduced by half if necessary and then bought by people who would not abuse the workers. If John Warland, the editor of the Whig *Courier*, berated him, he could stand it. Did not his listeners know that the marks on the newspaper man's face were caused by affairs with loose Mexican Creole women? The crowd roared, although one of Butler's candidates for the legislature decided he had enough and withdrew. The irrepressible orator himself promptly took the disgusted politician's place on the ticket.[15]

John Warland could hardly be expected to keep quiet after this performance. He decided to reply in kind, and on the day following the meeting at City Hall, he featured a prominent article in the *Courier*. Entitling it "Ben Butler," he wrote,

> This notorious demagogue and political scoundrel, having swallowed three or four extra glasses of liquor, spread himself at whole length in the City Hall last night. Nature herself has set her seal upon him by giving him a face which, like a wrecker's light, warns all whom it may concern to be on the

lookout while in its vicinity . . . . The uncouth figure of the demagogue, as he swung about, is said to have borne striking resemblence to that of a Bornese ape . . . .

An "epitaph" followed:

Here lies Ben Butler at last as you see
His miserable carcass just brought to the stand
His father was hung as a pirate at sea
And the son as a pirate on land.[16]

Eventually, that outburst was to involve the *Courier* in a libel suit. For the time being, however, only the war of words continued.[17] In spite of, or perhaps because of these torrents of abuse, the Ten Hour Ticket won again, although its leader was defeated.[18]

The personal reverse did not stifle Ben. Dramatic tactics and lurid publicity had brought victory to his party. If his measures were to succeed, if he were to stay in the public limelight, he would have to continue his agitation. At the very next session of the legislature, he demanded an inquiry into the charge that corporations had intimidated voters. Before a joint committee of the legislature, he submitted evidence that employers had handed to their employees envelopes with ballots enclosed. It was time to stop such practices, Ben said. Were not corporations creatures of the legislature, to be regulated at will by their creator? A bill embodying Butler's demands was introduced. It did not pass,[19] but he had again aired an abuse which needed correction.[20]

Butler did not allow people to forget him. Warland and his associate, Varney, had gone too far. Butler sued them for libel — nobody was going to besmirch his father and get away with it.[21] Varney was found guilty, but to Butler's chagrin, Warland was acquitted. Judge Ebenezer Rockwood Hoar agreed with the contention of the defense that the inflammatory article in the *Courier* did not necessarily refer to *the* Benjamin F. Butler present in court. Obviously, *that* Butler was no Bornese ape![22] Ben never forgave the Judge for this partisan decision, and the two became enemies for life.[23]

In 1853, Ben finally reaped a personal reward for his support of the coalition. He appeared as an assemblyman in the State House in Boston, where, before long, he established his position "as one of the leading debaters of the House."[24] Even those who charged that Butler merely introduced his bad manners into the legislature[25] could not deny that he fought vigorously for the groups which had elected him. To please the Irish, he introduced legislation recompensing the Charleston Ursuline Convent which had been burned twenty years earlier by a nativist mob.[26] To protect the workers, he not only appeared in the forefront of the fight for a ten hour law,[27] but tried tenaciously to prevent crippling amendments to the Secret Ballot Act. He would stay in the chamber until two o'clock in the morning to berate the Whigs for their cynical proposal to make the law optional instead of mandatory. And when Speaker George Bliss ruled against him, the scandalized Whigs reported that Butler had muttered, "I should like to knife the old cuss."[28]

As in the past, it proved easier to call attention to needed reforms than to bring them into being. Neither the Convent bill nor the ten hour law was passed in 1853, and the secret ballot did not remain mandatory. But Ben's agitation had not been in vain. Before the year was out, the Lowell corporations voluntarily reduced their employees' working day to eleven hours.[29]

There was one more forum at which the controversial Lowell statesman appeared that year. A convention to revise the Bay State's antiquated constitution was chosen in the spring. The election was the coalition's last success,[30] and Ben Butler was given a chance to try his hand at writing a fundamental law.

The convention which assembled in Boston in May, 1853, was a distinguished gathering. Among the delegates were such men as the venerable Robert Rantoul, Sr., father of the recently deceased reformer; Henry Wilson, anti-slavery cobbler from Natick; Anson Burlingame, soon to win fame in China; Charles Sumner, United States Senator and archfoe of slaveholders; Richard Henry Dana, author of *Two Years Before the Mast;* William Schouler, Butler's old Lowell antagonist; George Boutwell, ex-Governor and future Secretary of the Treasury; Rufus Choate, one of the foremost lawyers of the day; Otis P. Lord, renowned jurist from Salem; Nathaniel P. Banks, rapidly rising political leader from Waltham; Speaker George Bliss, General Caleb Cushing, and a host of others, including Benjamin F. Butler.[31]

Already known for his acid tongue, sarcastic wit, and facile way of routing his enemies in debate, Butler's behavior at the convention differed little from his antics in the legislature. As usual, he capitalized on strife, exasperating his opponents.[32] Judges should be elected, not appointed, he said; they would be less overbearing if they had to consider the wishes of the electorate. George Hillard, archconservative from Boston, thought he would silence Butler. "As long as we have jackals and hyenas at the bar," he cried, "I hope we shall have a lion on the bench, who with one stroke of his vigorous paw can . . . bring their scalps right down over their eyes." Butler was unruffled, remarking dryly that some members seemed to regard him as a hyena.[33] Actually, Hillard's attack was the type of encounter Ben loved.

When the convention adjourned, it had adopted a new constitution. Influenced in part by a plan submitted by Butler, the delegates had changed the old system of representation.[34] They had abolished obsolete property qualifications for office, and they had made less rigid the requirements for majorities at election time.[35] Judicial tenure had been made elective, a change Butler called *the* reform of the century.[36] But with the conservatives horrified by what they regarded as tampering with the privileges of the bench, and the Catholics resentful of the prohibition of state support for denominational schools, the constitution was defeated in the referendum held the following November.[37] However, many of its provisions were eventually adopted as amendments. The labors of the convention had not been wasted.

If the coalition had brought Butler fame and success, it had also brought him serious troubles. The national wing of the Democratic party, often called Hunkers in Massachusetts as in New York because they were said to be "hunkering" after offices, had been uneasy about alliance with the Free Soilers from the very beginning. After the passage of the Compromise of 1850, their opposition increased. They demanded that the party pass resolutions affirming the finality of the Compromise, notwithstanding the unpopularity of the new fugitive slave law, which was totally unpalatable to the Free Soilers. Butler was anxious to avoid a head-on collision with his old friend Caleb Cushing, who was already incensed by the election of Charles Sumner. Yet to prevent endorsement of the

Compromise and still remain in the General's good graces was impossible. Butler tried at the State Convention in 1851. He sought to soften the resolutions on slavery, but all that Cushing's men, led by Benjamin F. Hallett, would concede was the deletion of a phrase dealing with the finality of the Compromise. Otherwise they insisted on its unqualified endorsement.[38] Butler had to eat humble pie. Not only did he accede to Hallett's demands, but he even wrote an apologetic letter to mollify the powerful Hunker.[39]

Of course it was Cushing's friendship that Butler really wanted to retain.[40] Cushing had to be flattered, so when the victory of the Ten Hour ticket in 1851 gave Butler an opportunity for boasting, he wrote the General an enthusiastic letter. Calling the victory a great boon for the party, he assured the older man once more of his loyalty, the "troublous times" to the contrary notwithstanding.[41]

Cushing sems to have been impressed. At any rate, he remained close enough to Butler to allow the coalitionist to participate in the carefully planned movement to make their mutual acquaintance and fellow lawyer, Franklin Pierce, President of the United States. As the plotters had surmised, the Baltimore Convention of 1852 was looking for a dark horse candidate. It proved simple to present the New Hampshire statesman at the right moment and then prevail on the demoralized Whigs to send him to the White House.[42]

Relations with other Hunkers were more strained. They asked troublesome questions about the fugitive slave law at election time, and when the right answers were not forthcoming, they refused to support Butler in his bid for Congress in 1852.[43] After his defeat, the Hunkers succeeded in taking away his brother-in-law's office as sheriff of Middlesex County.[44] When Butler tried to obtain the Lowell Post Office for Hildreth instead,[45] they even attempted to undermine Ben's standing with Cushing. "Has Butler got the confidence of the legislature who vote with him?" they wrote,

> The answer is *universally NO* — The *ten hour* rabble and the Irish . . . *sustain him* — this for the moment gives him the balance of power in Lowell — But the anti-Catholic influence in his district is two to one against him and if he was up for the district this moment, he would meet with a disastrous defeat — the upper ten are opposed to him to a man — the great

middle *stratum* has *no confidence in him,* all below this is *drift* wood and in the times present and times to come will be controlled by the *middle stratum* — Therefore don't stake too much on the abiding influence of Mr. Butler — Let him and all men have their deserts — but do not commit yourself to any influence but the national.[46]

With good reason, Butler pondered the advice he had received only a short time before — to disregard the National Democrats and cast his lot irrevocably with the coalition. But he hesitated.[47]

Butler's caution was justified. The coalition was dying. If he wanted to weather the storm, he would have to effect a transition to the national wing. And at a time when his friend Pierce was President and his old mentor, Cushing, Attorney General, it was not easy to abandon the political ties of a lifetime. When Butler finally secured the postmastership for Hildreth — a decided success — it became clear that the Hunkers had not succeeded in turning the Administration against him.[48] He might fight once more in 1853 along the familiar lines, he might still engage in controversy with the *Courier* which now referred to him as "Kurnul Bootler,"[49] but he knew that the Hunkers were gaining strength.[50]

On October 29, 1853, the final blow fell. In a letter to the Boston *Post,* Caleb Cushing issued a "ukase" against further combination with Free Soilers. Calling coalition destructive to the Union, he threatened dire retribution to all who might fail to heed him.[51] At first Butler wanted to demur, but in a conference lasting all day, Hildreth convinced him of the futility of resistance.[52] Butler submitted, and by February 1854, he was ready to support the Kansas-Nebraska Act. Having lost his gamble on coalition, he had made up his mind that there was no future for him in the Democratic party unless he became a Hunker. If the Democrats had no chance of success in Massachusetts, they nevertheless controlled the national government, and Butler, abandoning his heresy and yielding to the wishes of the Administration in Washington, looked for rewards beyond his home state.

CHAPTER FOUR

## A Hunker's Tribulations

Cushing's "ukase" was a hard blow for Butler. He must have known that a party which failed to heed the rising anti-slavery spirit could not have much of a future in the Bay State. Even before 1854, the Hunkers had not been popular, and the Kansas-Nebraska Act did not improve their reputation. Stephen A. Douglas' popular sovereignty, involving as it did the repeal of the time-honored Missouri Compromise, was too much for many Northerners. The old political structure went to pieces, and men of varied political backgrounds joined to form the new Republican party. Many former coalitionists, among them Banks, Wilson, Boutwell and Sumner, soon played important roles in the new organization. But Butler remained outside, a Democrat and Hunker, with all that that implied.[1] Pierce no longer tolerated dissent.

Temporarily in somewhat of an eclipse even in his own party, the Lowell politician did not take a prominent part in the fall campaign. Actually, it would not have done him much good. Because of the general political confusion, the Know Nothings — prejudiced, bigoted, hating foreigners in general and Roman Catholics in particular — swept the state. Governor, Lieutenant Governor, most of the legislature and a substantial portion of the people now supported the intolerant party.[2] Under the circumstances, Butler decided to bide his time and build for the future, lest he lose the following he still retained. Because this following was partly Irish, Ben stoutly resisted the nativist craze. When Henry C. Gardner, the Know Nothing Governor, ordered the dissolution of the Jackson Volunteers, an Irish militia company, Colonel Butler refused to obey.³ Dismissed from the service for his pains,⁴ Butler still had the last laugh because the Governor was forced to reinstate him two years later when the Colonel was elected General by his brigade.⁵ While Ben appeared as counsel for Joseph Hiss, the Know Nothing Chairman of a legislative committee to investigate convents, he always maintained that he had accepted the case only to expose the secret order's hypocrisy.⁶ Had not the bigots told everybody that they would uncover shocking vice in the nunneries? And had they not made themselves ridiculous when Hiss was found entertaining a woman of dubious reputation at state's expense? The Irish appreciated Butler's efforts, whatever his motives were in the Hiss case.⁷ They remained his loyal supporters, though there was no real chance for Democratic success in Massachusetts for years to come.

The party's weakness in the Bay State was not surprising in view of the problems with which it had to wrestle. Even the Know Nothing excitement proved but an interlude, a temporary respite from the vexatious slavery question. Far from settling the affairs of Kansas, Douglas' formula of popular sovereignty had merely plunged the territory into civil war. It did not matter that the area contained only a few settlers; its woes surcharged the political climate of the country for many years. Andrew H. Reeder, Pierce's first appointee as territorial governor, made himself so obnoxious to the President's Southern advisers that he was removed from office, only to become a hero in the North. Yet unpopular as the Administration was, Northern Democrats were expected to defend it. That became Butler's task in 1855, and he vigorously upheld his party. In removing Reeder, he shouted, the President had merely done his duty. For who was opposed to this patriotic action? Nobody but fanatic abolitionists and bigoted Know Nothings. Such people, he declared, pursued a course synonymous with treason to the Constitution and to the Union.⁸ The voters of Massachusetts thought otherwise, and Governor Gardner was triumphantly reelected.⁹

Butler's loyalty to the Administration was not without its compensations. By 1856, he had again become an important figure in the party and headed the Massachusetts delegation to the Cincinnati Convention,¹⁰ where Stephen Douglas, Franklin Pierce, and James Buchanan were all actively seeking support for the Presidential nomination. Because of his acquaintance with the President, Butler might have been expected to stick by New Hampshire's favorite son, but he hesitated committing himself. For weeks, Douglas' emissaries had been writing that the Little Giant would either get the nomination or control the nominee. In either case, he would not forget the Lowell politician who, they had been told, controlled matters in Massachusetts.[11] Buchanan's managers seemed to share their rivals' opinions of Butler's importance. But they counted on him to keep New England in line for their candidate.[12] Ben was a much sought-after figure.

As the convention got under way, it became evident that neither Pierce nor Douglas had any chance. Deciding to climb on the handsome Pennsylvanian's band wagon, Butler rose to announce that Massachusetts would cast her thirteen votes for James Buchanan. She had shown her confidence in the President by supporting him in the sixteen preceding ballots, but now she was switching.[13] Again he had joined the winning faction. Some members of his delegation thought he should have abandoned Pierce earlier, but he managed to make his peace with these malcontents,[14] and he returned to Lowell to battle against Frémont and Republicanism.

Although there was no real hope of success in Republican Massachusetts, Butler worked hard. Seeking a seat in Congress again, he delivered speech after speech at one gathering after another. Peace would reign in Kansas, he maintained, were it not for the constant interference of the emigrant aid societies. If these troublemakers really wanted to do something for mankind, let them turn their attention to the evils of polygamy in Utah. They might send eligible bachelors there, but, he sneered, such worthwhile matrimonial enterprises would yield no political capital, and that was all he thought the professed friends of freedom desired.[15] Nor did he forget John C. Frémont's private life. Had not the Pathfinder run away with Colonel Benton's daughter? Let the fathers of Massachusetts beware![16]

Silly as these remarks were, they were overshadowed by the drama of a meeting which took place in Lowell in October. Rufus Choate had come to address the Democrats in Huntington Hall, but before he had even finished his introduction, he was interrupted by a noise. It appeared that the overcrowded building was in danger of imminent collapse, and an investigation convinced Butler that the audience would have to leave as quickly as possible. To the speaker, he said, "If I can't get this crowd out quietly, we shall all be in hell in five minutes." Publicly, he merely announced that it might be wise to clear the hall in an orderly fashion. He prevented a panic.[17] But in spite of all his drama and persistence, he still could not overcome the customary solid Republican majorities in Massachusetts.[18] Once again, he had to console himself with the knowledge that the Democrats had elected the President. Such was the lot of the Hunker.

The outgoing Administration did not seem to harbor resentment against Butler because of his swing to Buchanan. Cushing remained friendly, and Jefferson Davis, then Pierce's Secretary of War, appointed Butler a member of the West Point Board of Visitors, a group charged with responsibility for supervising the Academy's operations.[19] He had come a long way since that day over twenty years earlier when his efforts to become a cadet had failed, but his hostility to the Academy did not diminish.

Late in the winter of 1856/7, Butler went to Washington. He hoped to attend the inauguration festivities, but his stay in the capital was not a happy one. Together with many other guests at the National Hotel, he fell victim to the bad plumbing and suffered a severe attack of diarrhea which he was unable to shake off until his return to Lowell.[20]

However, a more fatal disease prevailed in the capital. Swarms of office seekers descended upon the city to put their factions' claims before the new Administration. Butler's friends were uneasy.[21] In spite of his surrender, in spite of his jettisoning of the coalition, not all the older Hunkers had forgiven him. The great influence they wielded became evident when Butler failed to obtain the coveted appointment as Federal District Attorney for the New England District.[22] If the Hunkers' intrigues were to be defeated, if Butler were to retain his standing in the party, he would have to show even greater firmness in support of Administration measures, obnoxious as these might seem to a majority of his fellow townsmen. Privately, he still expressed doubts about the denial of elementary legal safeguards to Negroes under the Fugitive Slave Law.[23] But publicly, he endorsed Buchanan's policies and ran for the State Senate on the Hunker ticket.[24]

It was during this period that Butler made many statements which afforded great merriment to his enemies later on. As he saw it, the Republicans not only erred on the free soil issue, but they were also responsible for widespread misery in the state. He maintained that their banks were flooding the country with worthless paper money for which they were able to show less and less specie coverage. "A dollar should be a dollar, and not a promise to pay," declared the future greenbacker, who still called a paper currency "not money, but rags."[25] Even though he was unable to make much headway and was, in fact, severely beaten,[26] nevertheless Butler held his own in the selective group which constituted the Hunker "Democracy".

It became clear in 1858 that this was a feat of considerable agility. Buchanan insisted that Kansas be admitted to the Union under the Lecompton Constitution, a document so unfair that the Free Staters had not even participated in the vote on its adoption. But since they had made an excellent showing in the elections for the territorial legislature, there could no longer be any doubt that freedom had more followers in Kansas than slavery. Accordingly, Senator Douglas — considering the proposed constitution a travesty on popular sovereignty, on the settlers' right to decide for themselves — refused to support the President. The result was a bitter feud between the two men, a rift destined to lead to utter disaster for both the party and the Union.

Like other Democratic leaders in the North, Butler was once more face to face with a serious dilemma. If he supported the Senator, he would lose Federal patronage. On the other hand, if he supported the President, his followers would desert him. Personally, he was disposed to favor Douglas. He wrote the Senator accordingly,[27] but his enemies within the party were anxious to repay old scores. They were again trying to displace his brother-in-law, this time to make J. C. Abbott, archfoe of the coalition, Postmaster of Lowell.[28]

To save his job, Hildreth rushed to the Capital. What he heard there left little room for doubt. He wrote to Butler,

... no Douglasism nor anti-Lecomptonism must appear in the Advertiser. Every man who does not sustain the Administration and the admission of Kansas under the Lecompton Constitution will be driven out of the Democratic party.[29]

Butler informed the Postmaster General that Abbott did not speak for a substantial portion of Lowell's "Democracy",[30] and Hildreth retained his position.[31]

Yet, as in 1852, the wily politician refused to burn all bridges behind him. He had maintained social relations with former coalitionists all along, even with abolitionists like Charles Sumner, whom he had visited in Washington when the Senator lay prostrate after having been bludgeoned by South Carolina's Representative "Bully" Brooks.[32] Butler might have abandoned the coalition, but he was still considered a liberal. Although he urged the nomination of Rufus Choate for governor in 1858,[33] he did not discourage the boom in his own behalf, inspired as it was by anti-Administration forces.[34] Throughout the summer, Douglas men talked of running Butler for the office,[35] and they made a strong showing at the Worcester Convention in the fall. Of course the President's control of the patronage was too strong. Butler himself was not ready to challenge the powerful Boston Customs House. He yielded first place to Erastus Beach; he did not demur at resolutions strongly endorsing Buchanan, but he remained popular with the Douglas faction.[36]

Butler was useful in the campaign. Though a minority party, the Democrats were at times able to win local contests. That fall, fighting for both a seat in Congress and the State Senate, Butler was determined to succeed. In view of Buchanan's lack of popularity, it was not necessary to emphasize the party's pro-Administration resolutions. Butler was even willing to concede that Kansas ought to be admitted without the most odious features of the English bill — the latest attempt to make the territory a slave state. But he could and did make the most of his friendly relations with the Administration when it came to issues other than Kansas. When Buchanan's friend, Senator Jefferson Davis of Mississippi, came north for a vacation, Butler was glad to obtain the Southerner's support for the party at a mass meeting in Faneuil Hall. And who was more likely to secure favors for Lowell, Butler asked — he, Buchanan's supporter, or the Republicans, the President's foes? Moreover, he assured his neighbors that he was not opposed to import duties. Revenue ought to be raised "by judicious protection," he said, expressing a point of view bound to appeal to a manufacturing population.[37] Even though his adroit trimming did not enable him to enter the House of Representatives, he managed to win a seat in the State Senate, the only Democrat in the county to do so.[38] His party would not be able to withhold its endorsement for higher honors much longer.

Butler's behavior in the legislature added to his stature. Although the General Court was strongly Republican, the Newburyport Daily *Herald* pointed out that

> when General Butler is in the Senate, and General Cushing in the House, there is a strong Democratic party — these two gentlemen in themselves making up in ability and energy, learning and eloquence, the lack of numbers.[39]

Successfully he labored for the establishment of a Superior Court; diligently he served on a committee to revise the statutes.[40] As behooved a good Democrat, he opposed a banking bill on the grounds that it would lead to inflation, and he showed nothing but scorn for a proposal to enroll Negroes in the militia.[41] But mindful both of his Jacksonian heritage and his popularity with naturalized citizens, Butler strove to uphold the Democratic suffrage, and when he attacked the literacy provisions of a proposed constitutional amendment, the galleries were crowded to overflowing. Many a Celtic heart must have rejoiced at the proud boast of the Senator from Middlesex that he, too, had Irish blood in his veins. Butler considered the right to vote a God-given privilege which no man could legitimately take away.[42] When the legislature finally adjourned, the admiring Newburyport Daily *Herald* did not hesitate to say,

> The leading mind and the leading man — the one rising far above all others, in each house, was a Democrat. General Butler of the Senate, possessed of more intellectual power, cultivation

and perception than any of his associates, stood out in bold relief and rendered the State much service.[43]

Even opponents admitted that he had displayed

> those traits of character which have attracted to him the circle of friends, which, like satellites, he has always carried with him in his social and political orbit.

With his ability to change in an instant from a well-mannered, affectionate gentleman to an insolent, brazen bully, his loyalty to his friends and his bitterness toward opponents, Butler was at once passionately loved and passionately hated. He was a man who left few people indifferent.[44] He was noticed, not only in the Senate, but also at the great encampment of the militia, where he proudly paraded his brigade before Governor Banks and the assembled notables.[45]

Butler's reward was soon forthcoming. In the fall of 1859, he received the Democratic gubernatorial nomination.[46] Irreconcilable conservatives might still be lukewarm,[47] a scurrilous pamphlet written by a Democrat might still call attention to Butler's "impossible combination of features" and his "harsh, cruel temper,"[48] but the powerful Benjamin F. Hallett himself praised him as a loyal Democrat, and General James G. Whitney, the President's favorite, seconded Butler's nomination.[49] Without losing the confidence of the Douglas men, he had been welcomed into the inner sanctum of the Massachusetts Democratic party.

If the Republicans expected a cut and dried campaign that fall, they were greatly mistaken. Butler's letter of acceptance was a fighting document. It castigated the tendency toward centralization within the State, and denounced once more the enrollment of Negroes in the militia. A tariff for revenue with incidental protection still expressed the candidate's views on the perennial issue of free trade. But on national matters, he was careful. By endorsing the Dred Scott decision with its apparent sanction of slavery in the territories, he seemed to agree with the President. Yet he also appealed to the followers of the Little Giant by declaring himself in favor of popular sovereignty.[50] The high point in his bid for the executive chair — an ambition he was not to realize until almost a quarter of a century later — was a great rally at Faneuil Hall on November 5.

There he was in his element. The lower classes of the city crowded the hall, and Butler knew how to appeal to them. The slavery question did not concern Massachusetts at all, he said. He was more interested in the welfare of the Whites at home than the condition of the Blacks in the South. By insurrection and bloodshed, the Republicans might succeed in carrying liberty to the slave, but it would only be the liberty of the grave. Did not all history show that if armed conflict arose between the races, "the inferior race, as God has made it, must yield as it ever has yielded?" Now the Republicans wanted to enroll Negroes in the militia. But how were they going to uniform them? Would they chalk the black soldiers or blacken the white recruits? He thought the proposal quite typical of a party which wasted the people's money on museums to house "bugs," state offices to enrich politicians, and reform schools to ruin poor boys. Let the voters support the Democrats, stop extravagance, and see the borders of the nation expanded as they should be. There was a great deal of applause,[51] but, as expected, Banks was reelected governor.[52]

Even while the campaign was still in progress, sensational news from Virginia overshadowed local affairs. John Brown had staged his "invasion" of the Old Dominion, and although he had not freed any slaves, the event created great excitement. When the old man was led to the gallows, many a bell tolled in the towns and villages of New England. But the Democrats fully approved the execution. They staged meetings to protest against manifestations of sympathy for the abolitionist, and reaffirmed their devotion to the Union. Butler was engaged in important cases at the time and had to be absent from a mammoth gathering at Faneuil Hall, but he made his approval of the meeting's purpose quite clear in a public letter. "Let everything be done to assure the South," he wrote,

> that in spite of the tolling of bells at the death of an executed criminal, or eulogistic speeches upon his treasons and murders, the great heart of the North beats true to its constitutional obligations . . . .[53]

Butler knew how to appeal to national Democratic sentiment. As long as straddles on popular sovereignty were still possible, as long as no clear-cut decision between Buchanan and Douglas would have to be made, he might continue indefinitely, a Hunker perhaps, but a powerful political leader at the same time.

CHAPTER FIVE

# The Great Decision

As the year 1859 drew to a close, Butler would have been justified in calling himself a success. A leading politician in his party, he had twice served in the state legislature. Even when not a member of that body, his opinion had often been sought on pending measures.[1] His profession, too, had brought him considerable fame as well as a steadily mounting income. People flocked to court in droves just to hear him speak, especially when he opposed such eminent attorneys as Rufus Choate.[2] Nor had he done badly in business. When the mismanagement of the Middlesex Mills had forced the factory to the wall, Butler had acquired a portion of the stock at depressed prices and taken a prominent part in the company's reorganization. As time went on, the Lowell mill's affairs improved, to the new directors' great profit.[3] Moreover, Butler owned considerable real estate.[4] His beautiful home, heated by steam as early as 1858, bespoke the affluence of its owner.[5] With an adoring wife, fast-growing, healthy children, and an important place in the community, Ben had every reason to be optimistic about the future.

However, there were storm clouds on the horizon. The rift between the President and the Senator from Illinois had not diminished. With an election approaching, the necessity for some sort of decision was imminent.

During the gubernatorial campaign, Butler had tried to straddle the dangerous question raised by the intra-party quarrel over the status of the South's peculiar institution. Without repudiating the decision of the Supreme Court that human property could not be kept out of the territories, he still endorsed the Freeport Doctrine[6] — the assertion that slavery could not exist unless local settlers passed laws for its protection — but at the same time, the platform adopted by the Massachusetts Democrats wholeheartedly endorsed the policies of the President.[7] And when local caucuses were confronted with motions favoring Butler for Governor and Douglas for President, the first was adopted, but the second, conveniently dropped.[8] With warnings from Washington that there was a strong movement to head off the Little Giant,[9] powerful influences pulled Butler away from the Senator,[10] although Douglas' managers still counted on the Massachusetts Democrat's support.[11] When he was chosen a delegate to the Democratic National Convention, Butler's public instructions were vague enough to permit last minute switches,[12] no matter what private pledges had been obtained by the backers of the rotund Judge from Illinois.[13]

It was only natural that Douglas should think of Butler as his staunch friend. Was popular sentiment in New England not strongly against Buchanan? Was it not true that the former coalitionist had many times voiced opinions similar to the Senator's own? Yet the Illinoisian failed to take into account the great agility of the man from Lowell who knew that Buchanan's supporters were raising heaven and earth to defeat their rival. They had not made General Whitney Collector of the Customs in Boston in vain, and the influence of the Customs House was not easily disregarded.[14] Moreover, there were increasing signs that Douglas might be defeated, a possibility which put cautious politicians on guard.[15] Consequently, the Lowell statesman traveled to New York in the company of leading Buchanan men from New England, and when he returned, there were rumors that he had tried to detach Democratic leaders in the Empire State from their allegiance to Douglas.[16]

Before Butler started out for Charleston in April, he was already lukewarm toward the Judge. He stopped over in Washington, where Cushing, reputedly in favor of the nomination of Jefferson Davis,[17] arranged for an interview between Butler and the future President of the Confederacy.[18] Ben was impressed. It was Davis who had appointed him to the West Point Board of Visitors, and had been instrumental in securing a favorable settlement of old Massachusetts claims against the Federal Government.[19] Davis had served with distinction in the Mexican War, and when Ben had met the future leader of secession in New England in 1858, the visitor had delivered patriotic speeches which seemed strongly pro-Union.[20] Davis might merit a New England vote, Butler thought, now more doubtful than ever about Douglas' chances.[21]

A visit to the Little Giant did not dispel Butler's doubts. Years later, Butler maintained that he had made his misgivings clear to the Senator, who had allegedly released him after a promise of support on five ballots.[22] In reality, however, Douglas continued to hope for help from Butler even after the balloting at Charleston.[23] Nor did Ben mention the supposed understanding between Douglas and himself in accounts of the interview delivered during the fall campaign. All Butler asserted was that Douglas had assured him that five ballots would cinch the nomination.[24] It actually appears that Butler went to Charleston prepared to desert Douglas,[25] but it is unlikely that the Senator knew about it.

After inspecting a fashionable Catholic boarding school at Georgetown to which he later sent his daughter, Butler joined the other Massachusetts delegates aboard a steamer at Baltimore. The voyage was stormy; many of the passengers were seasick, but with his healthy constitution and love for the sea, Butler was untroubled and ate five times daily.[26] Disembarking at Charleston, the travellers found themselves in a beautiful city of great charm, a place where time had not altered the appearance of Colonial grace and spaciousness. But neither had it softened the pervasive excitement of the Southern fire-eaters. These self-constituted guardians of what they conceived to be Southern rights were determined to defeat Douglas, and when the convention assembled in Institute Hall, the galleries were crowded with their fanatic supporters. They demanded not popular sovereignty, but Federal protection for their human property in the territories, an abstraction for which they were willing to disrupt both party and Union.[27]

For Butler, this situation was most disturbing. He wanted to minimize the slavery issue, not emphasize it. But on the platform committee, he found himself a minority of one. The majority wrote a report upholding the most extreme Southern contentions; the minority endorsed a plank leaving the question to the Supreme Court. Butler held out for readoption of the Cincinnati platform of 1856 — a simple declaration that the Kansas-Nebraska Act was the settled policy of the party.[28] In his one-man report he pleaded for this plank. How could good Jacksonians place such reliance on the Court, Butler asked the Douglas men who supported the minority resolutions. On the other hand, Butler queried the Judge's opponents, how could Southerners expect him to face his constituents with the majority plank? Let the convention beware of changing the platform. If the delegates could not agree on satisfactory resolutions, it would be better not to adopt any, and to unite on some acceptable candidate. In this way, Butler contended, the party would win again and the country would be safe for four more years.[29]

Butler's eloquence did not help him. The convention rejected his proposal twice. Instead, it adopted the minority report, whereupon many Southerners walked out. Protracted ballotting then engaged the attention of those who remained, but during fifty-seven ballots, Douglas could not obtain the necessary two-thirds.[30] Along with one other Massachusetts delegate, Butler, to his everlasting embarrassment, voted some fifty-odd times for Jefferson Davis, until the deadlocked convention adjourned to Baltimore.[31]

The interlude between the Charleston and the Baltimore conventions was not pleasant for Ben Butler. Douglas' managers still entertained the hope that Butler would in the end support them,[32] but most of the Democrats of Massachusetts were outraged at what they considered Butler's betrayal of the Little Giant.[33] He was hard-pressed to defend himself, a task which he undertook with great gusto on May 15. Conceding that he was addressing a constituency whose first choice had been Judge Douglas, he maintained that he yielded to no man in appreciation of the Little Giant. "It is not that we love Caesar less, but that we love Rome more," he shouted, explaining that he had decided to vote for Davis only to save the party, when it had become apparent that his first choice could not be elected. Expressing confidence that a compromise candidate would be nominated at Baltimore, he predicted that a reunited Democratic party would be victorious in November.[34]

Butler's explanations failed to convince Bay State Democrats. They published an open letter refuting his contentions, and demanded that he support the Senator at Baltimore.[35] At Douglas mass meetings, they condemned Butler's course,[36] and Murat Halstead, editor of the Cincinnati *Commercial*, accurately reported their feelings. Butler, he wrote,

> has repented. He is as pro-slavery as possible, and the little, brown mustache under his sharp, crooked nose would curl with wrath if he should be reminded of his record. He admits that he had a Free Soil attack — a sort of political measles — but considers himself all the better for having recovered from it.[37]

The final drama of the party's dissolution took place in Baltimore. Butler took no chances, popular dissatisfaction being what it was. Accompanied by a Boston prize fighter with a "bulldog expression of countenance," he swaggered down the aisles of the Front Street Theater where the convention was held.[38] So chaotic was the gathering, however, that not even a boxer was out of place. Rival sets of delegates had come from the South, both the original Charleston seceders and the elected substitutes friendly to Douglas. More determined than ever to nominate their candidate, the Little Giant's managers voted to admit the substitutes. The result was another bolt, only this time it was final. Even Caleb Cushing, though he had been presiding officer, joined the walk-out. When his successor, Governor Tod of Ohio, took the chair, Butler interrupted. Loudly calling for recognition, he announced that a portion of the Massachusetts delegation desired to retire. He was silenced temporarily by cries of "No"; the roll of the states was called. When the Secretary reached Massachusetts, Butler rose. Amid considerable confusion, he presented a protest against the admission of a pro-Douglas alternate for Hallett. Then he announced that he would withdraw from the convention. A majority of the states had bolted, he said, adding that he could not remain in a body some of whose members openly advocated the reopening of the African slave trade — piracy according to the laws of his country. Then he walked out, shaking hands right and left and remarking that he hoped for speedy reconciliation. Four Massachusetts Hunkers followed.[39]

The aftermath of this dramatic bolt was somewhat anticlimactic. The hater of African slave trade joined Southern ultras at the

Maryland Institute, where Caleb Cushing presided over a newly constituted "National Democratic Convention." After one last effort at a straddle by moving to dispense with a platform and to proceed immediately to the nominations, Butler calmly accepted the proslavery extremists' plank, pledging the Federal Government to protect slavery in the territories. Then, while the main convention finally nominated Douglas, the bolters agreed on John C. Breckinridge for the Presidency. The party had split asunder.[40]

From the point of view of a Massachusetts Democrat, Butler's behavior at Charleston and Baltimore was not illogical. Since Federal patronage was the sole tangible reward for Democratic leaders in hopelessly Republican Massachusetts, national party success was imperative for them. Therefore, when it became apparent that Douglas could neither be nominated by the united party nor elected by a rump, they tried to find some candidate acceptable to the South, some nominee capable of restoring harmony. Butler hoped James Guthrie, an elderly Kentuckian who had served in Pierce's cabinet, might be such a man, and, in order to demonstrate his good will toward the South, he voted again and again for Jefferson Davis. When, in spite of his efforts, the split finally did occur, he lent his support to the one candidate who still had a small chance to prevent the election of Abraham Lincoln, the Republicans' standard bearer. Should the election be thrown into the House of Representatives, as many of Breckinridge's supporters hoped it would be, the National Democratic candidate might yet win by a last minute combination of all anti-Lincoln votes.[41]

However, such considerations could not be expected to appeal to the Democratic rank and file in the Bay State. If Butler's course at Charleston had made his homecoming unpleasant, his desertion of Douglas at Baltimore raised his fellow citizens' anger to a white heat. His grandiloquent talk about the slave trade was met with scorn and derision. Douglas Democrats showed nothing but contempt for one who had prattled about the horrors of the traffic only to "go into the embrace of the Yanceyites."[42] When Butler tried to justify his course at a Breckinridge ratification meeting in July, Huntington Hall was crowded with angry Democrats cheering for the Little Giant. Groans and hisses greeted the speaker. After three quarters of an hour, the man who had probably become Lowell's most unpopular citizen, gave up, leaving the hall without further ado.[43]

There was little that Butler could do in his home state that fall. He finally did get a hearing at Huntington Hall in August, when he claimed that the National "Democracy" was the only true Union party, a sentiment that he reiterated in his letter of acceptance of the Breckinridge gubernatorial nomination.[44] But although he spoke for his candidates in various Northern communities,[45] he did not even bother to be present at the convention which nominated him at Tremont Temple.[46] He received whatever support the unpopular Buchanan Administration was able to give; he had the help of Collector Whitney, and of Southerners like William L. Yancey,[47] but he had no real hope of success. Toward the end of the summer, it had become obvious that not only would Butler make a poor showing, but that the Democratic party itself would be defeated by the followers of Abraham Lincoln.[48]

Election day told an irrefutable tale. John A. Andrew, Republican, received 104,527 votes for governor; as against the 35,197 cast for Erastus Beach, a Douglas Democrat. Amos A. Lawrence, Constitutional Unionist, received 23,816, but Butler, the Breckinridge Democrat, obtained only 6,000![49] Abraham Lincoln was elected President. The Administration and its backers were completely repudiated, and South Carolina proceeded to carry out her threats to secede with other Southern commonwealths prepared to follow suit. The continued existence of the nation seemed doubtful.

For the small band of Breckinridge Democrats in the North, these developments spelled utter ruin. Having staked their entire future upon continued cooperation with the slaveholders, they had made ever greater concessions to their demanding Southern friends until their following at home had virtually melted away. This political sacrifice could make sense only if their party, with its strength south of the Mason and Dixon Line, was in a position to capture the national government. In the absence of national victory, forlorn candidacies like Butler's could pay dividends only if there were some prospect of recapturing a reunited Democratic party in the future.[50] But if the South seceded, the National Democrats would be left stranded. Forsaken by the South, hated in the North for their collaboration with secessionists, they would have neither party nor influence left. Political oblivion stared them in the face.

Butler must have been well aware of the unpromising prospects of his party. Late in December, he went to Washington to confer with his associates. To his dismay, his acquaintances from Dixie openly avowed their secessionist sentiments and spoke of a new Southern confederacy which might even absorb certain portions of the North. While they foresaw no possible reunion with New England, they invited the few National Democrats in that section to make their homes in the South.[51] His friend Caleb Cushing had even been asked to participate in a parade in Charleston to celebrate the very secession he had been sent to avoid![52] Years later, Butler maintained that he had scorned these proposals and told the Southerners peaceful secession was impossible. He even recalled that he himself had vowed he would take an active part in civil war, should that calamity prove the only way of preventing secession.[53]

It is possible that Butler made these assertions, but the capital was hardly in a patriotic mood. Southerners had long dominated its social and political life, and as the city was completely surrounded by slave-holding states, they were confident of carrying the seat of government with them. They openly boasted of their plans and it was doubtful that the Stars and Stripes would ever float over a completed Capitol, then still under construction.

Washington's dominant Southern atmosphere was strongly reflected in the White House. The President — old, tired, disillusioned, and faced with the worst crisis in the Nation's history — was utterly bewildered by the radical turn of events. Only three of the members of his cabinet were Northerners; his closest advisers had been Southerners or Southern sympathizers; now, at the very moment he needed them most, they seemed to turn against him. Privately, he moaned that he was the last President of the United States; while publicly, he counseled Union but claimed that the Federal Government had no power to coerce rebellious states.

Buchanan might assert that he lacked powers of coercion, but South Carolina expected more from him than merely a passive attitude. She demanded that he order the evacuation of the Federal forts in Charleston Harbor, a proposition to which he could hardly accede as long as he maintained that secession was illegal. The touchy situation in South Carolina was complicated by Major Robert Anderson's removal of troops from indefensible Fort Moultrie to Fort Sumter, further out in the harbor. Secessionists sent three commissioners to Washington to negotiate, but they thought that the least the President could do was to order Anderson's return, pending the discussions.

When the commissioners came to Washington, Buchanan conferred with them. But his cabinet was badly divided on what action to take. The Secretary of War, John B. Floyd, a Southerner, counseled that Anderson be ordered back to Fort Moultrie, while the new Attorney General, Edwin M. Stanton, a Northern Union Democrat, vehemently opposed him. He maintained that the commissioners were traitors who ought to be treated as such.[54]

It was at this point that Butler became involved in the cabinet's difficulties. He had known Stanton for some time, and when he met the Attorney General shortly after a stormy cabinet session on December 27, he found his old acquaintance in a towering rage. How could Buchanan negotiate with the commissioners, the President's adviser demanded. Could Butler help convince the Chief Executive that they were traitors? At first, Butler thought it audacious to presume to advise the President, but he was impressed with Stanton's arguments and went to the White House.[55]

Exactly what he told Buchanan is not certain. In the three interviews he secured,[56] Butler probably conveyed Stanton's message, and if we are to believe his memoirs, he urged that the commissioners be arrested then and there to stand trial for treason, with himself ready to lend his legal talents to the Government free of charge.[57] Whatever may have been said, Buchanan's attitude stiffened somewhat. While he permitted the Carolinians to depart in peace, he refused to yield on the matter of the forts, and his cabinet was strengthened by the resignation of the Secretary of War.[58] For a moment, it was rumored that Butler might obtain the War Department,[59] but the President appointed Joseph Holt instead. The cabinet was becoming less defeatist.

Shortly before the New Year, Butler left for home. A last interview with Jefferson Davis and other Southern acquaintances had not made him very optimistic.[60] But he was no longer as conciliatory as he had been at Baltimore. According to the New York *Times*,

Even Gen. B. F. Butler, of Massachusetts, one of the most ultra of Breckinridge's supporters, and the bitterest of anti-Republicans, does not hesitate to assure Southern men that the Free States are forgetting all political parties and uniting as one man for the Union. Talking with a South Carolina Commissioner, the latter is reported to have told him that if Massachusetts should send 10,000 men to preserve the Union against Southern secession, she would have to fight twice the number of her own citizens who would oppose the policy. "By no means," Mr. Butler replied, "when we come from Massachusetts we will not leave a single traitor behind, unless he is hanging upon a tree."[61]

When he arrived home, he was convinced that armed conflict was more than likely.[62]

The three months which followed were as decisive for Butler as they were for the history of the country. While the cotton states were making good their threats of secession, Butler's old political associates in Washington were delivering farewell speeches to a Congress to which they never expected to return. And Jefferson Davis, for whom Butler and a sole colleague had so consistently cast their ballots at Charleston, assumed leadership of the new Southern Confederacy! Loyal Northerners would not be likely to forget who had supported the man they now considered the incarnation of rebellion. If Butler wanted to continue in public life, he would have to make a decision. To continue with the discredited ultra wing of the Democratic party would mean political impotence. But he still held one position of public trust — that of General in the Massachusetts militia, a post which might now be useful. As devotion to the Union had always been his philosophical justification for supporting the Hunkers, it would not be too difficult to rationalize continued support of the National Government, no matter how close his former association with Southern ultras had been. Consequently, he reasoned that he had been loyal to his obligations under the Federal compact. If Southerners now violated it, he was absolved from further loyalty to their interests.[63] He decided to swim with the tide and let the Governor know that he was ready to serve with his troops in any emergency.[64]

John A. Andrew, the new Governor of Massachusetts, was a Republican of the extreme school. A supporter of John Brown, he had long hated slavery and everything connected with it. He was determined not to be caught napping, and took steps to prepare the militia for any emergency.[65] When he met Butler, the most extreme of his antagonists from the previous November, and found him urging the very program he — Andrew — had in mind,[66] the Governor must have been more than pleased. General Schouler was now his adjutant; the former editor of the *Courier* also met his old opponent and was surprised to find him a changed man. The defeated Breckinridge candidate talked of the necessity of preparing for war; he even warned that his own political associates might attempt to prevent by force the inauguration of the President-elect.[67] And he was the moving spirit behind resolutions of support adopted by his brigade, resolutions which he now transmitted in person, along with the commander of the Sixth Regiment, who urged Andrew to hasten his preparations.[68]

Neither Schouler nor Andrew thought it wise to look this unexpected gift horse in the mouth. Not that they were willing to trust Butler,[69] but they knew that his influence with Democrats of the most troublesome type was great. Consequently, they agreed with his propositions, especially his warnings that the troops needed overcoats. The legislature made the necessary preparations, and a profitable contract for overcoats went to the Middlesex Mills.[70]

In the meantime, Lincoln had been inaugurated without the trouble predicted by Butler. A month of comparative inactivity followed, so that the Massachusetts legislature repealed its emergency appropriations.[71] On April 11, it adjourned, not suspecting the drama about to be enacted in Charleston Harbor. The North was divided. For the moment, it appeared that the "erring sisters" had really gone in peace.

However, it was only the calm before the storm. On April 15, news of the bombardment of Fort Sumter reached Boston. Had the Confederates deliberately tried to unify their opponents, they could not have accomplished their aim more rapidly than they did by their insult to the Stars and Stripes. The flag had been torn down. Lincoln issued his call for troops, and patriots replied with enthusiasm. Civil War had begun. The time had come to show devotion to Old Glory!

Ben Butler rose to the occasion. Amid intense excitement, he not only publicly avowed his intention to support the Administration and the Union, but declared that those who withheld their support were traitors deserving of a traitor's fate.[72] When he received orders to muster his troops on the Common, he was trying a case in Boston. Dramatically he asked for a postponement and stalked proudly out of the court room.[73] The cheering crowds outside were proof that the nightmare of political oblivion was ended.[74] Again he might enjoy popularity and perhaps win military glory as well. If only he could get command of the Massachusetts volunteers!

He acted fast to achieve this ambition. In order to overcome the rival claims of several officers who outranked him, he made good use of his contacts in Washington, — Charles Sumner, Henry Wilson, and the new Secretary of War, Simon Cameron.[75] But he concentrated on Andrew. Since the Governor alone had power to appoint Generals of the militia; it was he who would make the final decision. It was true that he had no love for Democrats in general and Breckinridge Democrats in particular,[76] but Butler, whatever his motives, had rendered valuable service to the country by setting a patriotic example for his political associates.[77] The very fact that he had been an ultra could now be turned to good account. The Republicans needed all the support they could get; considerations of national unity demanded the appointment of Democratic generals such as Butler and Cushing. But Cushing had made pro-Southern statements long after the November election, while Butler had already signified his willingness to let bygones be bygones.[78] Moreover, the contender from Lowell appeared at the State House with a note from James G. Carney, the President of the Bank of Mutual Redemption, who offered to lend the Commonwealth $50,000 to cover the unappropriated expenses of the state during the emergency.[79] Butler came at the right time. Popular with the troops, experienced in militia affairs, he was appointed to the coveted post by Andrew. He became Commanding General of the Massachusetts militia in the field,[80] and was ready to take his troops to Washington. Boston was treated to the rare spectacle of Butler, Schouler, and Andrew appearing together before the troops, complimenting one another as patriots, and agreeing on the one sentiment uppermost in everybody's mind: "The Union, now and forever, one and inseparable."[81]

CHAPTER SIX

# Washington and Baltimore

In the short but eventful history of Washington, no period is more remarkable than the third week of April, 1861. Totally surrounded by slave states, the capital was almost defenseless. Many residents were sure that it would only be a question of time before the Stars and Bars supplanted the old flag on top of the public buildings. With secessionist sentiment rife among the officers, the few regulars in town could not be trusted, and although loyal governors had responded enthusiastically to Lincoln's call for troops, day after day passed without any sign of a Northern army. When a regiment of Massachusetts militia finally did arrive, the sad tale of its encounter with a hostile mob in Baltimore, and the reports of torn railroad tracks to the North more than counteracted what little protection the troops afforded. Washington was truly isolated, a state of affairs which was brought home to all two days later when telegraph connections with the loyal states were also severed. Gloom and pessimism prevailed.[1]

While Washington was in the throes of despondency, Butler's southward progress was marked by ever mounting enthusiasm. In Boston, in Springfield, in New York, in Jersey City, everywhere there were cheering crowds to welcome the Yankees who had come to relieve the capital.[2] Not until he reached Philadelphia on the evening of April 19 did he learn that the Sixth Regiment had been fired upon in Baltimore and that communications with the South had been interrupted.[3]

His experience with strategy had not been great, but when unusual expedients had to be tried, he was quick to react. Closeting himself with an old Massachusetts acquaintance, S. M. Felton, President of the Philadelphia, Wilmington & Baltimore Railroad, he discussed the difficult situation which confronted him. How was he to carry out his orders to relieve Washington if the tracks were impassable beyond the Susquehanna? Felton pointed out that his company owned a large ferryboat at Perryville, on the near side of the river. Why not go there, put the troops aboard the steamer, and proceed to Washington by way of Annapolis, only forty miles from the capital? Immediately grasping the feasibility of this plan, Butler adopted it with enthusiasm. He even tried to persuade Marshall Lefferts, Colonel of the aristocratic Seventh New York, to join him. But, as was to be true on so many other occasions, Butler was unable to establish friendly relations with a fellow officer. Lefferts refused. He preferred to do things in his own way, which was to put his troops aboard a transport to reach Washington by water.[5]

Undaunted by this rebuff, the Brigadier General with his Eighth Massachusetts entrained for Perryville and seized the ferry steamer *Maryland* which was tied up at the pier.[6] The troops flocked aboard. Late that night, they arrived off Annapolis, capital of Maryland and home of the United States Naval Academy.

In spite of the late hour, the town seemed uncommonly active. The lights of the Academy were still burning, and before long, a small boat appeared in the bay. Asked for his identity, the small boat's occupant hesitated to reply. Threats of fire from the *Maryland* made him heave to, and he turned out to be a lieutenant from the Academy. The nocturnal visitor had been apprehensive lest the unknown ferryboat carried secessionists from Baltimore who had threatened to seize the historic frigate *Constitution*. "Old Ironsides" was then being used as a school ship by the midshipmen, so the lieutenant was actually encouraged by the appearance of loyal troops. They, too, were relieved to have encountered a friend, and the lieutenant quickly won their confidence.[7]

Even before the lieutenant's arrival, Butler had sent an advance party ashore. Early Sunday morning it returned, accompanied by the Commandant of the Academy who confirmed his subordinate's story. He begged the General to assist him in saving the *Constitution*, a task which did not seem too difficult for a regiment with many men from seafaring towns.[8] Butler agreed. A detail manned the historic frigate, threw useless impedimenta overboard, and stood by while the *Maryland* towed "Old Ironsides" into deep water from where she could be taken to safety.

So far, so good. On the way back, however, the *Maryland* itself ran into trouble. She was grounded on a mudbank, and no matter how hard they tried, the unhappy soldiers, — short of provisions and packed tightly like sardines — could not land. Butler was dismayed. Night was falling. The capital, less than forty miles away, remained unrelieved, while his soldiers were marooned aboard a stranded railroad ferry.[9]

It was a discouraging situation, but poor seamanship was not the only obstacle he encountered at Annapolis. Political problems were even more trying. It did not take long to discover that the city was not going to welcome the troops as had New York, Jersey City, and Philadelphia. Annapolis was a Southern town with an excited populace sympathetic to the South.[10] Even the Naval Academy had been affected by the prevalent secessionist sentiment. Not all the officers remained loyal, and families were divided against themselves.[11] Moreover, the city was the residence of Governor Thomas H. Hicks, fundamentally loyal to the Union, but irresolute in the face of almost insurmountable difficulties. Hounded by secessionists for his failure to take steps toward disunion, chief executive of a state which lay athwart all northern routes to Washington, he feared a repetition of the Baltimore riots.[12] He had implored Lincoln to prevent further passage of troops through the city, and on April 21, with Butler already anchored off Annapolis, the President granted Hicks' request. A contingent of Pennsylvania volunteers was recalled from Cockeysville, only fifteen miles from the disaffected metropolis.[13]

Under these circumstances, the appearance of the *Maryland* was most unwelcome to the Governor. If the Yankees landed, there might be trouble, and he advised Butler to take his troops "elsewhere," a suggestion he also forwarded to the Secretary of War. On the grounds that he had no cars for their transportation, the Acting Quartermaster seconded the Governor's request.[14]

Even if Butler had been willing to go elsewhere, he was in no position to comply. He was in dire need of supplies; his men were confined to an uncomfortable ferryboat, and he had to reach the capital. He so informed the Governor. To the Acting Quartermaster, he wrote that the troops could easily march to Washington if no cars were available.[15]

As he received no answer, the General wrote again on the next day, April 22. Making it clear to the Governor that his situation had not changed, he asked once again for permission to disembark, to pass quickly through the state on his way to Washington, and to purchase supplies as he proceeded. To correct the Executive's misapprehensions, he pointed out that his soldiers were not "Northern troops," but a part of the militia of the entire United States, obeying the call of the President. He suggested an interview and proposed the grounds of the Academy for a landing place.[16]

This time the Governor, accompanied by the Mayor, consented to meet the General. Once more he tried to dissuade the Northerners from landing, but in vain. In answer to his assertion that no one would sell them any supplies, he was told that hungry soldiers would find their own ways of provisioning themselves if offers of good prices were refused.[17] The argument was unanswerable, and although the Governor implored the President for help,[18] he yielded to the inevitable.[19]

For a man who had been the Breckinridge candidate for Governor of Massachusetts only five months earlier, the necessity of defying the authorities of a sovereign state was anything but easy. Butler was not yet the blustering radical who struck terror into the hearts of secessionists in New Orleans, nor yet the fiery leader who advocated arming Negroes. He had permitted negotiations to drag out for more than two days even though he was urgently needed in beleaguered Washington. When, because of sheer necessity, he finally did persist, he sought to appease the Governor as much as possible. Annapolis was rife with rumors of a threatened slave insurrection; unmindful of the consequences in Republican Massachusetts, the General assured the Executive that he was ready to assist in suppressing all unlawful combinations, servile uprisings included. His troops were armed only against the disturbers of the peace of the State of Maryland and the United States, an assertion which he hoped to emphasize with his dramatic offer.[20]

While Butler was still engaged in parleys with Hicks, another troop carrier arrived in the harbor. It was the *Boston* with the

Seventh New York, forced further up the Bay after an unsuccessful effort to sail up the Potomac. The New Yorkers were treated to a rare sight. Two ships were clearly visible in the Bay, the old frigate *Constitution*, now safe in deep water, and, half a mile distant, a long clumsy steamer, the stranded *Maryland*. They tried to assist the Massachusetts volunteers who could be seen marching to and fro in futile attempts to free the ferry, but their efforts were in vain. The steamer would not budge.[21]

Colonel Lefferts, too, was warned not to land, but he wasted little time and debarked his regiment at the Academy. Anxious to patch up his quarrel with the New Yorkers, Butler addressed them in a complimentary speech in which he appealed to their patriotism for cooperation. It was a striking scene — the group of officers listening to the unmilitary looking General, the broad bay in front, the sleepy city beyond, and the frowning crowd of civilians on a hill, watching each movement with unfriendly eyes. The New Yorkers liked the oratory, but they still refused to recognize Butler's authority over them.[22]

Late that night the Massachusetts volunteers, now pitch black with coal dust and parched for want of water, were landed with the *Boston's* assistance.[23] Hungry, thirsty, grimy as they were, they were in good spirits. "These fellows were GRIT," wrote the enthusiastic novelist Theodore Winthrop, a private in Lefferts regiment.[24]

While the soldiers of the two commands were fraternizing, their commanders were soon at odds again. The quarrel about the route to Annapolis still festered; new complications arose soon after landing. As the senior officer present, Butler considered himself in command of all troops called into Federal service, an idea which did not appeal at all to Lefferts and his officers. Their regiment had been called by the Governor of New York; it had not yet been mustered into the Federal service; consequently, it would obey only its own officers and the authorities of the Empire State. No brigadier holding a commission from the Governor of Massachusetts was going to tell them what to do, especially General Butler, whose military accomplishments had not impressed them.[25]

Under these circumstances, Butler and Lefferts found it difficult to get along. When the General insisted upon the seizure of the railroad to Washington, the Colonel pointed out that the wagon road was much shorter. He was determined to reach the capital by an overland march, a purpose he did not abandon until ordered to do so by General Scott.[26] But by that time, Butler had already taken steps to take possession of the railroad and he was convinced that Lefferts and his officers were cowards, afraid to venture into enemy country until others had made sure that there were no troops to oppose them.[27]

The line which played such an important part in this dispute was the Annapolis and Elk Ridge Railroad, a link between Annapolis and the main tracks from Baltimore to Washington. Confederate sympathizers had tried to destroy it, and as the bridges between Baltimore and Havre de Grace to the north were still unrepaired, it was essential to secure it in order to keep open the one remaining railroad to the capital.

Butler's troops proved themselves equal to the task. On April 23, they seized the terminus at Annapolis, where they found a partially damaged engine. By coincidence, it had been constructed in Marblehead, and Private Charles Homans of Company E had been one of the builders. In no time at all, he repaired the locomotive, and by April 24, it was ready for the trip to Annapolis Junction, the other end of the line.[28]

The ensuing march to Washington was as challenging as it was exciting. Closely followed by a train with Homans in the engineer's cab,[29] the Seventh New York and elements of Butler's Eighth Massachusetts marched cautiously along the tracks. As they moved forward, the troops repaired twisted rails, fixed broken bridges, and stood guard against possible hostile demonstrations. Not until the early morning of April 25 did they reach Annapolis Junction, where they found a train to Washington.[30] They arrived in the capital shortly afterward, hailed as deliverers of their country.[31] The Confederates had missed their chance. Never again was the city to be so defenseless.

Probably to his annoyance, Butler was unable to share in the honors of the triumphal parade along Pennsylvania Avenue. On the very day on which he secured the depot, two messengers arrived from Washington with orders for the General to remain at Annapolis to see that communications with the capital remained open.[32] Two days later, Scott sent him written instructions to make his headquarters at the little port.[33] In order that new regiments from the North might be forwarded along the route he had opened, Butler had to occupy and secure the captured railroad.[34] It is possible that Lincoln was not too anxious to station the contentious politician turned General at the seat of Government, but be that as it may, Butler could not be put off so easily. On April 27, the War Department issued an explanatory order creating a new command, to be called "Department of Annapolis."[35] Butler was still kept away from the capital, but he considered this a great victory and sent for his family to join him.[36]

His new command was by no means an uninteresting one. Made to order for a General with civilian rather than military experience, it required more political finesse than strategic know-how. While the reopening of rail connections between Washington and the North had relieved the capital from the most immediate perils, the threat of secession in Maryland remained. Determined to prevent this calamity, Lincoln was willing to be conciliatory as long as possible in order to give the Union element a chance.[37] Yet when public safety was threatened, he was prepared to empower commanding generals to suspend the habeas corpus in the state.[38] As hostile newspapers were quick to point out, such a procedure was of dubious constitutionality,[39] but the Administration went even further. Butler was given blanket authority to counteract any secessionist moves by the legislature. Should it arm the people against the United States, he even had instructions to bombard cities if necessary.[40] And he was the type of man to carry out such orders.

Fortunately for the peace of the state, this extremity did not arise. After many delays, Governor Hicks finally called the legislature in special session on April 23.[41] He informed Butler of the meeting, protesting at the same time that the seizure of the railroad would prevent members from reaching the State House. Despite Butler's assurances that he saw no reason why the legislators could not pass over the railroad in one direction when his soldiers had passed in the other,[42] Hicks decided to convene the legislature in Frederick instead of in the occupied port. Frederick was a center of Unionism, a consideration which may have had as much weight with the Governor as the presence of the Federal troops at the State House.[43] In his message, he strongly condemned the movement of soldiers through the state, submitted his correspondence with the General, but counselled a policy of neutrality and advised against rash action.[44] The lawmakers adopted resolutions favoring peaceable separation; they threatened, but did not pass an ordinance of secession.[45] Had they done so, Butler would have been ready to arrest them.[46]

The General was kept busy closer to his headquarters, too. He guarded the railroad as ordered, extended its tracks to tidewater, and forwarded many a regiment to Washington.[47] Though pompous and even theatrical, he was efficient.[48] On April 26, satisfied with his accomplishments, he sent a long report to Governor Andrew, praising not only the deeds of the men who had accompanied him to Annapolis, but those of the other regiments of the brigade as well. The Sixth had gained glory in Baltimore. The Third and Fourth had secured Fortress Monroe in Virginia. The Fifth had helped relieve Washington. The State could be proud of its sons.[49]

However, the Governor was far from satisfied. John A. Andrew was a man of principle. If there was one institution he hated, it was slavery. Butler's offer to use Massachusetts troops to help suppress slave revolts was more than the firm abolitionist could stomach. On moral grounds alone, he thought the idea an outrage.[50] But as his advisers pointed out, there was also a distinct possibility that Butler, the Breckinridge Democrat, had purposely placed the Republican party in the position of having either to sanction or disapprove the offer at a time when either course would undermine national support for the war.[51] In high dudgeon, the Governor rebuked the General, only to receive a spirited reply in which Butler prided himself on having kept Maryland loyal.[52] When the controversy appeared in the papers, more heat was engendered,[53] and although no further complications arose between the two men at this time, the clash was not to be their last.

In the meantime, the commander of the armies, Lieutenant General Winfield Scott — old, gouty, but still alert — had been pondering the problem posed by the situation in Baltimore. It was obvious that the route through the city would have to be reopened. Yet the Hero of Lundy's Lane still had hopes that the inhabitants might voluntarily abandon their opposition. If worse came to worst, he thought a joint movement of 3,000 men each from Washington,

## WASHINGTON AND BALTIMORE

York, Perryville, and Annapolis might secure the city. But, in full agreement with the President on the importance of the retention of Maryland, Scott was unwilling to take any unnecessary chances, notwithstanding the clamor in Northern newspapers.[54]

While Scott was engaged in these preparations, he received a visit from his impatient subordinate. Butler had come to Washington to urge an immediate advance upon Manassas Junction, only to be turned down on the grounds that Virginia's ordinance of secession had not yet been ratified.[55] When he returned on May 4, he saw Lincoln, dined with Secretary Cameron and General Scott, and was pleased to hear of the preparations to take Baltimore and the Gosport Navy Yard.[56] As a first move, the Administration wanted Butler to occupy Relay House, an important railroad junction eight miles from Baltimore, where the Baltimore and Ohio branched off to Harper's Ferry.[57]

Butler was ready, and two days later, he seized the place. It was high time, too, for Confederate sympathizers had sent supplies to Southern troops over the route. Butler effectively interrupted that practice, despite the protests of Maryland's legislature.[58]

Yet he was dissatisfied, tired of being in command of an inactive department, weary of serving as the guardian of a railroad junction only eight miles from a poorly defended city. While he might succeed in annoying hostile Marylanders — he warned them not to poison his soldiers lest he use the same weapon by inciting their slaves against them[59] — he could not secure much publicity in the North as long as he remained inactive. In order to remain in the public limelight, he would have to do something startling. And Baltimore was beckoning! To begin with, it was in his own department, a fact confirmed by Scott himself on May 13.[60] Furthermore, Massachusetts troops had been killed there, a crime which called for revenge. How fitting it would be if Butler could wipe out that stain and reduce the city to obedience.

It had already been ascertained by Captain Peter Haggerty of Butler's staff that the occupation would present few problems of a military nature. Disguised as an organ grinder, the Captain had wandered through the streets without encountering any hostile troops.[61] There were several tons of gun powder at Calhoun Street waiting for the enemy, as Scott himself pointed out,[62] but this information was merely an added incentive to go into the city and seize the stores of ammunition.

From a political point of view, the undertaking might prove more hazardous. Yet rash and impetuous as, on occasion, he could be, Butler was willing to risk it. Perfectly aware that Old Fuss and Feathers had his own plans and would never give his consent to more hazardous schemes, the Brigadier General decided to interpret liberally his superior's instructions. He had been ordered to seize secessionists in the city,[63] and, in the afternoon of May 13, he prepared a train at Relay House to carry out a coup. He entrained with about one thousand troops, feinted towards Harper's Ferry, and returned, reaching the unsuspecting metropolis at dusk.[64]

When he arrived, he found the streets virtually deserted. A thunderstorm was brewing, and it broke as the soldiers marched through the city. Amid the deafening noise of the thunder and the torrents of rain which drenched the men, their arrival went almost unnoticed. In utter darkness, interrupted only by frequent flashes of lightning, they found their way to Federal Hill, a strategic eminence overlooking the city. There they stacked arms, found what shelter they could in a public school, and awaited the actions of their General who had established himself in a nearby beer garden.[65]

In spite of darkness, rain and thunder, Butler was not idle. He wired to Pennsylvania for reinforcements,[66] and, to ensure the safety of his command, sent a message to the commander of Fort McHenry, the historic Federal stronghold in the harbor, informing him of the capture of the city. Should the enemy venture to attack during the night, Fort McHenry could always fire upon Monument Square.[67]

As it turned out, these precautions were unnecessary. In spite of rumors that Federal Hill had been mined to blow up the entire brigade, no untoward events occurred that night.[68] On the next day, the General issued a bombastic proclamation, assuring the populace that he had come as a friend, but prohibiting any manifestations of sympathy for the South.[69] In spite of considerable protest, he arrested several prominent citizens, confiscated a stand of arms, and threatened to hang Ross Winans, the elderly millionaire of Southern predilections whom he had seized at Frederick.[70]

Satisfied with these accomplishments, he rode to the Gilmore House for a leisurely meal. As he had some trouble mounting his horse afterward, Baltimoreans were convinced that he was drunk. But they were wrong. Cold sober, he rode back to his headquarters, elated that one of the largest cities in the country had yielded so easily.[71]

In the meantime, word of the successful if unauthorized occupation had reached Washington. General Scott was beside himself with rage. He had never had much use for volunteer officers,[72] but this Massachusetts brigadier had gone too far. Delicate negotiations between Maryland and the Administration might be endangered by his rashness, and a strong rebuke was in order.: "Sir," wrote the Lieutenant General,

> Your hazardous occupation of Baltimore was made without my knowledge, and, of course, without my approbation. It is a God-send that it is without conflict of arms. It is also reported that you have sent a detachment to Frederick, but this is impossible. Not a word have I heard from you as to either movement. Let me hear from you.[73]

When Butler received this communication, on May 15, news of his coup had reached the North, where the reaction to it was quite different from that in Washington. As loyal newspapers saw it, Baltimore had been secured. Rebels had been put in their place, and the forces of the Union had achieved a major victory. All this had been done by General Butler, the one General who accomplished things! Butler had captured the imagination of the Northern people.[74]

These developments created grave problems for the President. His General-in-Chief insisted that Butler be relieved, while the press clamored for his recognition. Moreover, the insubordinate brigadier had rallied the War Democrats less than two months earlier, and Lincoln could hardly afford to rebuke the popular hero in public. Consequently, he acted with characteristic diplomacy. He permitted Scott to send Butler a telegram at two o'clock in the morning asking him to issue no more proclamations.[75] He allowed the General to relieve the conqueror of Baltimore and send him to Fortress Monroe.[76] He listened to the entreaties of such distinguished Maryland Democrats as Reverdy Johnson to release Ross Winans.[77] But Lincoln also promoted Butler to be one of the ranking Major Generals in the country.[78] The public approved, and the recipient of the honor hastened to Washington to obtain the best possible terms from his embarrassed Commander-in-Chief.

If proof were needed of Butler's great popularity, the President obtained it when the General arrived. A vast crowd gathered in front of his hotel to serenade him. There were cheers and plaudits, and the hero, never at a loss for words, delivered a speech of great patriotic sentiment. He had become a power to be reckoned with.[79]

Butler was not easy to please. Hesitating to accept his promotion, he had a stormy interview with Scott. He was disgusted, and threatened to give up his military career, but Lincoln, Chase, and Cameron prevailed upon him to stay in the army. Yielding to his demand that he be given more than a mere fort, they promised to create a new department for Butler, with headquarters at Fortress Monroe. After consulting his wife, Ben finally gave in.[80] Amid the plaudits of the North and the imprecations of the South, he journeyed to Hampton Roads, hampered, to be sure, by insufficient troops, but vindicated in his own mind and ready for further martial and political laurels. By coming to the aid of an administration which he had fought bitterly, by relieving Washington, and by stirring popular imagination, he had performed an important service for the nation.

CHAPTER SEVEN

# Fickle Fortunes of War

In the dark days following the fall of Fort Sumter, an impartial observer of events might well have concluded that the chances of survival for the Union were very slight. Virtually all indications pointed to a Confederate victory. State after state seceded; one fortress after another fell; many of the ranking officers of the Army and Navy were placing themselves at the disposal of the Confederacy. With its interior lines of communications and its confidence in its cause and strength, the South felt safe in moving its capital to Richmond, only 150 miles from Washington. A rebellion of such dimensions had never yet been put down successfully.

Yet there remained a ray of hope for the Federal Government. Not only did it have greater potential resources, but it had retained command of the sea, an advantage which enabled it to blockade hostile coasts and control the broad estuaries of Southern rivers from which invasions could be launched. To exploit this superiority to the fullest, the Lincoln Administration was determined to hold and improve those coastal fortifications still in its possession.

Perhaps the most important of these bastions was Fortress Monroe. Located at the tip of a spit of land extending into Hampton Roads, it commanded the maritime approaches to Richmond, less than 150 miles up the James River. As a base for combined operations against the Confederate capital it was almost ideal. It had shortcomings — an insufficient water supply and no guns facing the shore[1] — but it was one of the strongest fortifications left to the Federal Government south of the Potomac.

The stronghold's external aspect was forbidding. Surrounded by a wide moat, its high walls enclosed eighty acres of ground. Solid ramparts with casemated flanks covered the land approaches, while the sea side was protected by two tiers of guns, one casemated, and the other "en barbette," as the 19th century was wont to refer to pieces mounted on elevated platforms.[2] The hexagonal structure as a whole looked like a big house with a basement and a garret in which the roof had been left off and the stories in between never inserted.[3]

To this bastion Butler was sent late in May, 1861. His interest in engineering served him in good stead. He proceeded almost immediately to remedy the water deficiency by ordering a pipe laid to a nearby well. Against the advice of the Post Engineer, he insisted that a railroad be built to connect the fort with the wharf, an experiment which proved extremely successful.[4] Telegraph lines soon linked his headquarters with the outside world,[5] and his organizational talent appeared to great advantage. Only his autocratic airs seemed somewhat out of place in a volunteer army.[6]

But engineering questions were merely of local importance. Butler was soon called upon to tackle problems which far transcended the immediate needs of the garrison, issues which were to plague the Administration for years to come. What to do with the enemy's human property was a question of the greatest delicacy, which neither the Government nor the soldiers were at all prepared to handle. Runaway Negroes would soon be encountered, but Lincoln had called out the troops to suppress a rebellion against the national authority, not to free slaves. Not only did he doubt his authority to do so under the Constitution, but he was loath to offend the border states which had remained loyal. Not till 1862 did he finally decide upon an emancipation proclamation of limited application.[7]

Butler could not wait so long. At Fortress Monroe, the question became acute on the second day after his arrival. A sentry saw three men creeping along a fence. He challenged them, and, getting no response, cocked his musket. "Don't shoot," cried the terrified strangers, three Negroes who had run away from their master. The sentry called the Captain of the Guard and the slaves were taken into custody.[8]

Butler interviewed them the next morning. All three agreed that their master, Colonel Mallory, had put them to work on Confederate fortifications. They had escaped because of fear that he would take them further south. Butler was in need of labor; the slaves had been used against the United States by their owners. Was he not empowered to impress this species of "property," like any other, into service for the United States? He decided that he was, sent a receipt to Colonel Mallory, and turned the Negroes over to his quartermaster.[9]

That afternoon, an emissary of the enemy arrived under a flag of truce. It was Major John B. Carey, a man Butler had last met at the Democratic National Convention.[10] He wanted to know upon what principles Butler proposed to conduct operations in the vicinity and what course he intended to pursue in regard to fugitive slaves. The answer was soon forthcoming. Butler assured his old acquaintance of his willingness to observe the amenities of war, but he refused to give up the slaves. He considered them contraband of war, and nothing the Southerner could say would change his mind.[11]

News of the parley spread like wildfire. Contraband — that was a fitting name for the ever-increasing number of fugitives from the peculiar institution. The term caught the popular imagination and soon became the general appellation for runaways.[12] "The emancipation of slaves is virtually inaugurated," exulted Count Adam Gurowski, the radical Polish refugee in Washington.[13] "Butler's fugitive slave law," said General Scott. The cabinet met to discuss the question, and although the President felt the problem required further thought,[14] he allowed the Secretary of War to approve of Butler's action.[15] For a second time in less than a month, the press outdid itself in praising the resourceful General.[16] And although there were others who claimed to have originated the term,[17] there can be no doubt that it was Butler who first successfully applied and advertised it.[18] As Theodore Winthrop, the General's devoted staff officer, exclaimed, "An epigram abolished slavery in the United States."[19]

In spite of his accomplishments, Butler must have strained at the leash at Fortress Monroe. His instructions gave him very little leeway. He was authorized to menace and recapture the Gosport

Navy Yard across the river; he was allowed to seize hostile batteries within a half day's march, but he had never been furnished sufficient horses or troops. And General Scott had pointedly warned him to communicate often with Washington. "Be sure to submit your plans and ask instructions from higher authority," Scott had written.[20] It would be difficult to surprise him again.

Butler was simply forced to wait. He occupied Newport News. He suggested a combined attack upon the Navy Yard.[21] He sent his brother to Washington to obtain horses. He even wrote to Montgomery Blair, the Postmaster General, who read his dispatches to Lincoln. But the General discovered that there was little hope. As Blair put it, Scott simply did not want Butler to succeed, and consequently Butler could do nothing until the old commander was superseded. Moreover, the Postmaster General cautioned Butler against chancing an undertaking while he lacked sufficient manpower and equipment. A disaster would only play into ill-wishers' hands.[22]

The General should have heeded this advice. But he was impatient by nature and stories were circulating that he had bragged he would be in Richmond within a few days.[23] Although there was no basis for these rumors,[24] the public expected action. The disaster at Big Bethel was the result.

Big Bethel was a small church near a bridge about one-third of the way to Yorktown, thirteen miles to the northwest. The Confederates had established a strong-point there, and Theodore Winthrop suggested that Butler make an attempt to dislodge them. Because it seemed reasonable that 3,500 men with proper artillery support ought to be able to overcome 1,400 defenders and one battery, Butler agreed to his staff officer's plan of a surprise charge.[25]

Almost from the very beginning, everything went wrong. With the exception of one regular battery — Lieutenant John T. Greble's — Butler's troops were green volunteers, while their opponents were commanded by such experienced regulars as John Bankhead Magruder, D. H. Hill, and George W. Randolph, soon to be Confederate Secretary of War.[26] A local resident betrayed the movement almost before it started,[27] and the last chance of surprise was lost when a regiment of New Yorkers, approaching a *rendez-*

*vous* with another detachment in the dark, mistook the friendly troops for the enemy and opened fire. For some unaccountable reason, its Colonel had not been informed of the password. He did not discover his mistake until one soldier had been killed and twenty-two wounded.[28] Thereupon General Ebenezer W. Pierce, the Massachusetts brigadier in command of the expedition, delayed the order for reinforcements.

When Pierce eventually reached Big Bethel, he was greatly discouraged. The enemy had had time to prepare, and the General was sure he could no longer succeed with a frontal attack. Accordingly, he attempted to turn the Confederate flanks,[29] but his troops, hungry and tired after marching all night, were in no condition to fight. Instead of actively supporting Greble's battery, one regiment sought shelter in the woods while another marched over an open corn field where it ran into heavy fire, and in the general confusion, two detachments again fired upon one another instead of at the enemy. After repeated failures to drive the defenders back, Pierce decided to call a halt. Refusing to countenance another charge which might still have saved the day, he hastened back toward Fortress Monroe, pursued by the exultant Confederates.[30]

The Southerners had every reason to rejoice. Not only had they routed a numerically superior force, but they had lost only eight men to the attackers' seventy-six. Among the dead was Lieutenant Greble, the regular artillery officer from Philadelphia who had accompanied the expedition, not to mention ardent young Winthrop, shot through the heart as he stepped on a log to get a better view of the Confederate position he had planned to capture.[31]

The disastrous skirmish was a bitter blow to Butler's prestige. He tried to minimize it by asserting he had never intended to occupy Bethel permanently,[32] but the North would not hear his excuses. As the affray had been one of the first of the war, its importance was exaggerated in both sections.[33] The New York *Times* demanded his recall, while the Boston Evening *Transcript* advocated a court martial. Both papers discussed the folly of civilian generals,[34] and Butler's popularity seemed to be vanishing as quickly as it had arisen.[35] With even radicals like Gurowski muttering about the inexperience of commanders,[36] Big Bethel almost cost Butler his confirmation as major general.[37]

Yet he weathered the storm. As on so many later occasions, he blamed subordinates for the disaster,[38] and his assertion that the skirmish had not been very significant proved correct. Immediately after the battle, Magruder, apprehensive of a new attack, withdrew his outposts from Big Bethel.[39] Butler remained in command of Fortress Monroe.

Nor did the setback dampen his ardor for new military movements. He continued to make plans — schemes for the capture of Portsmouth, Norfolk, and the Navy Yard on one side, and, on the other, the occupation of the Eastern Shore, across Chesapeake Bay.[40] If only he had sufficient equipment! Horses, artillery, suitable uniforms — all were lacking. He might attempt to overlook these deficiencies and to entertain the visiting Secretary of War royally. He might even have the assistance of the Postmaster General, but he could not obtain the supplies he needed to further his ambition.[41]

Whatever hopes he may have had were shattered by the Battle of Bull Run in July. The capital itself was believed to be in danger, and instead of receiving reinforcements, Butler was ordered to release four and a half regiments for the defense of the city.[42] Since many of the troops he retained were enlisted for three months only,[43] he had no recourse but to abandon the village of Hampton, where he had acquired an ever-increasing number of fugitive Negroes who had sought protection inside his lines.[44]

While these developments were distressing, Butler was not too upset about McDowell's defeat at Bull Run. After all, the disaster would make his own reverses look less significant, and as he wrote to Blair, he thought that Bull Run would have the same good effect on the Army that Big Bethel had had in his department — it would teach the troops wherein lay their weakness and the enemy's strength. Blair agreed, and assured Butler that he himself had always considered Fortress Monroe the proper base for major operations in Virginia.[45] That was a sentiment fully shared by the General.

In the meantime, the question of the "contrabands" had arisen once more. When Hampton was abandoned, the 900-odd Negroes whom Butler had settled there converged in panic upon Fortress Monroe.[46] Their presence created a difficult problem, but Butler made the most of the situation. In a long letter to Secretary Cameron, he demanded instructions and set forth his latest theories concerning the fugitives. Because many of them had not been used for military purposes, he admitted that they could not all be considered contraband of war. However, their owners had abandoned them, so they might be compared to a ship wrecked at sea — property legally salvageable by those who found them. And as their salvors did not consider human beings to be property, Butler continued, all proprietary relationship had ceased, with the slaves fully emancipated.[47] The radical Republicans would take notice of this proposal.

Shortly after sending off this missive, Butler left for Washington.[48] He thought his presence was required there, because Lincoln had not shared the Postmaster General's opinions about the importance of Fortress Monroe. No reinforcements had arrived,[49] and some of his ill-equipped troops were on the verge of mutiny.[50] Moreover, Congress was about to adjourn. He had to see to it that his promotion was confirmed,[51] and he wanted to be on hand to counteract his enemies.

When he arrived in the capital, his latest scheme for emancipation had already brought him good publicity.[52] The spectacle of the Hunker of yesteryear taking a position more radical than that of the Republican President may have seemed strange, but Congress was in a mood to listen. His rank was confirmed on August 5.[53] On August 6, Congress passed the first Confiscation Act, a measure which practically gave legal sanction to his theory of freeing slaves who could be considered contraband of war.[54] And although the lawmakers did not fully endorse his proposals concerning salvageable property in Negroes, Cameron finally gave him permission to retain fugitives, provided he kept careful account of their numbers.[55]

His dealings with the President seemed as successful as those with Congress. Lincoln was sorely in need of troops, and although Butler was advanced in his ideas on the subject of slavery, he could still use his position as a former Democrat to great advantage. Offering to raise five thousand volunteers, he asked the President to sign the necessary orders which he had drawn up in his own handwriting. Lincoln agreed, merely adding a proviso requiring the concurrence of the Secretary of War.[56] As the Secretary was absent, Butler left the endorsed authorization in the War Department for Cameron's signature, and, convinced that the Administration was not as hostile to him as had been reported, he returned to Fortress Monroe.[57]

But once there, in spite of the friendly reception in Washington, Butler was still woefully short of troops. And the Confederates knew it, as they demonstrated unmistakably after his return. Determined to prevent the use of Hampton as a shelter for fugitive slaves, they decided to burn the village. They carried out their mission so thoroughly that hardly a house was left standing. Butler might fulminate against what he called a "most heathenish outrage," but he could not hide the fact that he was so weak that the enemy was able to destroy a village under the very walls of his headquarters.[58] It was a vexing situation, especially as the paper he had left with the War Department failed to arrive.[59]

Actually, Butler had not been as successful in Washington as he believed. Lincoln had received him civilly enough, but the President was well aware of Scott's lack of confidence in the volunteer General. Because the inexperienced troops at Fortress Monroe seemed greatly in need of a regular officer to put them through their paces, the President authorized Scott to supersede Butler on the day following the latter's return to his headquarters.[60] Old Fuss and Feathers lost no time in making the necessary arrangements. General John E. Wool, a superannuated veteran of the War of 1812, was sent to take Butler's place.[61]

Ben was aghast. In an angry letter to Blair, he asked for an explanation. Had he not been promised troops only a week earlier?[62] Whatever the reasons for his predicament might be, Butler confided to his wife that he believed his stand on the slavery question had brought about his fall. He was certain of that, and although he had not heard anything from Washington, he was willing to accept the challenge. In spite of the Government's "namby-pamby" attitude, the Negro would be free, he wrote, and he predicted a fight at the capital which would settle his own future.[63] In his search for the dramatic, Butler was taking the first steps of a political somersault which would eventually carry him as far to the "left" as he had once been to the "right."

His family and friends shared his exasperation. They were agreed that he ought not to resign his commission under pressure, but they thought that he should return home to force the Administration to recall him to some active command. At the same time, Butler's business agent informed him that, with war orders pouring in, the Middlesex Mills were doing better every day. He certainly need not worry about financial matters![64]

In spite of his anger, in spite of the advice to return home, the General remained in Virginia. When his aged successor arrived, he treated him with great civility and accepted command of the volunteer troops in the Department.[65] In the long run, Butler had no intention of remaining a subordinate to General Wool, especially since the soldiers liked their old commander for his energy and rough treatment of the enemy,[66] but because he had succeeded in getting command of some nine hundred troops who were about to accompany the Navy in an expedition against Cape Hatteras,[67] he stayed on. It seemed like an excellent chance to wipe out the stain of Big Bethel.

On August 26, Butler left Fortress Monroe to join Commodore Stringham in his assault on the two sand forts which protected the inlet into Pamlico Sound in North Carolina. The General arrived on the next day, and although it was too late to land the troops that night, everything was made ready for an attack the next morning.

The sea was choppy on August 28. Nevertheless, three hundred and fifteen soldiers and marines, covered by the guns of the fleet, succeeded in reaching the hostile shore. After a severe bombardment, Fort Clark, the smaller of the two bastions, struck its colors. For a moment, it seemed as if its neighbor, Fort Hatteras, would follow suit then and there. But it held out another night, when it, too, had to yield to superior force. And when Flag Officer Samuel Barron, the ranking Confederate at the Fort, offered to surrender in return for permission to depart with his command, Butler refused. He would accept nothing but "full capitulation," terms which the harassed Southerner could not reject in view of Stringham's complete command of surrounding waters. The formal surrender took place aboard the Federal flag ship.

Butler was elated. His victory had been made possible by the Navy, but he could still pride himself on having taken two enemy forts, seven hundred and fifteen prisoners of war, a thousand stands of arms, five stands of colors, thirty-one cannon, and numerous supplies.[68] At a time when the North could boast of few victories, news of the successful engagement — though it was of minor importance — was most welcome. Determined that the papers should credit him with the victory, Butler sailed north as fast as he could get away.[69] Wool gave permission for a visit to Washington,[70] and Butler made his way to the capital.

He never forgot what followed. Thirty years later, he wrote vividly of his breakneck trip to Washington, his arrival early in the morning, and his visit to the Postmaster General. He found the latter in the company of Gustavus V. Fox, a fellow graduate of Lowell High School who had become Assistant Secretary of the Navy. Exhilarated by Butler's news of the victory, both men decided that the President must know about it at once. They took Butler across the street to the White House where, after some difficulties with the sleepy watchman, they finally roused the President. Looking even taller than usual in his nightgown, the delighted Lincoln fell into Fox's arms. The General, sitting on the sofa, roared with laughter as the lanky President flew around the room once or twice with the squat Assistant Secretary. It was a wonderful sight![71]

At a more reasonable hour, Butler reported his achievements to the cabinet. Forgiving him for his deliberate disregard of orders to sink sand-filled tugs in order to close the inlet, the assembled dignitaries agreed with the President that the forts the General had captured should be held.[72] Moreover, Butler was at last to have his way in the matter of recruiting troops in New England.

And why not? The lawyer turned general had brought the most cheerful news in many weeks. Skeptical observers might laugh at his anxiety to get to Washington before Stringham, in order to obtain all the credit for himself, but the public did not mind. The newspapers and periodicals had a new hero, and they outdid themselves in showering praise on the conqueror of Fort Hatteras.[73] "The people were jubilant," wrote William Howard Russell, the visiting reporter of the London *Times*, "and one might have supposed Hatteras was the key to Richmond or Charleston, from the way they spoke of 'this unparalleled exploit.' "[74]

The recipient of all this adulation was ready to go back to Lowell. This time his homecoming was different from his return from Charleston the year before. Enthusiastic crowds lined the streets while a military escort conducted him to the Merrimack House, where Lowell's famous son responded to the acclaim of his fellow citizens with a patriotic address. In the words of the city's historian, the return seemed like a "passage from the scaffold to the throne."[75] Butler's future seemed altogether bright. His Democratic friends were proud of him,[76] and radical Republicans were thrilled by his exploits.[77] The Administration would not dare slight such a popular hero!

CHAPTER EIGHT

# Preparing for the Great Expedition

The fall of 1861 was a period of comparative inactivity for the warring sections. But it was only a short respite — a lull before the storm. In less than a year, Grant was to capture Forts Henry and Donelson in the West, and Lee was to frustrate attempts to take Richmond from the East. Last but not least, Farragut, accompanied by Butler, was to take New Orleans in the South.

When Butler returned to New England in September, he was not yet thinking of New Orleans. What he had in mind was an operation on the Eastern Shore of Virginia,[1] an isolated area easy to pacify. Had he been able to carry out these plans, he might have succeeded, but his exploits would have been buried on the back pages of the newspapers. There would have been no great cities to administer, no foreign consuls to browbeat, no bankers to bully, no traitors important enough to be hanged. It was a God-send for Butler that his difficulties in New England delayed his expedition long enough to give General Dix a chance to occupy the peninsula before the Yankee troops were ready. And when they were, the Navy had other plans.

These developments, however, still lay in the future when the General arrived in Lowell. His request to raise troops in New England had not yet been acted upon to his satisfaction, although, as a former Democrat, he was in a strong bargaining position. The support of the political opposition was essential for victory, and Butler, even before his return, had sounded the keynote of no politics for the duration. In a public letter dated August 27, he had stated emphatically that he would not consent to run for governor on the Democratic ticket. Let the Republicans be given a chance to save the Union; were he at home, he for one would not vote against his old antagonists.[2] It was a strong bid for Administration support.

When he came back from his successful expedition against Hatteras, he repeated his appeal for a partisan truce. The peace Democrats might put a separate ticket into the field, but he announced publicly that his sympathies were not with them.[3] "That I am for a vigorous prosecution of the war is best shown by the fact that I am gone," he wrote to a Union rally at Faneuil Hall, and made good his boast by leaving for Washington to get full authority for his recruiting mission.[4]

Butler's task proved to be more difficult than he had anticipated. He had received permission to raise troops, but he had demanded a separate department for himself, and the War Department had not complied with his wishes.[5] Refusing to be a mere recruiting agent, he returned to Washington and this time he was more successful. When he saw the President, he repeated his offer of the previous month. Warning Lincoln against the dangers of partisanship in wartime, he proposed to raise volunteers among his Democratic friends in New England,[6] an offer the Chief Executive found difficult to resist. As it was, there were enough irreconcilable Copperheads, and he would have to avoid appearing partial if he wanted to obtain popular support for the war. The man who could give important commands to McClellan, McClerland, Logan, Dix, and Butler could not but welcome the enlistment of less prominent Democrats. If his visitor could succeed in making loyal soldiers of bitter opponents, so much the better. Accordingly, Lincoln permitted Simon Cameron to prepare a draft order. It contained the essence of the propositions submitted by Butler in August and gave him full authority to "raise, organize, arm, uniform, and equip" a volunteer force not exceeding six regiments in New England. The President did not endorse these orders until he had added a proviso making them contingent upon the Governors' approval,[7] but when all six New England chief magistrates replied in the affirmative to a telegram requesting their cooperation, he signed the directive.[8] Since Cameron issued even an additional order giving Butler the right to recruit as many troops as he needed for his expedition to the Eastern Shore,[9] the General left for New England well satisfied with his accomplishments.

By and large, the Governors kept their promise. They permitted Butler to enlist soldiers, granting him all the facilities at their disposal, and they did not even object when he asked them to commission his Hunker associates, their most hated political opponents. Thus he succeeded in raising regiments under such well known Democrats as Colonel Stephen Thomas in Vermont, Mayor Henry Deming in Connecticut, and his old associate at the Charleston Convention, George F. Shepley, in Maine.[10] In Massachusetts, however, he ran into trouble.

John A. Andrew had never been fond of Butler. He resented both the General's former association with the Hunkers and his offer of help to Hicks against insurgent slaves. But most of all, Andrew resented the General's interference with his lawful prerogatives of organizing, commissioning, and commanding the volunteers. At the very time Butler returned from Washington, the Governor's agents were in the Capital requesting the President to stop individual recruiting ventures. The Executive obliged with a general order placing all recruiting officers under the authority of state governors.[11] The directives to Butler still stood, although Andrew was determined to let him have only those regiments which the Governor himself had organized.

At first, everything seemed to be all right. Receiving the General with utmost courtesy, Andrew again pledged his cooperation and offered him two regiments then in formation.[12] But when he discovered that Butler proposed to commission the worst Hunkers in the state as colonels of the new units, the old abolitionist balked. No one was going to force him to place his confidence in people like Jonas H. French, a leader in the riots against a John Brown meeting at Tremont Temple less than a year earlier![13]

The result was a serious collision between the two men. Butler demanded the right to raise his own regiments in his own way, with officers of his own choosing, while Andrew vehemently refused to accede to these requests. The General managed to have himself appointed commander of the new Department of New England, with headquarters in Boston.[14] He received permission to give his men a month's pay in advance,[15] but he could not overcome the Governor's principal advantage. As commander-in-chief of all state forces, Andrew and Andrew alone had the right to commission officers of the Commonwealth, and he was in no mood to give up this prerogative.[16] When Butler came to call upon him he was conveniently busy; when Butler asked for offices in the State House, the Governor would not accommodate him.[17] Andrew's military secretary began to rake over the smoldering embers of the Hicks controversy,[18] and when Butler raised two regiments without official sanction,[19] Andrew not only refused to commission the officers but made it clear that he would deny the state bounty to the enlisted men.[20] For the Eastern Bay State Regiment at Lowell and the Western Bay State Regiment at Pittsfield, this was extremely bad news.

Butler was not the type of man to suffer rebuffs without retaliation. He decided to give up his pretense of courtesy and wrote a stinging letter to "His Excellency," a title he placed in quotation marks more than a dozen times. He demanded of the Governor a regiment of infantry and a squadron of cavalry with officers selected by himself.[21] And lest the troops worry about the Executive's threats, he issued a general order assuring them that they were entitled to the bounty, all the Governor's assertions to the contrary notwithstanding.[22]

Andrew did not reply immediately to Butler's insults. But he made it clear once again that only troops whose officers were commissioned by himself were entitled to the money voted by the state, and he refused to sign the commissions of the officers whom he disliked.[23] Moreover, he wrote a letter to the Boston *Journal* in which he intimated that Butler had been responsible for the faulty armament of Massachusetts troops at the Battle of Balls Bluff, the Union disaster near Washington. Had not the General kept at Fortress Monroe the rifled pieces of the three-month men when their terms of service had expired?[24] Butler's angry reply did not mollify the Governor,[25] and within a short time the public was treated to the unedifying spectacle of the General attempting to arrest members of another regiment on charges of desertion[26] while the Governor disputed his authority.

In the long run, it was inevitable that both contestants would seek to utilize whatever connections they had in the capital. As he had not yet cast his lot irrevocably with the Radicals, Butler relied on their opponents to help him. Pointedly he reminded the Secretary of State, William H. Seward, of his excellent work in preventing opposition to the Administration in Massachusetts;[27] hopefully, he relied on Montgomery Blair for assistance,[28] and when Butler himself arrived at the capital, he managed to spread the notion that he was being persecuted by a spiteful abolitionist.[29]

Andrew did not remain idle either. Perhaps he had no immediate political inducements to offer, but he had been one of the earliest Republicans, and he had friends in Washington. He hastened to send agents to the Potomac, men like the abolitionist merchant, Henry Lee, and the state's Attorney General, Dwight Foster. They were cordially received by the President, but Lincoln needed troops and he tried to ease tensions. After all, he said, General Butler was cross-eyed; perhaps he didn't see things the way other people did. The Assistant Secretary of War hoped that the controversy might be settled amicably and suggested that Andrew commission the officers. It would not be the Governor's fault, he pointed out, if any of them turned out to be bad.[30] But Andrew would not yield,[31] and although he consented to the consolidation of two competing Irish regiments, he still refused to let Butler pick his own officers.[32]

To Lincoln and the cabinet, the bickering in Massachusetts was very embarrassing. The President was grateful for Butler's past services, but he could not overlook the General's shortcomings. The regular Army distrusted the volunteer officer's military abilities, and Andrew loathed his imperiousness. Moreover, his high rank made his presence in the East uncomfortable for other generals. As Gideon Welles remembered years later, it was felt that

> all would be relieved were this restless officer sent to Ship Island or the far Southwest, where his energy, activity and impulsive force might be employed in desultory aquatic and shore duty in concert with the Navy.

Thus Lincoln finally did decide to give the General an assignment to go to Ship Island, off the coast of Mississippi, much further away than the Eastern Shore of Virginia. He was supposed to sail on November 20.[33]

For a moment, it looked as if Butler were to be shelved. But luck was with him again. It so happened that at the very time Lincoln sent him to the Gulf, the Navy was maturing plans for the capture of New Orleans. Possession of the city was indispensable for the effective implementation of the blockade, and its conquest would greatly enhance the prestige of the Union. To effect its surrender, Gustavus V. Fox and Commodore David Dixon Porter had drawn up plans to shell the forts guarding the Mississippi for forty-eight hours with a fleet of mortar boats. Afterward they thought the Navy could sail past the obstructions and take its objective. Gideon Welles, the Secretary of the Navy, considered the idea worthwhile. Lincoln was informed, and the President gave his approval during a conference in General McClellan's house on November 14.[34] With Butler's forces on Ship Island immediately available to accompany the fleet, the General was in a good position to be chosen to command them. And although McClellan was dubious at first — he maintained the expedition would require fifty thousand men — he was won over by the Navy's assertion that ten thousand soldiers in addition to the troops being raised by Butler would suffice. He seemed convinced, promised to supply this force, and the Navy proceeded with its plans in utmost secrecy. It decided to offer command of the fleet to Admiral David Glasgow Farragut, but not even the prospective army commander was informed of the proposed operation. Surprise was absolutely essential for success.[35]

Ignorant of these developments, Butler nevertheless took full advantage of the change in his assignment to Ship Island. On November 18, he sent a lengthy account of his recruiting activities to the War Department, informing his superior that he was ready to embark a portion of his command within a day. As for his differences with the Governor, he characterized Andrew's position as a doctrine of secession, no "more sound uttered by a John Brown abolitionist north of the Mason and Dixon line, than if proclaimed by Governor Magoffin south."[36] Moreover, he faced his opponents with a *fait accompli*. Notwithstanding the fact that some of his officers were still uncommissioned, he embarked the first contingent of his troops upon the steamer *Constitution*, ready to sail for Ship Island.[37] Their departure was delayed when Lincoln summoned Butler to Washington because of the *Trent* affair, a diplomatic crisis with Great Britain caused by Captain Charles Wilkes' seizure of two Confederate commissioners aboard a British mail packet,[38] but the troops remained aboard ship and sailed on November 21.[39] Six days later, the General deposited the roll of the Salem Light Artillery, one of the disputed units, with the Governor with a request for action upon the commissions.[40]

The controversy was now further than ever from solution. All that Butler had accomplished by his high-handed action was a renewed flare-up of the quarrel. Accusation followed accusation;[41] both contestants appealed to their friends in Washington,[42] and contradictory orders emanated from the capital.[43] Butler engaged in a squabble about etiquette with the Governor's secretary;[44] Andrew declared to Charles Sumner that he would never commission Jonas French.[45] The General managed to have Cameron send the Governor a list of officers for his action, a roster which included the controversial Hunker in a conspicuous place as commander of the Eastern Bay State Regiment,[46] but the Governor persisted in his refusal.[47] Nobody could force John Andrew to put his official approval on the appointment of the leader of the Tremont Temple riot.

This unsettled state of affairs was most disconcerting for the troops. They were worried about their bounty, and demanded that something be done. Butler assured them once more that they were entitled to their money; he even pledged his own fortune should there be any trouble,[48] but the Governor would not budge. When the legislature passed a bill which would have included the General's men among the recipients of a bounty, Andrew vetoed it and published the greater part of his correspondence with the Lowell volunteer.[49] And when Butler sought to counter this move with a public letter giving his side of the story,[50] he was further than ever from his goal of getting commissions for his political friends.

In the meantime, his expedition had been delayed again and again. In December, as war with Great Britain was still threatening because of the *Trent* Affair, McClellan thought Butler had best remain in New England. The brooding General-in-Chief was no gambler, and he did not wish to risk the danger of seeing the troops cut off on Ship Island by the British Navy. Nor could he make up his mind about Butler's forces after the danger of foreign hostilities had passed. So it was that although Butler had succeeded in collecting a second contingent of twenty-two hundred men for embarkation by January 1,[51] the unhappy troops had to stay in Boston harbor for almost two weeks while the authorities were trying to decide what to do with them.[52] When Butler was finally given permission to sail, he found to his chagrin that he was not to go further than Fortress Monroe. He therefore decided that his presence was urgently needed at the capital.[53]

His decision was sound. Hardly had he arrived in Washington than McClellan, slowly recuperating from an attack of typhoid fever, issued a new order. This time he diverted the New England troops to the command of General Sherman,[54] and if Butler wanted to save his role, he had to act quickly.

Of course he knew exactly what to do. He had been in politics long enough to learn how to check-mate dangerous opponents, and it had become obvious that McClellan was one. The self-styled American Napoleon had his own enemies, elements whom Butler could and did enlist on his behalf. The radicals in Congress could not but dislike a man whose exaggerated caution constantly antagonized them. For the specific purpose of infusing vigor into the prosecution of the conflict, they had created a Joint Committee on the Conduct of the War.[55] But McClellan continued to worry about more than one hundred thousand alleged hostile troops between Washington and Richmond while he retained the Army close to home.[56] Even the patient Lincoln was becoming exasperated with his dilatory commander,[57] and Butler made the most of the situation. Exuding self-confidence, he appeared before the Committee on January 15. How could there be as many men at Manassas as McClellan contended, he asked his listeners? He for one assured them that no more than seventy thousand held the strategic spot, an assertion which made an excellent impression upon such radicals as Ben Wade and Zach Chandler.[58] When he repeated his figures to Lincoln shortly afterward, his foes could not miss the point: a high ranking major general willing to take chances might prove a troublesome competitor for McClellan.[59] Butler must be sent away from Washington, the further the better.

It was at this very time that momentous changes were taking place in the cabinet. Butler's old friend and fellow Democrat, Edwin Stanton, took Cameron's place as Secretary of War,[60] an unexpected opportunity which Butler did not overlook. At a long, leisurely breakfast on January 19, he told Stanton about his woes,[61] and left a lengthy memorandum advocating the creation of a Department of the Gulf. The projected command was to comprise about fifteen thousand men, including the troops he had raised himself — a force strong enough to threaten any number of points along the Gulf coast.[62] Stanton was impressed, and within two days, McClellan's orders stopping Butler's expedition were countermanded.[63]

The new Secretary was not the type of man who did things half-heartedly. Butler had presented an interesting plan, but McClellan was yet to be consulted. Stanton promptly asked him for his opinion, only to receive a lengthy reply advising that the project be abandoned, on the grounds that the proper objective of any movement in the Gulf was New Orleans. Such an enterprise, wrote the General, required from thirty to fifty thousand troops — soldiers he could not afford to spare.[64] Apparently he had forgotten the conference of the previous November, and once again the great expedition hung in the balance.

Had he not been such a consummate politician, Butler might have been in serious trouble at this point. But in his anxiety to have McClellan's orders overruled, he had enlisted on his behalf not only the radical members of Congress, but also the Navy Department. With George Shepley, his Hunker friend from Maine, he appeared in Gustavus Fox's office. He asked his old schoolmate if he realized that McClellan was doing his utmost to wreck the expedition. That was disturbing news to Fox, who knew what neither his visitors nor the Secretary of War had been told — namely, that the operation's real objective was New Orleans, for which McClellan had promised the necessary troops only two months earlier. To save his project, Fox now revealed it to Stanton, whereupon the Secretary called upon the General-in-Chief for confirmation. What he heard convinced him. Enthusiastically endorsing the contemplated operation, he became one of Butler's most ardent supporters, overruled McClellan, and sent orders to allow the troops to resume their interrupted voyage from Fortress Monroe.[65] Butler, also, was told their true destination,[66] and he wasted no time in preparing for a third shipment of soldiers.[67] At long last, success was within his grasp.

With his troops finally off for the Gulf of Mexico, Butler's quarrel with Andrew also neared a solution. Lincoln was tired of the controversy. Anxious to have the matter out of the way as quickly as possible,[68] he arranged a compromise. The Department of New England was abolished.[69] Andrew accepted the disputed regiments as part of the State's regularly organized volunteer force, and commissioned all but the most objectionable officers.[70] However, Butler was permitted to appoint Jonas H. French to his staff, and, anxious to be off, he agreed to the settlement.[71] The wearisome contest was over.

All that remained to be done was to obtain final orders. McClellan was still hesitant, especially as he could not rid himself of the idea that the enemy's forces in Virginia were much stronger than they actually were, and he continually asked for more troops for himself. But Butler was a dangerous man to have about town. How could the General-in-Chief justify his own refusal to move when his impatient subordinate persisted in telling everyone willing to listen that it would be simple to dislodge the Confederates from Manassas? It was high time to get rid of the intruder,[72] and one day, after McClellan himself had failed to carry out Lincoln's orders for a push on Washington's birthday,[73] he issued the necessary instructions for the expedition against New Orleans. Butler was to receive more than fifteen thousand men to hold and occupy places captured by the Navy. New Orleans was the first objective, but other places might follow, with the opening of the Mississippi an eventual goal.[74] Without wasting any more time, Butler rushed to Fortress Monroe, where two days later he boarded the steamer *Mississippi*.[75]

CHAPTER NINE

# Off for the Father of Waters

Off for the Father of Waters at last! It was exhilarating to be at sea after the weary weeks of waiting in Washington, to be in command of fifteen thousand men aboard the *Mississippi*. And Sarah Butler was accompanying her husband on his most exciting mission — a major general had privileges in the nineteenth century.

The great expedition was by no means a simple matter. It was to be expected that the enemy would defend his largest city to the last. Farragut's fleet consisted of wooden ships. What if the Confederates had succeeded in building some steel monitors to guard the approaches to the Mississippi? Butler knew that he was sailing toward an uncertain fate,[1] but what he did not know was that his troubles would start even before he reached his destination. He had not been at sea for long when the *Mississippi* with her sixteen hundred passengers ran aground on a reef known as the Frying Pan Shoals, less than twenty miles off the shores of hostile North Carolina. To make matters worse, the ship's port anchor tore a hole in her bottom so that the forward compartment rapidly filled with water. The troops muttered that the captain, rumored to be a secessionist, had grounded the transport on purpose. Butler put him under guard, but his situation was not improved by this show of force. Fortunately for all aboard, the U. S. S. *Mount Vernon* sighted the stranded vessel. She tried to tow her to safety, and when that failed, she lightened the *Mississippi* by taking two hundred and fifty passengers off, among them Mrs. Butler and her maid. With considerable misgivings, she left her husband aboard the disabled vessel, but luck was with him once again. With the incoming tide, his efforts to float the *Mississippi* met with success, and, aided by the *Mount Vernon,* the transport reached Port Royal where the necessary repairs could be undertaken.[2] As this work was time-consuming, it was not until March 20 that the General arrived at Ship Island.[3]

His new headquarters was not very inviting. Ship Island was a barren, windswept spit of sand less than ten miles long, twenty miles from the town of Biloxi, from which it was separated by the waters of Mississippi Sound. With the exception of a brick fort at the western end and a wooden shed, there were no buildings on the narrow, ship-shaped dune, and the soldiers had to be satisfied with tents. The burned-out shell of a lighthouse at the eastern end served as a reminder of the war, otherwise not too noticeable on the isolated encampment.[4] Before Butler's arrival, the troops on the island had been under the command of Brigadier General J. W. Phelps, a dour Vermonter who had horrified the conservatives by a premature anti-slavery proclamation.[5] Now the Major General himself was to take over, an event duly marked by an artillery salute of thirteen guns.[6]

There was a great deal of work to be done for the General. The troops had to be whipped into shape, supplies had to be procured, and preparations had to be made for the assault. Annoyed though he was at the Senate's failure to confirm either Paul R. George, his quartermaster,[7] or his brother Andrew, now doubling as Commissary of Subsistence,[8] Butler attacked his problems with his usual energy. He organized three brigades under Generals Williams, Phelps, and Shepley,[9] he established contact with Farragut, and he even managed to offer the Navy some coal.[10] By March 30, he was able to inform the Flag Officer that six regiments of infantry and two batteries of artillery were in condition to set out for the forts.[11]

David Glasgow Farragut was a naval officer of considerable experience. In spite of many Southern family connections, he had proved his loyalty to the flag. When his neighbors in secessionist Norfolk had insisted that a man of his sentiments could not live among them, he had calmly replied, "Well, then I can live somewhere else," and removed to Hastings-on-Hudson.[12] After desultory service with the Naval Retiring Board, he had been selected by the

Navy Department to command the expedition against New Orleans, a lucky choice which enabled him to prove his worth under the most trying circumstances. For like Butler, he had run into trouble before he had even reached his objective. Had he been able to have his way, he would have attempted to run past the two forts guarding the entrance of the river without prior bombardment. But his foster brother, David Dixon Porter, a man as pugnacious as Butler, insisted that a fleet of mortar boats could reduce the forts beforehand. And as Porter enjoyed Lincoln's confidence, Farragut had to wait until a formidable flotilla of nineteen mortar schooners and six armed steamships had been collected to join his own fleet of seventeen men of war.[13]

New Orleans lies some one hundred and fifty miles northwest of the passes, as the many pronged mouths of the Mississippi are called. In 1862, it relied for defense on two forts slightly less than half way up the river. Fort St. Philip on the north bank was an irregularly shaped earth-work reinforced with brick, armed with about thirty-five guns. The more important Fort Jackson on the south bank was a pentagonal brick bastion, reaching a height of twenty-two feet and equipped with some seventy-five guns.[14] For defense of the forts, the Confederates counted on the fifteen hundred men within, as well as fifteen Southern naval vessels without. They were especially proud of the iron ram *Manassas* and the *Louisiana*, a peculiar looking floating battery.[15]

Formidable as these defenses appeared, Farragut found that mud and silt were almost more annoying. For days he was busy with the wearisome task of easing his fleet over the bar, and when he received Butler's message announcing the General's completion of preparations, he had to ask the Army to wait a little longer.[16] Much to the troops' chagrin, embarkation orders were countermanded.[17] The soldiers at Ship Island were impatient;[18] they had been waiting a long time. A minor diversionary action against Biloxi and Pass Christian[19] gave them something to talk about for the next few days, but it was a poor substitute for real combat.

In the meantime, their commanding general paid a visit to Farragut. He was accompanied by his engineer officer, Godfrey Weitzel, who had been stationed at the forts for five years before the war, and now his experience would be valuable. Farragut was interested in Weitzel's report. Who could give a better description of the enemy's defenses than a man who had himself worked on them? The Flag Officer listened attentively,[20] but it was not until April 7 that he succeeded in getting his ships over the bar. He would be ready within four or five days, he wrote to Butler, whom he cordially invited to come along.[21]

The General lost no time in accepting. After preparing two brigades for embarkation, he took the *Saxon*, his headquarters ship, up to the main fleet to witness the momentous battle that was about to begin.[22] Exactly what his own role would be he was not yet certain, but it had been agreed that he would attack the forts from the rear should the mortars fail to reduce them.[23]

Although these preparations should have warned the enemy, Mansfield Lovell, the commanding general at New Orleans, did not fully recognize the danger until it was too late. To be sure, he had asked for troops, but the authorities in Richmond had given priority to other theaters.[24] The very fact that Butler was in command of the land forces seemed to preclude anything of a very serious nature; as late as February 27, Lovell had written to Secretary of War Benjamin,

> I regard Butler's expedition as a harmless menace as far as New Orleans is concerned. A black Republican dynasty will never give an old Breckinridge Democrat like Butler command of an expedition which they had any idea would result in such glorious success as the capture of New Orleans.[25]

When Lovell finally realized his mistake, it was too late to rectify it. Woefully short of ships and men,[26] he had to rely exclusively upon the two forts and their defenders. Should they fail to prevent the passage of the fleet, the Confederacy's largest city must inevitably fall.

As a shortage of coal still delayed Farragut, it was not until April 16 that he appeared before the forts. For the next few days, Porter let loose a steady stream of mortar fire upon Fort Jackson while the men-of-war stood by to await the outcome.[27] Since the defenders found shelter in the casemates, however, the bombardment failed to reduce their bastion. Farragut, determined to wait no longer, decided to force a passage for the fleet no matter how doggedly the enemy might resist. He made final dispositions on April 23, and early on the next morning, he ascended the river with his vulnerable fleet.[28] Butler had left his transports twenty miles below,[29] just across the bar, but he had followed the Navy up to the forts in his headquarters ship. From there, he watched the momentous spectacle, although in later years, he retained only a very general recollection of what happened. "The moment Farragut's guns opened fire," he wrote,

> the smoke settling down made it impossible to see anything one hundred yards away, except the bright flashes, or hear anything save the continuous roar of cannon of the heaviest calibre.

He could do nothing but wait,

> but as the sun rose up in the heavens in the clear calm of a beautiful April morning, Farragut flashed back the signal of his triumph and victory by covering his entire fleet with flags and signals, as in the celebration of a gala day. That told the story.[30]

And what a story it was! Covered by Porter's mortar fire, the Flag Officer had run his wooden ships past the strongly resisting forts with minimum loss. Not only had he overcome the opposition from the shore, but he had completely overwhelmed the motley fleet of Confederate vessels which had sought to aid in the defense. At one time, it had looked as if the Flag Officer himself would perish amid the flames of his ship, but, coolly supervising the firefighting operations, he had brought the vessel safely above the forts. He had achieved one of the most brilliant victories of the war — a naval triumph of the first magnitude which placed New Orleans completely at his mercy.[31]

Butler was one of the first to send his good wishes. "Allow me to congratulate you and your command upon the bold, daring, brilliant and successful passage of the Forts of your fleet this morning," he wrote to Farragut. "A more gallant exploit it has never fallen to the lot of man to witness."[32] Privately, he was less enthusiastic. He considered it "an unmilitary proceeding" to run off and leave the forts unreduced, but such, he wrote to his wife, "is the race for the glory of the capture of New Orleans."[33]

The General himself was not idle in the "race for glory." Immediately after Farragut's victory, he went to see Porter who agreed that the troops should be landed from the Gulf side above Fort St. Philip, as had been planned earlier. With the mortar fleet on one side and the troops on the other, the defenders would be isolated, and their surrender only a matter of time.[34] To disembark the troops as close to the shore as possible, Porter gave his visitor a light draught vessel, and by eight o'clock in the morning, Butler was on his way to the head of the passes to pick up his transports. The small boat, a former New York ferry named *Miami*, grounded twice, but by April 27, he had established his headquarters on Sable Island.[35] Accompanied by their General, his men were landing near the quarantine station, just above their objective. They waded through the swamps, sometimes with water up to their waists, occupied both banks of the Mississippi, and closed the vise around the forts. Porter's ships guarded the approaches to the rear of Fort Jackson,[36] but the garrison made no attempt to escape. During the night of April 27, the enlisted men mutinied, spiked the guns facing upriver, and forced the officers to surrender.[37] The victory was complete,[38] only Butler, who had gone to see Farragut at New Orleans, was not aboard Porter's ship to share the honors of the formal capitulation.[39]

In spite of his unforeseen absence, the General always insisted that the victory was his and his alone. The Army, Butler reported to Washington, had waded through the swamps to isolate the enemy, and Porter's bombardment had proved utterly useless.[40] Porter thought otherwise. Fort St. Philip, the bastion he had not shelled, had inflicted most of the damage sustained by the fleet during the passage.[41] Let the Government try to rebuild Fort Jackson, which he had fired upon for days — the effort and the cost would prove the amount of damage. Resisting Butler's claims that he had done it all by himself, Porter wrote to Fox,

> If you could have seen the trouble I had getting old Butler and his soldiers up to the Forts, to take charge of them (after we took possession) you would laugh at the old fool's pretensions![42]

It was a quarrel which even the passage of a generation could not settle. Butler's friend Weitzel conducted a survey for the Army and found the fort virtually undamaged,[43] despite Porter's evidence to the contrary,[44] and the older the two men became, the more bitter the controversy grew. Eventually, Butler was to claim that Porter had not only failed to capture the forts, but had actually run away from the Confederate ram *Louisiana* after Farragut's passage.[45] Porter later asserted that Butler was not only an "imbecile," a "bird of ill omen," but that he had been drunk at the time of their first meeting.[46]

The quarrel was as unedifying as it was useless. Undoubtedly, Farragut's success ensured the capture of New Orleans, yet the final surrender of the forts was brought about by a combined operation. As in all such undertakings, cooperation of Army and Navy was essential for victory, and fortunately for the Union, Porter and Butler did work together while the campaign was still going on. Their collaboration and the news of the city's surrender[47] made their triumph possible, both having contributed to the final victory. Porter's bombardment facilitated Farragut's passage, while Butler's troops helped to drive the garrison to mutiny after it heard of Farragut's capture of New Orleans. The destruction of the fort was not total, but it had been helpful. Butler's troops were not the sole conquerors, but they deserved a portion of the credit for the bastions' surrender.

The actual fall of the Crescent City did not occasion much controversy among the victors in later years. At first the press was inclined to speak of the triumph as Porter's and Butler's,[48] but very soon the General's vigorous administration of the city made the country think of the expedition as his.[49] And because Butler became more and more convinced that Porter was his archfoe, he endeavored to remain friendly with Farragut, who was in truth the conqueror.[50] Farragut had steamed upriver shortly after the successful passage of the forts, had easily overcome feeble resistance at English Turn, and had appeared before the city on April 25.[51]

No one aboard his ships would ever forget the spectacle of the big city with the wharves deserted, burning cotton piled high on the river banks — a scene as eerie as it was impressive. Not a Confederate banner was in sight,[52] but a rough crowd in an ugly mood beat up the occasional loyalists who dared cheer the reappearance of the long-banished emblem of the Union.[53] It was evident that it would be no easy matter to re-establish national authority.

As the city had not yet surrendered, Captain Bailey and a lieutenant were sent to the City Hall to demand its capitulation. Surrounded by a howling mob shouting threats at the Yankees and cheering for Jefferson Davis, they made their way with difficulty, only to find that the authorities were almost as unreasonable as the populace. General Lovell declared that he would never surrender, but would evacuate the city since he had no means of defense. Mayor Monroe grandiloquently backed him up, on the grounds that as a civil magistrate maintaining his allegiance to the Confederate Government, he could not hand over the city. Only through the efforts of Pierre Soulé, former U. S. Senator and envoy to Spain, and the protection of an escort of Confederate officers did the shore party succeed in making its way back to the fleet.[54]

Farragut was not disposed to trifle with the contumacious Louisianans. Sending the Mayor a peremptory order to hoist the American flag over the public buildings, he declared that he had come to New Orleans to reduce the city to obedience and "to vindicate the offended majesty of the Government of the United States." He intended to brook no interference, and no flag other than the Stars and Stripes would fly in the presence of his fleet.[55] The Mayor remonstrated once more, but Lieutenant Stillwell and a Marine guard took possession of the Mint and raised Old Glory as ordered. The sailors then prepared for a divine service of thanksgiving for the victory.[56]

While they were assembled on the quarterdeck of the *Pensacola* for prayers, a lookout in the maintop shouted, "The flag is down, sir." A gambler named William Mumford had torn the Star-Spangled Banner from its mast atop the United States Mint; the cheering crowd tore the colors to pieces, and the perpetrator of the deed affixed its tattered remnants to his button hole. The observant sailor fired his piece while the men jumped to their guns, but as the gunner had removed the primers an hour earlier, New Orleans was saved from destruction.[57]

Although Farragut had to await the coming of Butler's troops to administer punishment to individual troublemakers ashore, he was able to force the city as a whole to obey his commands. He made this fact very clear to Mayor John T. Monroe, whom he informed without further ado that New Orleans would be shelled unless the fleet's orders were obeyed. Forty-eight hours were granted to the Mayor to evacuate women and children in case of non-compliance.[58] Notwithstanding his procrastination, Monroe soon realized that the game was up. On April 29, a force of Marines landed at the foot of Canal street, marched to the Customs House, Post Office, and Mint, and raised the Stars and Stripes once more. This time the national colors remained flying.[59]

While the warships were lying off the city, Butler arrived for a visit. Accompanied by long and loud cheers from the ships, he steamed through the fleet to confer with its commander.[60] Told of the desecration of the flag and the insults to the Navy, he vowed he would punish the offenders.[61]

After the surrender of the forts, his troops could at last be brought up to occupy New Orleans. When news of the victory spread to the fleet on April 29,[62] Butler had already hurried back to his temporary headquarters at Quarantine. There Farragut's clerk found him, "stretched on a hospital cot, sleeping noisily . . . [with] his head encased in a red nightcap." He was relaxing, his usual autocratic manner not at all in evidence. There was little formality at headquarters, and hardly any pretension. The clerk walked into the room, woke the General, and told him he was leaving for the North with dispatches. The sleeper was on his feet in an instant, and "a moment later the building was all agog with activity, everyone trying to get off his last letter before the trip to the final destination."[63] Butler himself penned a long report to the Secretary of War, giving a highly partisan description of the capture of the forts, and vowing again to punish the perpetrators of the outrages at New Orleans. "They shall fear the stripes if they don't reverence the stars," he wrote.[64] On May 1,[65] he took his troops upriver to take possession of the city and to carry out his threats.

CHAPTER TEN

# "Picayune Butler's Come to Town"

When Butler arrived in New Orleans, the city was in anything but a prosperous condition. With its trade ruined by war and blockade, hunger and starvation had replaced the city's former prosperity. Prices had risen to astronomical figures, banks had suspended specie payments, and the currency was in such confusion that street car tickets were being used for money.[1] Yet in spite of the city's plight, in spite of its poverty, the great majority of the population was intensely loyal to the Confederacy. Butler knew that it would not be easy to govern New Orleans, but he was anxious to try.[2]

It was toward evening on May 1 that he landed his advance guard and marched up to the Customs House which he formally occupied. The crowd yelled for the popular tune, "Picayune Butler," which he was willing to have the band play, but the musicians did not have the score, so they played patriotic strains instead. After this display of martial and musical energy, he returned to the fleet to spend the night aboard the *Mississippi*.[3]

On the next morning, the debarkation continued. Butler drove to the St. Charles Hotel, one of North America's most celebrated hostelries, where he obtained a better idea of the population's hostility. The inn keeper refused to serve him breakfast until Butler threatened to confiscate the hotel.[4] Moreover, the municipal authorities proved as obstreperous as the people. When Butler asked the Mayor to come and see him at the St. Charles later that day, His Honor sent word that his usual place of business was at the City Hall. Again it was not until the General had made it quite clear that such foolhardy demands were totally unrealistic that John T. Monroe, accompanied by Pierre Soulé, finally put in an appearance.[5]

Negotiations, however, were still impossible. Outside of the hotel, a large, unruly mob surged up and down the streets, causing such commotion that a serious conference could not be held. The mob threatened to tear to pieces a Southern Unionist who had to be protected by Federal troops and made so much noise that Butler decided the time had come for a showdown. Calmly turning to one of his captains, he gave orders to clear the streets with artillery. The Mayor turned pale. Begging the General to withdraw his order, he tried to address the excited crowd, but it would not listen. Amid loud jeers, it raised a clamor for "Old Butler" to show himself, only to find that the conqueror had his own way of complying with its requests. At the very moment when his artillery came rumbling down the streets, he stepped out on the balcony, cap in hand, to bid defiance to the angry spectators. They dispersed quickly, and four field pieces on the sidewalk in front of the hotel kept order thereafter.[6]

The mob had been cowed, but the city's spirit had not been broken, as the General and his wife discovered in person when they returned to the hotel from the transport. Not until he was threatened with a bayonet did their hack driver consent to take them to their destination.[7] Merchants throughout the city considered it their patriotic duty not to do business with the hated invaders[8] — a state of affairs which could not be tolerated if the occupation was to be a success. Butler was determined to break the population's obstinacy. Confiscating the goods of a shoe seller who had refused to serve a Yankee, he sold the merchandise at auction — thus providing a practical demonstration of the wisdom of cooperation with the conqueror.[9] When the proprietor of the New Orleans *True Delta* declined to print a proclamation to the people, his paper was closed and the Army ran off the document itself. In the face of such measures, the merchants' opposition soon became less overt.[10]

The proclamation which had caused so much trouble was Butler's first official address to the city. It established martial law, forbade public assemblies, prohibited the flying of colors other than the Stars and Stripes, and required all enemies of the United States to turn in their arms. But at the same time, it reassured the people that property would be secure and gave permission to the city government to continue its usual functions.[11] On the whole, it was a mild document.

Of course Mayor Monroe and Pierre Soulé did not see it in this light. When they returned to the St. Charles Hotel the evening after Butler's dispersal of the crowd, they protested the proclamation for two and a half hours. Soulé delivered a lengthy speech in which he asked for magnanimity, appealed to the conquerors' generosity, and suggested that the troops be withdrawn beyond the confines of the city. Butler, determined to maintain his authority, replied with firmness. He had heard threats from Southerners all his life, he said, but he would yield to them no longer. Whether Monroe or Soulé liked it or not, the troops would remain. All he was willing to concede was a temporary suspension of his orders against enemy currency. Otherwise the proclamation would stand. The Southerners had no choice but to agree to the proffered terms. Butler's rule of New Orleans had begun.[12]

Neither the General's refusal to allow Soulé to dictate to him nor his vigorous measures against recalcitrant businessmen meant that he intended to govern by force alone. On the contrary, during the first few weeks of his administration, he tried his best to win over his enemies. The *True Delta* was allowed to reopen,[13] the troops were so widely dispersed that only a mere handful were left in the city proper,[14] stern orders were issued against looting, and Butler reopened postal facilities. At the same time, he requested the Administration to lift the blockade.[15] A restoration of normal conditions in the captured city seemed imperative, whether the population desired it or not.

Not that a restoration was easy. The city was starving, and unless Butler took prompt relief measures, he would be faced with catastrophe. He did not hesitate. On May 3, he gave safe conduct to a ship which was to pick up previously ordered supplies in a Confederate port. On the same day, he reopened the Opelousas Railroad for freight traffic into rich western Louisiana, so that food, cotton, and sugar might be brought into the city. One week later, he issued instructions for the distribution of captured provisions to the poor. On May 4, he permitted the importation of cotton from beyond the enemy's lines,[16] and on June 1, the blockade was lifted.[17] Gradually, economic conditions improved,[18] but it was to take a long time before New Orleans recovered fully from its wartime depression.[19]

Even the most ardent Confederates had to admit that Butler's initial measures were marked by restraint.[20] To Northerners, his pacific course seemed offensive. "A man of words, not deeds, a tricky politician," wrote Farragut's surgeon.[21] However, the doctor had mistaken his man. Butler tried to conciliate as long as there was any chance of conciliation; when he failed, he changed his course. Moreover, because of his dislike for the aristocracy, he must have enjoyed bearing down on the former ruling classes of New Orleans.

And the city remained obstinate. Storekeepers and businessmen might yield outwardly in order to be able to earn their living, but their wives and daughters were under no such compulsion.[22] If a New Orleans belle chanced to meet a Union officer or soldier on the sidewalk, she contemptuously gathered up her skirts and walked away lest she be polluted. When Federal soldiers boarded a street car, female occupants would get off with great to-do.[23] Some even expectorated on the objects of their aversion.[24] One Southern girl, draped in a Confederate flag, walked up to a soldier standing guard, stared at him, turned toward the street, and, ostentatiously lifting her petticoats, spat in the gutter.[25] Not even the commanding general was spared. Years later, he remembered how he had passed six girls on a balcony, whereupon they turned around with a whirl, a shriek, and a sneer, throwing out their skirts "in a regular circle like the pirouette of a dancer." "These women evidently know which end of them looks the best," Butler said quite audibly.[26]

His rejoinder ended that incident, but the spitting and petty annoyance of the troops continued. The soldiers were sorely tried. It speaks well for them that they maintained their equipoise as long as they did. Yet the exasperating state of affairs could not continue indefinitely. Butler had to take drastic steps, but he had to be careful not to create martyrs, and he certainly did not want to fill the jails with protesting females. Finally, he hit upon a solution for his dilemma, an expedient which was to make him as famous in the North as it made him infamous in the South.[27] On May 15, 1862, he issued General Order No. 28,[28] in which he stated,

> As the officers and soldiers of the United States have been subject to repeated insults from the women (calling themselves ladies) of New Orleans, in return for the most scrupulous non-interference and courtesy on our part, it is ordered that hereafter when any female shall, by word, gesture, or movement, insult or show contempt for any officer of the United States, she shall be regarded and held liable to be treated as a woman of the town plying her avocation.[29]

It was a blow that hit its mark. If there was anything about which the nineteenth century Southerner was sensitive, it was the honor of his women. Butler's edict seemed to impugn that honor in some horrible way. Imagine treating spirited, noble Confederate ladies like common prostitutes! The very thought made the blood boil. To Southerners, the order's author became "Beast Butler,"[30] and at least one newspaper offered a ten-thousand-dollar reward for his head.[31] Confederate generals read the edict to their troops to spur their martial ardor;[32] the Governor of Louisiana proclaimed that the "annals of warfare between civilized nations afford no similar instance of infamy,"[33] and President Davis informed his Congress that there was one Federal general of "instincts so brutal as to invite the violence of his soldiery against the women of a captured city."[34] Mary Boykin Chestnut, the famous Diarist from Dixie, summed up her section's feelings when she said

> There is said to be an order from Butler turning over the women of New Orleans to his soldiers! Thus is the measure of his iniquities filled. We thought that generals always restrained by shot or sword, if need be, the brutal soldiery. This hideous, cross-eyed beast orders his men to treat the ladies of New Orleans as women of the town, to punish them, he says, for their insolence.[35]

Unfavorable comment was not confined to Dixie. Victorian England, too, was shocked.

> Haynau's lash tore women's back
> When she riz his dander
> Butler, by his edict black,
> Stumps that famed commander,

wrote *Punch*.[36] The London *Times* called Butler's order a "military rule of intolerable brutality,"[37] and Parliament echoed the cry. "An Englishman must blush to think such an act had been committed by a man belonging to the Anglo-Saxon race," said Lord Palmerston in the House of Commons, and his opinions were shared by Lord Russell.[38] Southern papers widely publicized these strictures, and they did not permit anyone to forget their hatred for the General who became the most detested man in Dixie — a veritable scapegoat for the ills of the Confederacy.[39]

In spite of abuse, in spite of vituperation, the order was effective. Insults to Federal soldiers ceased,[40] and, as Butler was wont to point out, his soldiers were well brought up. How did well brought up people behave toward women of the town plying their trade? They paid no attention to them whatsoever; the worst that could happen to any of the obstreperous ladies would be a night spent in the calaboose in accordance with an old municipal regulation. No untoward incident occurred, and the General never regretted his order.[41]

Nor did he have to. If the Confederacy and Great Britain thought the proclamation beastly, the North was thrilled by it. Here at last was a General who knew how to tame unrepentant rebels![42] Some might doubt his good taste,[43] but Butler proudly asserted that he did not fight a war with rose water.[44] The order's effectiveness was confirmed by the South's reaction to it. And if the English did not like it, so much the better for the General. They were notoriously friendly to the South. If they heaped abuse on Butler, he must indeed be a great patriot.[45] Even Secretary Seward, conservative as he was, refused to accept foreign criticisms. To the British envoy who had come to protest, he answered that he must

> ask his government, in reading that proclamation, to adopt a rule of construction which the British nation had elevated

to the dignity of a principle and made it the motto of their national arms — "Honi soit qui mal y pense."[46]

It was a fit rejoinder, and, in spite of pressure, the Federal Government never repudiated the edict.[47]

In New Orleans itself, the order hastened the Mayor's downfall. That incorrigible official had offended Butler again by tendering the freedom of the city to a visiting French fleet, an invitation the General considered an insult to the United States as well as to France. As he wrote to the Mayor,

> The offers of the freedom of a captured City by the captive would merit letters patent for its novelty. The tender of its hospitalities by a Government to which police duties and sanitary regulations are entrusted, is simply an invitation to the calaboose or the hospital.

He ordered the action of the City Council reversed.[48] But on that same day, the Mayor felt called upon to protest against the woman order.[49]

Sending for him at once, Butler threatened the head of the municipality with imprisonment at Fort Jackson. Monroe withdrew his protest,[50] only to renew it again when he returned to his own office. In a note to the General, he demanded that Butler state in writing that the order was not directed against decent ladies, a correction he expected to see in the newspapers.[51] Naturally, Butler refused, whereupon the Mayor retracted the apology he had written the day before and protested once more against the soldiers "being ordered to perpetrate unexampled outrages upon virtuous women." He was sure that the universal sentiment of the world would stamp the edict as inhuman and added that he would be at his office, ready to suffer arrest if Butler so ordered.[52]

He did not have to wait long. Within two days, he was summoned again to the General's office. Butler presented evidence that the Mayor had not only been insulting, but that six paroled Confederate soldiers intending to enter Beauregard's army had joined a company known as the Monroe Guards in expectation of pecuniary assistance from its patron. For these offenses and insults, the Mayor was arrested, together with his Chief of Police, his secretary, and Judge Kennedy, who had backed him. Butler sent the officials to Fort Jackson.[53] Henceforth, General Shepley was to be military commandant of New Orleans, and as Colonel French and Judge Bell had already been appointed provost marshal and provost judge, few functions remained for civilian officials.[54] The City Council functioned a little longer, but when its members refused to take an oath of allegiance, they too were relieved of their duties.[55] Butler now ran the municipal government in the spirit which he proclaimed in his office, where there was an inscription which read, "There is no difference between a he and a she-adder in their venom."[56] But even his enemies had to admit that the streets were safer at night than ever before.[57]

With the inauguration of a more stringent regime in New Orleans, the six Confederate soldiers who had broken their parole were tried before a military commission and condemned to death.[58] At the same time, the General apprehended William Mumford, the gambler who had torn down the American flag. Mumford, too, was tried and found guilty. Butler ordered his execution.[59]

The Confederates were aghast. To the last moment, they refused to believe that the General would carry out the sentence. Even Unionists asked for mercy, and the condemned man's family pitifully begged for his life. In spite of threats of retaliation and pleas for leniency, however, Butler remained firm.[60] He commuted the parole breakers' sentences,[61] but Mumford had to die. "If anyone attempts to haul down the American flag, shoot him on the spot," General Dix had said at the beginning of the secession crisis.[62] Butler, believing Mumford's execution necessary for the preservation of order in the city, was determined to carry out that widely hailed threat. Mumford was hanged on June 7, on the very spot where his crime had been committed.[63]

The crowd of spectators which had gathered at the mint was dumbfounded. Old Butler had really dared to defy them![64] It hardly mattered to his foes that the General could be equally harsh with members of his own command who perpetrated offenses no worse than looting, or that he allowed well-behaved Confederate sympathizers to depart without harm. Nor did his offer of safe conduct to General Beauregard to visit his sick wife in New

Orleans[65] make any impression. To his enemies, Butler remained a tyrant, a beast, and a barbarian worse than the hordes which overthrew Rome.[66] The Confederacy needed a martyr; Mumford filled the need.[67] He was apotheosized throughout Dixie.[68] Patriotic Southerners never tired of describing his last moments, and the story gained in drama what it lost in accuracy. It was said that Mumford had spurned a reprieve offered in return for a last minute confession and that he had turned to the spectators, asking them to remember "that the manner of my death will be no disgrace to my wife and children."[69] It was a stirring story, and loyal Southerners were convinced of Mumford's heroism as well as of his innocence.[70]

Of course the man who was responsible for Mumford's death became more hated than ever. The Government at Richmond, issuing threats of retaliation, instructed General Lee to protest to the authorities of the United States,[71] and after Butler had already been recalled from New Orleans, it singled him out in a grandiloquent order which pronounced him an outlaw and a felon, to be executed on sight.[72] Had Jefferson Davis deliberately tried to make his former friend more popular in the North, he could not have succeeded more readily than he did by these actions.

As for Butler, the incident always seemed an unpleasant but necessary duty. Convinced that Mumford's execution was effective in the preservation of peace in New Orleans, the General never regretted it as long as he lived.[73] Nor did he have any personal reasons for remorse. While serving to increase his popularity in the North, the affair did not constitute a violation of the law of nations. All Southern assertions to the contrary, Mumford was the one who had offended against the rules of war. If the flag was not secure, the Federal commander could hardly be said to be in control, and whether the offense had been committed prior to his arrival or not, it had occurred right under Farragut's guns, after the collapse of the Confederate defenses. Butler's position in a hostile city, held as it was with insufficient troops, was precarious at best. He had to demonstrate his power, and the execution served that purpose. No further disturbance occurred while he was in command.

The woman order and Mumford's death had shown the populace that Butler meant business. But there were to be still other measures to demonstrate his determination. The inhabitants were disarmed.[74] Confederate property had to be surrendered, and on June 10, all persons holding office or desirous of availing themselves of the protection of the law were required to take an oath of allegiance to the United States.[75] That was a harsh blow — in effect it gave Confederate sympathizers the choice of abandoning their cause or going out of business. Foreigners obtained slight concessions because of the representations of their consuls,[76] but for American citizens, there was no such easy way out. Eventually, in spite of public disapproval, some six thousand persons took the oath,[77] among them, much to Butler's amusement, Judah P. Benjamin's brother.[78] For those who refused, New Orleans offered little hope as long as Butler remained in control. At first, he merely forbade the evaders to engage in business, but eventually, he announced that they would be expelled from the city.[79] Only Butler's timely recall saved them.

Bankers also failed to escape the Federal commander's vigilance. Butler assured them that he would protect their bullion, their gold, and their silver as he would any other property, but warned them that he had come to retake, repossess, and occupy all . . . the property of the U. S." If they still had some obligation against the government, he would see to it that it was returned to its rightful owner. Doubtless, they knew what he meant: The deposits of the Confederacy would not be recognized.[80]

Within a few days after this announcement the General took steps to relieve the chaotic condition of the currency. On May 16, he forbade the circulation of Confederate bills after May 27, an edict which might not have troubled the bankers had he not issued a proclamation blaming them for the city's financial ills because of their introduction of Confederate money. He was unwilling to have the burden of conversion fall upon the poor, he said, and ordered the banks to stop paying but to continue accepting the banned currency until the deadline. No matter how much the financial community protested, he had his way,[81] and within a short time, he was able to abolish the troublesome shin plasters, as paper currency of low denominations was called.[82]

In other ways, too, Butler bore down on the banks. Contrary to his orders, they had not brought back all their hidden specie, but he was sure to find the hiding place. The Negroes knew their masters' secrets, and, as every Confederate knew, the General encouraged slaves to spy on their owners.[83] It was difficult to hide treasure from the Yankee commander. Once he uncovered secreted specie, he required strictest proof of ownership, condemning it as Confederate property on the slightest suspicion. In this manner, he seized from Smith Brothers two kegs containing fifty thousand dollars in gold on the grounds that the gold had been taken from the mint and was United States property. As he had no cash to pay his troops, he retained the confiscated funds and used them to cover his draughts for the soldiers' pay.[84] This transaction caused him great embarrassment later — so much so that he had to return the gold after a lengthy suit — but it solved his immediate financial difficulties.[85] Other banks still had outstanding debts to Northern creditors. He seized these too, sometimes under doubtful circumstances.[86] But he had his way and the city remained under his control.

Of course not every male offender could be punished as summarily as Mumford, nor could every "she-adder" be silenced by Order No. 28. Yet there were other ways. Archsecessionists like Pierre Soulé and his collaborator Adolphe Manzereau were sent north under arrest.[87] Less prominent persons were incarcerated within the department. There was a book seller named Fidel Keller who exhibited a skeleton with the legend Chickahominy; there was a well-known citizen named John W. Andrew who was accused of making a cross from the bones of a dead Federal soldier; there was a gambler's wife, Ann Larue, who dressed up in Confederate colors to distribute handbills announcing that McClellan had been captured. They were all arrested and sent to Ship Island.[88]

New Orleans buzzed with excited talk about these arrests, but what upset the city most was the punishment meted out to Mrs. Philip Phillips, wife of a former Congressman from Alabama.[89] High spirited and intensely loyal to the Confederacy, she had been in trouble before when she was apprehended for espionage in Washington.[90] This time, not espionage but merriment was to prove her undoing. Overheard laughing as the funeral procession of a Federal officer passed her house, she was taken into custody. Despite her protests that her gaiety had been meant for a children's party inside and not for the funeral cortege outside, she was brought before the General. Her refusal to apologize for an offense she insisted that she had never committed only caused Butler to fly into a violent rage. He called her not "a vulgar woman of the town, but an uncommonly vulgar one,"[91] and sentenced her to Ship Island, where she was not permitted to communicate with anyone except the General and her maid.[92]

It was a sentence as harsh as it was sensational.[93] Southerners talked of rescuing the lady, but they lacked the necessary ships and found it impossible to carry out their chivalrous plan. Butler pardoned her in September, two and a half months after her arrest,[94] but this action did not dispel the popular belief that he was a cruel tyrant.[95]

Actually, the General could — and did — offer clemency when he thought it appropriate. If Mrs. Larue wanted to behave, she could come back to New Orleans.[96] If his old friend and present enemy, Pierre Soulé, was suffering from imprisonment, Butler advised the Government to parole him to Boston.[97] When Mrs. Beauregard was sick, Butler let her remain in her house — even though it was forfeit because of her husband's "treason."[98] Only when viewed superficially did the General's measures convey the impression of a veritable reign of terror, but in effect, even after he had abandoned his early efforts at conciliation, his administration was much more moderate than Southerners were willing to admit.

In his treatment of the press Butler showed that he could still act with restraint. While he closed down the most incorrigible Confederate journals[99] and took over the *Delta* which he conducted in his own interest,[100] he permitted most of the newspapers to continue with a minimum of censorship. To the disgust of the New York *Tribune,* the *True Delta* was allowed to complain about "niggers" and "abolitionist madmen;"[101] the *Picayune* headlined a Confederate victory, "Later and Better,"[102] and the Daily *Advocate* was permitted to reopen after a brief suspension for speculating upon the increased chances for peace in view of Democratic gains in the fall elections.[103] Such indulgence was hardly typical of a mad tyrant!

His treatment of the clergy, too, was not exceptionally harsh, although most ministers were zealous supporters of the Confederacy. Butler forbade the observance of Jefferson Davis' Day of Fasting and Prayer on May 13, and he exiled a few obstreperous divines, but by and large, he interfered little with the exercise of religious functions.[104] The clergymen whom he did send to the North richly deserved their fate, as they had either refused to read the customary service for the President of the United States, or they had delivered particularly offensive anti-Union sermons.[105] In one church, a Federal officer, incensed at the insults to the national cause, actually rose in his pew to stop the service and arrest the minister.[106] But no matter how much Southerners might complain about what they called the "Battle of St. Paul's,"[107] they could not deny that Butler had permitted the most notorious secessionist clergymen to continue unharmed for months. And not only did the General leave Catholics undisturbed, but he took special pains to ensure their good will. He promised to repair the damage sustained by the Sisters of Charity during the bombardment of Donaldsonville,[108] he provisioned Catholic orphanages, and he treated the religious with utmost courtesy. It goes without saying that he never permitted his Irish followers to forget these services to the nuns of New Orleans![109]

It was in the administration of relief to the poor and in public sanitation, however, that Butler showed most clearly that he was not a mere heartless conqueror. The deplorable condition of New Orleans' lower classes was one of the most serious problems facing the occupation forces.[110] To be sure, it was not merely for humanitarian reasons that the General acted on behalf of the poor, but to those whom he helped, his measures were God-sends. He subscribed to the theory that the rich had started the "rebellion" and that whatever loyalty was left was to be found among the poor; consequently, it was to the lower classes that he looked for support. He continued to distribute rations, even appointing a superintendent of relief, and he saw to it that some eleven thousand families were supported in great part by the United States.[111] Although he did not have sufficient funds to care for all who needed assistance, he repeatedly ordered the city to put the unemployed to work.[112] When this system proved only partially successful, he decided to raise funds from the leading secessionists.

In order to determine who they were, Butler hit upon a novel expedient. Prior to the capture of the forts, the leading firms of New Orleans had not only contributed generously to a Confederate City Defense Fund, but ardent Confederate cotton brokers had signed a manifesto calling on planters not to bring their produce to the blockaded port. To Butler, such activities constituted *prima facie* evidence of treason. Cleverly playing on the Southern complaint that Fort Sumter had resulted in a rich man's war but a poor man's fight, he singled out for special levies to relieve the suffering poor all those who had contributed to the Defense Fund and had signed the manifesto.[113] Although the victims bitterly resented Butler's order, the General was unmoved, and he got his money.[114]

There was no lack of work for the unemployed. New Orleans was extremely dirty. Putrid, decaying animal matter cluttered up drainage canals and markets. It offended Butler's nostrils as much as his sense of proper sanitation. He was determined to have his bailiwick cleaned up, especially since summer, with its threat of yellow fever, was approaching. Actually, it was well known that Southerners were expecting the dreaded disease to wreak havoc among the Yankee troops, unaccustomed as they were to the climate of the Delta.[115] To keep this expectation from becoming a reality, the General put the unemployed to work removing the offending rubbish, and within a short time, canals, markets, and streets were as clean as those of any prim New England town.[116]

Nevertheless, these measures solved only part of the problem of keeping the city free from fever. Since both Army and Navy surgeons agreed that yellow fever was not indigenous but imported, they suggested the establishment of a rigid quarantine below the forts,[117] a bit of advice the General accepted with enthusiasm. No ship from an infected port was allowed to come upriver until forty days had elapsed; vessels from non-infected areas had to procure a clean bill of health from a visiting physician before they were cleared.[118] To Butler's great satisfaction, his efforts proved successful. Only two cases of yellow fever occurred in New Orleans during the entire summer.[119] The troops remained unaffected, and even his worst enemies grudgingly admitted that New Orleans had never been cleaner.[120] But that was as far as they were willing to go. They were determined to be rid of their conqueror, and it was with glee that they watched him become involved in serious difficulties.

CHAPTER ELEVEN

# "Butler Must Go"

"They may say what they please about General Butler, but he was the right man in the right place in New Orleans," Admiral Farragut said when the war was over.[1]

Though the Admiral's opinion may have been justified, there were many who disagreed as early as 1862. For one thing, there were constant rumors of large scale corruption in the Department of the Gulf. Opportunity for speculation was great at a time when cotton was almost valueless in the South but highly sought after elsewhere; when sugar sold for six cents in New York and three cents in New Orleans; when turpentine brought thirty-eight dollars on the Hudson and three dollars on the Mississippi; when flour was six dollars in the Empire State but more than twice as much in Louisiana.[2] Since the commanding general was in a position to issue permits for trade with enemy-held territories — to say nothing of his vast powers under the second Confiscation Act — it is certain that he was in a position to use his prerogatives corruptly. Whether or not he did so has never been proven, but circumstances looked so suspicious that not only his enemies, but even some of his friends expressed doubts concerning the General's activities. And with good reason, for Butler, never too careful about "respectable" people's opinions, was downright reckless in New Orleans. Even before reaching the city, he had engaged in private speculations of dubious propriety. He had bought a captured cargo of cotton and turpentine worth about five thousand dollars which he sent north from Ship Island in a Government vessel. Although the Quartermaster at Boston questioned the legality of the transaction,[3] the General made other private purchases in New Orleans and again sent cargo home as ballast in ships belonging to the United States. Considerable correspondence with the War Department ensued. Butler maintained that his purchases had greatly reassured planters and factors and had saved the Government the expenses of other ballast. The Department upheld him, declaring that his action had been wise and patriotic, but it warned that "he ought not to be involved in private trade and profits arising out of his official power and position."[4] The damage to his reputation had been done.

The incident should have been a warning, but Butler seemed undisturbed, and he continued to give his enemies ample opportunity to circulate the most damaging stories about him. His immediate entourage was in itself cause for suspicion. What could people think about the General's brother — "Colonel Butler," as he called himself? Jovial, fat and shrewd, Andrew Jackson Butler did not enjoy a good reputation.[5] His operations in the captured city were shady. He bought up provisions in Texas to sell to the officers in charge of New Orleans' poor relief;[6] as the commanding general's brother, he put pressure on frightened planters to sell him their crops for a pittance;[7] he engaged in contraband trade,[8] and if rumor is to be credited, the "Colonel" was engaged in a variety of illegal — and very profitable — activities.[9] Naturally, the conviction that the General was his brother's partner became ever more widespread.[10] And because some of his staff officers also engaged in suspicious transactions,[11] while Butler enforced with great rigor the Confiscation Acts passed by Congress to punish secessionists,[12] nothing he could say or do removed the clouds of suspicion that attached to his conduct.

It was inevitable that reports of the General's activities would reach Washington. The Treasury received detailed information from George Denison, the United States Collector of Customs and an admirer of Butler. But even Denison lost faith when evidences of illicit profits accumulated. He made no secret of his suspicions and included testimony which seemed to indicate that Butler, if not directly involved, at least winked at the laxity and corruption of his subordinates.[13] If generally friendly observers were suspicious, those hostile to Butler were certain that the General was corrupt.

Reverdy Johnson asserted that a state of fraud and corruption "without parallel in the past history of the country"[14] existed in New Orleans, while David D. Porter unmercifully castigated his adversary. As he wrote to the North,

> New Orleans will either be in the hands of the rebels in forty days or it will be burnt. Rest assured of that unless another man is sent in Butler's place. They are great fools for not wishing to keep him there as he is supplying the Rebels with all they want by way of Pearl River (salt, shoes, blankets, flour, etc.) for which he charges license, which goes God knows where.[51]

The impression created in Washington may easily be imagined.

Although none of these charges could be made to stick, it was not long before Butler's every move was subject to suspicion. When crooked offers were received in Richmond, Butler was believed to be behind them.[16] When he took over the former residence of General David E. Twiggs, the Creoles were convinced he did so for sinister reasons. He stole silver spoons, they said, and when Twiggs' valuable ceremonial swords disappeared, they knew that Butler looted weapons as well. It did not matter that he sent the swords to Washington for public disposal,[17] or that he turned over the Confederate General's property to the quartermaster upon his departure.[18] Even the fact that he had purchased the silver and sent it to his mother[19] failed to dispel rumors. His enemies were prepared to believe the worst, and as the plate of a Frenchman named Villeneuve was also confiscated,[20] the story that the General had stolen spoons became so widespread that his enemies called him "Spoons Butler" ever after. It made no difference that it was unnecessary for a man of Butler's power and wealth to steal anybody's spoons, or that he had documentary evidence of the falsity of the charges against him.[21] The rumors persisted.

Stories of peculation were not the only causes for the Administration's increasing concern about the Department of the Gulf. Seward knew well that the South was hoping for foreign intervention. Accordingly, he made every possible effort to keep the powers friendly. But Butler's treatment of the consuls in New

Orleans was so high-handed that the Secretary of State could not but wish for his removal.

Actually, the General did not act without provocation. Although they had to maintain an outward show of neutrality, the consuls were generally sympathetic to the Confederacy. Yet it would have been wiser to overlook some of their questionable activities. Butler, who distrusted the international financial community as he distrusted its American representatives, chose not to ignore the foreigners' activities, and the reaction of the State Department was anything but favorable.

His rows with representatives of foreign powers started immediately after he had landed. A "European Brigade" had kept order in the city during the interregnum,[22] and when it was disbanded, its members voted to send their arms to Beauregard. Upon learning of this partisan action, Butler ordered all those concerned either to surrender their weapons or leave the city. When the Acting British Consul, George Coppel, protested, his status was questioned. Resigning in a huff, Coppel was reinstated by his government, and Butler was forced to recognize him.[23] Neither this incident nor the imprisonment of British subjects at Fort Jackson facilitated future intercourse with Coppel.[24]

More serious was Butler's dispute with the Dutch consul, a liquor dealer named Amadié Couturié, who, prior to the arrival of the Federal troops, had hidden eight hundred thousand dollars' worth of Mexican silver taken from the vaults of the Bank of Louisiana. As the transaction looked suspicious, Butler decided to seize the money, despite Couturié's assertion that it belonged to the Amsterdam banking house of Hope & Company. A detail searched both the consulate and the consul's person, took the treasure, and left the outraged Couturié protesting against this invasion of his diplomatic immunity. He hauled down his flag, turned over his affairs to his French colleague, and informed the Netherlands legation in Washington.[25]

It was not long before the Dutch Minister, Roest van Limburg, demanded satisfaction from the Secretary of State. To make matters worse, van Limburg was backed by his British and French colleagues, for Butler had also sparred with Count Méjan, the French consul in New Orleans. That official, too, had received funds from a bank — money allegedly belonging to the firm of Dupasseur & Company. Because Butler suspected that it was to be used to purchase arms for the Confederacy in Europe, he had allowed the Count to keep it only on condition that none of the specie leave the consulate. But Méjan, who also resented Butler's order to saloon keepers to procure new licenses — an action which added to the expenses of French citizens — and who clashed repeatedly with the military authorities because of his countrymen's unneutral acts, protested vigorously both to Washington and Paris. Consequently, all three diplomats backed van Limburg when he demanded Butler's recall.[26]

The Administration was greatly embarrassed by these protests. While it could not heed all of van Limburg's demands lest it be considered too subservient to foreigners, it had to do something to appease the complaining diplomats. Lincoln solved the dilemma temporarily by appointing General Shepley Military Governor of Louisiana but leaving Butler in command of the Department of the Gulf, a change which could be represented to the foreigners as compliance with their wishes while at the same time not offending Butler, who had himself made his friend Shepley Mayor of New Orleans.[27] Moreover, Seward appointed a special commissioner to examine the matter of the seized funds.

The man he chose for this purpose was Reverdy Johnson, the widely known Maryland attorney of Democratic antecedents who had clashed with Butler in Baltimore. In making the appointment, the Secretary of State wanted it clearly understood that he was "by no means . . . prejudging Major General Butler, whose general course of administration [seemed to him] to have been eminently judicious and energetic,"[28] but the Postmaster General warned that Johnson was not to be trusted.[29]

Butler was under no illusions concerning the Johnson mission. The man who had prevailed upon Lincoln to free Ross Winans could hardly be expected to take a favorable attitude toward the General who had arrested the millionaire. Stanton might assure Butler of the Administration's goodwill, but the General distrusted Johnson and Seward from the very beginning.[30] Moreover, his relations with the consuls had worsened. They had complained about his order requiring foreigners to subscribe to a loyalty oath, only to be told by Butler that he would no longer countenance joint protests; they had been informed that many of the persons whom they attempted to protect were not foreigners at all, but had long claimed American citizenship, and they had been offended by the seizure of 3,205 hogsheads of sugar bought by the firm of Covas & Negroponte for several British, French, and Greek subjects on the grounds that the transaction had resulted in a sterling balance for the Confederacy. Butler was so convinced that the consuls were not neutral that he had even advised the Administration to withdraw their exequatur.[31] Under such circumstances, it was inevitable that Commissioner and General would clash, especially since the President had made it clear that he wanted foreigners well treated.[32]

When Johnson arrived in New Orleans late in July, he examined the cases brought before him. He sustained Couturié and recommended that his money be returned. He decided in favor of Méjan and counselled that the Dupasseur funds be released. He upheld Covas & Negroponte and advised that their sugars be given back to them. Nor did he confine himself to the consuls. The $8,948.50 which the General had confiscated from S. H. Kennedy & Company as the result of a blockade running venture was also ordered returned.[33] Although Butler engaged in a lengthy legal debate with the Commissioner,[34] and wrote angry letters to Washington,[35] he was unable to reverse Johnson's verdicts.[36]

These reversals did not make the General feel any more kindly toward the representatives of foreign powers. Irritations never ceased. While unrepentant secessionists sang Confederate songs aboard foreign warships,[37] the Spanish consul protested about quarantine regulations. A Spanish man-of-war tried to give asylum to a suspect wanted by the General,[38] and the Prussian consul became embroiled with the authorities about the clearance of a ship suspected of smuggling out Confederate property. The French consul protested against the imprisonment of Charles Heidsieck, of the famous champagne family, who was apprehended as a spy.[39] There was hardly a consul who did not clash with the General at one time or another,[40] and when Butler finally found proof that Count Méjan had actively assisted Confederates in transferring money abroad, he could not suppress a note of triumph. He had been right all along. As he wrote to the Secretary of War,

> I leave the consul to the Government at Washington. I will take care sufficiently to punish the other alien and domestic traitors . . . whom I have here.[41]

Such a commander was a constant source of irritation to the Secretary of State.

But in the War Department it was lack of military experience which undermined Butler's position. The President was anxious to reopen the entire course of the Mississippi — an operation requiring a general who knew his trade. To be sure, Butler agreed on the importance of opening the river; he had the will to fight, but it was questionable whether he possessed the prerequisites of a great strategist. And the campaigns he conducted in the Department of the Gulf were not particularly impressive.

After the capture of New Orleans, only limited operations were carried on in the Department. A portion of Butler's command, under General Williams, accompanied Farragut when he ascended the river early in May. Easily taking Baton Rouge, the combined forces arrived before Vicksburg on May 18.[42] There they ran into trouble. Situated on high bluffs overlooking the Mississippi, the city was a formidable fortress tenaciously defended by the Confederates. Its military governor boasted,

> Mississippians don't know and refuse to learn how to surrender to an enemy. If Commodore Farragut or Brigadier General Butler can teach them, let them come and try.[43]

For the time being, the Federal commanders decided not to accept the challenge. They wanted to await the outcome of the sparring for Corinth to the north, and as they considered the enemy's guns too high to be reached effectively by naval fire, they returned to Baton Rouge.[44]

Butler did not relish this setback. He was not easily discouraged, and if Vicksburg could not be taken by conventional means, he could always think of unconventional ones. The city was located at the far end of a sharp bend in the river. If a canal could be dug to straighten out the bend, the fortress would become useless to the enemy. The General decided to try, and offered to send seven thousand men to accompany the fleet, provided Porter send six to ten mortar vessels to bomb the heights.[45]

The expedition ran into trouble before it even got underway. Neither Farragut nor Porter was anxious to undertake it, because they thought that the water level was rapidly falling, and they were apprehensive lest Beauregard cut off their retreat. Moreover, Porter was annoyed about the Army's lack of cooperation in towing his fleet. Consequently, while Butler had his way, the mission was unpromising from the start.[46]

When the attackers reappeared below Vicksburg, they found that they could accomplish no more than they had the first time. They could not take the fortress. The tired troops detested their hard-driving General, Thomas Williams, and the canal could not be completed because the water level fell more rapidly than they were able to dig. Above all, the Federal forces were not strong enough,[47] and no matter how many requests for reinforcements reached General Halleck near Corinth, that cautious commander refused to deplete his own forces. He used his troops to occupy Corinth, then he scattered them and undertook no further offensive operations.[48]

Butler was extremely annoyed at this lack of cooperation. One month after the arrival of his men before Vicksburg, he sent peremptory orders for their return, on the grounds that they were in Halleck's department and were needed at Baton Rouge. He announced that he would leave Vicksburg to General Grant,[49] who took it almost a year later. But whether Butler blamed Halleck or not, he could hardly claim success for himself.

In the meantime, Butler's old political associate, John C. Breckinridge, had gathered a force of Confederates for the recapture of Baton Rouge. His army was hurled back on August 4-5, and Butler issued a grandiloquent order boasting of a great triumph,[50] but in reality, the outcome of the engagement was not wholly favorable, for Breckinridge also claimed victory.[51] General Williams was killed, and Butler evacuated the city shortly afterward. While he did so on the advice of subordinates who cited the action's military necessity,[52] Butler gained no laurels by this retreat. And since he was again engaged in controversy with the Navy[53] as the result of Porter's spreading tales in Washington about the corruption at New Orleans,[54] the General's reputation was not enhanced. He managed to justify himself by denying Porter's accusations,[55] but his constant rows did him no good.

During the remainder of the year, Butler turned his attention toward the east and west rather than toward the north. He thought of taking Galveston or Mobile, but he was still short of troops. No matter how much he tried or whom he enlisted in his behalf, he could not obtain reinforcements.[56] All he could do with his limited manpower was to send Godfrey Weitzel to western Louisiana in order to bring that region under Federal control. The expedition was successful. Donaldsonville, Thibodaux, Berwick Bay — all were taken.[57] However, the area was rich in sugar and cotton, and as widespread sequestrations followed, many believed that the operation's object had been commercial rather than military. Butler simply was unable to dispel the impression that he was not much of a soldier.[58]

Rumors of peculation, rows with consuls, lack of military experience — there were sufficient reasons to justify removing Butler from his command. But just as in the previous year, the Administration had to be cautious. 1862 was an election year; since Butler was still a nominal Democrat, he could not be shunted aside without serious repercussions. To further complicate the situation the radical Republicans were taking an ever more active interest in him. They were pleased with his rigorous enforcement of military law; they liked his rough treatment of the hated rebels. Moreover, they disliked Seward and did not sympathize with his policy of appeasement of foreigners. Above all they were thrilled by the General's successful employment of one of the first colored regiments ever raised in the United States.[59]

The Negro question had given Butler trouble from the day he arrived in Louisiana. With planters and many Federal officials in terror of a slave revolt, and with an increasing number of runaways drifting into his lines, he had to find some solution.[60] Only this time the answer was not as simple as it had been in Virginia. There were too many Negroes to declare them all contraband,

and as Lincoln had revoked General Hunter's orders for military emancipation, it was obvious that radical measures were not yet the order of the day.

At first Butler was hesitant. When General Phelps took matters into his own hands by preparing to recruit fugitive slaves into the Army, Butler ordered him to desist and asked him to put the men to work felling trees instead. The Vermonter demurred, offering to resign rather than obey these commands. When Butler forwarded Phelps' papers to Washington and the resignation was accepted,[61] the radical press criticized Butler severely.[62]

At first Butler was annoyed and complained to his wife about the prevalence of radical notions.[63] But it was not long before he, too, changed his way of thinking. The second Confiscation Act, providing for the emancipation of all slaves except those of loyal masters, gave the General an opportunity to demonstrate that plantations could be run with free labor. He abolished public whipping of Negroes,[64] and, short of troops, he finally came to the conclusion that the time was ripe to call on the colored population for military service.

The arrival at so radical a solution to the manpower problem by a former Breckinridge Democrat was one of the ironies of the Civil War. Butler knew he could not permit Phelps' method of enlisting fugitive slaves. Neither his troops nor the Government would have countenanced such a course at the time. But there was a sizeable population of free Negroes in New Orleans. They had served under Jackson in 1815, and even the Confederate Governor had permitted them to form two regiments of "Native Guards." These two incidents served as precedents for Butler, and he called into service the members of the former Confederate unit. In a flamboyant General Order dated August 22, 1862, he justified his course. If colored men could be called upon to fight for a Government founded upon the cornerstone of slavery and the inequality of races, there was no reason why they could not also be called upon to fight for one based on the Declaration of Independence.[65] Nobody inquired too closely whether or not the recruits were really free, but theoretically, the planters could not complain that the Federal Government was arming slaves. It goes without saying that the measure pleased the radicals.[66]

Butler had made a significant contribution to the solution of the racial problem.

Under these circumstances, the General felt that he could demand a clarification of his position. The constant rumors about his recall, and the warnings sent by friends from Washington,[67] had made him wonder about his future. For a time, he was undecided whether to recall Sarah, who had gone home to Lowell to avoid the yellow fever season, or to follow her. Sarah knew well what the trouble was: Brother Jackson and his speculations. She was sure that he would ruin Ben.[68] But her husband was notoriously loyal to his family, and he did not heed her advice to send his brother away. Jackson was allowed to remain, and in the belief that he himself would stay longer, Butler finally permitted Sarah to return.[69] He had written a sarcastic letter to Halleck, stating that he had read about his removal in the secession newspapers. As he put it,

> If that be so, might I ask that my successor be sent as early as possible, as my own health is not the strongest, and it would seem but fair that he should take some part in the yellow fever season.

The answer was wholly reassuring,[70] and he concluded that he was safe.

Yet, in spite of Halleck's reply, in spite of the radicals' support, his time was running short. Lincoln had his own ideas about emancipation — his proclamation was to go into effect that New Year — and he wanted to make a test case of Louisiana.[71] That state might well be brought back into the Union in accordance with his own mild policy of reconstruction. There was some Union feeling left in Louisiana,[72] and he was determined not to let it die. Butler might cooperate by arranging for elections and by seeing to it that two unconditional Unionists were returned to the House of Representatives,[73] but it was questionable whether he was the right man to foster Unionism and to administer the Emancipation Proclamation.[74] Chase might speak for him;[75] Stanton's attitude, however, was equivocal,[76] and Seward was hostile.[77] Consequently on November 8, shortly after the mid-term elections,

Lincoln issued orders to Nathaniel Banks to take over command of a greatly reinforced Department of the Gulf.[78] Butler was not informed, but he soon found out that changes were in the offing. Whether Banks was coming to lead an expedition into Texas, or whether he was coming to take over the entire department did not become clear until his arrival early in December. When he showed his order to Butler, the former commander knew that he had been superseded.[79]

Butler was furious.[80] He treated his successor courteously,[81] but to be removed without a word of explanation was more than he could stand. He could not even blame West Point — Banks, like himself, was a political general from Massachusetts — and he determined to find out the reasons for his downfall. He informed Washington that he was going home.[82] He was unwilling to remain in New Orleans in a subordinate position.

He did not intend to leave without a parting blow. In a stirring farewell address to his troops, he praised their great accomplishments under his leadership.[83] And lest the inhabitants of the city get the impression that he was leaving under a cloud, he issued a provocative proclamation in which he adjured them to return to their allegiance to the United States. "I do not feel that I have erred in too much harshness," he wrote,

> for . . . I might have regaled you with the amenities of British civilization, and yet been within the supposed rules of civilized warfare. You might have been smoked to death in caverns, as were the covenanters of Scotland by command of a General of the royal house of England; or roasted, like the inhabitants of Algiers during the French campaign; your wives and daughters might have been given over to the ravisher, as were the unfortunate dames of Spain during the Peninsular War . . . . Your sons might have been blown from the mouths of cannon, like the sepoys at Delhi; and yet all this would have been within the rules of civilized warfare as practiced by the most polished and most hypocritical nations of Europe.

But he had done nothing of the sort. He had fed the poor, cleaned the streets, and prevented disease.[84] It was a proclamation the country would not forget, and when he left the Crescent City on the day before Christmas, he left behind him not only the lasting hatred of secessionists,[85] but also his political past. Democrats had become his bitter enemies,[86] radical Republicans his fervent supporters.[87] The Hunker of yesteryear had become a radical of radicals.

Thus ended the most picturesque period of Butler's life. That his administration of New Orleans was not as bad as tradition has portrayed it has been proven repeatedly in recent times.[88] To be sure, corruption flourished, but it is questionable whether anyone could have prevented it. Moreover, it is doubtful that he personally profited greatly from the various deals which enriched his subordinates. He could and did make money in other ways.[89] He might have rid himself of dubious associates. But Butler was a criminal lawyer, and his profession had always brought him in contact with unsavory persons, who, to him, had always been a source of legitimate profit. What was true of private life seemed equally applicable in public affairs. If disreputable people could help a lawyer earn a livelihood, they might also serve a politician as a nucleus for a machine. In the long run, it was not their immediate profits which interested him, but their support in later years. In this he was successful. It might shock respectable people, but it was not at all unusual. And so Butler not only rendered a service to the Union by holding a rebellious city with insufficient troops, but he also helped himself by acquiring innumerable political friends and a reputation for uncompromising radicalism.

CHAPTER TWELVE

# From the Mississippi to the James

The month of December, 1862, was not a happy period for Abraham Lincoln. The Battle of Fredericksburg had shown that Burnside was no more capable than McDowell, McClellan, or Pope. The elections had been anything but encouraging, and the radicals in the President's own party were restless and dissatisified. Neither the political nor the military future looked particularly bright.

Under such circumstances, the President could hardly look with equanimity upon the return of the dispossessed commander of the Department of the Gulf. Butler was not the type of man to submit meekly to a rebuff, and as he had vociferous supporters, his recall was sure to stir up strife. Butler in Lowell might prove even more embarrassing than Butler in New Orleans. The President decided that he could not allow the General to go home without an interview, so he wired to him and asked Butler to come to Washington.[1] Even the Chief Executive had to admit that the man from Lowell had shown skill in discharging his civil duties in Louisiana. Perhaps he might send him back to the Mississippi Valley on a new mission.[2]

When Butler arrived at the capital, he was received with great cordiality. But he was in a sour mood. He wanted to know why he had been recalled, and why Jefferson Davis had been informed of his removal even before he himself had been told of it. Demanding an explanation, he questioned Lincoln, Stanton, Seward, and Halleck, but he found that nobody was willing to give him an answer. As he regaled the President with his radical views on emancipation, Lincoln tried to mollify the General by suggesting he accept a new command. The entire Mississippi Valley might be put at his disposal, and he might have full authority to raise Negro troops. But Butler refused. Convinced that Seward had sacrificed him in order to appease the French, he demanded nothing less than his old Department, and regardless of how earnestly the President explained that such a course might disgrace Banks, he persisted. When the conference broke up, Lincoln's offer stood, but nothing definite had been decided.[3]

Lincoln's misgivings about letting Butler go home without a command proved justified. People might argue about the merits of the General's administration of New Orleans, but no one could deny that his return was a complete success. In triumph he journeyed from Washington to Lowell. Wherever he stopped, enthusiastic crowds gathered to hail him.[4] That Jefferson Davis, on the very day on which Butler left New Orleans, had declared him a felon and an outlaw, only made the General more popular; that Southern gentlemen offered rewards of one thousand dollars for his capture only made him more interesting; that Southern ladies had volunteered to spin the cord to hang him only served to make him more deserving.[5] Here at last was a general who made rebels wince; a general who was able to cow the hated Southern aristocracy.[6] Formal votes of thanks were passed in state legislatures and in the House of Representatives.[7] The country was grateful; Butler was at the peak of his popularity.

Amid these signs of popular approval, the General did not remain passive. In town after town he delivered speeches, denouncing copperheads, heaping abuse upon secessionists, and calling for an end to slavery.[8] When he reached Lowell, Huntington Hall was packed to the rafters for the official welcome.[9] On his arrival in Boston, a mammoth meeting was staged in his honor at Faneuil Hall. Old enmities seemed forgotten when the Breckinridge gubernatorial candidate of only two years earlier presented a captured Confederate flag to the city as a memento of, and a warning against, secession. Dr. Oliver Wendell Holmes read a laudatory poem. When the former Hunker, after calling for payment of the war debt by a tax on cotton and making impassioned appeals for free labor, confidently predicted that the Union would emerge stronger than before, the old hall shook with applause.[10] He was the man of the hour.

Nor did he allow the Administration to forget it. Rumors were circulating that he was slated for a cabinet post,[11] and lest they die down, his quartermaster, Colonel J. W. Shaffer, planted new ones in the newspapers.[12] Shaffer knew the President, and he prevailed upon Simon Cameron and Republican members of Congress to call on Lincoln in person to protest against Butler's removal from his command.[13] Many others worked on Butler's behalf, among them John D. Sanborn, not yet notorious, but already an active supporter.[14]

For Lincoln, these developments must have been most embarrassing. After all, it was he who had recalled the irrepressible Yankee; it would be very dangerous to leave him sulking. The President was fond of Banks, but for a moment, it seemed as if he would have to sacrifice the "Bobbin Boy" from Waltham. "We cannot dispense with Butler's services," the Chief Executive wrote to Stanton,[15] and on January 23, he actually drew up a carefully worded order explaining his predicament to Banks. Until he could get an independent command in Texas, Banks might retain command of the forces in the field, but Butler would have to take over the Department of the Gulf.[16]

Although the order was not sent, Butler's position became even stronger during the following weeks. In a dramatic session, he testified before the Committee on the Conduct of the War. Declaring that he had no idea why he had been recalled, he launched upon a long defense of his administration in New Orleans, urged the employment of Negro troops, and altogether made an excellent impression on the radicals.[17] Lincoln could not but take note.

The President, however, could never see his way clear to issuing the order he had prepared. Doubts about Butler's military ability had not been dispelled;[18] nor had rumors of corruption died down.[19] Lincoln knew that the foreign powers would not take a favorable view of Butler's return.[20] Shortly after the General's appearance before the Committee, he saw Lincoln again, and the President now made a new offer. How would the General like to go to the Mississippi Valley on a personal mission for the Commander-in-Chief to report on conditions there? A pass had already been prepared for that purpose,[21] but Butler was reluctant. As he had heard from various sources that the President was about to send him back to New Orleans, he wanted a guarantee that the new assignment would lead to his restoration as Commander of the Department of the Gulf, with increased powers.[22]

A number of days passed. Butler saw various members of the cabinet, he dined at the White House,[23] and at last, a new draft order was drawn up. It embodied Lincoln's earlier plan of returning Butler to New Orleans but leaving Banks in command of the troops in the field.[24] Like its predecessor, however, it was never issued. Butler himself was unwilling to share power with anyone, least of all the man who had reversed his strict policies in Louisiana.[25] He would not go without additional troops, and the result was that he again left Washington with nothing more than a tentative offer.[26]

Failure to get what he wanted did not stifle the General's ambitions. The country was in such an unsettled state that there had long been talk of the possibility of the emergence of a dictator. In Butler's memoirs, he professed his horror of such a development,[27] but despite the General's strong warnings to Wilson against McClellan's ambitions,[28] he was not so perturbed about the trend toward one-man rule as he pretended to be at the time.[29] There were even predictions that he might be the coming strong man.[30] At any rate, people spoke of his chances for the Presidency.[31] His friends kept up the clamor for a place in the cabinet, especially during the chaotic weeks following the disaster at Chancellorsville,[32] and Butler himself did his best to remain on the front pages of the newspapers. In a widely publicized address at the Academy of Music in New York, he outlined a radical plan of reconstruction. Taking issue with conservatives but agreeing with Thaddeus Stevens, the emerging radical leader in the House of Representatives, Butler said that he for one was not willing to restore the Union as it had once been. Rebellion had obliterated the obligations of the North toward the South, he said. The seceded states had reverted to the status of territories, and ever since antiquity, the conqueror had had the right to take the possessions of the conquered. Let the Government confiscate rebel property, distribute it to loyal men, both Northerners and Southerners, and a new

Union — truly republican — would emerge.[33] It was a speech to fire the radicals' imagination.[34]

In his search for publicity, Butler had a stroke of good luck. James Parton, the country's most famous biographer, was impressed by his accomplishments and offered the General his services.[35] At a time when ever more vitriolic articles against him appeared in the anti-Administration press,[36] Butler welcomed such an opportunity. Inviting the author to his house, he gave him access to his papers and effects,[37] and a lifelong friendship sprang up between the two men. Parton went to work with enthusiasm, completing his book by late fall.[38] He called it *General Butler in New Orleans,* and although it was a campaign biography and hardly one of his best productions,[39] the book became an immediate success. It underwent many printings, greatly enriching its author[40] and keeping its subject prominently before an admiring public.[41]

In the meantime, Butler continued to deliver speeches advocating the enlistment of Negroes and punishment for conquered Confederates.[42] Before long, he was in demand as a campaign speaker for the hard-pressed Republican party,[43] his career received a favorable review in the *Atlantic Monthly,*[44] and he loomed larger and larger as a candidate for the highest office in the land.[45]

Yet Butler was not happy. No matter how hard he tried,[46] he could not get the New Orleans command on his own terms. The radicals on the Committee on the Conduct of the War sounded him out on the possibility of taking an army down the Mississippi Valley, but he was not enthusiastic. Insisting that the river could only be opened from the south, the General suggested that they provide him with enough troops to take Charleston instead. If he could cooperate with his old friend Farragut, he thought he would have little trouble taking that cradle of secession; moreover, the troops might later be led overland to attack Richmond from the rear.[47] Of course the Committee had no right to offer independent commands to anybody. That was the prerogative of the President, and nothing came of the plan.

Abraham Lincoln was sorely tried by Butler's restlessness. People were constantly asking him to send the dissatisfied political General somewhere — to prevent new draft riots in New York,[48] to supplant Schofield in Missouri,[49] or to resume the administration of the Department of the Gulf.[50] But the President took his time. After Gettysburg and Vicksburg, he could afford to delay his final decision. Now it was Butler who was worried, and finally he became so desperate that he even considered accepting the offer of the previous February, only to discover that it no longer stood.[51] Not until the eve of the November elections did the President finally decide to find a place for him. He was not permitted to go back to New Orleans — Banks could retain this command and Seward need not worry — but there was an opening for a new commander of the Department of Virginia and North Carolina. Weary of the long wait, Butler accepted, and early in November, 1863, he returned to his old headquarters at Fortress Monroe.[52]

Great changes had taken place since he had left Old Point Comfort two years earlier. The peninsula had become the main theater of operations during the spring and summer of 1862, when General McClellan had fought his way up to the very gates of Richmond. He had been forced to take his entire army back to Washington, and the area had become quiet again; but the department had been expanded. Norfolk, Portsmouth, Williamsburg, several coastal towns in North Carolina — all were now controlled by Union forces. Even though it was not an active area of war for the time being, the command had possibilities.

The new commander did not welcome this state of affairs. He had been inactive too long not to crave some action. Moreover, he had always thrived on publicity, and as no immediate military operations were planned, he had to think of other ways to remain in the public limelight.

As it turned out, he did not have to look far to exercise his talents. A problem as dramatic as it was complicated had arisen to plague the Administration. Ever since 1861, efforts had been made to effect the exchange of prisoners of war. In 1862, General Dix had negotiated a cartel providing for the speedy exchange of all captured personnel, the surplus on either side to be released on parole.[53] But the arrangement soon broke down. For one thing, the Confederates refused to treat colored troops as soldiers; nor could the belligerents agree exactly on who should be considered paroled. Furthermore, by 1863, the North held more prisoners than the South, and as time went on, the conviction grew that it would be to the Union's advantage not to continue with the exchange.[54]

To the public, the failure of the cartel was well-nigh incomprehensible. What was holding up an exchange which would have released the suffering soldiers from Andersonville and Libby? The press clamored for something to be done,[55] and if the people in control of the negotiations could not get results, there must be someone who could.

Butler thought he was that man. For one reason or another, he imagined that the Confederates might be induced to resume a man-for-man exchange, and he allowed his views to be circulated as widely as possible. The Secretary of War cautioned that the problem was not as easy as he imagined; the question of the disposition of colored troops constituted an insurmountable obstacle. Butler agreed that the Government could not deny protection to the Negroes who were fighting its battles, but he could not see why a man-for-man exchange could not be started. When all thirteen thousand prisoners held by the enemy had been returned, there would still be twice that number left in Federal hands in case the South made trouble about the colored men.[56]

At first glance this proposition seemed reasonable. But Butler had not really solved the problem. The Confederates had long insisted that no exchanges could be contemplated except under the provisions of the cartel calling for immediate release of all prisoners. The surplus on either side might be paroled, but not kept back. This problem, among others, had long held up negotiations, as Major General Ethan Allan Hitchcock, the exchange commissioner in Washington, hastened to point out. How did Butler propose to overcome this difficulty?[57]

To the General, these objections seemed spurious. Early in December, to demonstrate his ability to deal with the enemy, he arranged for a shipment of vaccine across the lines. The transaction's success was so encouraging[58] that on December 17, Hitchcock arrived to give him blanket authority to arrange for exchanges at City Point. The North was ready to waive all considerations save those which dealt with equal treatment of Negroes. If Butler could succeed in effecting a man-for-man bargain on that basis, the War Department would have no objections.[59]

It is doubtful whether Stanton, who opposed the cartel, ever believed that Butler could accomplish anything. The Hero of New Orleans was the most hated man in the Confederacy. It was unreasonable to assume that the authorities at Richmond would swallow their pride and deal with a commissioner whom they had publicly outlawed — a man they called "Beast." But the Secretary had little to lose. Negotiations had practically broken down; the public was clamoring for action, and if the Southerners refused to deal with Butler, they would be responsible for the consequences. The newspapers would then be able to explain the Government's failure in more personal, easily understandable terms.[60]

Butler knew that he would have to act fast to overcome the enemy's hostility to him. A *fait accompli* might accomplish more than long drawn out negotiations. His opposite was Judge Robert Ould, known to be a shrewd negotiator, but also reputed to be a practical man.[61] Christmas was approaching. Perhaps its spirit might work magic on the Confederates. Accordingly, the General not only informed the Judge officially of his assumption of his new duties, but confronted him with a boat load of some five hundred prisoners. He was willing to return them, provided an equal number of Federal soldiers could be assembled in exchange.[62]

The Confederates were annoyed. On the one hand, they were anxious to receive their prisoners; on the other, they were more than reluctant to deal with Mumford's executioner. Nor were they willing to waive their insistence upon the immediate release of all captives under the cartel. The situation called for the exercise of diplomatic finesse, a quality Judge Ould possessed. As a token of his willingness to resume negotiations, he sent back the required number of prisoners, but he refused to address his communications to Butler and demanded the appointment of someone else.[63]

This insult angered the new commissioner, especially as he had heard that the Richmond cabinet had decided to break off all exchanges as long as he was in control.[64] Although he had the Administration's backing,[65] an impasse had been reached. To break it, Butler suggested severe measures of retaliation. He even went to Washington in person to impress his views on the Government,[66] but nothing was done. Thereupon, having decided that a bold stroke might yet achieve his aims, he issued a unilateral declaration that he would exchange all prisoners received up to January 20, 1864, an action as hasty as it was unwise. As Stanton had not been consulted, he ordered the offer withdrawn, and Hitchcock engaged in lengthy controversy with the rash commissioner.[67]

Butler, however, was to experience at least a limited triumph. To the disgust of the Richmond *Examiner,* there were those in Dixie who openly advocated a reversal of the policy of non-recognition of the "Beast," and the Virginia House of Delegates, with Jefferson Davis' consent, passed a resolution calling on the authorities to negotiate with the "outlaw."[68] Ould himself thought he might accomplish something if he could deal with Butler, and although the proposition caused Secretary of War Seddon some misgivings, Ould finally justified it to Jefferson Davis on rather labored grounds.[69]

A meeting between Ould and Butler took place at Fortress Monroe on March 31, a conference which must have given the Federal commissioner great satisfaction. Here he was, conferring with a Confederate under a flag of truce — a memorable event for one who had been outlawed by Jefferson Davis. He had forced the enemy to recognize him, to take back the proclamation, if not formally, at least in fact. Nor did Ould cause much trouble. It was obvious that he was ready for an agreement on everything except the question of colored prisoners. Accordingly, Butler suggested to Stanton that all previously received captives be officially declared exchanged, and that the United States renew the offer to resume a man-for-man exchange under the cartel, while still insisting upon decent treatment for Negro soldiers.[70] He even wanted the President to come in person to examine the Confederate propositions.[71]

In the meantime, great changes had taken place in Washington. Ulysses S. Grant had become commander of the Union forces. Already known as "Unconditional Surrender Grant," the Lieutenant General had grasped the fact that modern war called for more than tactical maneuvers on the actual field of battle. He realized that it required the total energies of a nation — economic and political as well as military. Victory must surely follow if only the North's great superiority in men and materials could be applied exclusively to the task of weakening the Confederacy. An exchange of prisoners did not fit into this scheme. The Confederates would receive potential soldiers back in their midst, while the Federal Army would gain only starved, emaciated men, unable to fight for a long time to come. Grant was determined to stop the exchange, no matter how unpopular such a course might be in the North, where obloquy was poured on all who seemed to stand in the way of the liberation of the starving inmates of Southern prisons. He explained all this in detail to Butler on April 2, and to make sure his position was understood, two weeks later issued a formal order stopping exchanges.[72]

Thereafter, there could be little hope for successful rendition of captives. To be sure, Butler continued to meet with the Confederates to arrange for the transfer of invalids,[73] but he knew that nothing substantial could be accomplished. By August, Ould was ready to yield almost everything except the question of recaptured slaves, yet Grant remained adamant.[74] All that remained for Butler to do was to explain the stoppage in a manner which could be easily understood in the North, a task he performed in a lengthy letter to the Confederate agent. He insisted upon the rectitude of the Government's position on the question of colored prisoners,[75] but he could not reopen the negotiations.

Butler was anything but happy about Grant's decision. Always a man of action, he had sought the position of agent of exchange in order to accomplish something. Success would have increased his popularity, yet not only was he denied all opportunity to win fresh laurels, but he was put in the position of having to carry out a measure as unpopular as it was necessary. It was an obnoxious assignment, especially as the Navy saw no reason why it should not carry out its own exchanges. The General demurred,[76] but there was little that he could do. He was permitted to continue the transfer of sick and wounded;[77] he even had an understanding with Ould to produce all men called for by name on either side,[78] but all hope of effecting a general settlement had vanished. Perhaps he obtained some diversion by interviewing such interesting transients as Belle Boyd, the Confederate Mata Hari, and Edward Pollard, the historian of the Lost Cause.[79] All in all, however, his accomplishments as commissioner of exchange remained unimpressive.

CHAPTER THIRTEEN

# "Bottled Up"

Early in 1864, General Halleck unburdened himself to his friend William T. Sherman. "It seems but little better than murder," he wrote, "to give important commands to such men as Banks, Butler, McClernand, Sigel and Lew Wallace . . ."[1] Whether he was right, at least insofar as Butler was concerned, would have to be decided during that year — the first time that Butler had been given enough troops to show what he could do when there was no navy on hand to help him.

Cocky and self-confident, Butler was not disturbed by his lack of actual combat experience. Unwilling to wait until the spring campaign was under way, he was anxious to accomplish something as soon as possible. Consequently, when General Wistar, one of his brigade commanders, suggested a cavalry raid on Richmond to liberate the starving prisoners at Libby, and perhaps to capture members of the cabinet as well, Butler consented with enthusiasm, especially since Elizabeth Van Lew, the intrepid Union spy in the Confederate capital, had informed him that the city was poorly defended and that the prisoners were about to be evacuated. Success would have been conducive to good publicity, but the expedition failed. The enemy had received ample warning, and all Butler got for his trouble was the enmity of the commanders of the Army of the Potomac whom he had asked to undertake a diversionary movement.[2]

He could not grieve long about small skirmishes that winter.[3] With Union forces already in control of the Mississippi Valley and most of Tennessee, the time had come for a decisive campaign, and his mind turned to grand strategy. Combined operations of Army and Navy had always appealed to him; his greatest successes had been won in cooperation with the sister service. He thought he might now repeat earlier exploits, only on a larger scale. Since naval vessels were able to ascend the river to a point less than twenty-five miles from Richmond, it occurred to Butler, as it had already suggested itself to others, that the city might be taken by an amphibious operation. The troops might be landed near the confluence of the James and the Appomattox, where a number of peninsulas afforded excellent defensive lines from which to launch a short and successful overland movement against the Confederate capital.[4]

On April 1, General Grant, newly appointed to his post as general-in-chief, paid a visit to Fortress Monroe. When Butler outlined his scheme, Grant listened. It was a good plan, one which he had considered himself in the past,[5] and now that Butler suggested it, Grant not only indicated his approval, but saw no harm in allowing Butler to believe that he was its sole author.[6] Grant made it clear that the movement would have to be coordinated with the operations of other armies, especially those of the Army of the Potomac. That body was to move south against Lee until it forced his troops into the vicinity of Richmond, while Butler was to secure and fortify City Point. From there, he was to advance upon the Confederate capital along the south bank of the James, a march designed to bring about a junction of the two armies near their mutual objective.[7] As the Lieutenant General pointed out two weeks later, it might even prove feasible for the Army of the James — Butler's force — to invest Richmond from the south, enabling its left flank to establish contact with the Army of the Potomac's right flank above the city.[8] Richmond would be surrounded, and Sigel, Sherman, and Banks would be able to mop up their respective theaters of war.[9]

Butler was elated. He was now the commander of an army which was eventually to exceed thirty thousand men; he might even be the first to enter the enemy capital, and he worked day and night to prepare his forces for the impending campaign.[10] Two regular Army officers, Generals William F. Smith and Quincy A. Gillmore, commanded his two corps,[11] and although he suffered a minor setback when the Confederates captured Plymouth, North Carolina, he lost none of his eclat.[12] On April 28, he received word from Grant that simultaneous operations of the two armies would begin on May 4.[13]

The movement started under auspicious circumstances. As one of the participants recalled the scene years later,

> At daylight in the morning of the 5th of May this immense fleet of transports was assembled in Hampton Roads, stretching in a huge line from the mouth of the James, at the head of which lay at anchor the fleet of Admiral Lee . . . The day was perfect, not a cloud in the sky, with the sweet, balmy air of early spring . . . . At 5 o'clock General Butler ordered up anchor from his fleet and an hour later, every ship was in motion . . . Everything seemed to give promise of success . . . A sanguine and cheerful spirit pervaded the army; nor was there at this time lack of confidence in its commander and the two chiefs of the corps . . . Standing on the upper deck, his head bare, his long locks flowing back in the wind, General Butler then looked the picture of health, vigor and resolution as he waved his hat from east to west in unison with his swaying body, as if to indicate that "Forward, forward" was henceforth to be our motto.

In less than forty-eight hours, the armada had landed at City Point and Bermuda Hundred, one hundred and fifty miles upriver.[14] The first part of the plan had succeeded.

What happened during the next two weeks so shattered Butler's military reputation that he never regained the confidence of his army. There were fewer than ten thousand Confederate troops within fifty miles. Eight miles to the southwest lay Petersburg, an all important railroad junction in a virtually defenseless condition, its works manned by fewer than a thousand effectives. Richmond, some twelve miles to the north, was equally denuded of troops, not even five thousand being available to the worried Confederate authorities.[15] Yet for three days, Butler argued with his quarrelsome corps commanders, made ineffective demonstrations upon the railroad tracks, and kept his splendid army monotonously occupied with the construction of a strong line of fortifications across the neck of Bermuda Hundred peninsula.[16] Why he chose Bermuda Hundred for his main base is not quite clear. Had he followed Grant's instructions and established himself at City Point, he would have been much closer to Petersburg and in possession of a useful railroad.[17] But Grant had not mentioned Petersburg; he had spoken of Richmond, and Butler was anxious to effect a landing as far upriver as possible.[18] Years later, he remembered that he had suggested an immediate attack upon the capital, only to be told by his generals that such a movement was impossible.[19] Had he persisted, he might well have captured the city, and since he did not insist, he might at least have taken Petersburg. The city was within his grasp, and its fall would have shortened the war by many months. But he failed miserably.

The blame was not wholly Butler's. His corps commanders were regulars and might have been expected to make up to some extent for their General's lack of experience. But regular Army officers were notoriously suspicious of political generals, and neither Gillmore nor Smith knew how to handle their superior. Gillmore was a brilliant engineer who had graduated at the head of his class at West Point in 1849, but his talents lay in siege operations and defense, not in dashing attacks.[20] And "Baldy" Smith, though he had been successful at Chattanooga, was notoriously sharp-tongued and found it impossible to get along with persons of higher rank. Moreover, he too was an engineer, and although he was personally courageous, he disliked taking chances in battle.[21] Neither of the two generals showed much vigor after the landing, and it was difficult to induce them to cooperate, either with the commanding general or with one another.[22]

After an inconclusive fight at Swift Creek on May 9, Butler finally made plans to move against Petersburg by a joint operation on both sides of the Appomattox River. The corps commanders preferred a united march along the right bank.[23] This time Butler did not listen to them, and again he missed a perfect opportunity to walk into his objective. General Hincks, his old friend from Massachusetts, was ready to march and might even have taken the city, but at the last moment, Butler called him back.[24] For the Commander of the Army of the James was not only bedeviled by his subordinates, but also confused by his superiors. Telegrams arrived from Halleck announcing glorious victories of the Army of the Potomac; Grant himself was reported to be on his way to the James, and Lee was allegedly falling back on Richmond. On the basis of such reports, and worried about Lee's retreating army, Butler fumbled once more. He abandoned the effort to take Petersburg in order to move against Richmond before Lee could get there and effect a junction with Beauregard, known to be approaching from the south.[25]

Actually, Halleck's reports had been only partially correct. Grant's advance from the Rapidan had started simultaneously with Butler's move upriver. Then the Army of the Potomac had run into serious difficulty. It had slugged its way through the Wilderness, and fought an indecisive battle at Spottsylvania Court House, but it failed to destroy its opponents.[26] It was indeed on its way to join the Army of the James — but that made it even more necessary to seize Petersburg before Lee's arrival.

While Butler was wasting opportunity, the Confederates did not remain idle. General Beauregard had assumed command shortly before the beginning of the campaign, and the desperate situation in which he found himself spurred him on to Herculean efforts. Although he was unable to persuade Jefferson Davis to give him sufficient troops to destroy the Army of the James, he did succeed in so reinforcing his line that his opponent's numerical superiority vanished. He did not experience much difficulty in repairing the damaged railroads to and from Petersburg, so that by May 16, he was ready to meet Butler in full force at Drury's Bluff, a fortified eminence less than a dozen miles south of Richmond.[27] The day was foggy. The usual confusion reigned in the Army of the James — proper wire entanglements had not been erected — and before long, its right wing was forced back.[28] Having just heard that Grant would join him at City Point instead of waiting above Richmond, Butler ordered a retreat into the fortifications of Bermuda Hundred.[29] The withdrawal was successful; neither then nor later could Beauregard take the entrenched encampment. But, as General Grant later expressed it, Butler's army "was as completely shut off from further operations against Richmond as if it had been in a bottle strongly corked."[30] "Bottled-up Butler" was an epithet Ben would never live down.

# "BOTTLED UP"

Butler's failure, coupled with Sigel's reverses in the Shenandoah Valley and the Army of the Potomac's troubles north of Richmond, made Grant's original plans untenable. Forced to change front, the Lieutenant General determined to transfer his entire army to the vicinity of Petersburg.[31] What further part Butler might play in operations remained to be seen. Upon Grant's suggestion, Halleck sent an investigating board to report on the best way to utilize the bottled-up force. The board consisted of General Meigs, the efficient Quartermaster General, and General Barnard, one of the Army's most able engineers, and much to Butler's annoyance, it came to the conclusion that either "an officer of military experience or knowledge" be placed in command of the Army of the James, or the command be diminished by twenty thousand men.[32]

Grant accepted the latter alternative, at least in part, even before the report had been formally submitted. In need of men, he ordered the greater portion of XVIII Corps, Smith's force, to join him at Cold Harbor[33] — just at the moment when Butler had perfected a new plan for the capture of Petersburg. The irate army commander had no choice but to obey. Smith left, and the Army of the James was temporarily doomed to impotence.[34]

Butler, however, was stubborn. Petersburg had escaped him again and again, but he was unwilling to give up. After their victory at Drury's Bluff, the Confederates had again denuded the city of troops. Butler knew it, and, thinking his opportunity had come, he ordered Gillmore to try once more on June 9. Everything looked favorable. The cavalry under General Kautz made excellent progress, and although the defenders put old men and young boys into the entrenchments, they could not muster even half the number of the attackers. But weak as the Confederate hold was on the fortifications, they appeared formidable, and the overly cautious commander of X Corps decided that the town was too strongly defended. He retired in good order, again having thrown away an opportunity to take a city which held the key to Richmond.[35]

Butler was furious. He got rid of Gillmore,[36] but he had again failed to capture the elusive prize. Perhaps if he could get along with General Smith he might still take the city before its defenders returned from the north.[37] Once more, however, success would depend on speed, good staff work, and the cooperation of all concerned.

The final test came on June 15. Smith and his troops were returning from Cold Harbor; Grant's entire army was approaching the crossing of the James River, but Lee's forces had not yet arrived.[38] The Confederate Army of Northern Virginia might reach Petersburg at any moment — Butler was watching carefully from his signal tower overlooking both Richmond and Petersburg[39] — but as yet, the Confederate force was not there. This time it was Smith who was to make the assault. He was ordered to prepare for an attack posthaste, and early on June 15, he was ready to go. He, too, arrived before the city's defensive works. But there he halted. Careful as he was, he wanted to make sure of a feasible plan of operations. As he had already lost valuable time because the artillery had not been ready when the expedition started, his delay boded ill for the success of his mission. The colored troops, anxious to show their mettle, were eager to get at the enemy; conditions were most favorable, but Smith hesitated. He worked out a plan — he even advanced and took the main portion of the defenses' left wing — but then he allowed the troops to rest and wait for the next morning.[40]

Just why he made this fatal decision is still a matter of dispute. Years later, Smith maintained that he had had every reason to believe the works to be too strongly held. His troops were tired, and he wanted to make sure of the cooperation of II Corps, the vanguard of the Army of the Potomac which had arrived at the river crossing that morning.[41] It was commanded by General Winfred S. Hancock, an officer as able as he was intrepid, who might well have changed the outcome of the battle had he arrived in time. But he had been delayed by various misfortunes and did not reach Smith till after dark.[42] By that time, Smith considered it too late to undertake the risks of night fighting, and although the moon was shining brightly and Butler had told him repeatedly that no reinforcements had reached the enemy as yet,[43] he decided to wait until morning.[44] Had he but tried, he could have walked into Petersburg,[45] but he tarried, and his caution cost him the victory. During the night, the main forces of Lee's army moved into the beleaguered city. By sunrise the next morning, the attackers found themselves face to face with the battle-hardened veterans of the Army of Northern Virginia. They had lost the last opportunity to take Petersburg without a lengthy siege.[46]

This time, the fault was chiefly Smith's, but the disaster had occurred in Butler's command, and the senior officer found it impossible to escape censure. He might have retrieved his reputation somewhat if he had moved rapidly during the next few days, when Petersburg was attacked in force from the south by the entire Army of the Potomac. Yet in spite of the fact that the Confederates evacuated their entrenchments in front of Bermuda Hundred, and although he received strong reinforcements, Butler found it impossible to hold the former Confederate lines, not to speak of the vital railroad a few miles beyond. Within two days, he was back in his old entrenchments.[47]

Grant was very disappointed. He had entertained high hopes for the spring campaign, but now everything had gone awry. Butler had failed to live up to expectations, and Grant felt that it would be wise to replace him. Consequently, on July 1, the Lieutenant General wrote to Halleck,

> Whilst I have no difficulty with General Butler, finding him always clear in his conception of orders and prompt to obey, yet there is a want of knowledge of how to execute, and particularly a prejudice against him as commander that operates against his usefulness.

Praising Butler's great administrative ability, he suggested that the troublesome General be sent to some department where disaffected elements were to be controlled, but no battles to be fought.[48]

Halleck was not surprised. Considering Butler totally unfit, he had foreseen that the civilian-turned-general would create difficulty. He thought sending the General to Kentucky would cause an uprising, but if Grant wanted to spare Butler's feelings, Halleck suggested that the volunteer general might be sent to Fortress Monroe as titular command of the department, with somebody else in charge of the troops in the field.[49]

These ideas impressed Grant, and as Baldy Smith, also, complained about his commander,[50] Grant accepted Halleck's suggestions on July 6. Butler would go to Fortress Monroe, while Smith would obtain the tactical command.[51] The General Order, No. 225, was prepared in Washington. Lincoln himself saw and signed it,[52] and another political general seemed to have fallen by the wayside.

There was only one hitch in this plan — the personality of the general in question. No matter how much he lacked in military experience, Butler was no novice at politics. He was not a man to sit by idly while his opponents planned his ruin; nor was he averse to using whatever powerful weapons were at his command. 1864 was a presidential year, and Butler was the darling of the radicals whose hatred for Lincoln had become proverbial. His demotion would stir up a row which could not but prove embarrassing to the Chief Executive, already worried because of the approach of Early's forces to the outskirts of the poorly defended capital. Butler decided that no one would demote him with impunity.

There was no time to be lost. On June 9, he came to see the Lieutenant General to demand an explanation of General Order No. 225. Grant was embarrassed. "Oh, I did not mean that you should have seen this order," he said. "It is a mistake. I suppressed all the copies that were transmitted through me. How did you get this?" Butler's reply was frank. A friend in the War Department had sent it, he said. "Well," answered Grant, "I don't want this at all. I want Smith to report to you — you have the full command." Moreover, Grant promised to add the XIX Corps to the Army of the James.[53] For once, not the enemy, but General Grant had surrendered unconditionally.

The reasons for the Lieutenant General's sudden reversal have never been fully explained. Baldy Smith — angry, bitter, and smarting under his subsequent removal and censure by Grant[54] — claimed that Butler had seen his superior in a state of intoxication and blackmailed him by threatening to reveal the recurrence of Grant's old vice.[55] As Smith had exerted himself to the utmost to get rid of his commander, this story is open to question. It is much more likely that not until Butler walked into his headquarters on June 9 did Grant fully realize the personal and political implications of the orders he had requested for Butler. At a time when he was receiving frantic telegrams from the threatened capital,[56] it was hardly wise to add to Lincoln's troubles. Whether the coming election campaign or the prospect of even greater difficulty with Butler at Fortress Monroe swayed him cannot be determined;[57] yet it seems likely that all these factors entered into his decision not to go through with his plan. He kept Butler until after the November election; then he took advantage of the first opportunity to rid himself of his troublesome subordinate. U. S. Grant had become a good politician — at least while he was waging a war.

Butler was elated over his triumph. Upon his wife's advice, he wrote a fulsome letter of gratitude to the Lieutenant General whom he offered to serve "in all things."[58] To Colonel Shaffer, worrying at Fortress Monroe about rumors of impending disaster, he wired tersely:

> Do not trouble yourself about the order. It is all right now and better than if it had not been disturbed. Benjamin F. Butler, Major General, Comdg. all the Troops of the Dept. of Va. and N. C.[59]

He would watch out for his opponents in the future, and in spite of the oppressive heat and the alarming reports about Early, he felt happy, secure in the knowledge that he had won in a delicate situation.[60]

As for Smith, the disappointed commander of XVIII Corps was flabbergasted. He left for New York, convinced that Butler's influence over Grant was wholly sinister.[61] His own military career was arrested. The remaining years of his military service failed to provide him with an opportunity to regain his lost laurels.[62] Gillmore, also, had left the Army of the James,[63] and Generals Birney and Ord, able and less contentious, took over the two orphaned corps.[64]

Butler had won — Butler the politician, whom one observer described as the strangest sight imaginable on a horse. "It is hard to keep your eyes off him," wrote Colonel Theodore Lyman,

> With his head set immediately on a stout shapeless body, his very squinting eyes, and a set of legs and arms that look as if made for somebody else, and hastily glued to him by mistake,

he presents a combination of Victor Emanuel, Aesop, and Richard III, which is very confusing to the mind. Add to this a horse with a kind of rapid, ambling trot that shakes about the arms and legs, etc., till you don't feel quite sure whether it is a centaur, or what it is, and you have a picture of the celebrated General.

His appearance notwithstanding, Butler's political influence was a fact at which the Army marveled. Clearly, he was not a man to be underestimated.[65]

With its failure to take Petersburg, the Army of the James had seen its most dramatic period of the campaign. Henceforth, for all practical purposes, it merely constituted the right wing of the forces besieging Petersburg and Richmond. Whenever the Army of the Potomac planned any movements against Petersburg, Butler was expected to make a diversionary demonstration against Richmond. Moreover, he had to be ready to send reinforcements to Meade when needed.[66] As neither of the two cities could be taken that year, he was unable to gain any glory.

To follow in detail the minor movements and countermovements of the armies that fall is tedious. In order to carry out his diversionary mission, Butler established a bridgehead to the north bank of the James at Deep Bottom, where a pontoon bridge served as a route to the outer defenses of the Confederate capital. From this position, he launched several raids against the city,[67] but only one stands out in sharp relief — the capture of Fort Harrison on September 29. An action as gallant as it was costly, it resulted in the death of General Burnham, a severe loss to the attackers. Richmond itself had been the objective, but the heavy resistance at the fort and the injuries sustained by General Ord made it impossible to carry out the original plan,[68] although the Confederate authorities became panicky for a time.[69]

Though Richmond was not captured, the operation nevertheless proved beneficial. Butler had long contended that colored troops, generally despised by the Army, would fight if only they were given the opportunity.[70] Accordingly, he had hurled them against the strong fortifications at Newmarket Heights, east of Fort Harrison, on September 29. He proved his point. The Negro regiments fought as gallantly as any white soldiers. After a bayonet charge which proved extremely costly, they took their objective, to the immense satisfaction of their General. Butler could not promote Negroes to officer rank, nor could he authorize existing medals for them because of regulations, but he could and did strike his own decorations. The contrabands of yesterday had become the soldiers of today.[71]

Later in October, Butler undertook one more diversionary movement against the enemy capital. The defenses were too strong, however, and the attackers had to retire with considerable losses.[72] Thereafter, the Army of the James practically went into winter quarters. When it finally reached its objective in 1865, it had a new commander. Richmond was not to share the fate of Baltimore and New Orleans. Butler had missed his greatest opportunity. Once again he had proved what many people had believed for a long time: talented in politics and administration, a good friend to the Negro, Butler nevertheless was not gifted in strategy and military knowledge.

CHAPTER FOURTEEN

# The Election of 1864

Eighteen hundred and sixty-four was a bad year for Ben — not only for Ben the soldier, but also for Ben the politician. At first, his prospects looked bright enough. The Presidency, the Vice-Presidency, a cabinet post — all seemed attainable at one time or another. However, he failed to receive any political preferment that year, just as he had failed to capture Richmond and Petersburg. That these failures were closely linked must have been clear to a man of his intelligence, no matter how much he might protest his innocence of the military disasters.

Whatever else might be said of Butler, he could never be called modest. While he did not publicly avow himself a candidate for the Presidential nomination, he certainly failed to discourage the boom his friends created for him. There had been talk of his candidacy as early as 1863, Parton's book being little more than a campaign biography for that purpose. And since the radicals were anxious to shunt Lincoln aside, it was not at all improbable that they would turn to Butler, for whom their admiration increased in inverse proportion to the abuse poured upon him by their enemies.

The attacks on Butler had not diminished since his return to Fortress Monroe. None other than Fernando Wood, New York's stormy Copperhead, had introduced a resolution in the House of Representatives calling for an investigation into the General's conduct at New Orleans. The House had indefinitely postponed the inquiry, but for the radicals, the incident was merely confirmation of their good opinion of the author of General Order No. 28.[1]

Butler would make an excellent President, Count Gurowski confided to his diary, and he did not hesitate to inform his hero of his opinions.²

If the Pole and people of his type were thinking of Butler for the Presidency, others thought of him as a possible candidate for the second highest office.³ Early in 1864, when Salmon P. Chase seemed to be the leading radical contender for the succession, one of his supporters asked Butler if he would be willing to be the Secretary's running mate. Butler said no, explaining that he was not interested in any elective office just then, especially not the Vice-Presidency.⁴ Since the Chase boom was about to collapse, the field was open for other contenders. One never could tell . . .

Whether or not Butler disdained the Vice-Presidency, even Abraham Lincoln considered the possibility of enlisting the General as his running mate. Not that Lincoln had any exaggerated notions about Ben's character. He thought Butler was "like Jim Jett's brother . . . the damndest scoundrel that ever lived, but in the infinite mercy of providence, . . . also the damndest fool."⁵ However, the President knew how popular the General was, and in February, 1864, he had a long talk with his old acquaintance, J. Wilson Shaffer, now Butler's Chief of Staff. He was very complimentary to the General, and before Shaffer left, Lincoln gave him a signed statement concerning the interview. "Col. Shaffer has been conversing with me," he wrote,

> and I have said to him that Genl. Butler has my confidence in his ability and fidelity to the country and to me. And I wish him sustained in all his efforts in our great common cause, subject only to the same supervisions which the Government must take with all Departmental commanders.⁶

When Butler appeared before him in person, the President was equally friendly.⁷ Before long, consummate politician that he was, Lincoln sounded out the troublesome General about the forthcoming election.

As Butler remembered it, and as Simon Cameron and Alexander McClure corroborated, it was some time in March that the Chief Executive sent Cameron to Fort Monroe to ask the General if he would consent to becoming Lincoln's running mate. Butler said no,[8] and in later years, probably chagrined by the memory of a decision which may have cost him the Presidency, thought he recalled the exact words of his reply. "Please say to Mr. Lincoln," he said,

> that while I appreciate with the fullest sensibilities his act of friendship and the high compliment he pays me, yet I must decline. Tell him that I said laughingly that with the prospects of a campaign before me I would not quit the field to be Vice-President even with himself as President, unless he would give me bond in sureties in the full sum of his four years' salary that within three months after his inauguration he will die unresigned.[9]

Whether he really spoke in such unintentionally prophetic terms is questionable. However, since Lincoln was desirous of rendering Butler innocuous, it is not impossible that he approached the General for an office which seemed unimportant at the time but which might have catapulted Butler into the White House.[10]

No, Butler did not think the Vice-Presidency was the job for him. He knew that the political cauldron in Washington was boiling. Lincoln's renomination was not assured,[11] and radical newspapers were boosting the General for the higher office.[12] Moreover, when Chase took himself out of the race, Butler's chances for the nomination appeared to increase.[13] While friends boosted him in his home state,[14] Horace Greeley mentioned him favorably in New York,[15] and his agents were busy lobbying for him in Washington, where they maintained close contact with leading radicals.[16] The Butler boom was well under way,[17] and the General saw no reason why he should stop it.

Whether the enthusiasm could be maintained depended partially on developments within the Republican party. The President was still popular among the people, and if the convention were to meet in June as planned, there was little likelihood of sidetracking him.[18] For this reason, radicals in general and Butler men in particular tried to postpone the party gathering until fall.[19] But they failed, and Lincoln gained strength.

For a few extremists, the prospect of another four years of Abraham Lincoln was so unbearable that they nominated John C.

Frémont on a splinter platform late in May.[20] Like most important Republicans, Butler withheld his support. He was not anxious for a complete break with the President, especially when he was not the radical candidate and when rumors of his impending appointment as Secretary of War were again circulating.[21] He would bide his time.

In the last analysis, as Butler well knew, his political strength was closely connected with his military accomplishments. He needed good publicity, and although he was no great admirer of newspaper reporters, he was shrewd enough to treat them royally. He gave them accomodations on his own steamer, the *Greyhound;* he allowed them to maintain their own mess, and he tried to help those who were favorably inclined toward him when they got into trouble.[22] Yet in spite of these precautions, the military blunders of May, 1864, could not be kept out of the papers. Before long, devastating articles appeared in the leading journals of the country. Although Butler tried to justify himself in a letter to the editor of the New York Evening *Post*,[23] the damage had been done, and as the unfavorable publicity came on the very eve of the Republican convention, his advisers were sure that it constituted a deliberate plot to discredit him for political reasons.[24] Only Senator Davis' clumsy attempt to investigate Butler's administration of New Orleans — an attack which the General parried with a ringing challenge to have every act of his political life scrutinized — somewhat restored his fame.[25]

A few days later, the Union Convention met in Baltimore. Colonel Shaffer was at hand to look out for his Chief's interests,[26] but it had become obvious that the President could not be headed off. Lincoln was renominated on June 8. "This country has more vitality than any other on earth if it can stand this sort of administration for another four years," wrote the disgruntled Butler to his wife.[27] Publicly, however, he made the best of the situation and sent a congratulatory telegram to the President.[28]

In ordinary times, the intra-party contest would have ended with the selection of a candidate, but 1864 was not an ordinary year. Lack of military success in the summer did not make the President any more popular, and soon there was talk of prevailing upon him to withdraw. Some other candidate, more acceptable to the dissatisfied radicals, might be put in his place.[29] Ben Wade, the radical Senator from Ohio, for one, thought that Butler might fill the bill.[30] And as the Democrats had not yet held their convention, a Western radical suggested that Frémont withdraw to enable the war faction of the opposition party to join with the radicals in Butler's support.[31]

With such possibilities in the offing, the General's supporters did not remain idle. They canvassed the country; they prepared an appeal to the Union and War Democracy of the United States, and they were hopeful of success.[32] Lincoln's prospects looked so dark in August that he himself despaired of his re-election. Anti-Lincoln meetings were held in New York and Horace Greeley was sure that only with a ticket headed by Grant, Butler, or Sherman might the Republicans win.[33] Sarah Butler, convinced that her husband was the only man capable of saving the country, wrote to him to come home in order to take charge of his campaign in person.[34]

The General hesitated. "Meade does not go home, Grant does not go home. Why should I?" he replied,[35] and although he did come back for a few days toward the end of the month,[36] he preferred to rely on his agents.[37]

Once again, however, the Butler boom collapsed. While a few radicals did issue a call for a new convention to meet in Cincinnati late in September, the prospects of the movement looked so uncertain that Colonel Shaffer warned his chief to remain aloof for the time being.[38] The General's agents stayed in New York to take advantage of developments, but by the middle of September, they had to inform him that nothing further could be done. Lincoln was sure to make the race, and the best that could now be hoped for was a place in the cabinet.[39] With the adoption of a peace platform by the Democrats and the capture of Atlanta by Sherman, Lincoln's prospects looked infinitely better. The Cincinnati convention came to naught; Frémont withdrew, and even Zach Chandler and Ben Wade fell in line, although the bluff Senator from Ohio wished "the devil had Old Abe."[40] Butler probably agreed, but he, too, had no choice except to climb on the bandwagon.

So it happened that Butler became a supporter of an administration he considered an "abortion of government." Notwithstanding the General's machinations earlier that year, Lincoln could not but note with satisfaction that the ex-Hunker lent his aid to the ticket and publicly endorsed the gubernatorial slate in Massachusetts, though it was headed by his old antagonist, John A. Andrew.[41] And since Butler knew how to overawe disaffected elements, the Secretary of War thought he knew just where to send the General at election time. Stanton had had alarming reports of sedition from New York. Since riots had occurred in the city before, the Secretary prevailed on Lincoln to send Butler to the metropolis in order to ensure an orderly election.[42]

The mission was the type of operation Butler liked. Baltimore, New Orleans, and now New York! He would live up to his reputation and frustrate whatever plots the copperheads had hatched. A personal visit to Washington gave him a good idea of what the Administration wanted, and on November 2, he left for New York.[43] Establishing headquarters at Hoffman House, he awaited the arrival of some five thousand troops from Virginia.[44]

Stanton's fears had not been entirely without foundation. Normally a Democratic city, New York contained many rowdy elements who might be used to overawe voters who deserted their usual party affiliations. And since it was known that Confederate agents were making efforts to secure Lincoln's defeat, special care had to be exercised to keep both City and State from being thrown to McClellan by illegal means.[45] The secessionists had already made a number of raids along the northern border from hide-outs in Canada; they were planning to create a financial panic in Wall Street, and they had made preparations to set fire to the city on election day.[46] The appearance of the Hero of New Orleans might produce a salutary effect on the disloyal.[47]

There was a difference, however, between New York and the Crescent City. A northern community, already included within the command of General John A. Dix, could not be treated as arbitrarily as New Orleans. Butler could not maintain unchallenged sway, and jurisdictional disputes arose immediately. Dix suggested Butler's force be sent to the northern frontier; Butler demanded full territorial jurisdiction in the city. The result was that the local commander remained in control of the Department while the newcomer stayed in the city with the troops he had brought with him.[48]

It was an arrangement Butler heartily disliked.

The position of the State Militia further complicated the problem. Neither its commander-in-chief, Governor Seymour, nor its commander in Buffalo, John A. Green, was particularly fond of the Administration.[49] Worried about arms which had been sent to Green, Butler proposed to issue a general order placing all state troops under his own command, but neither Dix nor Lincoln was prepared to give his assent. So the General had to be content with a less specific order.[50] He proclaimed that

> there can be no military organization in any State, known to the laws, save the militia and armies of the United States.[51]

However, he warned militia officers privately that he would not tolerate any interference with the elections.[52]

The Confederate conspirators Butler handled with his accustomed vigor. Although he did not have sufficient authority to arrest the ringleaders, he succeeded in spreading rumors that he was looking for them. And when he cross-examined J. H. Lyons, former partner of the Montreal Confederate financial agent Porterfield, he made it quite clear that he was informed about the secessionist plot to create a panic by buying up gold. He would know whom to apprehend should the metal rise to three hundred, he said, and although Lyons had no connection with this particular scheme, the price of gold remained well below the crucial figure.[53]

It was not easy to control a disaffected city the size of New York. Unionists might be heartened by Butler's arrival,[54] but Democrats made no secret of their resentment.

> The appointment of this man, at this time, to this service is the most exasperating MENACE and the most insolent indignity that could be put upon this community,

editorialized the *World*.[55] Threats of assassination were commonplace, and Butler thought it necessary to visit the theater in full military regalia to counteract rumors that he had shut himself up in his headquarters in fear of violence.[56] It was obvious that he would have to exercise considerable care in disposing his troops on election day, lest their presence bring about the very riots he had been sent to prevent.

As usual, he found a solution. Major General Daniel Butterfield, a New Yorker familiar with conditions in his hometown, suggested that the troops be placed aboard ferry boats at strategic points surrounding Manhattan Island. Once aboard, they would not be in evidence in the streets, yet should any untoward incident occur, they could easily be called upon to intervene. Butler adopted the plan and disposed his soldiers accordingly.[57]

When election day arrived, New York was free from turmoil. The troops, carefully kept out of sight on their boats, had no occasion to interfere. The Republicans not only managed to carry the State for the President, but even to defeat the incumbent Governor, Horatio Seymour. Butler had accomplished his mission.[58]

To the more enthusiastic Republicans, the victory seemed attributable — to a large degree — to the General.[59] In gratitude, they tendered him a mammoth dinner at the Fifth Avenue Hotel on November 14. It was a convivial gathering, attended by such celebrities as Henry Ward Beecher, Theodore Tilton, Levi P. Morton, and a host of other influential New Yorkers. Butler responded handsomely. Appearing with his wife and beautiful daughter, he delivered an oration calling for an ultimatum to the South. Tell the Confederates to come back into the Union by January 8, he argued. If they heeded the call, the war would end, but if not, let the Government make it clear that there would be no mercy for any who held out longer. The enemy might then be driven out of the country altogether by relentless war, and his lands confiscated for distribution among the victors. The speech brought the house down, and, amid continuing cheers, Henry Ward Beecher rose to propose Butler for the Presidency in 1868.[60]

The next day, the General returned to Virginia. Rumors still circulated that he might be appointed Secretary of War, but as before, nothing came of these reports.[61] Whether he was aware of it or not, his chief hold over the Administration was gone. As long as Lincoln's re-election had been in doubt, Butler's support had been essential. But now, although he himself had helped to ensure the President's continuance in office, the Chief Executive no longer had to treat the troublesome political General with kid gloves. Butler's Civil War career was nearing its end.

CHAPTER FIFTEEN

# The Downfall of a Political General

It was a tribute to Abraham Lincoln's political sagacity that he put up with Butler as long as he did. No two men could have been more different. Where Lincoln was conservative, Butler was radical; where Lincoln was merciful, Butler was unforgiving; where Lincoln was patient, Butler was rash; where Lincoln was conciliatory, Butler was inflammatory. The two men had only one characteristic in common: Both were good politicians. They needed each other during the war; consequently the President refused to dismiss the General until he was absolutely sure of his case.

There had been complaints about Butler for a long time. As commander of the Department of Virginia and North Carolina, he behaved very much as he had when he was in charge of the Department of the Gulf. Again, there were charges of corruption. Because of its numerous inlets and sounds along the poorly guarded coast, the area was ideal for trade with the enemy — some of it licensed, but most of it illegal. Whether or not the General profited personally is impossible to tell, but it is certain that he was most liberal in giving permits of various sorts to friends, relatives, and political henchmen. His proteges seemed to receive an inordinate share of the spoils, and his growing machine did not suffer from the illicit trade.[1] In Washington, however, his standing did not improve.[2]

Complaints about contraband trade were not the only source of discontent in Butler's Department. Many of his measures were justified by the military situation, and were beneficial to the population. Nobody could deny that he prevented outbreaks of yellow fever,[3] aided public education, protected the rights of Negroes, and assisted the poor.[4] But no matter how much he advertised his achievements in the official Norfolk *New Regime*,[5] the inhabitants were not reconciled. All they could see were clergymen jailed for failure to give evidence of devotion to the Union;[6] citizens harassed and finally banished for refusing to take a loyalty oath;[7] liquor stores confiscated to make way for monopolies for Butler's friends.[8] Duties collected on exports and imports,[9] spies operating everywhere,[10] and levies upon dog owners for the payment of commutation fees lest every fourth pet be destroyed[11] did not make people more kindly disposed toward the General. Moreover, as he did not hesitate to put to work under enemy fire a man suspected of being Stanton's agent, the Administration was forced to take notice.[12]

The secessionists' hatred was to be expected, but unfortunately for the General's reputation, many Unionists, too, found fault with his methods.[13] Their dissatisfaction was due mainly to Butler's troubles with Francis H. Pierpont, Governor of the Restored Government of Virginia. An unflinching foe of secession, Pierpont had rendered valuable service to the Federal cause, both as the Father of West Virginia and head of the Government at Alexandria. The counties which acknowledged his authority were considered a nucleus around which Virginia might again become a loyal state, and he enjoyed the President's confidence. As Butler's establishment of monopolies deprived loyal Virginia of the taxes on spirituous liquors, and as his administration of the Department took little account of the prerogatives of the civilian government, he soon clashed with the Governor.[14] The resulting controversy between civilian and military authorities brought comfort to none but secessionists.

The first collision occurred shortly after the General arrived at Fortress Monroe where he protested against the Governor's desire to commission officers for the colored troops.[15] As the number of persons involved was small, this dispute might have been settled amicably, but when Pierpont came to Norfolk shortly afterward, he was appalled at the extent of Butler's power. The trading licenses, the taxes, the courts — such display of military authority was too much for him. He decided to appeal to the President.[16]

Lincoln was faced with a dilemma. He could not abandon Pierpont, Governor of the only Virginia recognized by the United States, since he considered the Alexandria government an important precedent for his reconstruction policy.[17] But neither could he afford to offend the powerful General. He wrote Butler a polite note asking for an explanation,[18] only to receive an answer of forty pages of billingsgate, in which the General suggested a plebiscite to decide whether civil government ought to continue in the department at all.[19] As an equally lengthy statement arrived from the Governor,[20] the President did not reply.

However, inaction was no solution for the problem. Interpreting the President's silence as tacit approval, Butler took matters into his own hands. Jealous of his prerogatives, he ordered the plebiscite held in July, and since Pierpont's supporters refused to participate, the General received three hundred and thirty votes to his opponent's sixteen. He thereupon suspended the civil government.[21]

Pierpont was outraged. He did not propose to permit the military to strip him of his authority, especially since Attorney General Edward Bates firmly supported him. Bates was convinced that the supremacy of civilian government was at stake, a point he emphasized at a cabinet meeting held on July 19. Secretaries Welles and Fessenden supported him, while Seward urged that the controversy be referred to Grant.[22] But Lincoln was still hesitant about interfering. Pierpont had to wait a little longer.

Butler may well have been encouraged by the President's silence. Determined to have his way, he ordered the arrest of Edward K. Snead, one of the civilian judges who had defied him by convening the district court in Norfolk. He interrogated the Judge, and let him go only after Snead had signed a promise not to cause further trouble.[23] Moreover, he wrote another long letter to Lincoln, in which he again gave vent to his dislike for Pierpont, Snead, and Bates, and maintained that the restored Government had no legal standing.[24]

This time it looked as if the President would have to act. Accordingly, he prepared a conciliatory answer. Pointing out that

## THE DOWNFALL OF A POLITICAL GENERAL

he had full confidence in both the Governor and the Attorney General, Lincoln asked Butler to disregard the results of the plebiscite. But he also assured the General of his goodwill, and finally, he decided against sending the letter at all — at least at that juncture. The month of August 1864 was hardly a good time to engage in a quarrel with Butler, and the missive rested in the Presidential files until after the elections.[25]

The result of the vote in November changed matters. Butler's hold over the Administration had disappeared, and Lincoln felt free to admonish him, especially as new controversies had arisen and Pierpont, in his address to the legislature, had launched a new attack on his antagonist.[26] The President now sent the letter, and he requested that no further plebiscites be held.[27] The Governor did not have his final triumph until Butler's dismissal in January,[28] but the controversy had already done tremendous harm to the General's reputation.

Other quarrels must also have annoyed the President. Just as Butler's high-handed methods had brought him into conflict with Pierpont, so his autocratic manner resulted in collision with others, even people who might ordinarily have been his friends. When he discovered that the articles criticizing his failure at Drury's Bluff had been written at Gillmore's request by Henry N. Hudson, a chaplain then absent without proper leave, Butler lost all sense of proportion and imprisoned the unhappy divine without bringing him to trial. As Hudson was a noted authority on Shakespeare with many important connections in the North, his plight aroused a great deal of sympathy, even among Republicans. No matter how hard Butler tried to justify himself by calling attention to his inability to convene a court martial in view of his personal interest in the case, he could not dispel the notion that his punishment of Hudson was a gross abuse of his power.[29] It was well known that the General would go to almost any length to protect reporters he liked.[30]

In spite of these blunders,[31] Butler might still have managed to retain his status had he been able to achieve some military success. He had failed to take Richmond or Petersburg, and although he lent his fertile imagination to ever more visionary schemes — flame throwers, artillery mounted on river boats, auxiliary railroads and canals[32] — he could not overcome the dislike of the regular Army. Moreover, while some of his experiments succeeded, the most spectacular of his enterprises was a failure. Amid much publicity, notwithstanding harassment by Confederate batteries, he had dug a canal across the narrow neck of Dutch Gap peninsula in order to enable the Navy to ascend the river nearer to Richmond. But when the engineers exploded the bulkhead on January 1, 1865, the dirt fell back into the excavation and the work had to be done over again. Another one of Butler's blunders, his enemies sneered, yet in later years the canal did become the main channel of navigation.[33]

However, the failure of the Dutch Gap Canal was not to be compared with the disappointing attempt to blow up Fort Fisher with a charge of gun powder. As the fort guarded the approaches to Wilmington, North Carolina, the last major port of the Confederacy, its capture had long been planned, but it was difficult to find the necessary troops.[34] Butler had become interested in the enterprise when he heard about the devastating effects of an accidental explosion in England; he wanted to demonstrate the feasibility of blowing up fortifications by exploding large masses of powder.[35] On his way to New York, he submitted his scheme to the President. Lincoln had misgivings,[36] but as the Navy Department, anxious to get troops for the expedition, was willing to support Butler if he could only induce the Army to cooperate,[37] the Chief Executive finally sanctioned the enterprise. "We might as well explode the notion with powder as with anything else," he said, and Butler had his way.[38]

Unfortunately, Butler's old antagonist David D. Porter, now an admiral, was in command of the naval forces along the Atlantic coast. At best joint operations are always difficult, but when the two commanders are at odds from the beginning, success is almost impossible. Not that they did not try. Swallowing his pride, the Admiral visited the General at Army Headquarters, where he found his host equally anxious to please.[39] The question was how long this cordiality would last under the stress of battle.

Explosives must have constituted one of the chief topics of conversation. The Navy agreed to stow three hundred tons of powder in an old tug which was to be brought as close to the fort as possible. Then it was to be blown up,[40] and as if to underscore the subject under discussion, Butler's steamer *Greyhound* exploded just as he was taking Porter back to Hampton Roads. The two commanders escaped unharmed, firm in their conviction that the experiment was feasible.[41]

General Grant did not share their faith. He wanted Butler to get ready as soon as possible, "with or without the powder boat."[42] On December 6, Grant issued final instructions. General Weitzel was to be in command of the expedition to close the port of Wilmington. He was to effect a landing

> on the mainland between Cape Fear River and the Atlantic, north of the north entrance of the river. Should such landing be effected, whether the enemy hold Fort Fisher or the batteries guarding the entrance to the river there, the troops should entrench themselves, and by cooperation with the navy effect the reduction and capture of those places.[43]

To order haste was one thing. Getting the expedition started was quite another. Countless delays frustrated the commanders, until at last the powder boat was ready. By that time, eager for glory, Butler had decided to accompany the expedition in person — a contingency Grant had not considered before. His subordinate informed him of the decision just prior to departure. Weitzel was but a young general, Butler pointed out. To observe the effect of the explosion and to handle Porter, a man of more experience ought to go along. Much as he regretted it later, Grant did not say no.[44]

In spite of the Lieutenant General's insistence on speed, Butler was not ready to sail until December 14. At first, he set course for the Potomac in order to mislead the enemy. Then he reversed his fleet,[45] but his precautions proved unavailing. The Confederates had been warned;[46] suprise was no longer possible. To bedevil the expedition still further, additional delays occurred when Butler failed to meet Porter at the rendezvous near the objective. The Admiral was still at Beaufort, and when he finally arrived, a severe storm arose. Notwithstanding the bad weather, Butler proposed to explode his powderboat at once. But since the waves made landing operations impossible, the experiment had to be put off again. Thereupon the General, in need of supplies because of the long wait, sailed his transports to Beaufort to take on coal and water.[47]

Porter did not wait for his return. At 2:10 A. M. on December 23, he exploded the powderboat *Louisiana*, not at the beach as intended, but in shallow water. As the powder did not ignite all at once, the effect was so slight that the Confederates believed a gun boat had accidentally blown up. The attempt to destroy Fort Fisher with one blast had failed, so the Admiral started a heavy bombardment.[48]

That evening, Butler returned. Mortified at the failure of the experiment, angry at Porter for not waiting for him, he ordered a landing for the next morning. Weitzel made the necessary preparations; one third of his men secured a foothold on the narrow peninsula north of the fort and captured prisoners as well as a flag. However, they were not to go further. Butler had lost heart. He was worried because the main works were still substantially undamaged. The obvious necessity for a long siege made him uneasy, and he felt insecure because the sea was too rough for further landings. Above all, he distrusted Porter, and so, hoping that Sherman would take Wilmington from the rear, he decided to disregard Grant's instructions. He ordered the troops to return to their transports, a course of action which was to give ammunition to his enemies for years to come. To be sure, both Weitzel and Colonel Comstock, an engineer officer on the Lieutenant General's staff, had advised re-embarkation. But they had not seen Grant's orders. Butler had kept those to himself, and not even Weitzel knew that he had been supposed to entrench. The expeditionary force returned to Fortress Monroe.[49]

Grant's chagrin at the failure of this assault knew no bounds. "Who is to blame I hope will be known," he wrote to the President on December 28. But on that same day, he heard that the Navy proposed to try again.[50] In utmost secrecy, he drew up a new set of instructions, making sure that Butler was kept in complete ignorance of developments and that Terry — not Weitzel — was placed in command of the second expedition. To Porter, he wrote that he was sending an increased force "without the former com-

## THE DOWNFALL OF A POLITICAL GENERAL

mander." This plan pleased the Admiral, who thanked Grant for rectifying a blunder — for having the wisdom not "to send a boy on a man's errand."[51] The expedition was to be more successful than its predecessor.

It had been clear to Butler from the moment he ordered the retreat that he would have a difficult time justifying himself.[52] He was pugnacious, however, and he quickly prepared two reports, both bitterly critical of Porter.[53] Determined to tell the Lieutenant General where blame lay, Butler pointed out that Colonel Comstock himself had testified to the correctness of his actions.[54]

For a moment, Grant seemed to hesitate. He forwarded Comstock's report; he even expressed the opinion that the Navy's delay had been fatal.[55] But he had more faith in Porter than he had in Butler,[56] and his doubts soon vanished. Whether bitter comments from General Sherman[57] or the fiasco at Dutch Gap contributed to his decision to oust Butler is unimportant. The Major General had been causing him uneasiness since July; if he had kept Butler in command, it was not because he had faith in the General's military accomplishments. Now Butler had gone too far. Grant could not feel free to leave Virginia as long as his high-ranking subordinate would automatically become commander during his absence. Nor had Grant dreamed of the possibility of Butler accompanying the expedition to Fort Fisher until the last moment.[58] It took Grant a long time to make up his mind, but once he had made the decision, it was final. He was determined to let Butler go, and on January 4, he wrote to the Secretary of War:

> I am constrained to request the removal of Major General B. F. Butler from the command of the Department of Virginia and North Carolina. I do this with reluctance, but the good of the service requires it. In my absence, General Butler necessarily commands, and there is a lack of confidence in his military ability, making him an unsafe commander for a large army. His administration of the affairs of his department is also objectionable.[59]

And to make sure of his case, he put a devastating endorsement upon Butler's Fort Fisher report. The Major General had disobeyed orders.[60]

When Grant's request reached the capital, conditions were very different from those prevailing the previous summer. The President had just been triumphantly re-elected; no enemy threatened the city. Since Lincoln had been willing the previous summer to grant the Lieutenant General's wishes, he could not refuse now. Nor did he wish to, as his strictures upon the Major General during the cabinet meeting on December 30 had indicated.[61] Butler had caused too much trouble. The regular Army distrusted him; Pierpont hated him, and the victims of his harsh measures constantly complained about him. Rumors of illicit trading in his department could not be quashed, and now that the Fort Fisher expedition had failed, Grant himself wanted to get rid of him. The President granted the request. On January 7, by Lincoln's direction, Butler was relieved of his command. He was ordered to "repair to Lowell . . . and report by letter to the Adjutant General of the Army."[62] Lincoln had removed the last of the civilian generals from an active command.[63]

Butler was stunned by the news. With the war drawing to a close, there was a chance that his army might still be the first to enter Richmond. He would have been delighted to become the conqueror of the enemy capital — Butler, the man whom the Confederates had outlawed and called beast. Lincoln's decision to remove him from command shattered all his hopes for glory, for personal victory, for a triumphant climax to his military career.[64] The publication of Porter's report before his own did not make things easier, and insult was added to injury when a reporter procured copies of Butler's recall orders before the General had seen them himself.[65] However, he refused to give up. Copperheads might exult; his enemies might rejoice;[66] but Butler still had friends. Bitterly castigating West Point — he blamed the regular Army for his discomfiture — Butler gave vent to his feelings. He would show his opponents a thing or two, for he knew he could count on the radicals giving him a favorable hearing.[67] All he needed to do was demand the opportunity to state his side, and demand it he would. He was determined to fight back.

Butler's counterattack was launched on January 8, when he published his farewell order. "Soldiers of the Army of the James," he said,

Your commander, relieved by the order of the President, takes leave of you.
Your conduct in the field has extorted praises from the unwilling . . .
Your deeds have rendered your name illustrious . . .
To share such companionship is pleasure.
To participate in such acts is honor.
To have commanded such an army is GLORY.
*No one could yield it without regret.*
Knowing your willing obedience to orders: witnessing your ready devotion . . . I have been chary of the precious charge confided to me. I have refused to order the useless sacrifice of the lives of such soldiers, and I am relieved from your command. The wasted blood of my men does not stain my garments. For my action I am responsible to God and my country![68]

The allusion to Generals Meade and Grant, both of whom had been attacked because of their high casualty rates, was too blunt to remain unnoticed.[69]

One week later, Butler left Fortress Monroe — not for Lowell, but for Washington, where the Committee on the Conduct of the War was ready to listen to him. Dominated by such uncompromising radicals as Senators Chandler and Wade, the Congressional group was an excellent sounding board for the General. He appeared well fortified with maps, documents, and depositions. Making a strong plea for his justification, he defied criticism of his administration of his department, and he made it very clear that it was not his fault if Union soldiers were still languishing in Confederate prison pens.[70] To be sure, Terry's capture of Fort Fisher added an unexpected anti-climax to the hearing; for just as Butler finished demonstrating that the bastion could not be taken except after a long siege, a newsboy was heard to shout, "Fort Fisher done took."[71] Nonetheless his testimony was effective. The radicals agreed that the circumstances surrounding Terry's expedition were entirely different, and no matter how many subsequent witnesses testified to the contrary, the Committee upheld the General in its final report.[72]

The controversy about Butler's dismissal was not confined to the committee rooms. His enemies had seen to that when James Brooks, a New York Democrat, had launched a bitter attack upon him on the floor of the House. A "bold robber," he called the General. Butler demanded an explanation, and Brooks renewed his assault on January 23. The words used had not been "bold robber," but "gold robber," he said, reminding his audience that Butler had been charged with stealing the Smith gold. It was an accusation which could not be left unanswered, and the radicals, led by George Boutwell, rushed to the General's aid. They flung epithets at Brooks; the New Yorker countered with the fifty-odd votes for Jefferson Davis and the rumors of contraband trade. Not until Thad Stevens himself joined the fray did the debate come to a close. Butler had friends, and even his downfall did not diminish their admiration.[73]

The General, of course, did not rely entirely on others to carry on his fight. When he returned to Lowell, his fellow townsmen arranged for the traditional reception in Huntington Hall. It was a gala affair, which the guest of honor exploited to full advantage. In a bitter speech, he again contrasted his own unwillingness to spill the blood of his brave soldiers with the methods of other generals, who not only suffered bloody losses on the field of battle, he said, but were callous of the suffering at Andersonville.[74] It would have been difficult to wound Grant more grievously.

The radicals applauded,[75] but Grant had had enough. Not only did he lend support to an investigation of Butler's conduct of affairs in Norfolk,[76] but he also urgently requested that no new command be tendered to the General.[77] Lincoln complied. The President might still receive Butler with great courtesy; he might still listen to his proposals for the punishment of Confederates and the employment of Negro troops for the construction of a canal across the isthmus of Panama,[78] but Lincoln did nothing for Butler. Neither the post of provost marshal at Charleston, nor a command in Kentucky, nor a seat in the cabinet — all under discussion at various times — ever materialized.[79] Butler was not even able to put an end to the inquiry at Norfolk, although he managed to have

Congress give him a clean bill of health concerning his activities there.[80] The time for political generals had passed.

Thus ended the military career of Major General Benjamin F. Butler. Though found wanting as a strategist, his example to his fellow Breckinridge Democrats of unhesitating support of the Union, his prominent part in the relief of Washington, his firm administration of New Orleans, and his championing of the rights of the Negro had strengthened the national cause. In his own way, he had contributed to the final victory.

CHAPTER SIXTEEN

# Return to Active Politics

On April 9, 1865, Robert E. Lee surrendered his army to U. S. Grant. The terms were easy; Grant was a magnanimous victor. But magnanimity was not yet the order of the day. Four years of civil war are not conducive to a forgiving frame of mind. War-time propaganda whips up a spirit of hate that makes it difficult to separate emotions from reason. And when, on April 14, 1865, President Lincoln was shot in Ford's Theater, the bitter feelings already aroused by the War became irresistible. John Wilkes Booth's crime seemed to stamp the South not merely as a nest of rebels, but as a den of assassins as well. Currents of popular opinion were running strongly against a soft peace; the radicals knew it, and they were anxious to take advantage of their unforeseen opportunity.

It is not surprising that Butler became one of the radicals. His whole life had been devoted to extreme causes of one sort or another. When he upheld the rights of labor in conservative Massachusetts, he was an extremist; when he stood for the rights of slaveholders in abolitionist New England, he was an extremist; when he pronounced slaves contraband, he was an extremist; and when he later came out for emancipation, he was still an extremist. Nor was his extremism always a matter of expediency. He happened to be with the majority after the Civil War, but within a short time, he was to embrace monetary views of such unpopularity as to render his political position insecure. There is no doubt that he really believed in the necessity for radical reconstruction in order to secure civil rights for Negroes in the South, although he was animated by practical considerations of party politics as well. And since he throve on notoriety, he flourished in a period when spectacular radicalism was common.[1]

The years immediately following Lincoln's assassination were such a time, and it did not take Butler long to grasp this fact. In search of something to do, he had been in Washington during the week preceding the catastrophe. There he had delivered a speech advocating harsh punishment for the leaders of secession and friendship for loyal freedmen,[2] and when he had seen the President, he suggested his plan for an Isthmian canal built by Negro regiments. Lincoln referred him to Seward, but the Secretary of State was inaccessible because of a carriage accident, so Butler took a train back to New York on April 14.[3] Not until he reached Jersey City did he hear the momentous news of the tragedy.[4] He decided to return immediately, although he found time for some oratory in New York, where he addressed an angry, saddened crowd in Wall Street. Woe to those who would strike down the most merciful of men! Let the audience decide what would be done with them. "Hang them, hang them," his listeners chorused.[5] The General was in his element, and he hurried back to Washington.

In the meantime, Butler's friends in the capital had not been inactive. J. K. Herbert, his chief agent, had sought out Zach Chandler immediately after hearing the news of the assassination and "talked Secretary of State or Sec. of War . . ." He had also established contact with other radicals,[6] so that George Julian, Ben Wade, and Henry Winter Davis, along with a few colleagues, agreed to bring pressure to bear for the General's appointment as Secretary of State.[7] Butler himself arrived shortly afterward. Declaring publicly that the crime ought to show the North that it was folly to speak of the Southern states as erring sisters, he proposed that the only relations that should exist between the two sections were those which normally prevail between conqueror and conquered.[8] Privately, he informed Andrew Johnson of his availability for the cabinet.[9]

The President would not commit himself. He received Butler cordially. He even asked the General what obligations rested upon the United States as a consequence of the liberal terms granted at Appomattox, only to be told that the war had ended and that there were no longer any prisoners. Butler wanted to hang Lee.[10] The President listened, but he said nothing about the cabinet post. Nor did he act later, in spite of continued pressure to make the General one of his official advisers.[11]

Butler, however, saw no reason to give up hope. After all, Johnson's career had been similar to his own. The Tennessean also had fought the conservative Whigs, supported Breckinridge, and remained loyal in the nation's darkest hour, doing his utmost to bolster an administration he had fought hard to defeat. Johnson also had preached hatred of the rich and at the same time was skillful in haranguing the poor; the President also insisted that treason ought to be made odious and that traitors ought to be punished. Why should two men of similar antecedents not cooperate in the future? "I am pleased to learn that you . . . are on intimate terms with President Johnson, the President of the Massachusetts State Senate wrote to the General,[12] and many radicals said, "Amen."

Others, however, were not so sanguine. After Butler's return, Colonel Shaffer went to the capital, and what he saw did not please him. "Wade tells me that Johnson talks first rate but don't just say the word," he wrote,

> but to be frank with you, I have no more faith in him [Johnson] than when here before. I don't like the Blairs and King being so close to him. I don't believe he is big enough. There is a determination however on the part of our friends to stick and hang until he decides matters for or against them.

He added that there would be a "smash up" within a month and advised Butler to come as soon as Stanton retired.[13]

Shaffer was more astute than most radicals. Johnson was not willing to play their game. Southern born and Southern bred, he had little sympathy for their views on the race question. He hated secession; he hated the wealthy slave owners who had supported it, but he wanted to restore the Union much as it was. In Lincoln's spirit, he wanted to effect reconstruction as quickly as possible — even before the next Congress met. It would then be the Executive and not the Legislative branch which would reestablish loyal commonwealths in the defunct Confederacy.

It was well known that this plan was distasteful to the radicals. They had entirely different ideas. As Butler put it, they thought the President had no right to bring any states back into the Union. Let the Executive establish military rule in the seceded commonwealths; let newly elected legislatures adopt a constitution outlawing slavery, repudiating the Confederate debt, disenfranchising Confederate officers, and declaring secession unconstitutional. Under such conditions they might be restored to full representation.[14] But the President did not heed this advice. Within thirty days of Butler's speech advocating the radical program, Johnson announced a policy of far reaching amnesty to ex-Confederates and a Presidential plan of reconstruction for North Carolina. Similar proclamations for almost all other Southern states followed, and collision with the radicals became almost inevitable.

However, Butler was still hesitant about breaking with the Chief Executive. The President's policy might be merely experimental and the South would probably behave so badly that Johnson would soon realize his error. Although the General professed to have faith in the Tennessean,[15] he himself advocated a policy of redistributing confiscated Southern lands to black and white soldiers alike.[16] He traveled to Washington once more to advocate a public trial by military commission for Davis and Lee, but the President was not in favor of this scheme.[17]

Butler settled down to wait, although he was not inactive. That was not his nature. His financial affairs had prospered during the war; Middlesex Mills had done very well.[18] Now was the time not only to resume his profession — a pursuit he preferred to all others — but also to engage in a number of business ventures which were to yield him handsome profits. Having heard that bunting had to be imported, he established a firm for its manufacture at home,[19] and within a few years, he had become interested in such varied enterprises as a cartridge company, a river navigation firm, a company to exploit the resources of Lower California, and investments and property in the "late rebellious states." As his knowledge of business was extensive, these undertakings prospered.[20] Money was not a problem in the Butler household.

To be sure business and law did not absorb all his energies. Butler could not leave politics alone, and in speech after speech, he called for the direst punishment of leading ex-Confederates. But while he expressed his distaste for the President's mild policies, he still hoped that Johnson would remain true to his announced principles of detestation of "traitors and treason." "Loyal suffrage" without inequality of race and color was Butler's prescription for reconstruction, and amid great applause, he told the 1865 Massachusetts Republican State Convention that "by the abandonment of the democratic party," he had "nowhere to go" but into their ranks.[21]

In spite of Butler's hope for a change, Johnson remained steadfast. Neither the election of outstanding Confederates, nor the enactment of degrading black codes in the South made him reverse his policies. Convinced of the rectitude of his stand, the President persisted — often with more courage than tact. The result was that when Congress met in December, all the states but one were ready for readmission — provided Congress agreed.

But of course the radical members of Congress were totally unwilling to agree. Not for them a policy which would have brought back the defeated "rebels" unchastened; not for them a policy which would have exalted the Executive branch over the Legislative, or restored the Government to Democratic control. The radicals insisted that they not only be consulted, but that they alone formulate reconstruction policies. Their measures would exclude as many ex-Confederate whites as possible and include — in the South — as many blacks as feasible. Thad Stevens, now the radical leader of the House of Representatives, was not a man for trifles; he girded himself for an all-out struggle with the President, and, in a manner unmatched by any representative before or since, he rose to domination over the Government. The old man was as stubborn as Johnson, but he was also a better politician.

Congress opened early in December. None of the Johnson states was recognized. Stevens organized his Joint Committee of Reconstruction, and the Legislative branch served notice to all that *it* would determine the conditions of readmission. It was not yet clear what these were going to be, but the Commoner, as Stevens was called, had checkmated the President.

Butler had been on good terms with Stevens for some time. Now that their interests merged more than ever before, the two men drew closer. Not that the General went quite as far as the Pennsylvanian — Butler, unlike Stevens, did not insist on universal Negro suffrage[22] — but he drew up the draft of a civil rights bill which he sent to the Commoner shortly before the opening of the new Congress. The measure contained the chief features of the bill which was passed later.[23] Moreover, convinced that there was no further hope of being appointed military governor of one of the Southern states, Butler finally resigned his commission as Major General.[24]

Not yet a member of Congress, Butler did not play a major role in the establishment of the Joint Committee of Fifteen on Reconstruction. Shortly after Congress assembled, however, Grant published his final report. Butler's repeated failures to take Petersburg and Richmond, the disaster at Fort Fisher, the inglorious recall — all were included.[25] The Major General did not appear to advantage; the phrase, "a bottle strongly corked" was an expression which delighted his enemies. Spoons Butler, Beast Butler, and now Bottled-Up Butler, "Hero of Fort Fisher."[26] The epithets stuck.

Butler was stunned. Convinced that he had been wronged, he determined to get even with Grant, whatever the cost. He consulted Parton and began to collect material for a devastating book on his antagonist.[27] When Grant invited him — belatedly — to a social function in January, 1866, he sent a curt reply:

> General Butler has the honor to decline the invitation of Lieut. Genl. Grant. Genl. Butler has now no desire for further acquaintance.[28]

"I never forget nor forgive until reparation is made," he wrote to a friend, "and in Grant's case it never can be."[29] He worked hard on his book,[30] but the polemic was never published. Events were moving too quickly, and Butler had to change his mind.

Grant's final report was not the only document he transmitted that winter. He also sent another paper to the President in which he endorsed the Executive's mild policies toward the seceded states. It is to be surmised that this development did not endear Johnson to the Major General.

In the following March, Butler's pride received another blow. The Supreme Court handed down its decision in the Milligan Case which tested the legality of military tribunals when civil courts were open. Butler had represented the Government; he had strenuously upheld its contention that military commissions were constitutional, but the Court was unconvinced. It decided once and for all that no American might be deprived of a civil trial when civil courts were available, and Butler's ideas about the punishment of the leaders of the Confederacy were no longer tenable.[31] Johnson had not taken his advice in 1865; now it would no longer be possible to carry out the General's proposals even if he were willing to do so.

In spite of these disappointments, Butler still had some lingering hopes that the breach between the two coordinate branches of government would not become final.[32] He did not consider a rupture imperative at that time,[33] possibly because he still hoped for a position in Johnson's cabinet. At any rate, he continued to maintain social relations with the White House and persisted in attempts to prevail upon the President to work with Congress.[34]

He was not alone in his efforts to keep his party from splitting. Although Johnson's veto of the Freedmen's Bureau Bill and his ill-advised remarks on Washington's Birthday diminished chances for success, many persons thought that some accommodation might still be possible, at least during the first quarter of 1866. First Senator Stewart of Nevada proposed a measure of reconstruction which coupled Negro suffrage with amnesty and reunion; then Robert Dale Owen suggested a similar compromise,[35] and finally — with the Reconstruction Committee ready to report what was later to become the Fourteenth Amendment — Ben Butler made his last effort to induce Johnson to cooperate. His plan also called for a Constitutional amendment. It would have forbidden the payment of the Confederate and the repudiation of the Union debt; it would have left the question of suffrage to the states, but prohibited the exclusion of more than one half of the males over twenty-one with automatic reduction in representation for all persons disenfranchised. Moreover, he suggested that these measures be coupled with amnesty for all except the leading participants in the Confederate or Southern state governments and those who had violated a previous oath to support the Constitution. In order to allow these arrangements to take effect, he thought Congress ought to adjourn for three months after the passage of the amendment, then reassemble and pass an enabling act restoring the seceded commonwealths.[36] He was convinced that the President would have accepted the plan had Congress only stood firm on impartial suffrage, but, as he put it, "the Committee on Reconstruction have reported giving up the suffrage question."[37]

In some ways, Butler's proposal did possess elements of a compromise. Because of its prohibition of disenfranchisement of more than half of the qualified electorate, it protected Negro suffrage in the South to a greater extent than the Civil Rights Act or the Fourteenth Amendment; it contained the same sweeping disqualifications of ex-Confederates, but at the same time, it did provide a speedy method of reconstruction which most radicals, unwilling to allow the Southern states to come back into the Union in the immediate future, had not included in their plans.[38] However, this concession was not enough for Johnson. Congress might repass the Civil Rights Bill over his veto, but he was in no mood to abandon his opposition to measures he considered destructive to the Constitution. He believed that Butler's plan was such a measure.[39]

Under these circumstances, Butler's hesitation to break with the Chief Executive disappeared. His efforts to bring the President into the radical camp had not meant that he was not in sympathy with extreme measures. His active role in the Milligan case, his known friendship for the Negro, his publicly announced determination to hang Jefferson Davis and his radical orations all made this abundantly clear. Therefore it was not surprising that he made no further efforts when it became apparent that Johnson would not yield. Like Stevens, Butler called Southern states conquered provinces, for as he told a huge crowd in Boston in 1866, the United States had by conquest acquired full title to all privileges that the South had ever possessed. Moreover, although he might be willing to compromise somewhat on Negro suffrage, demanding merely that all freedmen able to meet fair election tests be admitted to the polls, he did not think that the proposed Fourteenth Amendment went far enough. He preferred his own plan. Equality of right, equality of protection, equality of power under the government —

these were the principles upon which he chose to stand,[40] and after May, 1866, there were no further reports that he was advising the President.[41]

The radicals appreciated his efforts. Stevens might have some misgivings,[42] but in the last analysis, he found it easy to cooperate with a man who could hate as he himself hated. The legislature of Massachusetts elected Butler Major General of the militia;[43] Williams College conferred an honorary degree upon him,[44] and by August, he had become one of the principal speakers in the campaign against the President.[45]

It was no ordinary campaign — that campaign of 1866. The riots against Negroes in Memphis and New Orleans, the President's swing around the circle — a trip which he utilized to deliver undignified speeches comparing his foes to Judas — the pro-Johnson convention in Philadelphia where the delegates from South Carolina and Massachusetts appeared arm-in-arm — all provided ammunition to the radicals. To them, such antics merely seemed to prove their opponents' depravity. Moreover, the radicals could organize conventions of their own. Early in September, "loyal Unionists" met in Philadelphia in a counter-demonstration, where Butler made himself conspicuous by paying great attention to the famous Negro leader, Frederick Douglass.[46] The General had become known as the spokesman for those most insistent on dire punishment for the fallen foe, and, his violence possibly heightened by a desire to head off a Presidential boom for Grant, the man who had permitted the enemy to go home in peace, Butler's speeches became more and more extreme.[47] He himself could swing around the circle as well as the President, and wherever he appeared there were cheering crowds. There was even talk of Butler as the next Chief Executive,[48] and when an anti-Johnson Soldiers' and Sailors' Convention met in Pittsburgh, the General was very much in evidence. His speech and resolutions were as uncompromising as anything Stevens had produced,[49] and before long, he took the ultimate step by calling for the impeachment of the President.[50] So effective were the General's appearances that many a Republican candidate asked him for help in local campaigns.[51] He readily complied; moreover, desirous of personal preferment, he decided to run for Congress himself.

The idea of running for Congress was nothing new to Ben, but a candidacy with a possibility of success was an innovation. The only trouble was that the Middlesex District — his own — was represented by his friend George Boutwell, whom he was unwilling to edge out. In this quandary, Butler's fertile imagination hit upon a novel expedient. There was a vacancy in the neighboring Essex district, and in 1863, he had bought a plot of land near Gloucester, an area ideal for summer vacations. "The tent on the beach" he called it — a picturesque locale from which to launch a political campaign. There was no prohibition against such a procedure in the Massachusetts Constitution. The Republicans were willing, and Butler, anything but reluctant, entered the lists as a carpetbagger against the Essex Democrats, ably supported by his old political associate, Dr. George Loring.[52]

So sure was the General of success that he did not even bother to concentrate his attention upon his new bailiwick. He campaigned throughout the country, calling for the impeachment of the President and pointing out that the Republican party was the old Democratic host of Jefferson and Jackson, since it stood for universal freedom, universal justice, and universal protection to all men under the law. He characterized the conquered South as a "camp of paroled prisoners," an appellation of which he thought all but copperheads ought to approve.[53] He considered equal rights the privilege of the Negro as well as the white man, and if he did not yet demand complete suffrage for all freedmen, he did insist upon voting rights for all those who had fought for the Union.[54]

That Butler's bold attacks would not please all Republicans — not to speak of the Democrats — was to be expected. The General had too many enemies for that. Neither William Schouler nor Andrew's Secretary, A. G. Browne, had ever forgotten his conduct as commander of the Department of New England. Moreover, conservative businessmen found it hard to overlook the General's advocacy of radical labor legislation.[55] His financial views were known to be unorthodox even before he became a leading greenbacker,[56] and his hatred for Grant offended many. Schouler published an open letter in which he advised Republicans to vote against Butler on the grounds that he was not a resident of the district which he proposed to represent, that he was pledged to impeach the President, and that he was a sworn enemy of Grant.[57] However, Schouler's strictures could not really harm the General. Butler was too popular with the rank and file.

As so often in the past, the General's enemies helped him retain his popularity. When he campaigned on his party's behalf in New York, he found himself faced with a hostile crowd of hecklers in City Hall Park. He knew exactly what to do. When an apple was thrown at him, he quietly pared it, and munching it, remarked that it tasted fine. Then turning to his assailants, he savagely attacked Tammany Hall. "I charge the blood of the children murdered here in 1863 upon Horatio Seymour," he said. Groans greeted this thrust. But he continued,

> This is a miserable scene . . . the men who are now hollering and hooting are the men who in 1863 were killing children, men who were murdering babies . . . Why, you poor fools, I have faced your masters in Baltimore and New Orleans. I have hung your betters, and if you don't behave yourselves I fear I shall have the chance some day to do the same to you. Do you suppose that I will flinch before you? A man who has smelled gunpowder can stand rum and garlic. You think yourselves the equal of the negro. No, no; the negro is immeasurably your superior as heaven is above the hell where you are going. I do not fear you. You cannot overpower free speech and free thought . . . . Now then, men of the Five Points, bullies of the bawdy houses, thieves of the lobby and burglars of the Toombs, I simply declare here, as the voice of this nation, that you are not fit for the elective franchise. That fact could be no better demonstrated than it has been here today.[58]

It is not surprising that Butler had no difficulty in refuting Schouler's charges in Massachusetts. On Election Day, he rolled up a handsome majority.[59] The radicals had acquired a new leader in Congress.

CHAPTER SEVENTEEN

# Radical of Radicals

With their victory in the Congressional elections of 1866, the radicals threw all caution to the winds. They had nothing to fear from the President any longer; their two-thirds majority in both houses gave them unchallenged control of Congress. Now it was possible for them to show their true colors. Anyone who had thought the Fourteenth Amendment was all Stevens would require of the South soon saw how wrong he had been. The Amendment was only the beginning; military government and Confederate disenfranchisement with full Negro suffrage became the aim of the dominant party. In the Reconstruction Act finally adopted by Congress in March, 1867, there was no mention of Butler's talk of equal voting qualifications. It was quite clear that now the goal was a maximum number of black, and a minimum number of white, voters, at least in the Southern states. And Butler who said little about this change was now considered one of the most radical politicians in the country.

After his election in November, he had made many public appearances. In a speech to a large audience in Brooklyn, he listed the charges he wanted to prefer against the man whom he now called "King Andrew the Indecent." Drunkenness, indecent harangues, usurpation of power — these were the high crimes and misdemeanors for which the General demanded impeachment.[1] His closest advisers warned him against constant reiteration of this theme,[2] but he disregarded their counsel.[3] And it was clear that Butler had great influence; Adjutant General William Schouler discovered that when he was dismissed from office at the turn of the year.[4]

The radicals in Congress took full advantage of their victory. Their Reconstruction Act was only one of the extreme measures passed during the short session. The Tenure of Office Act making Senate consent necessary for Executive removals from office, an army appropriation act which required the President to transmit all military orders through the General of the Army, and an act which provided for the immediate assembly of the new Congress were all rushed through to shackle Johnson. And if Butler called for the President's impeachment at informal gatherings, Representative James M. Ashley of Ohio began an investigation for that purpose in the House of Representatives. He was unable to find anything very significant, but he refused to be discouraged. Butler would soon be in Congress to help.[5]

March 4, 1867, was a day of considerable interest in Washington. The galleries of the Capitol were crowded with people who knew that the spectacle about to take place would be well worth watching. As soon as the thirty-ninth Congress expired, the clerk called the roll of the Fortieth, and the members were sworn in. There were the familiar faces of Thad Stevens, John Bingham, James Garfield, and Schuyler Colfax; there were also some newcomers, among whom Butler was the most notable.[6] What would that controversial politician do in his new surroundings? The excited spectators watched him with anticipation.[7] They could not overlook the ever active Representative, with his half bald dome, his famous squint, his ungainly countenance, and his unparalleled repartee in debate. Enemies might deplore his election as a sad commentary on the times,[8] but friends expected him to play a leading role in the House from the very beginning.[9]

The General did not disappoint the onlookers. Within three days of his arrival at the Capitol, he arose to deliver a fiery speech in support of the resolution to continue the impeachment investigation. He accomplished his purpose, and henceforth he was to be ever more active in the search for evidence against Andrew Johnson.[10] But this oration was only the beginning. Strife had always been his element — in the law, in politics, in the Army. Now that he was in Congress, Butler could hardly be expected to change. In row after row with various fellow lawmakers, he kept himself constantly in the limelight; as long as he was in Congress, the dullest debate might become lively at a moment's notice.[11]

To the edification of the curious, the first altercation was underway before Butler had been in his seat for a month. Anxious to find some substantiation for impeachment, he began to pursue Ashley's fantastic hypothesis of Johnson's complicity in Lincoln's assassination and stumbled upon the fact that Booth had left a diary from which eighteen pages had been removed. Here was a sensational bit of information which he quickly sought to expose. The opportunity to do so arose when John Bingham, one of the leading prosecutors in the trial of the assassin's accomplices, opposed the General on a measure for the relief of the Southern poor. Noticing that his antagonist had wandered over to the Democratic side of the House, the General taunted him with having "got over on the other side not only in body, but in spirit." Angrily, Bingham replied:

> . . . it does not become a gentleman who recorded his vote fifty times for Jefferson Davis, the archtraitor in this rebellion, as his candidate for President of the United States . . . to cast an imputation either on my integrity or my honor. I repel with scorn and contempt any utterance of that sort from any man, whether he be the hero of Fort Fisher not taken or Fort Fisher taken.

However, Butler could not be silenced. When he obtained the floor again, he struck back. Yes, he had voted for Jefferson Davis, he said, but he had supported Davis when the Mississippian still claimed to be loyal to the Union. Bingham on the other hand, was upholding him now, "when he is a traitor." That was the difference; moreover, he, Butler, had done his part during the war, "but the only victim of the gentleman's prowess . . . was an innocent woman hung upon the scaffold, one Mrs. Surratt."

Bingham was taken aback. He demanded evidence of wrongdoing, only to elicit a further challenge from his antagonist the next time the matter came up. There was evidence, Butler shouted, a diary which Bingham had never produced. "Who spoliated that book," he roared,

Who suppressed that evidence? Who caused an innocent woman to be hung when he had in his pocket the diary which had stated at least what was the idea and the purpose of the main conspirators in the case?

Livid with rage, Bingham denied that he had been remiss. "Such a charge," he exclaimed,

> is only fit to come from a man who lives in a bottle and is fed with a spoon.[12]

Bingham, perhaps, had the last word, but Butler had the publicity.

To Butler, the altercation with Bingham constituted merely an incident in his effort to impeach the President. Absurd as the hypothesis was, the General assured his friends that Johnson was in some way implicated in Booth's plot — a theory he was determined to prove.[13] Since the Judiciary Committee had decided against impeachment in June, Butler prevailed upon the House to adopt a resolution authorizing a new investigation, this one to unearth evidence concerning the assassination. As Chairman of the Special Committee appointed for this purpose, the General spent much of the summer looking for clues.[14] Letter upon letter arrived from people who asserted they had information, but these leads proved uniformly disappointing.[15] For a moment, the statements of a convicted perjurer, Sanford Conover, seemed promising. The man was willing to swear to any falsehood to get out of jail, and Ashley tried to get him a pardon from the President. But the slippery convict then sought a new approach. In a letter to Johnson, he charged Butler and Ashley with deliberate attempts to manufacture evidence.[16] The Committee, its reputation damaged despite Butler's vehement denials, had to look elsewhere.[17] Its efforts produced nothing, and impeachment failed when Congress reassembled in the fall, although by that time the majority of the Judiciary Committee had reported in favor of the measure.[18] Butler had to bide his time a little longer.

Butler's failure to sway Congress in the matter of the impeachment was not the only cause of his annoyance during his first term. Jefferson Davis was released on bail in May; there were rumblings of discontent at home,[19] and, worst of all, the radicals were wooing Grant.[20] Butler was so distressed that he went to see Secretary Welles to tell him he was not in agreement with the First Reconstruction Act, no matter what people might say. Much to the Secretary's astonishment, the General even suggested that the President might have his policies tested by the courts.[21]

Whatever the purpose of this strange visit, Butler's worries about Grant did not cease. His manuscript of accusations against the General was ready;[22] but the wisdom of publishing it was questionable under the circumstances. Perhaps it would be far better to head off his enemy in a different, more indirect manner. An Indianapolis supporter suggested that it would be advantageous to publicize Grant's responsibility for the breakdown of the prisoner exchanges.[23] Butler snapped up this idea and tried hard to circulate his information on the matter.[24] Then Johnson, tired of the opposition of Secretary of War Stanton, the radicals' representative in the cabinet, replaced him with the Victor of Appomattox. It was a situation which called for care, so Butler commented upon the appointment in a guarded way which left him free to take any necessary future action.[25] But he continued to shadow Grant with detectives.[26]

With this state of affairs, the resourceful Representative of Essex County sought variation by devoting his attention to new issues. He had always fancied himself a student of finance;[27] now questions of the currency were assuming an importance second only to those connected with reconstruction. In an expanding country, slight inflationary measures might have been beneficial, but the business interests of the East demanded deflationary policies, and only a minority opposed them. With complete disregard for the prevailing notions of his section, Butler embraced monetary schemes calculated to appeal to Western farmers, a decision which was to put him beyond the pale of respectable Republicanism. As a manufacturer, he might have profited by inflation; as a politician with national ambitions, he had long been anxious for popularity in sections other than his own. Moreover, the protagonists of deflation were the Brahmins whom he disliked. So he boldly advocated the payment of the interest on five-twenty bonds in greenbacks, on the grounds that there was no legal obligation to pay in coin.[28] Technically, he was right; politically, he committed a grave blunder. Radical periodicals like *Commonwealth* and *Harper's Weekly* severely castigated him;[29] radical statesmen like James G. Blaine and James A. Garfield took issue with him,[30] and Jay Cooke, the country's leading banker, was excited enough to write to him in dismay.[31] Yet the General refused to budge, and from that day on, he supported every inflationary measure that came up in the House.

By the time Congress reassembled in the fall, Butler was a radical of the deepest hue in respect to finance as well as impeachment. He agitated for both,[32] but it was impeachment which soon came to a head. The Senate refused to concur in Stanton's removal; Grant relinquished his office, broke with Johnson, and the Secretary resumed his functions. As the President was determined to bring the reconstruction issue, and especially the constitutionality of the Tenure of Office Act, before the courts, he did not propose to permit Stanton to remain in the cabinet. After an unsuccessful attempt to appoint either General Sherman or Thomas Ewing, he chose the aged Adjutant General, Lorenzo Thomas, to serve as Secretary *ad interim,* and again dismissed Stanton. As the Secretary of War refused to yield, and as the Senate upheld him, the President, instead of getting his difficulties into the courts, merely presented the House with an opportunity to impeach him.

The radicals were quick to react. Against a background of serio-comic drama — Stanton refusing to leave his office day and night lest Thomas gain physical possession — the House adopted a resolution to impeach the President for "high crimes and misdemeanors." Excitement was at a fever pitch; Stevens and Bingham were appointed to notify the Senate, and a committee was appointed to prepare the formal articles.

Butler did not play a leading role in these developments. To be sure, his speech in support of the resolution was violent, and replete with rhetorical references to George III, Charles I, and James II,[33] but in spite of his prominence as one of the earliest and most insistent advocates of impeachment, he was not on the original committee to implement the charges. Now that the General of the Army had turned against the President, Butler's enmity for Grant made the member from Essex an embarrassing candidate for such a post.[34] Nor was Butler's offensive language acceptable to many who might otherwise have agreed with him.[35] Had he been less adroit, or had Stevens been in better health, the General might well have missed a chance to play a leading role in this dramatic trial.

But the Commoner was ill; he needed help, so he turned to Butler. "As the Committee are likely to present no articles having any real vigor in them," he wrote,

> I submit to you if it is not worth our while to attempt to add at least two other articles (and as many others as you choose) in the House as amendments, and see whether they will adopt anything worth convicting on. Had I my usual strength, I would not ask you to undertake this movement, but I deem it so important that I send you copies which may serve as hints for you to act upon.[36]

The General did not have to be asked twice. Convinced that indictable charges were unnecessary for conviction, he was disappointed by the articles prepared by the Committee. Tortuously legalistic, they arraigned Johnson in various ways for the violation of the Tenure of Office Act and for plotting illegally with the Army.[37] "Naked bones and sinews," he called them, asking that they be clothed "with flesh" so that posterity might know the real reason for impeachment.[38] To make this possible, he introduced an additional article. "Said Andrew Johnson," it read,

> did attempt to bring into disgrace, ridicule, hatred, contempt and reproach the Congress of the United States.

As proof, it cited "intemperate, inflammatory, and scandalous harangues" delivered to jeering crowds during the Swing Around the Circle. The House hesitated; in spite of Butler's impassioned pleas, it voted the article down, but there would be another chance. The General succeeded in being elected to the Board of Managers who were to try the case.[39]

During the next few days, he worked as he had never worked before. He was determined to play a leading role in the trial; only a short time was left, and his colleagues were not anxious to prepare the opening argument. Butler maneuvered things in such a way as to receive that honor for himself, knowing full well that it would give him an opportunity to introduce subsequent evidence as well.[40] Moreover, with Stevens' aid, he convinced all the managers but one of the value of his article of impeachment, and finally, the House accepted it. It became Article Ten, and was followed by another, the Commoner's catch-all Article Eleven.[41] Butler had maneuvered himself into the spotlight.

March 4, 1868, was the day set aside for the formal presentation of charges. It was a splendid scene; the trial had become the social event of the season. Washington society, the diplomatic corps, and as many visitors as managed to procure the coveted tickets filled every seat in the Senate galleries. The seven managers, accompanied by the House organized as a Committee of the Whole, made their appearance. Butler entered arm in arm with his antagonist of the year before, John Bingham. The other managers — Boutwell, Williams, Logan, and Wilson — followed. Stevens, too weak now to walk, was carried behind. Bingham read the accusations; the Senate listened gravely. The spectators were not disappointed.[42]

Even more dramatic were the events of March 13, the day upon which Johnson had been summoned to appear. After the senators had filed in, the Sergeant-at-Arms loudly called the President's name. Expectant faces awaited his entrance, but the Chief Executive did not come. Instead, his attorneys asked for a forty days' adjournment, only to be rebuffed by the managers. "Forty days! As long as it took God to destroy the world by a flood . . ." Butler protested, insisting upon the utmost speed to ensure the continuance of government. The Senate granted ten days,[43] and after further preliminaries, the General was ready for his opening on March 30.

For Ben the lawyer, that afternoon was the most dramatic of his career. As he described it more than twenty years later:

> When I entered the Senate chamber from the vice-president's room the scene was almost appalling to one who had to address such an audience. The floor of the Senate chamber was filled because the House attended in committee of the whole; the

galleries were also crowded with those interested in the case, and the ladies' gallery shone resplendent with bright, beautiful women in the most gorgeous apparel. I came as near running away then as I ever did on any occasion in my life. But summoning up such courage as I could, I stuck to my post and addressed the Senate in a speech of two hours' length.[44]

At first, those who had come to witness an exhibition of typical "Butlerisms" were disappointed. Dry, legal arguments predominated. Butler proudly contrasted the sublime scene of one of the world's greatest nations' removing its chief magistrate by legal process devoid of violence with the convulsions which would have attended such changes elsewhere; then he launched into a lengthy discussion of Anglo-Saxon impeachment precedents with special emphasis on the trial of Warren Hastings. Coming more directly to the point, he gave his definition of an impeachable crime. As he put it, it was

> one in its nature of consequences subversive of some fundamental or essential principle of government or highly prejudicial to the public interest . . . a violation of the Constitution, of law, of an official oath, or of duty, by an act committed or omitted, or, without violating a positive law, by the abuse of discretionary powers from improper motives, or for improper purpose.

Not for him the doctrine that high crimes and misdemeanors had to be clearly recognized transgressions. Nor was he willing to admit that the Senate was a court. To him, it was but a political body conducting an inquest of office, bound by no law, except by "natural principles of equity and justice." Accordingly, he insisted that Johnson's guilt did not have to be proved beyond reasonable doubt; all that was needed for conviction was preponderance of evidence. He did not want to take any chances.

When he reached the specific charges against the President, he tried to make the most of what was, in essence, a very weak case. If the power of removal were in the hands of the Executive, he argued, the government would become an unmitigated despotism. As long as Congress had refrained from legislating on the subject, he admitted that Presidents could remove at will, but he denied that a power not exercised was a power surrendered. When Congress had passed the Tenure of Office Act, it had resumed a power which it had always possessed. Therefore, by disregarding the Act, Johnson had violated the Constitution. Cavalierly dismissing the objection that Stanton, as Lincoln's appointee, was not covered by the measure — to Butler, Johnson appeared to be merely serving out Lincoln's term — the General turned to the question of criminal intent. He denied the President's right to bring a law before the courts in any way other than by process of *quo warranto*, with due notice to the Senate. This Johnson had not done, therefore his intentions were not proper.

Those technical arguments were not what the galleries expected; but Butler was Butler, and he was only awaiting the right moment. Indeed, he had come to the conclusion to "try the case upon the same rules of evidence, and in the same manner, as . . . a horse case," and when he reached Article Ten, the one he had inserted himself, he gave the listeners what they were waiting for. Castigating the President's behavior during the Swing Around the Circle, he waxed eloquent. Deploring the disgrace of Johnson's speeches, he professed shock at the defendant's blasphemous references to his enemies as Judases. Did the Tennessean dare compare himself to the Lord? "By murder most foul he succeeded to the Presidency, and is the elect of an assassin to that high office," Butler shouted, declaring that anyone who failed to do his duty by voting for conviction was voting to establish tyranny in the land. He was proud of his work, and, confident of victory, sat down among the managers in front of the presiding officer's chair. He hoped it would not be long until Benjamin F. Wade, President *pro temp.* of the Senate, succeeded to the Presidency.[45]

The following days were taken up with the presentation of evidence, not so much of Johnson's criminal intent, but simple proof of incidents which had led up to the trial. The President's removal of Stanton, his appointment of Lorenzo Thomas as Secretary *ad interim*, his speeches to excited crowds — all were put into the record.[46] As Butler had intended, he became the *de facto* leader of the managers. Having delivered the opening address, he had the right to substantiate his accusations, and the publicity was largely his.[47]

His task, however, was not easy. The President's counsellors were men of great experience and legal talent. William M. Evarts, witty, adroit, with a political record of unquestionable Republicanism, was a leader of the New York bar. Benjamin R. Curtis, ex-Justice of the Supreme Court and famous dissenter in the Dred Scott case, was one of the most noted lawyers in Massachusetts and in the nation, while Henry Stanbery had only just resigned his position as Attorney General of the United States to defend his chief. Of lesser stature, but nonetheless able, were the President's fellow townsman, T. A. R. Nelson, and former Congressman William Groesbeck.[48] And, in the last analysis, the law was on Johnson's side.

Butler's chief difficulty lay in the weakness of his case. The removal of one of Lincoln's appointees was not a clear-cut violation of the Tenure of Office Act, as John Sherman, Republican Senator from Ohio, had specifically stated at the time the measure was adopted.[49] Moreover, the Act itself was of doubtful constitutionality, and Butler himself had intimated as much a year earlier, when he had expressed the opinion that the President, without criminal intent, might seek a decision from the Supreme Court.[50] Furthermore Butler's own article of impeachment was so weak that even many radicals doubted the wisdom of its introduction.[51] The habit of free speech was too deeply rooted in America to convict easily on the basis of speeches, no matter how obnoxious. Finally, the General's insistence that misdemeanors did not have to be defined was in itself an admission that the "Great Criminal" had not sinned so grievously after all. It was also an extremely doubtful doctrine.

Still, Butler had reasons for hope. If the law were not on his side, party sentiment certainly seemed to be. If he took full advantage of these prejudices, he might obtain the necessary two-thirds vote for conviction. He conducted himself accordingly.

It was patent that he tried hard. Determined to press to the utmost his insistence that the Senate was not a regular court, he delivered an impassioned plea to reduce the powers of the Chief Justice to those of a mere figurehead, a contention the Senate did not entirely accept.⁵² Moreover, he had not introduced the Tenth Article for nothing. Since it afforded an excellent opportunity to remind the Senators of Johnson's offensive remarks, Butler was able to inject drama into what was essentially a dreary procession of uninteresting witnesses.⁵³ Even the submission of routine evidence could be enlivened with humor. By eliciting the world-shaking fact that one George W. Karsner had encouraged his fellow Delawarean, Secretary *ad interim* Thomas, with the statement, "The eyes of Delaware are upon you," Butler produced general merriment. The Senate responded with uproarious laughter.⁵⁴

While these antics were newsworthy, they could not obscure the lack of real evidence. The witnesses called by the managers testified to the events leading up to Stanton's dismissal; they revealed the fact that Thomas was a garrulous, foolish old man; they attested to the accuracy of the official version of Johnson's messages, telegrams, and speeches. However, they could not produce anything startling. The managers had created much heat but little light, and, after calling a postmaster whom Johnson had dismissed, the prosecution rested on April 9.⁵⁵

That afternoon Benjamin R. Curtis opened for the defense. In a speech lasting the better part of two days, he demolished the prosecution's contentions. Pointing out the inconsistency of charging Johnson with violation of the Tenure of Office Act when Sherman himself had not considered that measure applicable to Stanton, he defended the President's right to test unconstitutional acts in the courts. To Curtis, Stevens' catch-all article in itself was proof of the flimsiness of the other charges. Johnson's actions might at best be called differences of opinion; they certainly did not constitute high misdemeanors.⁵⁶ It was a powerful argument, and after Curtis had finished, even Butler had to admit that "nothing *more* was said in his [Johnson's] behalf, although in the five or six closing speeches by his other counsel much *else* was said."⁵⁷

The witnesses summoned by the defense were well qualified to disprove allegations of Johnson's criminal intent. General Sherman, members of the cabinet, Presidential secretaries — all stood ready to testify that the Executive's purposes had been entirely legitimate, Stanton himself having considered the Tenure of Office

Act unconstitutional. Determined to allow their antagonists as little leeway as possible, the managers sought to parry this blow to their case by resorting to technicalities. Time after time Butler rose to object to witnesses and to testimony. Ordinarily, the Senate upheld him, but try as he might, the General could not entirely prevent the introduction of unfavorable evidence, and the defense succeeded in proving that Johnson had never contemplated the use of force.[58]

That things were not going well for the managers became evident as the trial went on. Privately, Butler himself admitted to Evarts that he wished he were on the other side,[59] but publicly, he put up a stiffer front. He badgered witnesses; he delivered a lengthy harangue about the crimes of unrepentent Southerners,[60] and he engaged in furious rows with his opponents. William Evarts, James Brooks, Reverdy Johnson all battled with him,[61] and if his antics did not lend dignity to the trial, they certainly kept things lively. The only question was whether they might not do more harm than good.

At last, after the introduction of additional written evidence, the closing arguments began. Boutwell, Stevens, and Bingham made impassioned pleas for conviction; Nelson, Groesbeck, Stanbery, and Evarts summed up for the defense. Little was said which had not been elaborated upon before; the managers tried to make up by oratory what they lacked in law, while their opponents made the most of the obvious flaws in the prosecution's case.[62]

Butler did not play a major role in the closing scenes. He read part of Stevens' closing argument because the old man was now too sick to do so in person, but because he had delivered the opening speech, he had no claim to participate in the summation. Yet once again he became the center of controversy. Since the managers had sneeringly referred to the fact that Jeremiah S. Black had withdrawn from the defense at the last moment, T. A. R. Nelson thought he ought to reply. Had not Butler, supported by other managers, signed a paper urging Johnson to seize the Dominican guano island of Alta Vela in which both Butler's friends and Black's clients were interested? Johnson's refusal had cost him Black's services. The President could not be used to "carry on a speculation," exclaimed Nelson, who implied that Butler had tried to make a corrupt deal with the defendant. The angry colloquies which followed, Butler's outraged denial, talk of a duel, and the uproar in the Senate, added considerable drama to the proceedings.[63]

With the completion of the final pleas, the time for balloting drew near. Excitement increased from day to day. How would the Senators vote? Butler thought he knew. "The removal of the great obstruction to peace and quiet is certain," he wired to the Republican State Convention of New Hampshire. "Wade and prosperity are sure to come in with the apple blossoms."[64] However, there was an element of doubt. If a few uncertain Republicans voted for acquittal — and several preliminary conferences had indicated this possibility — impeachment would fail.[65]

The managers were in no mood to take chances. As Butler wrote to John R. Young of the New York *Tribune,*

> We should go through barring corruption. Money is here to be used like water. Denunciation for those who have betrayed the country is the only path to safety. The reasons why we are betrayed should be shown that other true men may avoid the pit into which others have fallen. Spare not. I speak the voice of our friends.[66]

The *Tribune* complied,[67] and the managers exerted enormous pressure on Senators suspected of lack of firmness.[68] Butler might rush into the House, shouting, "We are sold out,"[69] but he remained sufficiently confident to bet on conviction.[70]

And well he might, for Ben Wade's cabinet had already been picked, and there were rumors that none other than the Essex statesman was to be Seward's successor.[71] Leading radicals confidently predicted success;[72] Butler's greatest case might net him his greatest fee.

At last the great day — Saturday, May 16 — arrived. The Senate met, and as the Eleventh Article seemed the most promising, it was voted upon first. Breathlessly, the audience awaited the replies of the Senators. "How say you? Is the respondent, Andrew Johnson, President of the United States, guilty or not guilty of high misdemeanors as charged in this article?" Senator after Senator replied to this question — the Democrats in the negative, most of the Republicans in the affirmative. Since this response had been expected, it caused little surprise. But when the doubtful Senators rose, suspense mounted. Fessenden, Fowler, Grimes, Henderson — one after the other they disappointed the radicals. At last the clerk reached Edmund G. Ross, junior Senator from Kansas. Without his vote, there would be no conviction, and although he had given some assurances a few days before, his statements had been very vague. The Senator rose. Deathly silence ensued. "Mr. Senator Ross, how say you?" . . . Every eye, every ear was upon the Kansan. "Not guilty," came the reply. Impeachment was as good as finished, and when the total votes were counted, they fell one short of the necessary two thirds.[73]

The radicals were furious. One vote! Rumors of bribery had been rampant for some time; now Butler, whose opinion of human nature had never been high, thought he was certain of their truth. "How does it happen," he wrote,

> that just enough and no more republican Senators are convinced of the President's innocence. Why have not these conscientious convictions on which the seven act struck any more of them? Is conscience only confided to just enough to acquit the President?. . . I think we shall be able to show where some of these men got their consciences and how much they are worth.[74]

And as the court had adjourned till the 26th, he went to work to prove his allegations. The managers, acting as a committee, scanned every scrap of evidence to fasten a bribery charge upon their opponents. They impounded telegrams; they unearthed bank records; they arrested one Charles Woolley who had gambled heavily on the President's acquittal after withdrawing money from his bank in New York. But when Butler presented a report to the House on May 25, he could not produce any evidence of bribery.[75]

Failure to prove their charges did not dampen the managers' ardor. If one single Senator could be induced to change his vote, Wade might yet become President. The result was that the seven recusants were subjected to incessant pressure.[76] Ross especially found himself hounded by spies, threatened with political oblivion, and exposed to never-ending abuse. "Tell the damned scoundrel that if he wants money there is a bushel of it here to be had," was a message he received from Butler.[77] But he remained firm. When the final vote came on May 26, this time on Article Two, the result stood as before. The managers tried once more, on Article Three, but they could do no better. Then the Senate, sitting as a High Court of Impeachment, adjourned *sine die*.[78]

Butler had lost his greatest case. In impotent rage, he continued the investigation to unearth evidence against the recusant Senators, but so little turned up that his associates did not even sign the final report. Butler did, although the document retailed nothing but slander and did not even call for action on the part of the House.[79] Impeachment was over. Actually, it was partially his own fault that the outcome was so disappointing. For in spite of the shortcomings of the indictment, in spite of the weakness of the case, he might conceivably have won. The President was so unpopular, times were so exceptional, party spirit was running so high, that a partisan verdict, — regardless of evidence or law, — might have been obtained. But Butler's histrionics, his outbursts, his undignified attempts to try the President of the United States as a horse thief might be tried, had been totally out of place.[80] His tactics were ill suited to win over the doubtful Senators,[81] and although he had received publicity as a politician, he had mismanaged his case as a lawyer. However, he remained one of the leading radicals of the day.

CHAPTER EIGHTEEN

# Grant's Lieutenant

Failure to impeach the President was only one of Butler's disappointments in the spring of 1868. Much to his disgust, he had been unable to prevent Grant's nomination, and, to make his chagrin complete, the Republican party had accepted a platform with a conservative financial plank.

It was no news to Butler that Grant's star had been on the ascendant. He had been warned by friends,[1] and as early as December, 1867, he had reconciled himself to the unpleasant possibility of having to vote for his antagonist.[2] But he continued to give vent to his bitter feelings about the prospective candidate,[3] until the certainty of the impending nomination caused him to be cautious. Then sheer political necessity forced him to desist.[4]

To many radicals, the rift between the two generals seemed deplorable. George Wilkes, editor of the radical *Wilkes' Spirit of the Times*, for one, thought that it was imperative to bring the two men together. As he told Grant, the common cause required reconciliation; nor did he believe the points at issue were insurmountable. Grant agreed; he explained that he had meant no harm when he had used the term "Bottled up," and he disclaimed any intentional insult in the matter of the delayed invitation.[5] The delighted Wilkes hastened to inform Butler, but he discovered that the Major General was not so forgiving as his former superior. Although he was prepared to accept Grant's explanations about the "bottle" and the invitation and was willing to apologize for his rude rejection of Grant's hospitality, Butler nevertheless demanded satisfactory clarifications of other unfavorable references in Grant's report. He was not going to crawl back into his foe's favor, at least not for the time being.[6]

Wilkes forwarded this reply to Grant,[7] and on June 19, the Presidential candidate gave his answer. While he expressed satisfaction that two issues were out of the way, he refused further explanation. As he put it,

> in regard to other matters in my report of the operations of the armies for the last years of the war to which General Butler alludes, I must decline to open discussions.[8]

And no matter how strenuously Wilkes urged acceptance of the proffered hand, Butler remained intransigent.[9]

At this juncture, part of the story leaked to the press. Featuring it prominently, the Boston *Advertiser* voiced the belief that reconciliation was an accomplished fact.[10] Wilkes, who suspected Schuyler Colfax of the indiscretion, spent some uneasy hours worrying lest Butler do something "anti-climactic,"[11] but his fears proved unfounded. The *Advertiser*, professing ignorance of Butler's position, retracted part of the story; yet it continued to assert that Grant had said he had no quarrel with his old opponent.[12] Under the circumstances, the Representative from Essex, faced with an approaching Congressional campaign and unable to back the Democrats because of their hatred for radical reconstruction, publicly announced his support of the Republican candidates.[13] Reconciliation was far from complete, but the first steps had been taken.

That his position was hateful to Butler may well be imagined. He might settle his differences with Grant, but the stumbling block presented by the deflationary platform remained. There seemed to be no real place in either party for radicals like himself — men whose devotion to greenbacks and taxation of national bonds was secondary only to their insistence on equal suffrage. Depressed as he was, he thought he would take little part in the forthcoming canvass.[14]

However, he was mistaken. His enemies would not permit him to remain inactive. Offended by his harangues, furious about his advocacy of soft money, they hoped to rid themselves of the Representative who defied the conservative economic traditions of the Commonwealth. Grant's nomination encouraged them, and when Butler, despite their efforts to defeat him, received the regular Republican nomination in his district, they bolted. Richard Henry Dana, lawyer, writer, and author of *Two Years Before the Mast,* became their candidate.[15] Grant secretly approved,[16] and Dana prepared to give battle to his opponent. Contending that Essex had been utterly misrepresented by the incumbent, Dana condemned Butler's hatred for Grant, his financial heresies, and his offensive ways.[17] And lest the challenger be at a loss for campaign speakers, his backers asked two of Butler's most bitter foes, Generals Gordon and Kilpatrick, to come into the district and aid Dana. Both complied with alacrity, and, in speech after speech, raked over all the old charges of corruption against the former Commander of the Department of Virginia and North Carolina.[18]

A campaign of this type had to be countered. Never one to avoid a head-on collision, Butler saw no reason why he should not reply in kind. After all, he had publicly endorsed Grant and he was in demand as a campaign speaker in other states.[19] If he permitted himself to be defeated at home, his political career would be over, but if he triumphed over his enemies, his position would be overwhelming, and, as Henry Adams remarked, he would go to Washington carrying their scalps in his belt.[20] Moreover, the odds were greatly in his favor. The leading journals of Boston might be against him, the leaders of Massachusetts society might berate him,[21] and "Brick" Pomeroy, vitriolic Democratic New York editor, might make him the main target of his sarcasm, but the people of Essex resented outside interference.[22] To them it mattered little that the country did not care for the General. Perhaps his notions on money were queer — ordinary people did not understand such things anyway — but the rebels hated him more than they did any other Yankee, and he had taught rich secessionists what it meant to defy Old Glory. These facts made him popular in Essex. Let him be called a spoon thief, let him be called "a bottled curiosity of nature." He was sure to have a ready answer, and, effective speaker that he was, he never bored his constituents.[23]

Butler threw himself into the campaign with great zest. Dana symbolized everything he hated. An aristocratic old Whig, a respectable conservative in financial matters, Cambridge born and Harvard bred, the luckless author became a perfect target for the General's barbs. Hammering away at his opponent's patrician origin, Butler made fun of Dana's pretensions, until at last the challenger was provoked to unwise replies.[24] The writer said it was true that he wore white gloves when he was in polite society, but he had also spent two whole years before the mast and had got as dirty as any of his listeners.[25] With such statements, he could not hope to win, and when election day came, he ran a poor third, polling 1,819 votes to Butler's 13,000.[26] The triumphant General returned to Washington as the unquestioned leader of his district;[27] office holders who had opposed him found themselves without jobs,[28] and General Kilpatrick had to fight hard to retain his post as Minister to Chile.[29] For years to come, Butler was to wield a powerful influence in the Republican party of Massachusetts.

The General's victory over Dana hastened the reconciliation with Grant. In order to obtain political patronage Butler needed the support of the President-elect, and he could now approach Grant from a position of strength. Accordingly, he called upon the General for the first time since the war, and although he was unable to obtain an interview — Grant was just dressing for dinner — the courtesy was noted.[30] Moreover, Butler embarked on a deliberate campaign of flattery in Congress, where he, of all people, introduced a bill for the unconditional repeal of the Tenure of Office Act, a measure close to Grant's heart.[31] Whatever he might think privately,[32] publicly he made it known that he had more confidence in the new President than in the old.

Grant responded handsomely. To show that he was ready to let bygones be bygones, he in turn left his card at Butler's house.[33] Butler might still have misgivings, — he made a surprise appearance at Johnson's New Year reception, a sensational visit which might be interpreted as a slap at Grant[34] — but by February, the press was able to report that the General and Mrs. Grant had called upon Mrs. Butler.[35] The breach was healing.

To the amazement of friend and enemy alike, once the ice had been broken, the two generals became more and more intimate. As time went on, Grant tended to rely increasingly upon the ingratiating Representative from Massachusetts.[36] Butler's foes were sure that his hold over the President was proof positive of blackmail, but such an explanation is most unlikely.[37] Given Grant's childlike reliance on rich men, to say nothing of his inexperience in politics, it is not surprising that he became dependent upon Butler. For the Major General not only flattered the President's ego, but, in spite of military shortcomings, he excelled in the two fields in which Grant was least successful — business and politics. The victor of Appomattox was impressed.

Of course Butler did not allow Grant to forget that he was willing and able to be of service. Because of the Senate's jealousy of its prerogatives, Butler's original effort to repeal the Tenure of Office Act had failed. Grant, however, wanted the measure repealed in its entirety, and Butler was anxious to cooperate. Accordingly, within five days of the inauguration, he again introduced his two-line bill for repeal. The House was willing to pass it, but the Senate still had misgivings. And no matter how hard he tried in the committee of conference, the Upper House would not yield. The most he could obtain was a compromise restoring the President's prerogatives for all practical intents and purposes; the Senate insisted on maintaining its ultimate right to supervise removals.[38] His foes chortled at what they considered his defeat;[39] yet in a larger sense, it was not a defeat at all. The compromise afforded an excellent opportunity for continued agitation for total repeal, and the Essex member did not propose to let the matter rest. Again and again he introduced his measure in the House.[40] If the Senate took no action, he did not particularly mind. Grant would be pleased with the effort.

In other ways, too, Butler made himself useful to the President. Early in his Administration, Grant had become vitally interested in the purchase of the Dominican Republic, the eastern end of a tropical island which he believed to be immensely valuable. He referred the Treaty of Annexation to Charles Sumner, Chairman of the Senate Foreign Relations Committee, who promised to take it under careful consideration. Upon close examination, however, Sumner developed such a decided dislike for the measure that his attacks upon it brought about a complete break between him and the President[41] — a development Butler knew how to utilize for his own purposes.

Annexation of territory had always been part and parcel of the General's creed. He belonged to the spread-eagle school of diplomacy; as he expressed it, he hoped that

> within my day I shall see the Stars and Stripes floating as evidence of our control and beneficent power at the Isthmus of Darien while the traveler at the North Pole shall mistake its red and white for the glow of the Aurora.[42]

It is true that he had opposed the purchase of Alaska — that "land, or rather the ice," as he called it.[43] But Johnson had been President when that issue had arisen, an unsettled American claim in which the General was involved had beclouded the matter,[44] and he had been jealous of the prerogatives of the House.[45] None of these considerations applied to San Domingo. Even before Grant's inauguration, Joseph W. Fabens, one of the original speculators in Dominican real estate, had interested Butler in the island; the General had accepted a piece of land in the republic and had become one of the principal advocates of annexation.[46] Therefore, when Sumner's opposition made it certain that the necessary two thirds could not be procured for the Treaty in the Senate, Butler again appeared as the Administration's counsellor. The Senate might not ratify the Treaty, he said, but had not Texas been annexed by joint resolution? He advised a similar procedure with respect to the Caribbean island and went ahead to introduce the necessary legislation in the House. He tried no less than nine times, much to the President's satisfaction, but the opposition proved too strong and San Domingo remained independent.[47]

Butler, however, derived benefits from his action. What did it matter whether or not one small island belonged to the United States if his influence with the Administration was increasing so steadily?[48] If Sumner broke with Grant, Butler was not overly disturbed; relations between him and the Senator had never been too cordial. For a time, the General might attempt to patch up the quarrel, but then it was gratifying to him to see a man close to such people as the Hoars, the Andrews, the Danas — all rabidly anti-Butler — get into trouble.[49] The Representative from Essex knew how to retain patronage in Massachusetts, whatever the relationship between her senior Senator and the President.[50] Moreover, his arch foe, Judge E. R. Hoar, who had been appointed Attorney General in Grant's cabinet, had agreed with Sumner; now Hoar's opposition to San Domingo could be turned to good effect, and before long, the Judge was forced to resign. That was a greater victory for Butler than annexation could ever have been.[51]

So it was that the man whom Grant had ordered home in disgrace, the man who thought that there was little difference between a "drunken tailor and a drunken tanner,"[52] became one of the chief spokesmen of the Administration. A frequent visitor to the White House, he maintained close personal relations with the Chief Executive.[53] In Congress and out, he could be relied upon to defend the President from calumny. When Chairman Henry L. Dawes of the Appropriation Committee implied that the Administration was not careful with money, Butler had an answer ready: Grant was not extravagant; if the budget seemed greater than anticipated, that was due to Johnson's dishonest estimates.[54] When Congress wished to expel West Point cadets because of misbehavior, Butler, knowing full well that Grant's son was implicated, rushed to the defense of the culprits, notwithstanding his hatred of the Academy.[55] When General Logan berated the Administration for failure to extend belligerency to Cuban rebels, Butler, though an annexationist, arose, dramatically holding high some Cuban bonds, and engaged in a furious row with the opponents of the policy of the Secretary of State.[56] Since the President lacked newspaper support in New York, Butler contributed to a new pro-Administration organ established by John R. Young.[57] "The entente cordiale is strengthening everyday between me and the executive," he wrote to his wife in 1870, and he was not mistaken.[58]

To his enemies' dismay, Butler's influence with Grant brought great rewards. His political power extended far beyond the confines of his district. Applicants for office turned to him, not only in Essex, but in the South, the West, and even the East.[59] It was obvious that Butler's friends were well looked after; he was known to cultivate close relations with Secretary of the Treasury George Boutwell and his successor, W. A. Richardson. Roland Usher, Butler's faithful lieutenant in Lynn, became U. S. marshal, J. H. Chadwick, another devoted supporter in Massachusetts, State Director of the Boston and Albany Railroad, and Colonel Shaffer, Governor of Utah.[60] Butler's family benefited also. His nephew George was appointed consul in Alexandria; his brother-in-law Webster, consul in Frankfurt, and his brother-in-law Parker was on the public payroll in New Orleans.[61] Butler was influential, and even though his power was not as extensive as was commonly believed,[62] it was still far greater than that of any ordinary Congressman.

These were good years for the General socially and professionally also. His law practice flourished, and he lived in great style. The "tent on the beach" had become a splendid granite summer house called Bay View;[63] the Lowell mansion had lost none of its grandeur, and a magnificent residence on Fifteenth Street bespoke the General's influence in the capital. His parties were the talk of the town, especially since his daughter Blanche was one of the most admired beauties in Washington.[64] When in 1870, she was married to General Adelbert Ames, Republican Senator from Mississippi, her father staged a gigantic three-day wedding celebration in Lowell, with enough dignitaries present to give the affair the appearance of a chapter out of the Arabian Nights.[65] Ben basked in the glory of his proximity to the throne.

Yet these festivities could not obscure the fact that reconstruction was still the country's most pressing problem. Thad Stevens had died in August, 1868; yet his spirit lived on. He had bequeathed his seat in the House to Butler,[66] and when Congress met in December, the General tried to assume the Pennsylvanian's mantle of leadership as well.[67] As radical reconstruction and protection of the Negro had been the Commoner's chief concerns, so they became the mainstay of Butler's politics. Not that he was especially concerned about the legal niceties involved in carrying out his ideas; what really interested him was the establishment of a healthy Republican party in the South, an organization which would be strong enough to safeguard the civil rights of its members, both black and white, and sufficiently powerful to assure victory over the Democrats in national elections. To make such a development posible, the Negro must be allowed to vote on equal terms, and Butler was determined to see that he did.[68]

Practical as may have been his interest in the freedmen, the General's concern about the rights of colored people appears to have been genuinely based on principle. The events of the Civil War had profoundly altered his views on the relations between the races, from the moment he declared the first fugitive a contraband until the impressive charge at Newmarket Heights. On that day, he wrote later,

> as I guided my horse this way and that way that his hoof might not profane their [the Negro soldiers'] dead bodies, I swore myself an oath . . . that they and their race should be cared for and protected by me to the extent of my power as long as I lived.[69]

And whether his recollections were entirely accurate or not, he certainly maintained the substance of the oath. He remained the most ardent defender of the Negro in the House of Representatives.[70]

When Butler returned to Washington after his victory over Dana, the reconstruction machinery set up by Congress had already been functioning for some time. The South was bitterly resentful; it hated the carpetbag governments which had been instituted, and the Democrats tried by all means, fair and foul, to recapture control. Although the original Ku Klux Klan had allegedly been disbanded, outrages against Negroes continued — proof positive to Republicans that the hooded order and the evil spirit of rebellion were unconquered. Then the legislature of Georgia expelled several Negro members; an outcry arose against the recalcitrant state, and Butler, determined to make an issue of the matter, introduced remedial legislation.[71] When Congress met in joint session to count the electoral vote for President, he insisted the tally of the offending commonwealth be excluded. The Senators retired; the Representatives upheld him, but when the Upper House returned, Ben Wade overruled him. The General was on his feet in an instant. Throwing back his head, pushing up his coat cuffs, squaring himself before his desk, he shouted his protest. "Let us see whether we have any rights in the House or not," he exclaimed. Bedlam reigned for more than half an hour. Wade finally announced that Grant and Colfax were elected,

"Whether Georgia be counted or not,"[72] so that Butler failed to carry the immediate point at issue; yet while he was severely censured for his behavior,[73] he had again succeeded in capturing headlines and in dramatizing the continued need for protection of the Negro in the South.

When Grant became President, Butler saw no reason to abandon his radical policies. True, the Chief Executive was not by nature a vindictive man; he might even have supported Johnson had the Tennessean been more adept. But when Johnson intimated that Grant had broken his word by permitting Stanton to resume his office, the General was so hurt that he never forgave his predecessor and made common cause with Congress. He was nominated on a radical platform, accepted radical support, and was committed to the reconstruction acts. If he still expressed his desire for pacification, extremists like Butler knew how to handle him. The Essex statesman shrewdly used his influence with the President to accomplish his aims, and, aided by politicians of similar views, succeeded in committing the Executive to a radical policy.[74] And if opponents of these measures attacked the Administration, Butler could conveniently pose as its defender. It was a process which netted benefits to the General, for Grant always appreciated those who supported him. Moreover, it made certain of the continuation of the policy of proscription of former Confederates.

A major role in the reconstruction program was assured to Butler when he became Chairman of the Reconstruction Committee in Grant's first Congress.[75] It was partially on his insistence that new and more onerous conditions were imposed on the remaining unrestored states;[76] it was his bill which remanded Georgia once more to military rule from which she was relieved only after the adoption of additional safeguards against backsliding.[77] And the passage of the Fifteenth Amendment finally embodied his philosophy of equal suffrage in the Supreme Law of the Land, even before he took over the Chairmanship of the Committee. Grant seemed to approve.

Continual outrages against freedmen served to justify to some extent Butler's radical course. Southerners were not willing to recognize Negroes as full citizens, so that it is doubtful whether a policy of mild reconstruction could have secured for the former slaves even the limited protection of the Fourteenth and Fifteenth amendments. For Butler, recurrent atrocities provided numerous opportunities to wave the bloody shirt, and although two so-called Enforcement Acts were passed in 1870 and 1871, he wanted to go further. What he desired was legislation to smash the Ku Klux Klan, and when the House, unmoved by his oratory, refused to approve of a Senate bill for that purpose, he provoked a bitter row with the Speaker, James G. Blaine. He declared that he for one would not serve on a committee of investigation which had been proposed as a substitute for the measure, for, he said, Blaine's failure to support the bill was nothing but a trick, a barter for votes for the tariff. "For ways that are dark and tricks that are vain I will name Speaker —," he shouted. The Plumed Knight, exasperated by the accusation, left his chair to answer the "insolence of the Gentleman from Massachusetts,"[78] but Butler had his way. In a lengthy harangue a few weeks later, he conjured up the villainies of the masked riders, the perfidy of the Democratic party, and the unregenerate treason of the South. The oration, the furious exchanges with Senator Garrett Davis and Representative Swann which followed, gave him much publicity;[79] the two Houses agreed on a compromise, and a Ku Klux Bill was finally passed.[80] If it fell short of what he had wanted, Butler nonetheless took full credit for it just the same.[81] The lawless band eventually disappeared, its epitaph luridly embodied in the majority report of the investigating committee, signed, among others, by the man who had vowed he would not serve on it — Benjamin F. Butler.[82] His admirers of both races were pleased, and Grant signed the bill.

In one respect, Butler was willing to implement, at least partially, Grant's desire for mercy. As early as November, 1869, Horace Greeley had asked him to couple a measure of universal suffrage with universal amnesty for former insurgents.[83] At that time, the man who wanted to hang Davis was not yet quite ready to forgive the bulk of the Confederates,[84] but as time went on, he changed his mind. He knew amnesty would please Grant, and so many bills to remove the disabilities imposed by the Fourteenth Amendment had cluttered up the Congressional calendar that it was expedient to enact a general measure. Charles Sumner's insistence on linking amnesty with a civil rights bill held it up for a time, but finally, in 1871, Butler succeeded in piloting it through the House. It extended forgiveness to all but seven hundred-odd Confederates, a show of mercy more generous than that evident in the settlement of most civil wars.[85]

This gesture of magnanimity reflected credit on the Administration. But it came too late. Tired of war, reconstruction, and the Negro problem, the liberal Republicans became increasingly critical of the President and the spoilsmen who surrounded him. They decried his policies, especially the harsh treatment of the South. Yet Grant as much as Butler had become committed to these measures.[86] Attacks upon them were as attacks upon himself, and his detractors were unable to break the bond that tied him to Butler. The reconciliation between the two men had become permanent.

CHAPTER NINETEEN

# Enfant Terrible of the Republican Party

> History deals with Benedict Arnold, with Aaron Burr, with the evil counsellors of Charles I and Charles II, with Robespierre, with Barère and with Catiline . . . without considering the fact that they are dead. . . . I repeat what I said of General Butler in his lifetime . . . that the success of his attempt to use and consolidate the political forces of Massachusetts would have been the corruption of her youth, the destruction of everything valuable in her character, and the establishment at the mouth of the Charles River of another New York with its frauds, Tweed rings and scandals.

So wrote George F. Hoar in 1903,[1] and his opinion was not at all atypical. The conservatives of Massachusetts — the rich, the well-born, the well-educated, the refined, generally agreed with him. They might put up with the eccentricities of a Sumner; they might be satisfied with the plebeian Wilson, but they would never reconcile themselves to Butler.

And how could they? Whether or not they were aware of Butler's hatred for them, they liked people of breeding, men who knew how to behave themselves. They could hardly overlook the fact that Ben was involved in rows in almost every session of Congress while he was a member. He fought with Blaine and Dawes; he quarreled with General Farnsworth and Senator Davis; he provoked John Logan and John Young Brown, and the language he used was rarely dignified. Pithy replies were his forte; few could flatten an opponent as quickly as he, who, scarcely taking note of Samuel S. Cox's attacks upon him, merely said, "There is no need for me to answer the gentleman from New York. Every Negro minstrel just now is singing the answer, and the hand organs are playing the tune, 'Shoo fly, don't bodder me!' "[2]

These sallies might have been forgotten had their author merely dealt with insignificant questions. But Ben was involved in the most vital topics of the day, and his ambitions extended beyond Massachusetts. Just as, before the war, he had supported slavery in abolitionist Massachusetts, he now advocated inflation in the hard money Bay State. To many of his enemies, this was a sin which outweighed all others,[3] but he refused to desist. His speeches in favor of paying in greenbacks the interest on the five-twenty bonds and his advocacy of taxation of national bonds had been bad enough; but they had been only a beginning. In January, 1869, he developed his ideas further. To the horror of conservatives,[4] he delivered an impassioned oration proposing the revision of the entire currency structure of the nation. "I stand here," he shouted,

> for inconvertible paper money, the greenback. . . . I stand here for a currency by which the business transactions of forty million people are safely and successfully done, which, founded on the faith, the wealth, and the property of the nation, is at once the exemplar and engine of its industry and power — that money which saved the country in war and has given it prosperity and happiness in peace. To it four million men owe their emancipation from slavery; to it labor is indebted for elevation from that thrall of degradation in which it has been enveloped for ages. I stand for that money, therefore, which is by far the better agent and instrument of exchange of an enlightened and free people than gold and silver, the money alike of the barbarian and the despot.[5]

Of course, his bill embodying his ideas of a dollar at once elastic, stable, and inconvertible, never became law,[6] but his advocacy of inflationary schemes never ceased. He was one of the few Republicans who voted against the deflationary Public Credit Act in March, 1869; he was the only Republican from Massachusetts who supported expansion of the currency in 1870, and he ardently advocated the most extreme version of the Inflation Bill of 1874.[7]

He remained a fanatic proponent of soft money for the rest of his long career.

What the General's advocacy of inflation was to the conservative financier, his espousal of labor legislation was to the conservative employer. Butler was opposed to the peculiar type of *laissez-faire* endorsed by so many Republicans — tariffs and subsidies for business coupled with a hands-off attitude toward labor. He had not forgotten his struggles in behalf of the mill girls of Lowell; if business had grown, so had labor, and he thought Government had a distinct duty to protect the underdog. He considered hours, conditions, and a fairer distribution of profits fit subjects for legislation — let the aristocrats say what they pleased.[8] And although he did not believe strikes were necessary in a country with universal suffrage,[9] he successfully intervened with Grant in favor of an eight-hour day for Government employees at unreduced wage scales. Moreover, he publicly praised the Paris Commune.[10] It would have been difficult to express sentiments less congenial to the Brahmins.

There was also the question of women's suffrage. This was not so dangerous a subject as greenbacks or the rights of labor, but when Ben Butler appeared as the champion of a suffrage petition advocated by Victoria Woodhull, the brazen champion of free love and other causes unmentionable in a Victorian community, well brought up people might well shudder.[11] The man had no sense of decency.

Moralistic though the age was in respect to the relation between the sexes, its public standards of ethics were not high. It was a period of the most widespread corruption in American history; rarely had politicians been more cynical in their insistence on the spoils of victory. Many a respectable citizen, unable to reconcile himself to such conditions, felt that there ought to be a limit, an end to ceaseless plunder of the public treasury. The result was a powerful movement for civil service reform, a crusade to which Grant gave lip service at first, but which he eventually abandoned. Why he changed his mind seemed patent to the reformers: He was too dependent on spoilsmen like Conkling Cameron, and last but not least, Butler.[12]

That Butler was a spoilsman cannot be denied; he reveled in the acceptance of favors for his machine, in punishment for enemies no less than in jobs for friends.[13] But whether he was really very different from others is questionable. What others did quietly, he did openly; what others did sanctimoniously, he did brazenly. Others might pay lip service to civil service reform; he, with his contempt for causes advocated by "reputable" reformers, attacked it unceasingly.[14] As he said in the House in 1872,

> this "civil service reform" I characterize as a political trick. It is always popular with the outs and never with the ins, unless with those who have a strong expectation of soon going out.[15]

Moreover, he generally castigated civil service reform as an attack not only on the integrity of the President, but also upon poor, maimed soldiers, displaced by unworthy academy students.[16]

Butler loved to flaunt his disregard for respectable opinion. Legal representative for the advocates of innumerable shady claims, he defied his foes to investigate him; and since his profits generally accrued not from the original corrupt bargains but their legitimate defense in court afterward, it was impossible to pin anything on him.[17] In 1870, a particularly persistent representative from Illinois, John Farnsworth, tried, only to find that he could not get very far. Not that he did not have enough material. It was rumored that Butler had procured a profitable contract for the supply of granite for the new Boston post office to Jonas French's Cape Anne Granite Company; it was said that he himself had an interest in that enterprise,[18] and there was incessant criticism of his conduct as President of the National Home for Disabled Volunteer Soldiers. To say the least, the bookkeeping methods employed by that institution were peculiar. Its funds had been mingled with those belonging to its President; moreover, one of the branches had been established on land in which Butler had an interest.[19] Farnsworth put the worst possible interpretations upon these facts;[20] yet none of the accusations could be made to stick. Denying personal ownership of the granite company, the General readily admitted having helped his friend with the contract, the cheapest and best bid, he said.[21] He remained President of the Home, a Congressional committee having absolved him from all wrongdoing.[22] Attacks upon him in Congress were violent, as were his replies,[23] but as in so many suits brought against him for alleged wartime irregularities, he generally prevailed.[24] While none of his victories, in Congress or in the courts, ever dispelled entirely the clouds of suspicion which hung about him,[25] they gave him unceasing publicity. He had always thrived on that.

Outraged as the "better people" were at Butler's domestic policies, they could find little to cheer them in the field of foreign relations. Always a violent Anglophobe, he gave free rein to his dislike for all things British. Irish causes won his unwavering sympathy,[26] and the complaints of fishermen against Canada received his constant attention.[27] Like Charles Sumner, the General believed the only proper compensation for Britain's hostile attitude during the Civil War was the cession of all Canada; but unlike the Senator, he considered "the Springfield musket" and the "ten pound Parrot" the "only negotiator on this subject."[28] By proposing non-intercourse with England in order to force her to quit the North American continent, he was perfectly willing, for partisan reasons, to risk war with a kindred nation.[29] When, despite his opposition, the Treaty of Washington was finally negotiated, he continued to denounce it and tried hard to block appropriations for carrying it into effect.[30] It was not an edifying spectacle for believers in pacific diplomacy.

While many of his most flamboyant attacks on respectability did not come until Grant's second Administration, the struggle between Butler and the Brahmins increased in intensity long before. Dana's raid, the greenback speech in 1869, spats with Dawes and Schenck, the struggles over reconstruction in general and Georgia in particular, all heightened tensions. Butler did not take a prominent part in the election of 1870 — he was too annoyed at his Republican foes for that[31] — but they were continually frightened by rumors of his elevation to the cabinet, perhaps even to head the Department of State.[32] Moreover, while he himself remained somewhat in the background, his friend and supporter, Wendell Phillips, the abolitionist orator and now a radical of radicals on the labor question, was very active. The Brahmins were sure that the orator's nomination by the Prohibition and Labor Reform party was merely a "breaker-up of the ground" for the General.[33]

Their fears proved well founded. In a Lyceum lecture on the "Present Relations of the Parties" in November, 1870, the General declared that with the settlement of the questions of the war, the old issues were dead. Problems of the day cut across party lines. What was needed was an anti-British foreign policy, a course which would solidify the Republican party, right the nation's wrongs, and bring the Irish into the fold.[34]

This address was merely the opening blast. Ever since 1858, Butler had been ambitious to become Governor of Massachusetts. At that time, he was a Democrat with little chance of success, but now he was a Republican. Why should he not realize his ambition at last? There were issues enough; the party had been in power so long that it was easy to attack "the state house ring." And since the faction opposed to him had held many of the offices, its misdeeds might help him attain the highest office in the Commonwealth. Many of the Irish, labor, temperance men, veterans, and Federal job holders were with him; the field looked promising, so he decided to try.

What followed was a free-for-all rarely seen in Massachusetts. One man, largely unsupported by press and party, brought the Republicans of the Bay State to such straits that, in desperation, they had to jettison all personal differences and combine. Otherwise they could not hope to defeat the audacious interloper.[36] When the idea was first broached, early in spring, the conservative Springfield *Republican*, one of the papers most actively opposed to Butler, rallied the opposition. "To him quite as much as to any other person is due the conspicuous failure of General Grant's administration," wrote the editor,

> The worst appointments made by the President were at Butler's suggestion; the worst acts of Congress have been passed under Butler's whip and spur; this whole broil about the Southern states is due almost entirely to Butler . . .[37]

That such a man was to aspire to John Andrew's chair was too much to contemplate. The Boston *Advertiser, Journal, Herald,* and

*Transcript,* all sought to blacken Butler's reputation.[38] Finally, the editors of the *Chronicle,* charging him with a secret deal with George Loring, asked the General openly if he intended to run. To their dismay, he replied with an unmistakable "yes." Reports of an understanding between him and Loring were falsehoods, he said, and to agitate still another troublesome issue, he added that he would enforce the prohibition law. Then, if the people did not want it, it might still be repealed.[39]

From that day on, he campaigned vigorously, making it quite clear that he would base his bid for office upon the advocacy of many issues long ignored by the party — the rights of labor, woman suffrage, and prohibition.[40] It was a frightening spectacle to his foes, so frightening that they dug up all the old slanders about him that they could find, including the apocryphal tale about his father's death.[41] As they should have known, that story was the one charge he never overlooked. On August 24, in a crowded meeting in Springfield, he delivered his reply. He would tell the audience why the leaders of the Republican party, the State House ring, were abusing him, he said. They hated him because of personal spite. Mr. Sanborn, of the *Republican,* had collided with him during the John Brown affair; "Warrington" had clashed with him in Lowell years ago, and General Hawley, of the Hartford *Courant,* had been displaced by him for incompetence in Virginia. These were the reasons why his opponents attacked a man who had served his country faithfully in war and peace, a man who was an outstanding supporter of the Administration. Avowing that he would never yield, he asserted again that he was an old-fashioned Democrat who believed the poor man had "equal rights with the rich." Sanborn tried to interrupt but was not given a chance. Butler ridiculed the *Republican* by reading some of the then usual sensational advertisements from it. Nor did Hawley's angry denial make any difference. It was clearly the General who had received the publicity.[42]

Stumping the state, Butler repeated his pithy charges about his adversaries wherever he went. The real culprits, he said, were the capitalists and their allies among politicians and editors, bloated exploiters of honest workingmen.[43] Such speeches warmed the hearts of labor reformers like Wendell Phillips,[44] but they goaded the opposition to desperate measures.

The leaders of the Republican party were in a difficult situation. Governor Claflin, then in his third term, had made many enemies among the very groups now wooed by Butler. For some time, there had been talk of replacing Claflin with somebody else — George Loring, Alexander H. Rice, Harvey Jewell, or William B. Washburn. The newcomers could always withdraw at the last moment to enable the Governor to run again.[45] But now that Butler had become such a threat, his enemies had to make haste to combine against him. Moreover, they enlisted the state's two Senators, Sumner and Wilson, on their behalf. The Senators signed a joint statement deploring Butler's methods;[46] "Warrington" ceaselessly attacked him,[47] and when the State Convention opened in Worcester, the opposition was able to muster about as many delegates as the General.[48]

Excitement ran high in the densely packed hall. Butler entered, greeted by deafening cheers. If he could prevail on the Convention to seat a number of contested delegates, he would carry off the prize, but the opposition had labored well. Not only had the conservatives managed to bring together all of Butler's rivals, but they had placed his bitter foe, George Hoar, into the Presiding Officer's chair. Hoar and Dawes could be trusted to outmaneuver the challenger. Butler's motion to admit to the galleries "the people — largely his henchmen — was carried; yet through judicious adjournments, the conservatives prevailed upon the two leading anti-Butler candidates, Loring and Rice, to withdraw. They then united on William B. Washburn, a man after their own heart from the western part of the state, so when the Convention reassembled, the General was outvoted. He accepted the verdict in a bitter speech. However, notwithstanding rumors to the contrary, he refused to bolt.[49] His enemies must have known that he would try again.

1872 was a Presidential year. It had become obvious long before that the anti-Grant movement would be formidable,[50] and when Sumner, Bowles, and other reformers opposed to Butler deserted Grant for Greeley, the nominee of both the Liberal Republicans and the Democrats, the General was not at all sorry. He might have preferred a candidate other than Henry Wilson for the Vice-Presidency — it was painful to swallow the "Natick

Cobbler" in addition to the man he still, privately, called "Galena James"[51] — but the President had been helpful in the past and might be more so in the future. Therefore Butler dramatically refused to be a candidate for the governorship lest the Republican party be split still further,[52] and after some hesitation,[53] he helped rally the country to the Administration. When the campaign was over — he himself had easily been re-elected to Congress — he was stronger than ever.[54]

To the dismay of conservatives, his strength added to his audacity. Hardly had the President been chosen for a second term when the Crédit Mobilier scandal broke. The construction company by that name, controlled by the same men as the Union Pacific Railroad, had fleeced investors of millions, and, as it developed, Representative Oakes Ames of Massachusetts had distributed many a valuable share among members of Congress. Colfax, Wilson, Logan, Bingham, Garfield, Brooks, all were besmirched by the scandal; a committee of investigation was appointed, and when it recommended Ames' expulsion from Congress, Butler rose to defend his old friend. Ames was merely the scapegoat for the real offenders, he said, an honest man who had told the truth when others had lied to protect themselves.[55] But it was with pleasure that he contemplated the discomfiture of many of his old enemies.[56] He himself had been much too clever to take any of the tainted stock. The money he had made on the Union Pacific was the fee for his legal service, a reward to which he had been entitled.[57] To see Butler unscathed while his enemies were caught, to have him defend a man who had debauched Congress, was hardly an edifying spectacle for the conservatives. For they considered him the worst "corruptionist" of all.

If the General's defense of Oakes Ames shocked the Brahmins, his leadership in the salary grab outraged them. Everybody knew that Grant would appreciate a raise in salary, twenty-five thousand dollars being hardly sufficient for the head of a great nation. But Butler, whether to implement his belief in higher wages, or whether to make sure that the bill for the President's salary increase passed the House, became the mastermind behind a scheme to raise Congressmen's salaries also, not merely for the future, but for the past two years as well. After considerable debate, a bill doubling the President's salary and giving every Congressman an additional twenty-five hundred dollars, was enacted into law.[58] Grant was pleased; the conservatives were affronted.[59]

The abuse which was poured upon the General because of the salary bill failed to discourage him. He would try again for the governorship, this time with the White House under greater obligations than ever before. Moreover, he had been instrumental in enabling George Boutwell to overcome his opponents and become Wilson's successor in the Senate.[60] The Senator was not likely to forget, and as for Sumner, he was not even able to prevail on the legislature to expunge the resolution of censure for his proposal to return Confederate battle flags.[61] Accordingly, in the spring of 1873, Butler announced that he would run again.[62]

Except for a demand for government ownership of the roadbed of railroads, the issues were the same as in 1871. But since 1873 marked the beginnings of one of the worst depressions America had ever experienced, the General's challenge to the possessing classes would have been more effective had it not been for the salary grab. With millions of people destitute, the thought of Congressmen enriching themselves at taxpayers' expense was not attractive. Moreover, Butler was too close to the Administration and to various railroad companies to convince all voters that he was a true friend of the oppressed.[63]

The General's opponents made good use of his weaknesses. They issued an address to the people, savagely attacking the "claimant," as they called him.[64] Washburn must be reelected, they said, for Butler was a "corruptionist," a repudiator, and a war profiteer. George F. Hoar characterized the General's career as one of "swagger, quarrel, failure;"[65] "Warrington" again lent his pen to the attack, the core of his charges being the salary grab, and an entire pamphlet was issued to prove the General's responsibility for the measure.[66]

The General fought back. Vigorously defending the salary bill — he himself did not need the money and decent wages were opposed only by grabbing capitalists — he loudly called for economic reform. He thrust again at his opponents in general and the "gentlemen Hoars" in particular,[67] but he fared no better than he had two years earlier. When the Convention met at Springfield, he found himself unable to muster enough votes for a resolution against bolters, a move he deemed necessary because of threats of non-support should he be nominated, and so at the last minute he withdrew his name. The conservatives had beaten off his second assault, but they could no longer disregard the demand for a ten-hour day for women. The measure was enacted in 1874.[68]

As in previous years, he was not chastened by defeat. His relations with the President had not suffered, nor did he cease to be of service to the Executive. When popular resentment forced a repeal of the salary grab, he saw to it that Grant's compensation remained at fifty thousand dollars a year, much to the gratification of its recipient.[69]

Rewards came quickly. The Collector of the Port of Boston was about to retire — pushed, some said, by Butler, who felt that the Customs House had not supported him sufficiently in the gubernatorial contest. However that may be, Butler had a hand-picked candidate for the post, William A. Simmons, a devout Methodist with unimpeachable personal habits, but a leading figure in Butler's machine. To the mortification of Boston's mercantile community, the General prevailed upon the President to nominate Simmons for the vacant office.[70]

The conservatives were not willing to take this affront lying down. Determined to prevent what they called the "Butlerization" of the Customs House, if not of the entire state, they sought to prevent ratification at all costs. Protest meetings, petitions, irate editorials in the leading newspapers — all the pressure of an organized party were brought to bear upon Senate and Executive. George F. Hoar went to see Grant to ask him to withdraw the nomination; yet as Sumner had opposed it, Grant who considered the Senator his mortal enemy, refused. The clamor was nothing but an attack upon Butler, he said. If any wrong-doing on the part of Simmons were brought to his attention, he would withdraw the candidate's name; otherwise, he saw no reason for complying. As Hoar recalled, the President and he passed Lafayette Square just at that time, and Grant,

> with great emphasis, . . . shaking his closed fist toward Sumner's house, said; "I shall not withdraw the nomination. That

man who lives up there has abused me in a way which I never suffered from any other man living."

Hoar desisted. It was clear that Butler had made the most of Sumner's defection.[71]

Final confirmation was up to the Senate, where things did not look promising. Boutwell, in spite of threats of retaliation, joined Sumner in opposition by reporting against confirmation. Yet, unlike his colleague, he did not appeal to the courtesy of the Senate, and because of Grant's attitude, Sumner's appeals carried little weight at that time.[72] Moreover, Butler, correctly considering the opposition an undisguised attack upon himself, moved heaven and earth to secure the necessary votes. Indefatigable, he "walked the lobbies, puffing and snorting like a healthy sea lion," cornering a friend here, whispering to a Senator there, until the full chamber, badgered, wheedled, brought into line by his incredible exertions, voted to confirm.[73] It was a triumph of the first magnitude.

And yet disaster lay ahead. The Brahmins did not mean to give peace to the man they detested. They were merely biding their time to deliver what they hoped would be a knock-out blow. Butler had suffered a setback in January when Grant had been forced to withdraw the nomination of Caleb Cushing for Chief Justice,[74] but more serious were the revelations about the operations of one of Butler's henchmen, John D. Sanborn. That shady individual had succeeded in obtaining a contract from the Treasury to collect delinquent taxes under the existing moieties system which guaranteed large percentages to an informer. Of the $427,500 Sanborn had collected, he had kept $213,500, and he had paid large sums to unnamed counsel. The suspicion that some of this money had found its way into Butler's pockets was widespread; obloquy and abuse were heaped upon him, and an investigation committee sought to unearth evidence connecting him with the scandal. The committee could not find anything, but the attacks continued.[75]

As revelation followed revelation, it became known that Butler would deliver a spirited defense of Sanborn and the moieties system. But early in May, he fell sick, so that it was not until one month later that he finally rose in the House to reply to his detractors.

In spite of the stifling heat, the galleries were crowded; the eager spectators waited with anticipation.[76] How would "Old Cockeye" get out of this scrape? They were not disappointed. Butler was as defiant as ever. Sanborn had done no wrong, he said; his maligned lieutenant had acted within the letter of the law. The real wrong-doers were the big merchants, "respectable businessmen," like the owners of Phelps, Dodge and Company, who tried to defraud the Government of taxes and were now anxious to deflect attention to poor Sanborn. "For myself," he continued,

> I defy investigation. For fourteen years . . . I have lived under the focus of a microscope, magnifying and distorting every action of mine a million times, except, perchance, it was a good one, which it blurred and covered altogether. Living under such inspection, therefore, whether I would or not, I must lead an honest and upright life, or some man would in all those years have got "a rap at old Cock-eye."[77]

All this may have been effective oratory. Whether it contributed greatly to the speaker's reputation was a different matter.

What really boded ill for the confirmed greenbacker was Grant's veto of the inflation bill of 1874. Butler might plead and shout; the hard money Republicans, especially Judge Hoar, had the last word. They committed the party to deflation.[78]

The General expected his foes to try to take advantage of his discomfiture. There were intimations enough of their intentions;[79] nor did the 1874 Senatorial contest bring much cheer. The leading candidates for Sumner's seat — the great abolitionist had died — were Dawes and George F. Hoar, one more objectionable than the other from Butler's viewpoint. He decided to throw his influence behind Dawes whom he considered the lesser of two evils, but he was outmaneuvered. William B. Washburn, a man who hated him "with an evangelical hatred," won the prize.[80] It was discouraging, and at times, the General thought of retiring altogether.[81]

But then he again considered the governorship. He kept his foes guessing — now they thought he would try, now they were certain he would not.[82] Attacks upon him did not diminish, General Hooker going so far as to charge that the commander of the Army of the James had embezzled money belonging to colored soldiers.[83] But since he was constantly in the public limelight — he had taken a prominent part in the sensational adultery trial of the Reverend Henry Ward Beecher which had given him much publicity[84] — the opposition decided not to take any chances. The conservatives prepared to defeat him in his own bailiwick.

At first his enemies' efforts proved feeble. With powerful speeches and efficient organization, Butler frustrated their attempts to rob him of the nomination in his district. But then the incredible happened. He was unable to prevent the adoption of an unequivocal hard money plank by the State Republican party,[85] and as the campaign progressed, it became evident that the usual enthusiasm was lacking.[86] The large spoons which his opponents lowered behind his back while he spoke could be laughed away,[87] but the depression, the poor record of the Administration, the scandals blamed by many upon Butler — all seemed to point to a Democratic victory. It was difficult to obtain money,[88] and when the election returns were in, the General had been defeated, beaten by less than 1,000 votes in a contest from which his Republican foes had absented themselves in order to give victory to Charles P. Thompson, a war Democrat of excellent reputation.[89] Mortally offended by what he considered rank ingratitude, Butler blamed the capitalists for his defeat.[90] It was no consolation that the midterm elections had brought disaster to Republicans throughout the nation, or that the Democrats had captured the Governorship of Massachusetts. He had at last suffered a severe setback at the hands of the conservatives, and he was not in a forgiving mood.

Though mortified, Butler did not remain silent during the lame duck session of Congress. If he must leave, he would depart in a blaze of glory. The Democrats would have a majority after March 4; since Sumner's Civil Rights Bill had not yet been passed, it would have to be pushed through now or never. Equality for the Negro in public places, street cars, inns, bars — equality in fact as well as in name — was the purpose of the measure, a program heartily endorsed by Butler. While the conservatives fumbled, he utilized all his parliamentary cunning and oratorical strength to assure its adoption.[91] He waved the bloody shirt; he battled furiously with the representatives of Southern states. They might call him a murderer, an apologist for thieves, a prodigy of vice and meanness, but they could not prevent him from forcing the Civil Rights Bill through the House.[92] It became law shortly afterward,[93] and although it may have been ahead of its time, its principles were worth fighting for. The General had rendered his parting service as a Representative from Essex County.

During the next two years, Butler held no public office. He continued to dabble in politics, upsetting conservatives by angling for new nominations,[94] by trying, though unsuccessfully, to defeat Alexander H. Rice for the governorship,[95] and by continually advocating his financial theories of a stable paper curerncy.[96] But his foes could console themselves with the realization that the party's *enfant terrible* was in retirement.

Although no longer a member of Congress, Butler continued to spend much time in Washington. In defiance of society's preference for residences near the White House, he built himself a tremendous granite house opposite the Capitol, at New Jersey Avenue and B Street S. E. There he could be seen with the inevitable carnation in his buttonhole, leaving in his handsome French coupé, ever busy on some case. For he still had an extensive practice, and he still gave advice to the President. As a private citizen, he fought bitterly and successfully to prevent the confirmation of Richard H. Dana as minister to Great Britain.[97] And from there he watched with anxiety his wife's failing health.

Sarah had long suffered from a tumor in her throat.[98] But in 1876, her spirits as well as her physical condition were at a low because of the troubles of her son-in-law, Governor Ames of Mississippi. As a result of the redemption of his state by the Democrats, Ames was impeached, and although he resigned before the case could come to trial, Sarah was sorely worried.[99] Her throat grew progressively worse, and in March, her health reached a critical stage. She needed an operation; Ben, in desperation, took her home to Massachusetts, only to have her die upon arrival. It was a blow worse than any he had ever sustained.[100]

And yet, unhappy though he was, Butler, still driven by political ambition, decided to attempt a comeback in politics. Not in Essex — he was through with that district — but in Middlesex, where he had lived all his life. Boutwell no longer represented that area, and Butler thought he had a good chance of getting the nomination.[101] Trial balloons among the faithful had encouraging results. Many were anxious to help, only they warned the candidate to keep quiet about the greenback question. The bloody shirt was a much better issue,[102] and nobody could wave it more adeptly than Butler.

With local backing assured, Butler turned to the National Committee. William S. Simmons went to see Secretary Chandler and his associates. The General asked for nothing, said the Collector; Butler was willing to abide by the party platform, including the money plank. All he wanted in return was to be left alone. Should that request be refused, he was ready to spend five hundred thousand dollars to defeat Massachusetts Republicans. The answer sounded encouraging.[103]

As in the past, the campaign got off to a lively start. At a flag raising ceremony at Lawrence on August 22, the candidate spoke at length about the crimes of Southern Democrats. Did his audience want to see American citizens murdered on American soil? Did his listeners wish unreconstructed rebels to dictate to them? If so, let them vote for his opponent. But if not, let them send him back to Congress. "I have no hesitation in speaking about it," he said, "I am not a maiden, but more like a widow, for I know what I want and I am not afraid to ask for it." The country roared with laughter, and he appeared henceforth as "Widow Butler" in many a cartoon.[104]

Yet the currency issue caused trouble. Butler went so far as to pledge support of resumption, but only, as he put it, to give people a chance to see how harmful this policy really was. To that extent, he was willing to make good Simmons' promises,[105] and he obtained the nomination.[106] But his equivocation did not satisfy the conservatives. Unwilling to support him, they bolted, nominating Judge E. R. Hoar instead.[107]

With two such antagonists in the field — the Democratic incumbent, John K. Tarbox, was less controversial — sparks were sure to fly. Charges and counter-charges filled the air. In an open letter, Butler wrote a savage review of Hoar's career. Hypocrite, incompetent, schemer, he called him,[108] and although the Judge tried to reply in kind, he was not as adept in the rough-and-tumble of dirty politics as the General. He might ridicule Butler's financial views and castigate Butler's connection with innumerable scandals; he might receive handsome contributions from leading capitalists; yet he could not overcome the handicap of his irregular nomination.[109] Butler was not above raiding the Democratic party; popular with the Irish, he distributed handbills asking Tilden men to vote the straight Democratic ticket, with the exception of himself, for Congress. Moreover, he obtained the endorsement of labor and the aid of such outstanding colored leaders as Frederick Douglass, and he agitated the Southern question with hyperboles of Ku Klux terror.[110] The result was that he was re-elected, his last victory as a Republican.[111] He was still the bane of the party he would soon forsake, but the issues he had raised could never be ignored again.[112]

CHAPTER TWENTY

# Return to the Democrats

Butler had won again, but whether the party had also prevailed was questionable. That would depend entirely on who counted the electoral votes of Florida, Louisiana, and South Carolina. The Democrats, who controlled the House, were convinced that Tilden had carried these states; on the other hand, the Republicans, who controlled the Senate, were equally certain that Hayes had won. What the truth was is difficult to determine. Considering only the votes actually cast, Tilden was the victor, but many Negroes had been kept from the polls. A maze of corruption made a genuine count all but impossible.

Ordinarily, an issue of this type would have fascinated the General, but since both candidates were "reform" politicians of the type he abhorred, he took little part in the controversy.[1] Privately, he advised the seating of Tilden so that a Republican more congenial than Hayes might, in 1880, benefit from the probable revulsion against the Democrats;[2] publicly, however, he voiced no such opinion. Stories leaked out that he thought Tilden had won — rumors which he promptly denied. All he had said, he maintained, was that the issue ought to be decided by a new election in accordance with a law dating back to 1792.[3] When this proposal found no favor he relapsed into silence. As he put it, "I shall always remain in the rear when George William Curtis and Carl Schurz speak for the Republican party."[4]

While Washington was engrossed in watching the spectacle of the deadlocked House and Senate, Boston was the scene of a political struggle of a different sort. The full term for the Senatorship had to be filled, and Butler, having forgiven Boutwell for his part in the Simmons affair, was pushing him as a candidate. However, the anti-Butler forces in the State had become stronger than he, and so, to the General's intense mortification, his enemy George F. Hoar received the prize. Butler's hold over Bay State Republicans had become very precarious.[5] Soon it would disappear altogether.

When Hayes was finally inaugurated, the future did not look encouraging for a radical like the Lowell Representative-elect. Seated with the tacit consent of conservative Southern Democrats, the new President was representative of a group somewhat analogous to the old Whig party.[6] His inaugural address and his subsequent policies showed that his position on the Negro, civil service reform, finance, and labor was diametrically opposed to Butler's. Stalwart Republicans and radical greenbackers were equally in disfavor, and sooner or later a break had to come. Butler paid a perfunctory visit to the White House a few days after the inauguration,[7] but his lack of influence was patent from the very beginning. In spite of opposition, Hayes selected a cabinet wholly distasteful to the General. With William Evarts as Secretary of State, Carl Schurz, Secretary of the Interior, Charles Devens, Secretary of War, and a Confederate brigadier Postmaster General,[8] he could not expect much from the new administration.

However, the President made one friendly overture to Butler. Although he knew full well that George Butler, the General's nephew, was a drunkard who had disgraced himself as consul in Egypt, he gave him a temporary position with the Post Office Department. Butler might have been pleased, but within a short time, George fell victim to his vice once more. His dismissal did not endear Hayes to the uncle.[9]

It was evident by the President's Southern policy that radicals and Stalwarts were passing from the scene. Within a few weeks of the inauguration, he withdrew the remaining troops from South Carolina and Louisiana, an action which doomed local Republican governments. Intended as a gesture of goodwill toward the South, this course brought nothing but sneers from Butler. A "dreadful and shameful bargain" he called it, vowing that he for one would not be reconciled to the assassins of loyal Negroes.[10]

He made good his boast. In an open letter to Marshal Pitkin of New Orleans, he charged that Louisiana Republicans were being sacrificed to carry out Hayes' deal with the South. Had not Wayne McVeagh, the Philadelphia lawyer who had arranged matters for the President in New Orleans, promised money to Republican state legislators to induce them to go home? An angry exchange of letters between the General and McVeagh followed, but it was merely the precursor of more vitriolic attacks.[11] A complete break with the White House seemed only a matter of time, especially since Hayes believed also in civil service reform, hard money, and the suppression of strikes with Federal troops.

The final rift came in December. Speaking at Boston's Middlesex Club, Butler severely criticized the Administration. Civil service reform, the withdrawal of troops from the South, financial policies — all came in for their share of obloquy.[12] And as the President did not seem to take heed, the General recurred to his theme two weeks later. If Hayes had been honestly elected, he declared, Packard, the deposed Republican Governor of Louisiana, had been chosen also. But Packard had been abandoned, and the speaker, for one, had no respect for "a man who will dishonor his mother's marriage certificate," a pointed reminder of charges that Hayes' title to office rested upon the same evidence as Packard's.[13] Like his friend Conkling, the Stalwart Senator from New York, the General was now in open revolt.

To be in opposition to an administration was by no means a new experience for Butler. He had fought Johnson for two years and radicalism had prevailed; perhaps he might succeed again. Yet there was a difference. In 1866, the majority of the party had opposed the President on the question of reconstruction, an issue upon which Butler had been sound according to Republican canons. But now there was no such rapport between the General and the leaders of the party. It is true that Conkling's Stalwarts broke as completely with Hayes as Butler ever did, and the love of Blaine's Half-Breeds for the Executive was no greater, but the primary issues of the day were no longer those bequeathed by the Civil War. Economic problems had taken their place, and the General was completely at variance with the party on questions of finance. Whether free coinage of silver should be restored, whether specie payments should be resumed — these were issues upon which he saw eye to eye neither with the party managers in Washington nor with his constituents at home.

For a while he had tried to live up to his pledge to abide by the party's hard money platform. In spite of his positive views on the subject, he had abstained from voting on the repeal of the Resumption Act.[14] But the temptation to advocate his financial notions once again was too great. As an inveterate inflationist, he had moved with the times to take up the cry about the "crime of 1873," the demonetization of silver.[15] And when Representative Richard P. Bland's bill to restore the unlimited coinage of silver at the old ratio of sixteen to one was emasculated in the Senate, he threw all caution to the wind. Pleading for the original, radical proposals, he gave free rein to his monetary theories, and although he finally voted for the compromise Bland-Allison Act, he again sought to convince Congress of the merits of his "American" system of finance. The unredeemable greenback, the free coinage of silver, the appeal to the debtor, were all included, despite his election pledge to the contrary.[16]

His foes within the Republican party in Massachusetts were greatly strengthened by this course. They had already seen to it that Hayes refused Butler's request for a postmastership in Methuen;[17] now they had their full revenge. Simmons was not reappointed Collector of the Port of Boston.[18]

Having burned his bridges behind him, the General had to look for new sources of support. Gradually but surely he would have to join another party, either the new greenback-silverite organization[19] or the Democrats, awkward as that might be after all these years.

Consequently, the House of Representatives witnessed strange behavior on the part of the arch-radical. A disputed election had taken place in Boston, as a result of which both W. A. Field, Republican, and Benjamin Dean, Democrat, claimed victory. In complete disregard of party obligations, Butler supported the Democrat. Because Dean was a friend and Field close to the anti-Butler Republicans, this decision was easy to understand, but it caused comment nonetheless.[20] A few days later, the General astonished his colleagues again. While the House was debating the election of a new Doorkeeper — the Democrats wanted a Confederate veteran — Butler demanded the office for General James Shields, an Irish Democrat and wounded veteran of two wars on behalf of the Union. Shields was rejected, but Irish Americans were grateful.[21]

Whatever leading Democrats might think about these maneuvers, they were quick to make use of Butler's disaffection. As a nominal Republican, he might render them great service on committees, especially on matters connected with the disputed election. An investigation of that issue was very much on their minds, and they appointed him to serve on the Potter Committee to look into the matter.

Butler accepted gladly. Determined to embarrass the President, he turned the investigation into a veritable circus. Browbeating witnesses, haranguing his colleagues, he sought evidence and publicity.[22] And when his friend William E. Chandler, Republican committeeman from New Hampshire, deposited in Butler's office the cipher dispatches sent by Democrats to election officials in Southern states, he lived up to his reputation of being able to break any code whatsoever.[23] Although the dispatches showed that neither party had a clean record, he submitted his doubts about the President's title to office as an individual member of the Judiciary Committee long before the Potter group rendered its report, and proposed to have the dispute adjudicated by the courts.[24] One year later, when the Potter Committee published its final conclusions, he again wrote a separate opinion, more severe than that of the majority. Hayes' title to the Presidency he thought fraudulent; Packard's title to the Governorship he thought legitimate.[25] It was a strange conclusion, indicative of his abnormal position between parties.

On the remaining issue between himself and the Administration — the question of the relations between capital and labor — he also tangled with the conservatives in 1878. Congress found it convenient to pass legislation to refund the debt of the Union Pacific Railroad — everybody knew that the hated Jay Gould opposed that measure.[26] But when more specific proposals concerning the rights of labor were made, few were willing to commit themselves, and Congress did not oppose Hayes' high-handed treatment of strikers. Butler, however, acted differently. In complete defiance of popular prejudice against Gould, the General heeded the financier's request and voted against the funding bill;[27] yet he had always considered himself labor's friend and had never stopped agitating on its behalf. He thundered against violations of the eight-hour day for Federal employees, and when the Army Appropriations Bill came up for discussion, he surprised the House by a forceful plea for government aid to the poor. Not overproduction, but underconsumption, ailed the country, he said. Business had always been helped by the State; why should not labor get similar support? Let the money spent on maintaining an army in the West be used to settle Eastern workers on public lands. Then the settlers' purchasing power would be restored, the Indian frontier would be defended, and in time, the beneficiaries would become self-sustaining. As a practical solution, the scheme was chimerical, but it was an attractive talking point.[28]

Lesser men who defended Jay Gould might have had trouble with labor afterward. But Butler dared where others hesitated, and on July 4, he made a new bid for the workingman's support. Not all capitalists were the foes of labor, he said, merely the idle ones, coupon clippers who wasted their lives in sloth. Bondholders had caused a depression because of their insane hard money policy, and workers ought to do something about it. Not that he advised strikes — such measures were not for freemen who had the ballot. Only let workers vote properly and his program for the issue of four hundred million dollars in non-interest bearing bonds to settle the unemployed on public lands might yet be realized. He thought it was time for a change, in Massachusetts as well as in the nation, and he believed himself the man to accomplish it.[29]

As the speech was well received, he sounded out the Democrats on the possibility of support. It became evident that while the Irish wards were with him, the Brahmins who controlled the party loathed him.[30] However, since they were in a minority, he determined to seek the governorship, whether they liked it or not. Declaring that he had left both parties,[31] he permitted himself to be petitioned by some fifty thousand citizens who asked him to become a candidate. He replied in a public letter. He was willing to serve the people, he wrote; his platform would be the old one of equal rights, equal privileges, and reform of the state government. Abolition of useless commissions, an overhauling of the administration of charities and the tax structure, drastic economy, and protection of labor's rights — he promised all these.[32] The Greenback party endorsed him without trouble.[33] But he still wanted the Democratic nomination, despite his claims to the contrary.

It was certain that his desire would be difficult to realize. The Brahmins in the Democratic party had not become reconciled to him, and Butler did not endear himself to them by his indefatigable campaigning on behalf of his radical principles.[34] He had even received the support of Dennis Kearney, sand-lot agitator and scourge not only of Chinese but also of respectability, who had come from San Francisco to visit his mother in Boston. Kearney's behavior was not the sort of thing which went over well in the Hub, and Butler should have known it.[35] But he was determined to capture the Democratic party, by fair means if he could, by foul means if he must.

So it was that when the Democratic Convention was about to assemble in Worcester in September, he was prepared for every eventuality. As in previous years, there were again a number of contested delegations, and if the Butler men could be seated, the General would prevail. On the evening before the formal opening of the gathering, the conservative Democratic Executive Committee voted against the General's delegates; the Brahmins seemed to have won, but they had reckoned without their foe. Early in the morning of September 18, long ladders went up to the second floor windows of locked Mechanics' Hall, the Convention's meeting place. Assiduous politicians climbed up in great haste, and when, at a more reasonable hour later that day, the regular delegates arrived, they found that the Butler men had captured the hall. They — not the conservatives — now examined credentials, threw out opposing delegations, and amid deafening cheers, nominated their hero for the highest office in the Commonwealth. The regulars, under the leadership of Judge J. G. Abbott, adjourned to Faneuil Hall in Boston, where they nominated their own ticket and denounced the usurpation. But they had no real following.

Butler had carried off the bulk of the Democratic party.[36]

Winning the election proved more difficult. He campaigned strenuously; yet his foes, Democrats and Republicans alike, fought back. The coup at Worcester afforded them endless opportunity for attacks;[37] nor were the old scandals overlooked. Butler's assailants accused him of underpaying his workers at the Middlesex Mills; they passed resolutions calling upon him to resign his Congressional seat on the grounds that he had betrayed his constituents; they called him a demagogue, a plunderer, and a liar.[38] And although he replied in kind, charging employers with bulldozing their workers to vote against him, his exertions were in vain.[39] His opponents vowed that the Hero of Fort Fisher would never sign his name to the traditional Thanksgiving Proclamation of the Governors of Massachusetts,[40] and that year at least, they made good their vow. To the infinite relief of conservatives in general and the President in particular, Thomas Talbot, the Republican candidate, won.[41] As in the past, however, Butler had shown such strength that his demands for reform were productive of much good. Many of the measures he advocated — retrenchment, a more effective ten-hour law, and the reorganization of state penal and charitable institutions — met with success in the legislature of 1879, and the Springfield *Republican* conceded that Butler knew how "to stir up the dominant party to at least a pretense of reform."[42]

Disappointed as he was, Butler was not without hope for the future.[43] Politics was not his sole concern; his law practice was still his first love. Remunerative cases involving wills, real estate, and divorces swelled his income; criminal trials of all sorts provided an outlet for his histrionics, and patent suits gave him an opportunity to exercise his love for inventions.[44] For recreation, he went sailing on his yacht *America,* a splendid craft which won many a race and also the admiration of sports fans.[45] In India rubber coat and southwester, his face as red as a lobster, he would emerge from the yacht in many an Atlantic port and have a wonderful time.[46] He was getting a little older, stouter, and more deaf, but the old acuteness was still there.[47] Southerners might decorate their chamber pots with his pudgy visage, but in Washington, he was still a major tourist attraction.[48]

His relations with his family remained very close. General Ames and Blanche now lived in the North with an ever-growing number of children; Paul, Butler's older son, was successful in the cartridge business, and Benny, the younger, graduated from West Point in 1878.[49] Ben had never overcome his grief for the loss of Sarah, but there were rumors that he had taken an interest in Anna Dickinson, the impassioned advocate of women's rights whom he had helped out of many scrapes[50] — defeat or victory, it could not be said that he lived a dull life.

Shortly after the elections of 1878, he went to Washington for his last session in the House. His incongruous position as a repudiated Republican did not faze him. He still stood for the greenback; he heaped abuse upon Chinese coolies, and he tried to besmirch the President through the Potter Committee. What amused his colleagues most was his advocacy of pensions for disabled Confederate soldiers — an obvious bid for Democratic support.[51] But nothing about Butler really surprised the country any more. His antics had become part of the political scene.

The great success achieved by Greenbackers in the West in 1878 must have encouraged him. At any rate, he was determined to try once more to satisfy his political ambition. This time he would not make the mistake of campaigning with Kearney; nor did he want the regular Democrats to hold aloof if he could avoid it. Therefore he supported their candidate for Mayor of Boston in 1878,[52] delivered his Confederate pension address in Congress, and damned Hayes in the Potter report. And if his wooing proved vain, 110,000 voters still constituted a good base upon which to build. A few more would give him victory, even on an independent ticket.

In many respects, the campaign of 1879 was a repetition of the contest of the year before. This time, there were no stolen halls; but there remained the same charges, the same replies. Both sides printed campaign literature in unprecedented quantity. A full-sized biography of the General appeared,[53] and violent rejoinders followed.[54] The regular Democrats, now led by John Quincy Adams, Jr., still withheld their support, but the overwhelming majority of the party, especially voters of Irish descent, were again with him.[55] Ex-Collector Simmons and Roland Usher lent their services in the organization of a small group of Butler Republicans,[56] while the bulk of the opposition supported John D. Long, the regular Republican nominee, who was brilliant, popular, and eminently acceptable to the conservatives. As economic conditions had improved, and as some of Butler's planks, especially his demand for economy, had been taken over by his foes, he could do no better than the year before. He received 109,149 votes to Long's 122,751 and Adams' 9,989, an amazing tribute to his ability, but not enough to win.[57] However much he vowed to continue the contest, he would be impelled to seek regular party support first.

It was in 1880 that he finally returned to the party of his youth. In a Presidential year, unity within the Massachusetts "Democracy" seemed essential for success, and a marriage of convenience was arranged between Butler's followers and the conservatives.[58] The General himself held somewhat aloof at first; he enjoyed himself hugely on a trip to California and did not appear willing to commit himself.[59] But when the Republicans nominated James A. Garfield, the hard money Half-Breed who had opposed him in Congress for years, he abandoned his reserve. He had no use for such a candidate; moreover, open endorsement of a Democrat might finally gain for him the good will of the old party. Therefore, in a widely heralded speech, he came out for General Winfield S. Hancock, his old comrade in arms. The Republican party was bankrupt, he said, for it had betrayed the Negro, the farmer, and the worker — elements for whom he expressed his undying devotion. Within the "Democracy," he would henceforth work for their welfare.[60] His old associates might laugh, his new friends might be somewhat dubious,[61] but when the State Convention met at Worcester that fall, a reunited Democratic party gave the old man a deafening ovation. Some said he could have had the nomination for Governor then and there; but he endorsed Charles P. Thompson, the man who had beaten him in 1874.[62] And although the Republicans won that year, he had the satisfaction of having gained control of the Democratic party of Massachusetts, an accomplishment which might yet make success possible in the future. The prodigal had returned.

CHAPTER TWENTY-ONE

# Climax and Anticlimax

For the next year or so, Butler was not very active in politics. He practiced law, tended to his private affairs, and went yachting.[1] However, his chances to realize at last his ambition of almost a quarter of a century, the Governorship of Massachusetts, were improving. In 1882, the tide was turning against the Republican Administration in Washington, where the passage of a particularly offensive Rivers and Harbors Bill had aroused the reformers' ire. Moreover, the Republicans of the Bay State were in an embarrassing position as their leading contender for the gubernatorial nomination, William Crapo, had voted for the controversial measure in the House of Representatives.[2] And should Butler win as a Democrat in a normally Republican state, he would have a good claim upon the party for consideration for higher office in 1884. His friends advised him to try again.[3]

At first, he was dubious.[4] He was getting along in years, and personal sorrows had left their mark. Many of his intimates had died. His wife, his mother, Colonel Shaffer, Caleb Cushing, and finally, just on the threshhold of a legal career, his youngest son, Ben Israel.[5] Young Ben's death had been a cruel blow, but the General was resilient, and personal misfortunes had never kept him from seeking political preferment. He therefore decided to accept his friends' counsel.

Since the Democratic party was now beholden to him, it was not difficult for him to secure the nomination. Butler accepted in a decorous letter. Condemning the Rivers and Harbors Bill, he proposed economy in government, reform of the tax structure, and the time-tested principles of equal rights. Even the Democratic civil service plank received his endorsement, although he promptly interpreted it in his own way.[6] The Brahmins would have to fight him again.

As Butler's friends had foreseen, the Republicans were handicapped from the very beginning. Already disconcerted by national issues, they were further weakened by the nomination of Robert R. Bishop, President of the State Senate, a man of aristocratic habits who offended the followers of Representative Crapo. Butler made the most of these difficulties. Observers did not believe that the Democrats could capture the legislature or the council, but the political currents seemed to flow in the General's favor. "Let's elect the old man and see what he will do," was a sentiment as widespread as it was shocking to the Brahmins. The result was Butler's victory in November, an unprecedented personal tribute, for he was the only Democrat to win that year. He had his chance at last.[7]

It was to be expected that he would promptly try to carry out his program. However, his constitutional powers were not great. The Governors of Massachusetts were generally dignified figureheads, totally dependent upon their legislature. They were expected to write the annual Fast Day and Thanksgiving proclamations, but they were not permitted to make any appointments without the advice and consent of the Council. And since both General Court and Council were in hostile hands, Butler seemed foredoomed to impotence. Butler, however, thought otherwise. The people had elected him "Supreme Executive Magistrate," as he liked to call himself, and Supreme Executive Magistrate he would be.[8]

If anyone doubted his determination to be Governor in fact as well as in name, the inauguration dispelled all such uncertainty. Long before the new Executive was ready to take the oath of office, dense crowds of his supporters, eager to share his great triumph, milled about the State House. It was a beautiful day, with the golden State House dome glistening in the sun, and the rush was so great that the police had trouble keeping order. The Governor-elect arrived at half past eleven, wrapped in fur cap, fur coat, and the customary dress suit. The crowd cheered lustily, unmindful of the fact that "Boston was agitated to the very social basis of things" about Butler's success.[9] There had never been an inaugural quite like it.

Once inside the State Capitol, Butler conducted himself with his usual self-possession. Greeting the outgoing Governor with great civility, he impressed bystanders with his charm and delivered a lengthy inaugural address. He lambasted the poll tax requirements which still disgraced the Commonwealth; he presented his demands — a mandatory secret ballot law, woman suffrage, protection for laboring women and children, a ten-hour day for railroad workers, and he scathingly attacked the state's charities, especially the poorhouse at Tewksbury. It was an occasion few would ever forget.[10]

Nor would old Bostonians fail to remember the months — the year — that followed. Accompanied by messages of great verbiage, veto upon veto was sent to the State House, and although most of the vetoes were upheld, they caused unending comment.[11] The first one was of dubious validity, the Governor having been out of the state at the time of its submission.[12] Others were less controversial; however, one of the messages referred to precedents set by third century Christian emperors in Rome, a slip in chronology Massachusetts did not overlook.[13] Then there were two bills which disappeared from the Governor's desk. Their whereabouts remained a mystery until stable attendants found them on the seat of his carriage![14] And the Governor's pious Fast Day Proclamation was most offensive. His warning to the clergy not to meddle in politics rendered him the subject of many hostile sermons on the traditional holiday. "When the wicked beareth rule, the people mourn," was the text of one such disquisition, and with great emphasis, ministers read the customary closing sentence of the proclamation, "God save the Commonwealth of Massachusetts." However, the Governor had the last laugh. He announced that he had copied the document from one issued by Governor Gore in 1810.[15]

Butler's foes did not appreciate his antics. They were determined to fight him, and fight him they did. When Butler appointed Noah Plympton insurance commissioner, they refused to confirm that most faithful of Butlerites. When the Governor proposed a Negro of Democratic antecedents for a judgeship, they turned him down.[16] Few of the measures he advocated were enacted by the legislature,[17] and his attempts to end inefficiency in the state government were met with scorn. How dared the Executive chide clerks for being a few minutes late when he himself was frequently absent on private business?[18]

But in spite of setbacks, Butler's term was not barren of accomplishments. His methods might offend good taste, his measures might be temporarily rejected, but in the long run, his dramatic airing of abuses did result in reform. It was Butler who appointed the first judge of Irish origin in Massachusetts; it was Butler who appointed the first Negro to judicial office in the Commonwealth by substituting a Republican for the rejected Democrat.[19] Even if he did not succeed in his attempt to ameliorate labor conditions in 1883, even if poll taxes and the open ballot did not disappear immediately, these reforms could not be held up indefinitely once he had given them publicity. With the passage of time, the eight-hour day became the law of the state; health conditions were improved, children were forbidden to slave in the factories, and suffrage was extended to all.[20] Last but not least, the abuses of the state's eleemosynary institutions — abuses which had not been corrected by the reforms of 1879 — received extensive scrutiny. And although some of his accusations were exaggerated, the Governor's appearance before the committee investigating the almshouse at Tewksbury did much to bring about long overdue reforms.

The asylum at Tewksbury was a home caring for the poorest of the poor — unwed mothers, unwanted children, the indigent aged, and the physically and mentally ill. Over the years, the relatives of the Superintendent, Captain Thomas Marsh, had secured many of the offices at his disposal. The mortality rate was high, medical care poor, and sanitary conditions unsatisfactory. These shortcomings had been pointed out by a Republican legislature and Governor several years earlier, but the result had been disappointing. Butler now made the most of this neglect. He sought to present evidence that not only graft and peculation flourished at Tewksbury, but that infectious diseases were transmitted among the inmates through use of common bathtubs, that the bodies of the dead — babies and adults alike — were sold to the Harvard Medical School, and that their skins turned up as tanned leather. And he knew how to present his evidence dramatically. A prostitute from New York served as his star witness, and when his opponents attacked her testimony by calling attention to her unsavory profession, he managed to voice his disapproval of yet another state institution, the Normal Arts School. No one could blame the witness, he said, when the poor girl had been led astray by the Commonwealth itself in a tax-supported school in which pupils were taught to "model nude figures in clay." His opponents might object; they might point out that lack of money was the cause of conditions at Tewkesbury, but they could not compete with the sensational Governor. The poorhouse as well as the state board responsible for its management were thoroughly overhauled.[21]

Penal institutions also aroused the Governor's interest. When the warden of the prison at Concord had trouble with the inmates, Butler ordered all letters of complaint forwarded to the State House. When the Republican official did not comply meticulously with these instructions, he found himself supplanted by Roland Usher, the stalwart from Lynn, who pacified the prisoners.[22] Although this appointment was a political one, the selection of Clara Barton as superintendent of the women's prison was not. Even the conservatives were unable to complain about that.[23]

The Barton appointment was an exceptionally good one, but the Brahmins were not reconciled. That the man who had humbled them should be the recipient of the customary honorary degree from Harvard was more than they could stand. Almost from the day on which Butler was elected, the problem of the degree was debated in the clubs. President Eliot thought tradition ought to be maintained, but the Hoars, Moorfield Storey, and other distinguished alumni were dead set against conferring the degree. The Tewkesbury investigation, with its assaults on Harvard Medical School, strengthened the cause of the Governor's foes, who eventually convinced the President.[24] Thus Butler, who was proud of the fact that he, unlike most of his predecessors, would have been able to read the citation in Latin, was the first Governor not to be honored by the University. He turned the tables on his antagonists by appearing in full regalia to deliver a dignified address on commencement day,[25] and he attacked Harvard's Unitarianism at Williams College shortly afterward,[26] but Harvard never again gave a degree to a Governor of Massachusetts *ex officio.*

By the time the administration was half over, "respectable" people were agreed that something would have to be done to prevent Butler's re-election. If they failed, the Governor would be a powerful contender for the Democratic Presidential nomination in 1884, a contingency which they were determined to prevent. The anti-Butler Democrats could do little more than withhold their support — the party was completely controlled by the Governor — but the Republicans worked as they had never worked before. Early in the summer they began to organize, to approach men of wealth, in order to collect money.[27] Moorfield Storey, veteran of many a campaign against the Lowell statesman, spared neither effort nor funds;[28] George Hoar brought up the old accusations,[29] and young Henry Cabot Lodge enthusiastically threw himself into the fight. As its standardbearer, the Republican party nominated George D. Robinson, a Congressman as popular as he was capable.[30] Butler must go, the press screamed; Butler must go, the campaign speakers echoed; Butler must go, the conservatives throughout the country prayed.[31]

Butler sought to meet this assault with his customary methods. Again he stumped the state, again he harangued the crowds.[32] Tewksbury became a lively campaign issue, and the Democratic State Committee published a pamphlet replete with horrible illustrations of inmates eaten by rats, babies sold to the medical school, and sandals made of tanned human skin.[33] But these methods evoked more disgust than enthusiasm.

> George D.
> Robinson, he
> Will squelch the hero
> Of Tewksbury,

said the Republicans, and they were right.[34] Although more people turned out for the election than during the last Presidential year, Butler was defeated.[35] With his 150,000 votes, he might claim that defeat was victory, Bunker Hill and not Waterloo, but he must have known that his political future was no longer rosy.[36] Never again was Benjamin F. Butler to hold elective office.

There was, however, to be an anti-climax. Somehow or other, Butler could not rid himself of the notion that, because of the unusually large vote he had polled, he still had considerable influence. With discontent great among farmers suffering from declining prices, a firebrand like Butler might yet have a chance, and people continued to tell him that he was the only possible candidate to attract the anti-monopoly and labor vote in 1884.[37] In view of the deep-seated hostility of the South, to say nothing of his defeat at the polls, all thoughts of the Presidency or Vice-Presidency were unrealistic; yet whether he really believed in his chances or whether he merely wished to fish in troubled waters, it was not long before he was angling for the highest office in the land.[38] Publicly, he might disclaim all further political ambition;[39] privately, he was less coy.[40] And as he was rich, professed reform principles, and was willing to support impecunious reformers, there was no lack of minor party interest. Many a Greenbacker, many a labor leader, many a disgruntled politician, wrote that there was a groundswell for the General, especially in the Midwest. If only Butler would lead them![41]

Nor were these the only radicals who sought help in Lowell. The growth of industrial concentration had provoked such widespread criticism that an Anti-Monopoly party had been formed. By his testimony against the Standard Oil Trust before a Congressional Committee in 1880 and his condemnation of the polarization of wealth,[42] Butler had made a good impression on the leaders of the new organization. If they were upset by his support of railroad land grants, money and persuasion helped them to forget it.[43]

So it was that before the major parties had made their choice, the Greenbackers at Indianapolis and the Anti-Monopolists at Chicago nominated the General for President.[44] Instead of accepting, however, he wrote non-committal replies.[45] It was obvious that he was waiting for the Democrats to convene in Chicago, where he hoped to make a good showing with his assorted nominations.

In 1884, the Democrats were in a good position to win, but the party was rent by factionalism, feuds which the General hoped to exploit to his own advantage. The emergence of Grover Cleveland as the leading contender for the nomination was bound to offend both the protectionists, led by Representative Samuel Randall, and Tammany, controlled by John Kelly. To Butler, also, the Governor of New York was anathema. Like Randall, the General, — long an opponent of free trade — could not be expected to favor a candidate supported by low tariff men; like Kelly, he was bound to detest a politician favored by the foes of machine politics, Democratic and Republican alike. He had made his position clear to both Randall and Kelly as prospective allies long before the Convention met.[46] Butler was willing to go to any length to defeat Cleveland, even to support an old opponent, Senator Bayard of Delaware.[47] Moreover, he thought he still had influence himself, for there were still advisers who told him not to give up hope. If only he could show some strength at Chicago, Noah Plympton wrote, many of the Western delegates would go for him.[48]

To secure election to the Convention had not been difficult. The General appeared on the scene in fine spirits, harangued the crowds, cooperated with Kelly, and tried his best to head off the avalanche for Cleveland.[49] As a member of the platform committee, he argued strenuously for his pet principles, especially a plank for "customs duties . . . adjusted to promote American enterprises and industries . . . and to cherish and foster American labor" by taxing luxuries but not necessities. Yet neither his demand for an incidental tariff nor his proposal for an arbitration panel for the settlement of strikes found favor. The party endorsed a tariff plank even more meaningless than Butler's straddle, said little about labor, and nominated the Governor of New York. After submitting a minority report, the General withdrew in a huff. John Kelly, too, was sulking, but the Mugwumps, as the Republican bolters were called, announced their support of the Democratic nominee.[50]

At this juncture, it would have been wise for Butler to give up. Had he endorsed Cleveland, as Kelly eventually did, the new President would have been under obligations for the removal of the third party threat. Moreover, the Massachusetts "Democracy" would have remained in his control so that he might have wielded power for some time to come.[51] Butler, however, hated the New Yorker; he detested the Mugwumps who flocked to his standards,[52] and he received letters of encouragement from the Greenbackers and Anti-Monopolists.[53] Moreover, he thought he might still exert some influence as an independent. Fusing with Democrats in normally Republican states and with Republicans in normally Democratic commonwealths, the minority party might win local victories and reward its allies with a few votes in the electoral college. As a result the race might then be thrown into the House where Butler hoped to have the balance of power.[54] Yet such a gamble would cost money, and, though he was rich, he was not too eager to spend a great deal on what was at best a doubtful proposition. He decided to wait a little longer.[55]

In the meantime, the Republicans had run into serious trouble. At long last they had nominated James G. Blaine, but the Mugwumps' bolt and the general discontent gave them pause. They would have to do something to overcome these handicaps. Butler's candidacy might prove the answer. Would he not be able to make inroads on normally Democratic areas?

To negotiate with the General, they chose his old friend, William E. Chandler, now Secretary of the Navy. After a preliminary meeting in New York early in July, the two men conferred again, this time at Portsmouth, New Hampshire, aboard the U. S. S. *Tallapoosa*. They parted amicably; Chandler sailed to Bar Harbor to visit Blaine, and returned on August 4, in order to welcome the Arctic explorer, A. W. Greely. Butler was present also; once more he boarded the *Tallapoosa*. Chandler took him back to Gloucester,[56] and a few days later, the General finally published his long awaited letter of acceptance of the nominations of the previous May.[57]

This chain of circumstances looked suspicious from the very beginning. For months, representatives of various interests had tried to induce the General to commit himself. He had never done so,[58] and now, after hobnobbing with leading Republicans, he decided to make the race. *Harper's Weekly* thought it had the answer. In order to throw a few doubtful states to Blaine, the Republican National Committee must have agreed to pay for Butler's canvass.[59] The rumor would not die down, although the General promptly denied all reports of a deal aboard the *Tallapoosa*. Chandler knew why he kept silent;[60] for Butler had in fact accepted money for his campaign.[61] Thus the new People's Party was launched under a cloud; it would never be able to convince the voters of the rectitude of its intentions.

As the campaign progressed, it became evident that the new party's best chance lay in Michigan, where the Greenback-Democratic Governor was friendly.[62] But it was in New York that the race would be decided, so the General concentrated on the Empire State.[63] He maintained a subsidized paper in New York City, he enjoyed the support of Charles A. Dana of the *Sun*,[64] and, to lend color to the canvass, he toured the state in a luxuriously equipped private car.[65] It did not seem to bother him that such ostentation was hardly fitting for a People's Party candidate.

The election, however, did not turn out as expected. Not only did Butler fail to throw New York to Blaine, but with fewer than 200,000 votes, he did not even equal the record of General Weaver, the 1880 Greenback candidate.[66] Nowhere did he capture a single elector, and whatever strength he may have taken away from the Democrats was counterbalanced by the appearance of a prohibition candidate who cut into the Republican vote. Not only had the Portsmouth interview proved damaging to his popularity,[67] but thousands of Irish-Americans had voted for Cleveland after reading about the Reverend Samuel D. Burchard's unwise remarks concerning the Democrats' love of "rum, Romanism, and rebellion." Butler charged that his ballots in the Empire State had not been properly counted in order to cheat Blaine,[68] but few took his accusations seriously. He had led his followers into a political wilderness from which there was no return.

An old man returned to Lowell that winter. His fall from power had been swift. Only a year earlier, he had still been Chief Executive of the Bay State, with powerful support in both parties. Now he had polled hardly more votes in the entire United States than he had obtained for Governor in Massachusetts alone. His erratic ways, his shifts from party to party, his disregard for convention, could help him no longer. Indeed, these eccentricities were now the principal cause for his downfall. A new generation, unfamiliar with the old issues of Big Bethel, New Orleans, Fort Fisher, and the bloody shirt, was growing up. Butler's day was done;

only the law and his far flung speculations remained to keep him occupied.

Not that Butler forsook all interest in politics. He lent his legal talents to the anarchists involved in the Hay Market riot,[69] he continued his agitation for the annexation of Canada,[70] and he remained adamant in opposition to free trade. Seeing eye to eye with the Republicans on the tariff, he even campaigned for Benjamin Harrison in 1888 and induced his former supporters in Michigan to break up their coalition with the Democrats.[71] The final switch came in 1892, when he supported the Populist General Weaver.[72] Only no one cared any longer.

His political career was practically over, but his old combativeness remained. For years, he had been trying to get even with Admiral Porter, going so far as to propose the abolition of the grade of admiral during Grant's Administration, when Porter's unflattering letters about the President had come to light.[73] However, the Admiral's popularity had remained undimmed. Much to Butler's chagrin, Porter, in 1885, published an article containing the Navy's version of the capture of the forts along the Mississippi.[74] The General merely awaited a suitable opportunity to make a fitting rejoinder. Finally in 1889, at the celebration of the twenty-fifth anniversary of the capture of New Orleans, he voiced his charge that the Admiral had run away from the enemy's fleet. He created a sensation; Porter answered in kind, and the result was that both principals made themselves ridiculous at the very end of their careers.[75]

As time went on, Butler took on fewer and fewer legal cases. He was anxious to write his memoirs, an undertaking for which he needed time. The materials for his book were available — some two hundred boxes of letters preserved to this day — so, early in 1891, he went to work in earnest. Wildly gesticulating, he marched up and down the room while dictating his tome.[76] No ghost writer found employment with him, for none could write as pungently as he, and when the book was ready, it bore evidence from beginning to end of the author's peculiarities. The swagger, the conceit, the hatred for aristocrats, the appeal to the underdog, the interest in things military, technical, and legal, the bitter feuds — they were all there. Even the garish but nonetheless fascinating illustrations were typical of the General's taste. No one would ever lay down the book for lack of interest in the writer.

In the meantime, Butler had prepared to retire. He had announced that he would take no more criminal cases,[77] but he still had so many others that he did not stop practicing until the week of his death. His intended exit from the Massachusetts courts was not what he had expected, however. Judge George M. Carpenter was so annoyed at counsel's persistence in a perjury case that he had the old man ejected from the court room after Butler had refused an admonition to sit down. It was said that tears stood in the General's eyes when he was thrown out, and expressions of sympathy poured in from all over the country.[78] Yet, as so often in the past, he had the last laugh. His client was freed a few months later, and the old attorney, wearing an enormous slouched hat, beamed with evident satisfaction.[79]

Time had told on his appearance. He was more obese than ever, and there were frequent reports of his ill health.[80] The famous drooping lid had been subjected to an operation, but the characteristic strabismic appearance remained to the end.[81] Although he had sold his granite house to the Government at an enormous profit,[82] he spent more and more time in Washington, where his nieces kept house for him. There he reviewed G. A. R. parades with great gusto,[83] attended to his cases, and conducted his business affairs. His seventy-fifth year, however, did not find him in good health.

On January 10, 1893, the old General, plagued by a cold, made his last appearance before the Supreme Court. It was not a successful case; he lost an appeal concerning a will. Afterward, in spite of the inclement season, he went to the War Department on legal business. When he came home, he was not well. His faithful Negro servant helped him to bed. "That's all, West," he said, "You need not do anything more." Shortly afterward, the valet was awakened by heavy breathing. In great alarm he hurried into the General's bedroom. The old man was unconscious, and his nephew rushed to get help, but when the doctor arrived, it was too late. Benjamin Franklin Butler, Major General of U. S. Volunteers, ex-Governor of Massachusetts, ex-Congressman from Essex and Middlesex, renowned member of the bar, and one of America's most picturesque politicians, had died in his sleep at one o'clock that morning.[84]

Death did not end the controversy that raged about him during his lifetime. For years, efforts were made to erect a statue to his memory in Boston, but no success attended these exertions. The Brahmins of Massachusetts would not have any memorials to their dead antagonist, no matter how staunchly his grandchildren defended his memory.[85] Yet he does not really need a statue. The reforms he advocated have been accepted. Women now vote, labor is strong, the Negro has made progress, and the Government considers itself responsible for the protection of the weak. If Butler's methods were often those of a demagogue and his motives frequently those of a self-seeking politician, his flair for publicity nevertheless turned the spotlight on many abuses. And the positive accomplishments of his career — the rallying of the Breckinridge Democrats to the Union, the maintenance of order in a hostile city under difficult circumstances, the passage of legislation to protect Negroes and workingmen — constitute a sufficient monument for him. For these achievements he deserves credit, no matter what his motives. So we leave him, slightly tarnished perhaps, but productive of good nonetheless.

GRAPHIC STATUE NO. 60—AN INTERESTING WIDOW, BEREAVED BUT NOT INCONSOLABLE.

"YOU SEE I HAVE NO HESITATION IN SPEAKING ABOUT IT. I AM NOT LIKE A YOUNG MAIDEN, I AM MORE LIKE A WIDOW. I KNOW WHAT I WANT AND I AM NOT AFRAID TO ASK FOR IT."—*Butler's Speech at Lawrence, Mass., August 21.*

# THOMAS NAST CASTIGATES *WIDOW BUTLER* IN 1876, DAILY *GRAPHIC*, SEPTEMBER 5, 1876

THE HIGH COURT OF IMPEACHMENT.

(THE ARTIST MADE A JOURNEY TO WASHINGTON ON PURPOSE TO MAKE THE DRAWING—IT IS RELIABLE.)

## IMPEACHMENT OF JOHNSON — BUTLER ADDRESSING THE SENATE

(From J. T. Trowbridge, *A Pictorial History of the Desolated States and the Work of Restoration, 1865-1868*)

BUTLER'S TURNOUT--TRICKY HORSES AND DOUBTFUL FOOTMEN

ANTI-BUTLER CARTOON IN 1884, NEW YORK EVENING *TELEGRAM*, OCTOBER 18, 1884

DEFENSES OF RICHMOND AND PETERSBURG.

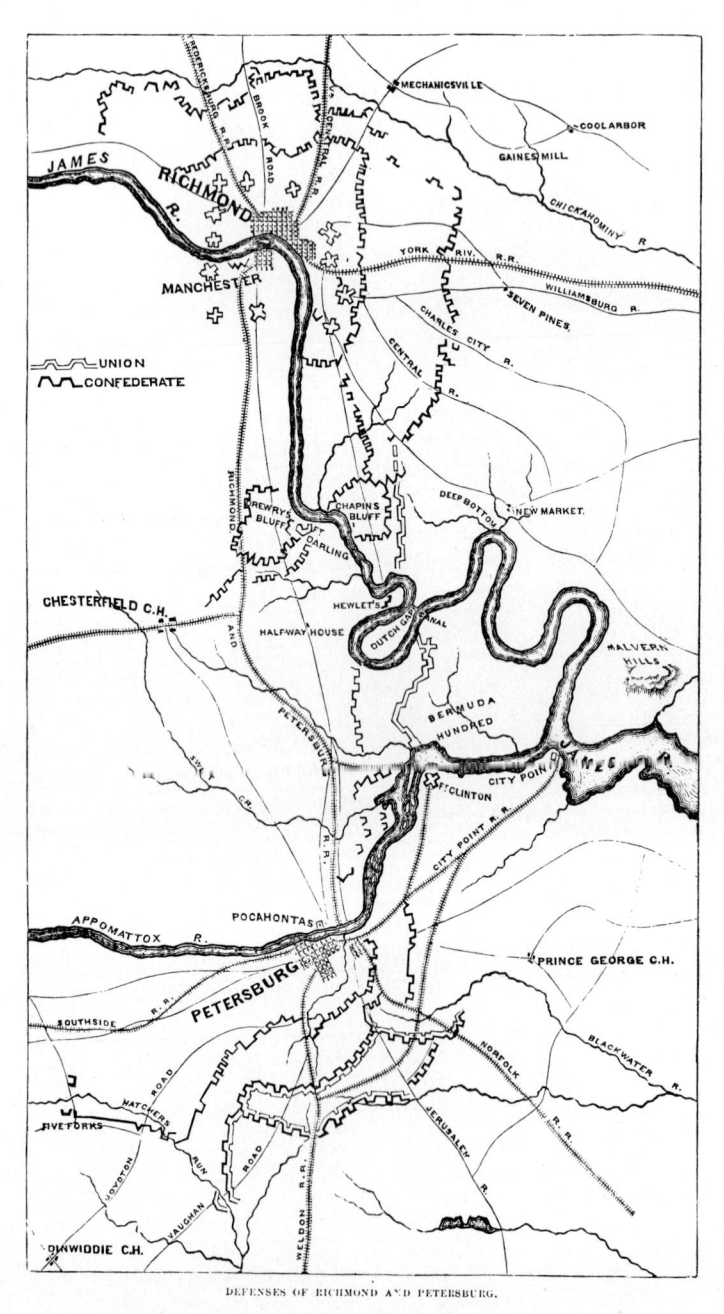

## RICHMOND-PETERSBURG AREA IN 1864
(From B. J. Lossing, *Pictorial History of the Civil War*)

PANORAMIC VIEW OF NEW ORLEANS—FEDERAL FLEET AT ANCHOR IN THE RIVER

# THE FEDERAL FLEET BEFORE NEW ORLEANS
(From H. Johnson, *Campfire and Battlefield*)

ORIGIN OF THE WORDS "CONTRABAND OF WAR," APPLIED TO SLAVES—FIRST USED BY GENERAL BUTLER

## ORIGIN OF THE TERM CONTRABAND
(From H. Johnson, *Campfire and Battlefield*)

MAP OF LOWER MISSISSIPPI RIVER.

APPROACHES TO NEW ORLEANS
(From *Butler's Book*)

BENJAMIN F. BUTLER, POLITICIAN
(Photograph by Warrens, Boston, in Prints Division,
New York Public Library)

# Notes

### CHAPTER I  *Youth*
(Pages 17 to 24)

1. Benjamin F. Butler was born on November 5, 1818. Benjamin F. Butler, *Butler's Book* (Boston, 1892), 41.
2. *Ibid.*, 43; Lowell *Journal & Courier*, November 21, 1851; M. M. Pomeroy, *Life and Public Services of Benjamin F. Butler* (New York, 1886). Pomeroy was Butler's arch-enemy and his book consists of the wildest rumors. The charge that John Butler was hanged as a pirate is probably spurious. Isaac Hill knew him and recommended Ben to Caleb Cushing in 1835. It is unlikely that he would have done so had the Captain's career ended so ignominiously. Isaac Hill-Charlotte Butler, September 30, 1835, Butler MSS, Library of Congress, Washington, D. C.
3. *Butler's Book*, 44-45.
4. Blanche Butler Ames, *The Butler Ancestry of General Benjamin Franklin Butler* (Lowell, 1895); Elliott C. Cogswell, *History of Nottingham, Deerfield, and Northwood* (Manchester, N. H., 1876), 172, 183-84, 195.
5. *Butler's Book*, 41-44; Butler-Charles Sumner, December 19, 1853, Charles Sumner MSS; Harvard University, Cambridge, Massachusetts.
6. *Butler's Book*, 44-51.
7. Butler-J. P. Casey, April 21, 1883, letterbooks, Butler MSS.
8. *Proceedings of the City of Lowell At the Semi-Centennial Celebration of the Incorporation of the Town of Lowell*, March 1, 1876 (Lowell, 1876), 36 ff.
9. Allan Macdonald, "Lowell: A Commercial Utopia," *The New England Quarterly*, X (March, 1937), 37-62.
10. Henry A. Miles, *Lowell As It Was And As It Is* (Lowell, 1846), 67 ff.
11. Hannah Josephson, *The Golden Threads* (New York, 1949), 58 ff., 286 ff.; Macdonald, *loc. cit.*
12. John Greenleaf Whittier, *The Stranger in Lowell, Whittier's Works* (Boston, 1892), V, 354.
13. Letter from E. L. Magoon, *Contributions of the Lowell Historical Society*, II, 325 ff. (January, 1883).
14. Charles Cowley, *History of Lowell* (Boston, 2d ed., 1868), 111 ff.
15. *Ibid.*, 69-86.
16. *Butler's Book*, 52.
17. Cowley, *op. cit.*, 116 ff.

18. *Ibid.*, 106; James S. Russell, "Reminiscences of the Lowell High School," *Contributions of the Lowell Historical Society*, II, 13-33 (November, 1883); D. M. Patterson, "Reminiscences of the Early Physicians of Lowell and Vicinity," *ibid.*, II, 428 ff. (November, 1883); C. C. Chase, "Reminiscences of the High School," *ibid.*, III, 113-144 (July, 1885); Mary Clark Sturtevant, *Thomas March Clark* (Milwaukee, 1927), 20.

19. Chase, *loc. cit.*; George L. Balcolm-Butler, September 29, 1836, 1954 boxes, Butler MSS; examples of the themes in the same place.

20. Butler-Mrs. Abbie E. Packer, February 2, 1892, letterbooks, Butler MSS.

21. George L. Balcolm-Butler, September 29, 1836, 1954 boxes, Butler MSS.

22. Z. E. Stone, "General Jackson in Lowell," *Contributions of the Lowell Historical Society*, I, 105 ff. (February, 1876).

23. *Butler's Book*, 42, 47-48, 85.

24. George L. Balcolm-Butler, September 29, 1836; Butler-Mrs. Abbie E. Packer, February 3, 1892, Butler MSS, 1954 boxes and letterbooks. One of the twins later married a Southerner, moved to New Orleans, and spread tales about the General's childhood pranks all over the city.

25. *Butler's Book*, 52.

26. *Ibid.*, 57.

27. Dr. Theodore Edson wrote that Ben was "a person of great moral character . . . and promising talents." Letters from Edson, January 26, 1836; William Graves, January 22, 1836; S. R. Hanscom (a teacher at the High School), January 23, 1836, Butler MSS. These references would seem to cast doubt on stories that Butler was an obnoxious child, his enemies' assertions to the contrary notwithstanding. Cf. Springfield *Republican*, November 9, 1874.

28. Isaac Hill-Charlotte Butler, September 30, 1835; Caleb Cushing-Butler, February 17, 1836, Butler MSS.

29. Edwin Carey Whittemore (ed.), *The Centennial History of Waterville* (Waterville, 1902), 300 ff.

30. James Parton, *General Butler in New Orleans* (New York, 1864), 16 ff.; James Dabney McCabe, *Behind the Scenes in Washington* (Washington, 1873), 208-09; *Butler's Book*, 60-63.

31. Erastus Everett-Butler, July 19, 1862, Butler MSS.

32. Henry W. Scott, *Distinguished American Lawyers* (New York, 1891), 100-01; theme in 1835 box, 1954 boxes, Butler MSS.

33. Boston Daily Evening *Transcript*, November 26, 1859; *Butler's Book*, 65; Whittemore, *op. cit.*, 300 ff.

34. *Butler's Book*, 69; Moses J. Kelley-Butler, November 25, 1871, 1954 boxes, Butler MSS. The suit became a matter of controversy, as Butler's enemies maintained that he left college without settlement of his debts after abandoning a fiancee. The charges concerning the girl are probably false, but he did leave Waterville before he had satisfied his creditors, the total amount being $2.29. F. G. Cook-Butler, September 11, 1839, 1954 boxes, Butler MSS.

35. Parton, *op. cit.*, 16.

36. *Butler's Book*, 69-71.

37. *Ibid.*, 63-64; *Dictionary of American Biography* (New York, 1928-1937), XII, 366.

# NOTES

38. *Butler's Book,* 71-73; William S. Smith-Butler, November 22, 1839, 1954 boxes, Butler MSS; New York Weekly *Tribune,* June 1, 1861.
39. Samuel P. Hadley, "Historical Sketch of the Police Court of Lowell," *Contributions of the Lowell Historical Society,* N. S., II (October, 1926), 36-81.
40. Butler-R. J. Holcomb, October 4, 1883; Butler-H. Holton, January 5, 1891, letterbooks, Butler MSS.
41. *Butler's Book,* 73.
42. Lowell *Courier,* February 1, 1883.
43. Fisher Hildreth was a Democratic politician and newspaperman. Alfred Gilman, "The Newspaper Press of Lowell," *Contributions of the Lowell Historical Society,* II, 261 ff., (May, 1882).
44. *Butler's Book,* 78-79; *Commonwealth,* December 17, 1864; Butler-B. G. Libbie, February 23, 1892, letterbooks, Butler MSS. A sympathetic sketch of Sarah Butler was written by her husband's critic, Gamaliel Bradford. Gamaliel Bradford, *Wives* (New York, 1925), 199-235.
45. Butler-Eliza Dexter, June 18, 1840, 1954 boxes, Butler MSS.
46. *Butler's Book,* 79.
47. *Vital Records of Lowell, Massachusetts, To the End of the Year 1849* (Salem, 1930), II, 115.
48. Boston *Herald,* February 9, 1879; R. M. Balch-Butler, March 3, 1879, 1954 boxes, Butler MSS. Mr. Balch, of the *Herald,* wrote: "I trust that the article (on Butler's good homelife) may show that even if 'we' do not believe in General Butler as a politician we can at least admire him as a man and example in private life."
49. D. Hamilton Hurd, *History of Middlesex County, Massachusetts* (Philadelphia, 1890), I, xxiii; *Butler's Book,* 75-77.

CHAPTER II  *Young Lowell Lawyer*
(Pages 25 to 33)

1. Henry A. Miles, *Lowell As It Was and As It Is* (Lowell, 1846), 58 ff.
2. Lowell *Advertiser,* July 12, 1842.
3. *Butler's Book,* 986 ff. Pomeroy maintains that he enabled a thief to escape instead of defending him in court. Pomeroy, *op. cit.,* 10.
4. George F. Hoar, *Autobiography of Seventy Years* (New York, 1903), I, 330; Scott, *op. cit.,* 107 ff.; New York Weekly *Tribune,* June 1, 1861; Lowell *Advertiser,* July 15, 1842.
5. Alfred Gilman, "The Newspaper Press of Lowell," *loc. cit.*; William S. Robinson, *"Warrington" Pen-Portraits* (Boston, 1877), 439 ff.; Frazer Kirkland, *The Pictorial Book of Anecdotes and Incidents of the War of the Rebellion* . . . (Hartford, 1869), 607.
6. Lowell Daily *Courier,* September 19, 1845; Lowell *Advertiser,* September 18, 1845; Robinson, *op. cit.,* 574.
7. Butler MSS, 1954 boxes, September 7-15, 1847.
8. *Butler's Book,* 985 ff.; Parton, *op. cit.,* 33 ff.
9. Lowell Daily *Courier,* July 16, 1845.

10. Hoar, *op. cit.*, I, 330; Springfield *Republican*, August 15, 1884. Some of his enemies, however, did concede his legal talents. Gamaliel Bradford, *Damaged Souls* (Boston, 1926), 225.

11. Appointment dated May 16, 1842, 1954 boxes, Butler MSS, and February 25, 1843, 1954 boxes, Butler MSS.

12. Lowell *Advertiser,* October 1, 1846, February 15, 1851; Levi S. Gould, *Ancient Middlesex, With Brief Biographical Sketches of the Men Who Have Served the County Officially Since Its Settlement* (Somerville, Mass., 1905), 251. Cf. the 1850 boxes in the Butler MSS for his growing practice. Parton maintained that Butler had the "most lucrative practice in New England" in 1861 and netted $18,000 a year. Parton, *op. cit.*, 35. While Parton probably exaggerated his hero's importance, Butler's practice was undoubtedly extensive.

13. Butler-Fay, January 17, 1881, Butler MSS, letterbooks.

14. 1843-1853 folders, Butler MSS; Cowley, *op. cit.*, 92-93; 120-21; John Coolidge, *Mill and Mansion* (New York, 1942), 201.

15. Lowell *Courier,* February 1, 1883.

16. George Hedrick, "Reminiscences and Recollections of Lowell, Since 1831," *Contributions of the Lowell Historical Association,* I, 360 (May, 1879).

17. *Butler's Book,* 123-27; Parton, *op. cit.*, 24; by 1841, he had become clerk of the City Guards. *Vox Populi,* October 16, 1841.

18. *Vital Records of Lowell, Massachusetts, to the End of the Year 1849,* I, 51; *Butler's Book,* 79 ff.

19. Josephson, *op. cit.*, 204 ff.; Miles, *op. cit.*, 101.

20. Josephson, *op. cit.*, 217 ff.

21. *Commonwealth* v. *John Hunt & Others,* 4 Metcalf, 45 (1842); Oscar and Mary Handlin, *Commonwealth* (New York, 1947), 245-46.

22. Charles Cowley, *History of the Ten Hours Movement,* in *Lowell, A City of Spindles* (Lowell, 1900), 247 ff.

23. Cowley, *History of Lowell,* 138; George F. O'Dwyer, *The Irish Catholic Genesis of Lowell* (Lowell, 1920).

24. Lowell *Advertiser,* December 5, 1842; Cowley, *History of Lowell,* 158 ff.; Hurd, *op. cit.*, 58 ff.

25. Arthur B. Darling, "Jacksonian Democracy in Massachusetts, 1824-1848," *American Historical Review,* XXIX (1929), 271-81.

26. James C. N. Paul, *Rift in the Democracy* (Philadelphia, 1951), 68-69. In Massachusetts, the faction friendly to Calhoun was known as the "City Faction," led by David Henshaw. The opposing County Faction was led by Marcus Morton. Cf. Russel B. Nye, *George Bancroft* (New York, 1944), 89, 114 ff.

27. Lowell *Advertiser,* October 12, 1840. Fisher Hildreth served as a Democratic member of the General Court.

28. Lowell *Advertiser,* November 2, 3, 1840; Robinson, *op. cit.*, 20.

29. *Butler's Book,* 77.

30. Lowell *Advertiser,* February 15, 1841.

31. Z. E. Stone, "Lowell's Once Popular Newspaper, *Vox Populi,* 1841-1896," *Contributions of the Lowell Historical Association,* VI, 172 ff. (May, 1898); Butler-Vox Populi Press, May 22, 1891, letterbooks, Butler MSS.

32. *Vox Populi,* June 12, 1841.

33. Hurd, *op. cit.*, II, 192; Cowley, *History of Lowell,* 124.

# NOTES

34. *Vox Populi,* May-August, 1841.
35. Lowell *Advertiser,* June 21, 1841.
36. George S. Boutwell, *Reminiscences of Sixty Years in Public Affairs* (New York, 1902), I, 91.
37. Butler-Vox Populi Press, May 22, 1891, letterbooks, Butler MSS.
38. Lowell *Advertiser,* October 3, December 5, 1842; August 9, 19, September 4, 1844.
39. *Ibid.,* March 22, 1844. He was the speaker at the Lowell Irish Benevolent Society's St. Patrick's Day dinner.
40. Cowley, *History of the Ten Hours Movement, loc. cit.,* 250 ff.
41. In spite of his solicitude for the factory workers, Butler was not averse to representing the corporations. Lowell *Advertiser,* September 15, 26, 1846.
42. *Ibid.,* June 12, September 4, 1844.
43. *Ibid.,* November 2, 1840.
44. J. G. Abbott-George Bancroft, June 9, 1845, George Bancroft MSS, Massachusetts Historical Society, Boston.
45. Butler's Book, 1007. He was mistaken when he maintained that Levi Woodbury was his sponsor. That honor belonged to John Y. Mason. December 16, 1845, Butler MSS.
46. Butler-James K. Polk, December 19, 1845, including petition, Bancroft MSS. The Butler-Hildreth faction of the Lowell Democrats tried to convince the President to remove Postmaster Stephen S. Leary. Leary held office from 1845 until 1849. Cf. C. C. Chase, "Life of the Postmasters," *Contributions of the Lowell Historical Society,* IV, 128-41 (August, 1889).
47. Fisher Hildreth-Samuel J. Varney, May 30, 1845, Butler MSS; Lowell Tri-Weekly *Advertiser,* August 14, 1845. Hildreth also published the *Republian,* a weekly. Gilman, *op. cit.*
48. Charlotte Butler-Butler, September, 1846. Butler MSS, 1954 boxes. Charlotte was worried about her older son and wrote: "I was very much shock and grieved to think . . . Andrew should take the course he has to leave his wife and child to the mercy of the wourld and throw his life away in that miserable Mexican war and bring upon me sorrow upon sorrow. I want you to rite him immigiately and try to persuade him not to go."
49. Lowell Tri-Weekly *Advertiser,* June 2, 1846, October 16, 1847; Claude Fuess, *The Life of Caleb Cushing* (New York, 1923), II, 64 ff.
50. *The Campaign* (Washington, 1848); Lowell Tri-Weekly *Advertiser,* July 25, 1848.
51. *Ibid.,* June 24, 25; October 14, 26, 28, 1848.
52. *Ibid.,* November 9, 14, 28, 1848.

## CHAPTER III  *Coalitionist*
### (Pages 34 to 41)

1. Scott, *op. cit.*, 106-07.
2. Cases in 1845-1860 folders, Butler MSS; Butler-Horace Wentworth, November 5, 1885, letterbooks, Butler MSS.
3. Hoar, *op. cit.*, I, 171; Fuess, *op. cit.*, II, 98; *Butler's Book*, 93 ff.
4. Boutwell, *op. cit.*, I, 119.
5. Hoar, *op. cit.*, I, 170.
6. Albert B. Hart (ed.), *Commonwealth History of Massashusetts* (New York, 1930), IV, 19; Boutwell, *op. cit.*, I, 115.
7. In Middlesex County, both parties held their conventions at Concord on the same day, Butler presiding over the Democrats and George F. Faley over the Free Soilers. Lowell Daily *Journal & Courier*, October 21, 1850; Lowell Tri-Weekly *Advertiser*, October 10, 1850; Henry Wilson, *The History of the Rise and Fall of the Slave Power* (Boston, 1874), II, 345.
8. *Ibid.*, Boutwell, *op. cit.*, I, 115. Boutwell became Governor; Wilson, President of the Senate, and Banks, Speaker of the Assembly. Cf. *Commonwealth*, January-February, 1851.
9. *Butler's Book*, 114; Butler- ?, November 18, 1851, 1954 boxes, Butler MSS.
10. *Butler's Book*, 99 ff.; Lowell *Advertiser*, November 18, 1851.
11. *Ibid.*
12. *Butler's Book*, 99 ff.
13. Lowell *Advertiser*, November 25, 1851.
14. *Ibid.*, November 18, 1851.
15. *Ibid.*, November 25, 1851.
16. Lowell *Journal & Courier*, November 21, 1851.
17. *Ibid.*, November 20-28, 1851; Cowley, *History of Lowell*, 144-45.
18. Lowell *Journal & Courier*, November 28, 1851.
19. Lowell *Advertiser*, March 9, 11, 13, 18; April 6, 1852. One of the witnesses made himself ridiculous when it was discovered that he had had to borrow his coat from Representative Brown of Lowell.
20. He also challenged successfully the exclusion of the voters in Ward Four. Lowell Election Case Brief, 1841-1851 box, 1954 boxes, Butler MSS; Lowell *Advertiser*, January 31, 1852.
21. Z. E. Stone, "Lowell's Once Popular Newspaper, *Vox Populi*, 1841-1896," *loc. cit.*, 175.
22. Lowell *Journal & Courier*, March 4, 5, 12, 1852; Lowell *Advertiser*, March 2, 1852. It was especially annoying to hear witnesses testify that in Deerfield, there were unpleasant rumors about the exact manner of the elder Butler's death.
23. *Butler's Book*, 109.
24. Lowell *American*, January 15, 1853. However, the Whigs had recaptured the Legislature. Godfrey T. Anderson, "The Slavery Issue as a Factor in Massachusetts Politics From the Compromise of 1850 to the Outbreak of the Civil War," unpublished doctoral dissertation, University of Chicago, 1944, 54.
25. *Commonwealth*, January 12, 1853.

## NOTES

26. *Ibid.*, February 1, 2, 8; April 9, 12, 14, 1853; Lowell *American*, February 11, 18, 1853; Lowell Daily *Advertiser*, March, 22, 23; April 9, 11, 13, 15, November 8, 1853; Butler-John Boyle O'Reilley, April 30, 1884, letterbooks, Butler MSS.
27. Journal of the Massachusetts House of Representatives, 1853, State House, Boston, 91, 186; Boston *Journal*, January 19, 1853, May 23, 1853; Lowell Daily *Advertiser*, April 15, 27; May 25, 1853.
28. *Ibid.*, February 19-26, 1853; Lowell *American*, February 18, 1853; Springfield *Republican*, August 24, 1871; *Commonwealth*, February 16-29, 1853. Butler said he had merely meant to knife the decision.
29. Cowley, *History of the Ten Hours Movement, loc. cit.*
30. Boston Daily *Advertiser*, March 8, 9, 1853; Hoar, *op. cit.*, I, 174.
31. *Ibid.*, 178-79; James Schouler, "The Massachusetts Convention of 1853." *Proceedings of the Massachusetts Historical Society*, 2d Series, XVIII (1903-1904), 30-48; Boutwell, *op. cit.*, I, 218.
32. For examples, *Official Report of the Debates and Proceedings in the State Convention*. . .(Boston, 1853, III, 204, 223, 424; Hurd, *op. cit.*, I, xvii. Yet Richard Henry Dana, no friend, said: "Butler has behaved quite as well, perhaps, on the whole, a little better than was expected of him. He has not been ill-mannered except to men who have fought him in his own way, or men against whom he has an old hostility. He has shown great power of will, strength of mind and industry." Charles Francis Adams, *Richard Henry Dana* (Boston, 1890), I, 249.
33. *Official Report of the Debates and Proceedings in the State Convention*, II, 473-74, 528.
34. *Ibid.*, II, 152; John Gorham Palfrey, *Remarks on the Proposed State Constitution by a Free Soiler From the Start* (Boston, 1853). The coalitionists in general and Butler in particular were anxious to increase the representation of outlying districts, where their strength was greatest. Anderson, *op. cit.*, 67.
35. Schouler, *op. cit.*, 41 ff.; *Official Report of the Debates and Proceedings in the State Convention*, I, 274-76, 416-18; II, 278; III, 87, 578.
36. *Ibid.*, II, 787-92; Hoar, *op. cit.*, I, 174. Hoar believed Butler and J. G. Abbott thought up this scheme in order to have their revenge upon a judge who had offended them. But it is more likely that the Democrats simply sought a means of escape from the inevitability of the appointment of Whig judges.
37. *Ibid.*, I, 176; Boutwell, *op. cit.*, I, 220.
38. Lowell *Advertiser*, August 19-28, 1851.
39. Butler-Benjamin F. Hallett, August 25, 1851, 1954 boxes, Butler MSS. He claimed he had prevailed, but the Whigs laughed at his contention. Lowell Weekly *Journal & Courier*, August 29, 1851.
40. Fuess, *op. cit.*, II, 117.
41. Butler-Cushing, December 1, 1851, Caleb Cushing MSS, Library of Congress, Washington, D. C.
42. Roy Frank Nichols, *The Democratic Machine, 1850-1854* (New York, 1923), 81, 133-34; Butler-William C. Todd, May 2, 1891, letterbooks, Butler MSS; James G. Blaine, *Twenty Years of Congress* (Norwich, Conn., 1884), I, 100; Fuess, *op. cit.*, II, 117; *Proceedings of the Democratic National Convention Held at Baltimore, June, 1852* (Washington, 1852), 15 ff.

43. I. W. Beard, Joseph Holbrook, J. C. Abbott-Butler, October 27, 1852, 1954 boxes, Butler MSS. The ultra-Hunkers seceded from the Fitchburg convention rather than endorse coalition.
44. Cowley, *History of Lowell*, 122; Lowell Daily *Advertiser*, March 12, 1853.
45. Butler-Cushing, Cushing MSS, May 2, 1853.
46. H. I. Merriam-Cushing, March 7, 1853, Cushing MSS.
47. He urged Cushing that both Hunkers and coalitionists be appointed to office and was willing to effect a truce with some of his foes. Butler-Cushing, April 4, May 2, 1853; H. I. Merriam-Cushing, May 1, 1853, Cushing MSS.
48. Lowell Weekly *Journal & Courier*, October 21, 1853; A. J. Cass-Butler, December 21, 1853; Sumner-Butler, December 22, 1853, Butler MSS; Butler-Sumner, December 19, 1853, Sumner MSS. The Senate almost failed to confirm him.
49. Lowell Daily *Advertiser*, October 20, November 14, 1853; Lowell Weekly *Journal & Courier*, September 6, 30, November 12, 1853.
50. Hamilton-Butler, August 15, 1853, Butler MSS, 1954 boxes.
51. Lowell Daily *Advertiser*, November 4, 1853; Fuess, *op. cit.*, II, 139-40.
52. Lowell Weekly *Journal & Courier*, November 11, 23, 1853; Hamilton-Butler, November 4, 1853, 1954 boxes, Butler MSS.
53. Lowell Daily *Advertiser*, February 25, 1854.

CHAPTER IV  *A Hunker's Tribulations*
(Pages 42 to 51)

1. Cf. Boutwell, *op. cit.*, I, 246, 247; Fred Harvey Harrington, *Fighting Politician, Major General N. P. Banks* (Philadelphia, 1948), 18.
2. Wilson, *op. cit.*, II, 420; Hoar, *op. cit.*, I, 189; G. H. Haynes, "The Causes of Know Nothing Success in Massachusetts," *American Historical Review*, III (1898), 67-68.
3. Lowell Daily Evening *Advertiser*, January 11, 12, 23, 1855.
4. Boston *Bee*, February 10, 1855; Lowell Daily *Journal & Courier*, February 7, 16, 1855; Hurd, *op. cit.*, II, 156-57.
5. *Butler's Book*, 121; notification and commission in Butler MSS, May 26, June 16, 1857.
6. Butler-Thomas J. Gargan, October 8, 1876, letterbooks, Butler MSS.
7. For the Hiss case, cf. G. H. Haynes, "A Know-Nothing Legislature," *American Historical Association Reports*, IV (1896), 177 ff.; Boston *Bee*, May 12, 1855, May 26, June 2, 1855; Lowell Daily Evening *Advertiser*, May 12, 15, 16, 1855; Lowell Daily *Journal & Courier*, April 14-May 11, 1855.
8. Lowell Daily Evening *Advertiser*, August 27, 1855.
9. Boston Daily Evening *Advertiser*, November 7, 1855.
10. Butler-F. R. Rice, February 15, 1886, letterbooks, Butler MSS.
11. A. J. Cass-Butler, May 15, 20, 1856, 1954 boxes, Butler MSS.

**NOTES** 265

12. N. E. Upham-Butler, May 24, 1856, 1954 boxes, Butler MSS.
13. *Official Proceedings of the National Democratic Convention, Held in Cincinnati, June 2-6, 1856* (Cincinnati, 1856), 47.
14. Griswold-Butler, September 12, 1856, 1954 boxes, Butler MSS. Griswold had originally feuded with Butler and had tried to defy his dictum that the Massachusetts delegation observe the unit rule. Lowell Daily Evening *Advertiser,* June 3, 1856; *Official Proceedings of the National Democratic Convention . . . 1856,* 14-15.
15. Lowell Daily Evening *Advertiser,* June 18, October 17-29, 1856. A. J. Cass even thought Butler had a chance. A. J. Cass-Abbott, Butler MSS, 1954 boxes, September 25, 1856.
16. Boston *Bee,* September 6, 1856.
17. Claude Fuess, *Rufus Choate* (New York, 1928), 216. Choate remarked to Butler afterward: "Brother Butler, when you told me that we should all be in five minutes in that locality unmentionable to ears polite, did you have the slightest idea of insinuating that both of us would go to the same place?"
18. Butler received 3,686 votes to his opponent's 9,621. Lowell Daily Evening *Advertiser,* November 5, 1856.
19. Jefferson Davis-Butler, February 21, 1857; Cushing-Butler, February 23, 1857, Butler MSS.
20. A. J. Cass-Butler, March 15, 1857, Butler MSS; McCabe, *op. cit.,* 66-67.
21. A. J. Cass-Butler, March 15, 1857; other letters to Butler from various applicants for positions, 1857 folder, 1954 boxes, Butler MSS.
22. Lowell Daily Evening *Advertiser,* April 4, 1857. C. L. Woodbury received the appointment.
23. Butler-Cushing, April 10, 1857, Cushing MSS.
24. Lowell Daily Evening *Advertiser,* September 22, October 22, 1857.
25. *Ibid.,* September 22, October 21, 1857.
26. *Ibid.,* November 3, 1857. The results were: Bonney (Republican), 2,023; Butler (Democrat), 1,766; Wright (American), 60.
27. Butler-Stephen A. Douglas, December 18, 1857, Stephen A. Douglas MSS, University of Chicago; George Fort Milton, *The Eve of the Conflict* (Boston, 1934), 279.
28. Butler-A. V. Brown, February 18, 1858, 1954 boxes, Butler MSS.
29. F. A. Hildreth-Butler, January 27, 1858, 1954 boxes, Butler MSS.
30. Butler-A. V. Brown, February 18, 1858, 1954 boxes, Butler MSS.
31. C. C. Chase, *op. cit.,* 128-41.
32. Butler-Sumner, May 27, 1856, Sumner MSS; Butler-F. R. Rice, February 15, 1886, letterbooks, Butler MSS; Dewitt C. Butler-Butler, October 28, 1874, 1954 boxes, Butler MSS. While passing through Washington on his way to the Cincinnati Convention, he publicly denounced the outrage and carefully selected a cab driven by a Negro to visit the Senator. Moreover, he counselled Anson Burlingame to accept Brooks' challenge to a duel. Cushing also sent his regrets, but he did not offend the Democrats by publicly calling upon Sumner. Fuess, *Cushing,* II, 157.
33. J. S. Whitney-Butler, June 5, 1858, 1954 boxes, Butler MSS.
34. Lowell Daily *Journal & Courier,* September 3, 1858.
35. Boston Daily Evening *Advertiser,* August 30, 1858.

36. Moses Bates-Butler, August 17, 1858, Butler MSS, 1954 boxes; Lowell Daily *Journal & Courier*, September 2, 3, 1858. Lowell Daily Evening *Advertiser*, September 2, 1858.

37. *Ibid.*, October 7, 18, 1858; Varina Howell Davis, *Jefferson Davis* (New York, 1890), I, 594. Lowell Daily *Journal & Courier*, November 2, 1858. The *Journal & Courier* expressed pleasure at Butler's opposition to the odious features of the English Bill, but it did not believe he was the right man to stop the South.

38. *Ibid.*, November 3, 1858. The figures for the Congressional race were: Train (Republican), 5,968; Butler (Democrat), 3,512; Temple (American), 522.

39. Newburyport Daily *Herald*, January 5, 1859.

40. George Lowell Austin, *The History of Massachusetts* (Boston, 1885), 484; Hart, *op. cit.*, IV, 66 ff.; Boston *Post*, January 18, 19, 20; March 31, July 26, September 7, November 3, 1859; Boston Daily Evening *Transcript*, October 14, December 7, 1859; Edward P. Conklin, *Middlesex County and Its People* (New York, 1927), I, 202; Butler-Lemuel Shaw, June 11, 1859, Lemuel Shaw MSS, Massachusetts Historical Society, Boston. Remembering Judge Hoar's charge to the jury, Butler saw to it that in the future judges' charges became restricted to questions of law.

41. Boston *Post*, March 5, October 20, 1859.

42. *Ibid.*, February 19, 1859; Newburyport Daily *Herald*, February 21, 1859.

43. *Ibid.*, April 11, 1859.

44. Hurd, *op. cit.*, I, xviii. The character sketch was written by William T. Davis, who had been a Republican member of the same legislature.

45. Boston *Post*, September 8-10, 1859.

46. *Ibid.*, September 16, 1859.

47. Boston Evening *Transcript*, November 7, 1859.

48. J. Q. A. Griffin, "A Portrait of Benjamin F. Butler. By A House Painter," Charleston City *Advertiser*, September 7, 1859, copy in Butler MSS.

49. Boston *Post*, September 16, 1859.

50. *Ibid.*, October 8, November 2, 8, 1859; Boston Evening *Transcript*, October 11, 1859.

51. Boston *Post*, November 7, 1859.

52. Boston Evening *Transcript*, November 10, 1859. The figures were: Banks (Republican), 58,839; Butler (Democrat), 35,317; Briggs (American), 14,457.

53. Boston *Post*, December 9, 1859.

**NOTES** 267

CHAPTER V  *The Great Decision*
(Pages 52 to 64)

1. Butler helped to draw up liquor control legislation in 1855. Butler-Editor, New York *Voice*, December 16, 1889, letterbooks, Butler MSS; Lowell Daily Evening *Advertiser*, June 27, 1855.
2. *Ibid.*, August 27, 1857.
3. *Ibid.*, December 8, 31, 1857; June 19, 1858; Boston *Post*, December 29, 1859; Boston Evening *Transcript*, December 13, 1859. Conklin, *op. cit.*, II, 473; Hurd, *op. cit.*, II, 76 ff.; Cowley, *History of Lowell*, 53; Hildreth's proxy, April 11, 1859, Butler MSS.
4. Accounts from June 1, 1859-June 1, 1860, totalling $3,692.83, Butler MSS.
5. Memorandum, June 5, 1858, Butler MSS.
6. Boston *Post*, October 8, 1859.
7. *Ibid.*, September 16, 1859.
8. A. J. Cass-Butler, January 25, 1859; September 19, 1859, Butler MSS, 1954 boxes.
9. Boston *Post*, August 19, 1859.
10. Milton, *op. cit.*, 418-19.
11. A. J. Cass-Butler, September 5, 1859; October 7, 1859, Butler MSS.
12. Boston *Post*, September 16, 1859.
13. John W. Mahan-Douglas, April 17, 1860; Moses Bates-Douglas, March 5, 1860, Douglas MSS; Milton, *op. cit.*, 418.
14. *Ibid.*
15. Butler was warned of all these developments, but he was also cautioned that Douglas' defeat might well mean Lincoln's victory. A. J. Cass-Butler, September 19, 1859, 1954 boxes, Butler MSS.
16. Milton, *op. cit.*, 419. He was alleged to have tried to undermine the loyalty of the leader of the New York Softs, Dean Richmond. H. H. Coates-Douglas, February 22, 1860, Douglas MSS.
17. Fuess, *Cushing*, II, 244.
18. Davis-Cushing, April 15, 1860, Cushing MSS.
19. Butler-Albert J. Chapman, August 22, 1889, letterbooks, Butler MSS.
20. Davis, *Jefferson Davis*, I, 594, 608 ff.; Clarence C. Buel and Robert U. Johnson (eds.), *Battles and Leaders of the Civil War* (New York, 1887), I, 102.
21. Butler-Albert J. Chapman, August 22, 1889, letterbooks, Butler MSS.
22. *Butler's Book*, 135-36.
23. H. W. Bishop-Butler, May 22, 1860, 1954 boxes, Butler MSS.
24. Boston *Post*, October 5, 1860.
25. Butler-Albert J. Chapman, August 22, 1889, letterbooks, Butler MSS. He was hoping for the nomination of James Guthrie of Kentucky.
26. Jessie Ames Marshall, *Private and Official Correspondence of Gen. Benjamin F. Butler During the Period of the Civil War* (cited as *Butler Cor.*) (Norwood, Mass., 1917), I, 1-2.
27. Roy Frank Nichols, *The Disruption of the American Democracy* (New York, 1948), 288 ff.

28. *Official Proceedings of the Democratic National Convention Held in 1860 in Charleston and Baltimore* (Cleveland, 1860), 38-39. The idea seems to have been Hallett's. B. F. Hallett-Butler, April 17, 1860, 1954 boxes, Butler MSS.

29. *Official Proceedings of the Democratic National Convention Held in 1860 in Charleston and Baltimore,* 56 ff.; New York Weekly *Tribune,* May 5, 1860.

30. Murat Halstead, *Caucuses of 1860* (Columbus, 1861), 52-97; Boston Evening *Transcript,* April 30-May 3, 1860.

31. *Ibid.* For his alleged reasons, cf. Butler-Albert Chapman, August 22, 1889; Butler-L. G. Stafford, January 5, 1879, letterbooks, Butler MSS; *Butler's Book,* 138 ff.; note 34 *infra.*

32. H. W. Bishop-Butler, May 22, 1860, Butler MSS, 1954 boxes.

33. Milton, *op. cit.,* 459. Reverdy Johnson came to Boston to denounce him.

34. Boston *Post,* May 16, 1860. Trying to explain his votes for Davis, Butler said the Senator from Mississippi was a man with whom he disagreed in some things, but with whom he could act in most; a man who loved his country first and his section next, a man who had been instrumental in obtaining hundreds of thousands of dollars for Massachusetts.

35. *Letter of the Honorable Whiting Griswold in Reply to the Speech of Hon. Benjamin F. Butler, Delivered at Lowell, May 15, 1860, on the Proceedings of the Charleston Convention* (Boston, 1860).

36. Boston *Post,* May 21, 1860; Moses Bates-Douglas, May 7, 1860, Douglas MSS; Milton, *op. cit.,* 459. Yet he seems to have continued his search for a candidate acceptable to the administration, perhaps Horatio Seymour of New York. George Fort Milton calls this the "Seymour plot." *Ibid.,* 462.

37. Halstead, *op. cit.,* 22.

38. *Ibid.,* 206.

39. *Official Proceedings of the Democratic National Convention Held in 1860 in Charleston and Baltimore,* 156-57; Nichols, *Disruption of the American Democracy,* 314-22; John Bassett Moore (ed.), *The Works of James Buchanan* (Philadelphia, 1910), XII, 66.

40. *Ibid.,* 68-69; *Proceedings of the Conventions at Charleston and Baltimore* (Washington, 1860), 241 ff.; Milton, *op. cit.,* 474-477.

41. Alexander H. Stephens, *A Constitutional View of the Late War Between the States* (Philadelphia, 1868), II, 276.

42. Boston *Post,* June 30, 1860.

43. Lowell *Advertiser,* July 27, 1860; Boston *Post,* July 27, 1860; Boston *Herald,* July 27, 1860; Cowley, *History of Lowell,* 173-74.

44. Boston *Post,* August 11, 13, 1860; Lowell Daily Evening *Advertiser,* August 13, 1860; *Proceedings of the Massachusetts National Democratic Convention and of the Mass Meeting for the Ratification of the Nominations of Breckinridge and Lane, Held at the Tremont Temple, Boston, September 12, 1860* (Boston, 1860), 67-69.

45. Boston *Post,* October 1, 1860; Isaac I. Stevens-Butler, August 3, 9, 1860, 1954 boxes, Butler MSS.

46. *Proceedings of the Massachusetts National Democratic Convention,* 17-20.

47. Boston *Post,* October 13, 1860.

# NOTES

48. P. R. George-Butler, September 23, 1860, 1954 boxes, Butler MSS.
49. Boston Evening *Transcript,* November 9, 1860.
50. P. R. George-Butler, September 23, 1860, 1954 boxes, Butler MSS.
51. *Butler's Book,* 149 ff.; *Butler Cor.,* I, 6-14. No contemporary record of these conversations has been found. There is no mention of them in the biographies and reminiscences of the alleged participants, an omission which may be due to the hatred with which they pursued Butler later on.
52. Milton, *op. cit.,* 511.
53. *Butler's Book,* 149 ff.; *Butler Cor.,* I, 6-14.
54. Philip G. Auchampaugh, *James Buchanan and His Cabinet on the Eve of Secession* (Lancaster, 1926).
55. Frank Abiel Flower, *Edwin McMasters Stanton* (New York, 1904), 89.
56. Willis Weaver, "A Criticism of Butler's Book," MSS in Personal, Miscellaneous file, Library of Congress.
57. *Butler's Book,* 151 ff. Butler maintained he himself thought of the idea of trying the commissioners and originally said so to Attorney General Jeremiah Black. He did indeed see Black, but in an earlier account, written by himself, in Flower, *Stanton,* 89, he credits Stanton with the idea. Weaver, *op. cit.,* is a fairly convincing piece of detective work comparing the two accounts. The author arrives at the conclusion that Stanton gave Butler the idea; that there were three distinct interviews between Butler and Buchanan, only the last of which was scheduled beforehand and witnessed by John Cochrane as attested by the letter dated July 11, 1893, from Cochrane to Butler in *Butler's Book,* 156.
58. Fletcher Pratt, *Stanton* (New York, 1953), 108-10.
59. Boston *Herald,* December 31, 1860.
60. *Butler's Book,* 159 ff.; Parton, *op. cit.,* 65.
61. New York *Times,* January 3, 1861.
62. *Butler's Book,* 161.
63. Albany Evening *Journal,* August 10, 1878.
64. William Schouler-Butler, August 3, 1870, Butler MSS.
65. Henry Greenleaf Pearson, *The Life of John A. Andrew* (Boston, 1904), I, 168 ff.
66. *Butler Cor.,* I, 6-14.
67. William Schouler-Butler, August 3, 1870, Butler MSS. When Schouler, the wartime Adjutant General of Massachusetts, published his *History of Massachusetts in the Civil War* (Boston 1868), he did not refer to Butler's efforts to aid in preparing the Commonwealth. On July 10, 1870, in the letter quoted in *Butler Cor.,* I, 6-14, Butler protested. Schouler agreed to have this correction appear in the newspapers. The General's recollections are probably highly slanted in his favor, especially as he hated both Schouler and Andrew and maintained that his enemies had abstracted the papers in question from the State Archives. Schouler did concede, however, that a conversation between him and his correspondent had taken place substantially as Butler described it. Cf. *Butler's Book,* 161 ff.; Schouler-Butler, August 3, 9, 1870, Butler MSS.
68. George W. Nason, *History and Complete Roster of the Massachusetts Regiments, Minute Men of '61* . . . (Boston, 1910), 190; B. F. Watson, *An Oration Delivered at Huntington Hall, Lowell, Massachusetts, by Colonel B. F. Watson of New York City, April 19, 1886* (New York, 1886), 14.

69. Augustine Jones-John F. Andrew, October 7, 1876, John F. Andrew MSS, Massachusetts Historical Society, Boston.

70. *Butler Cor.*, I, 6-14; Boston *Post*, March 27, 1861; Louis Taylor Merrill, "General Benjamin F. Butler As A Radical Leader During the Administration of President Andrew Johnson," unpublished doctoral dissertation, University of Chicago, 1936, 29-30.

71. Pearson, *op. cit.*, I, 174.

72. Boston *Post*, April 16, 1861.

73. *Butler Cor.*, I, 15; *Butler's Book*, 170. Butler asserted that the case remained unfinished ever after, but according to the Boston *Post*, he appeared in the case of *David Cleary* v. *Hon. McGreevy* in Superior Court on April 15, a case which was decided against him on the next day. Boston *Post*, April 16, 17, 1861.

74. *Ibid.*, April 16, 1861.

75. *Butler Cor.*, I, 6-14; *Butler's Book*, 170-73; Parton, *op. cit.*, 68-69.

76. Pearson, *op. cit.*, I, 183 ff.

77. G. W. Van Horn-Editors, Springfield *Republican*, September 24, 1868, Butler MSS. Even Butler's implacable enemy, George Hoar, gave him credit for this deed. Hoar, *op. cit.*, I, 332-34.

78. Fuess, *Cushing*, II, 269 ff.; 278; Pearson, *op. cit.*, I, 183 ff., 198. According to Pearson, Andrew thought Cushing beyond hope. Knowing Butler less well, he was willing to take a chance on him but regretted it later.

79. He always claimed he had suggested this course to Carney. *Butler's Book*, 170-72. Pearson calls the story ridiculous. It is probable that Butler did indeed carry a note offering financial support from Carney, a circumstance which caused him to conclude that Andrew appointed him for that reason. Many years later, when preparing his memoirs, he requested George C. Carney to search for his father's note which he, Butler, remembered having carried to the Governor. Butler-George C. Carney, January 19, 1891, letterbooks, Butler MSS. Andrew, however, was well aware of the importance of rallying potential troublemakers to the flag. William J. Stillman, *The Autobiography of a Journalist* (Boston, 1901), I, 334. Cf. C. P. Headly, *Massachusetts in the Rebellion* (Boston, 1866), 103-04.

80. *Butler Cor.*, I, 15-16.

81. Boston *Post*, April 19, 1861.

CHAPTER VI *Washington and Baltimore*
(Pages 65 to 76)

1. Margaret Leech, *Reveille in Washington, 1860-1865* (New York, 1941), 46-73.

2. Boston *Post*, April 19, 1861; New York *Herald*, April 19, 1861; Nason, *op. cit.*, 231; *Butler Cor.*, I, 23; Parton, *op. cit.*, 70 ff.

3. *Butler Cor.*, I, 16-17.

4. According to Butler, he thought of this plan first. Theodore Winthrop, the New York novelist who fell under his spell, agreed with him. The preponderance of evidence, however, indicates that the railroad authorities suggested it. For Butler's version, cf. *Butler's Book*, 176 ff.; Theodore Winthrop,

**NOTES**

*Life in the Open Air and Other Papers* (New York, 1876), 223-24. For contrary evidence, cf. Sarah Forbes Hughes (ed.), *Letters and Recollections of John Murray Forbes* (Boston, 1889), I, 189; Wilmington Morning *News*, January 29, 1889; Schouler, *op. cit.*, I, 99; *War of the Rebellion, Official Records of the Union and Confederate Armies* (Washington, 1880-1901), Series I, II, 596-97. (Cited as *O. R.*)

5. *Butler Cor.*, I, 18; for a less favorable version, cf. William Swinton, *History of the Seventh Regiment, National Guard, State of New York, During the War of the Rebellion* (New York, 1870), 53 ff.; Emmons Clark, *History of the Seventh New York Regiment, 1806-1889* (New York, 1890), I, 476.

6. *Butler Cor.*, I, 29-30.

7. *Ibid.*, I, 25; *Butler's Book*, 183 ff.; Parton, *op. cit.*, 75-80.

8. Butler-Andrew, April 26, 1861, Butler MSS.

9. *War of the Rebellion, Official Records of the Union and Confederate Navies* (Washington, 1894-1922), Series I, IV, 315, 398. (Cited as *O. R.* [Navies]); Edward W. Hincks, *The Forty-fifth Regiment Massachusets Volunteer Militia* . . . (Cambridge, 1883), 12 ff.; Winthrop, *op. cit.*, 225-28; *Butler Cor.*, I, 25.

10. Elihu S. Riley, "The Ancient City," *A History of Annapolis in Maryland, 1649-1887* (Annapolis, 1887), 281. For the hostility of the inhabitants, cf. MSS Diary of Philip Woodruff Holmes, April 9-June 30, 1861, New York Public Library.

11. James Soley, *Historical Sketch of the United States Naval Academy* (Washington, 1876), 105 ff.; *Butler's Book*, 193.

12. George L. P. Radcliffe, *Governor Thomas H. Hicks of Maryland and the Civil War, Johns Hopkins University Studies in Historical and Political Science*, Series XIX (November-December, 1901), *passim*.

13. John G. Nicolay and John Hay, *Abraham Lincoln* (New York, 1914), IV, 125-32; J. G. Randall, Lincoln, *The President* (New York, 1945), I, 364-66.

14. *Butler Cor.*, I, 18.

15. *Ibid.*, 20, 22.

16. *O. R.*, Series I, II, 589.

17. *Butler Cor.*, I, 47-48; *Butler's Book*, 195; Parton, *op. cit.*, 82. According to a clipping from the Washington *Post*, April 27, 1892, Butler MSS, Butler offered an exorbitant sum for a broken old nag. The owner overcame his hostility, and thereafter the General could make his own terms. The matter came to light when the Treasury Department questioned the price.

18. *O. R.*, Series I, II, 588. He also suggested the British minister be asked to mediate between the sections. Secretary of State Seward replied that there had been times when "a general of the American Union with forces designed for the defense of its capital was not unwelcome anywhere in the State of Maryland;" nor did he think domestic matters were the business of foreigners. Frank Moore, (ed.), *Rebellion Record* (New York, 1861-1869), I, 133; Nicolay and Hay, *op. cit.*, IV, 138-39.

19. Still, he sent another protest and cautioned Butler to take his troops through town as quickly as possible. *O. R.*, Series I, II, 589.

20. *Ibid.*, Series II, I, 750.

21. Clark, *op. cit.*, I, 482-85; Swinton, *op. cit.*, 67 ff.; Winthrop, *op. cit.*, 225.

22. Clark, *op. cit.*, I, 487 ff.

23. Swinton, *op. cit.*, 70 ff.; *Butler Cor.*, I, 34.

24. Winthrop, *op. cit.*, 232.
25. Swinton, *op. cit.*, 85-90; Clark, *op. cit.*, I, 487-90. As the Seventh New York Regiment was not mustered into the service of the United States until after its arrival in Washington, it was able to resist his pretensions to command.
26. Clark, *op. cit.*, I, 487-90; *Butler Cor.*, I, 22-23.
27. *Ibid.*, I, 34; Butler-Francis H. Harris, February 11, 1889, letterbooks, Butler MSS; *Butler's Book*, 200 ff.
28. Hincks, *op. cit.*, 14-15; Winthrop, *op. cit.*, 234 ff.; Clark, *op. cit.*, I, 490 ff.
29. He was accompanied by Andrew Carnegie, then a young representative of the Pennsylvania Railroad. Andrew Carnegie, *Autobiography* (Boston, 1920), 99.
30. Winthrop, *op. cit.*, 237 ff.; *Harper's Weekly*, V, (May 18, 1861), 317.
31. Leech, *op. cit.*, 66 ff.; Winthrop, *op. cit.*, 240 ff.; Nicolay and Hay, *op. cit.*, IV, 155.
32. *Ibid.*
33. Lincoln issued this order on April 24. Order No. 3, April 24, 1861, Butler MSS. Scott's order is in *O. R.*, Series I, II, 600.
34. *Ibid.*, Series I, LI, Part I, 1273.
35. *Ibid.*, Series I, II, 607. It consisted of a strip of territory twenty miles wide on both sides of the railroad.
36. *Butler Cor.*, I, 52.
37. Randall, *op. cit.*, I, 363.
38. *O. R.*, Series II, I, 567.
39. Nicolay and Hay, *op. cit.*, IV, 174 ff.
40. *O. R.*, Series II, I, 675.
41. Radcliffe, *op. cit.*, 68; Baltimore *South*, April 29, 1861.
42. *Butler Cor.*, I, 28.
43. Radcliffe, *op. cit.*, 68-69.
44. Moore, *op. cit.*, I, 159.
45. New York *Times*, May 11, 1861.
46. Butler-Belknap, December 29, 1882, letterbooks, Butler MSS. The Great Seal of the State was deposited with him for safe keeping.
47. *Ibid.*, Joshua Brown-Butler, April 23, 1861, Butler MSS. An interesting account of the difficulties encountered by his soldiers while guarding the railroad may be found in James Butler MSS, Thomas F. Madigan Collection, New York Public Library.
48. Carl Schurz, *The Reminiscences of Carl Schurz* (New York, 1909), II, 225.
49. Butler-Andrew, April 26, 1861, Butler MSS.
50. Pearson, *op. cit.*, I, 284.
51. D. L. Child-Andrew, April 26, 1861, John A. Andrew MSS, Massachusetts Historical Society, Boston.
52. *Butler Cor.*, I, 37-41.
53. *Ibid.*, 76, 93-4, 100; Boston Daily Evening *Transcript*, May 17, 1861; Schouler, *op. cit.*, I, 159-60.
54. *O. R.*, Series I, II, 608, 619. For Northern impatience, cf. *Harper's Weekly*, V (May 4, 1861), 274.
55. Parton, *op. cit.*, 105; *Butler's Book*, 222-23.

# NOTES

56. *Butler Cor.*, I, 64-65.
57. *O. R.*, Series I, II, 620.
58. *Ibid.*, 629; Series II, I, 568; *The South*, April 24, May 6, 9, 19, 1861; *Harper's Weekly*, V (May 18, 1861).
59. *Butler Cor.*, I, 71-73; *The South*, May 19, 1861.
60. *Butler Cor.*, I, 80.
61. Washington *Post*, April 27, 1892, Butler MSS. This incident, too, came to light when the Treasury questioned the expense for the hand organ.
62. *Butler Cor.*, I, 80.
63. *Ibid.*; *Butler's Book*, 226-27. Butler admitted that "it is but fair to say that I had the strongest possible suspicion that if I asked General Scott for orders to occupy Baltimore he would refuse them." He was aware of the fact that Scott was engaged in careful preparations to facilitate the transit of troops through the city. *O. R.*, Series I, II, 608, 619.
64. *Ibid.*, 30; *National Intelligencer*, May 15, 1861; Parton, *op. cit.*, 110 ff.
65. *National Intelligencer*, May 15, 1861; *New York Herald*, May 15, 1861; *The South*, May 14, 1861; *Butler's Book*, 229 ff.
66. *O. R.*, Series I, II, 636.
67. *Butler Cor.*, I, 81.
68. Parton, *op. cit.*, 112; *Butler's Book*, 232-33.
69. *Butler Cor.*, I, 82-84.
70. *The South*, May 14, 1861; Baltimore *American*, May 14, 1861; Jacob Frey, *Reminiscences of Baltimore* (Baltimore, 1893), 126-27.
71. Parton, *op. cit.*, 115.
72. Charles W. Elliott, *Winfield Scott* (New York, 1937), 718-19.
73. Scott-Butler, May 14, 1861, Butler MSS; *O. R.*, Series I, II, 28.
74. *New York Herald*, May 15, 16, 1861; *Harper's Weekly*, V (May 25, 1861, June 1, 1861). The June 1 number contained a huge portrait of the General, admiringly called "The First Hero of the War." A flattering biographical sketch followed.
75. *O. R.*, Series I, II, 28.
76. *Ibid.*, 636, 638.
77. Carl Sandburg, *Abraham Lincoln, The War Years* (New York, 1939), I, 275-76. The millionaire was ordered released on parole.
78. *O. R.*, Series III, I, 207. The decision was made on May 15. Ever after, Butler insisted that he was the ranking Major General of the Army. *Butler Cor.*, III, 66-70, 85.
79. *Boston Daily Evening Transcript*, May 17, 1861.
80. *Butler's Book*, 237-42; Otis P. Gunn, "A Great American," paper read before the Farragut Post, G. A. R., February 9, 1893, Butler MSS; *Butler Cor.*, I, 95-97; *O. R.*, Series I, II, 41, 603. Although orders to that effect had not yet arrived, Butler, in his first General Orders, styled himself "Commanding General of the Department of Virginia." Although the War Department failed to address him in these terms, he persisted and demanded the confirmation which he maintained had been promised to him. The issue was not fully resolved until General Wool, upon arrival, also styled himself "Commander of S. E. Virginia." As such, the Department was later listed in the O. R. *O. R.*, Series I, II, 643; IV, 601.

CHAPTER VII  *Fickle Fortunes of War*
(Pages 77 to 87)

1. *O. R.*, Series I, II, 648; *Butler's Book*, 246.
2. H. K. W. Patterson, *War Memories of Fort Monroe and Vicinity* (Fort Monroe, 1885), 72; Charles W. Betts, *Visitors' Handbook of Old Point Comfort, Va.* (Hampton, Va., 1885), 18 ff.
3. Winthrop, *op. cit.*, 295-97.
4. *O. R.*, Series I, II, 648; *Butler's Book*, 246.
5. Robert Arthur, *The History of Fortress Monroe*, (Fortress Monroe, 1930), 86.
6. William Howard Russell, *My Diary North and South* (Boston, 1863), 406 ff.; *Battles and Leaders*, II, 146.
7. Randall, *op. cit.*, II, 126 ff.
8. John M. Deane-Butler, March 14, 1891, 1954 boxes, Butler MSS. Deane was the commanding officer of the company.
9. *Ibid.*, *O. R.*, Series I, II, 648.
10. Parton, *op. cit.*, 126 ff.
11. *O. R.*, Series I, II, 648; *Butler Cor.*, I, 102-03. The first source is Butler's report of the incident to the War Department, May 25, 1861; the second, a letter from John B. Carey to Butler, March 9, 1891, in which he maintains Butler mentioned the word "contraband." Cf. Carey's report to Colonel Magruder, May 24, 1861, *O. R.*, Series I, II, 870-71.
12. Allan Nevins and Milton H. Thomas (eds.), *The Diary of George Templeton Strong* (New York, 1952), III, 192; Nicolay and Hay, *op. cit.*, IV, 389.
13. Adam Gurowski, *Diary* . . . (Boston, 1862, New York, 1864), I, 50.
14. *Butler Cor.*, I, 116-17.
15. *Ibid.*, 119, 120-21.
16. William Knott Harding, "Contemporary Opinion of General Benjamin Franklin Butler During the Civil War," M. A. essay, University of Wisconsin, 1929, 21; Boston Daily Evening *Transcript*, March 27, 1861; New York Weekly *Tribune*, June 1, 1861.
17. Much to Butler's disgust, the question of the authorship of the expression became a subject of considerable dispute. It appeared first in a dispatch from a *Tribune* reporter in the New York *Tribune*, on May 27, 1861, but neither Butler nor Carey used it in their reports of the interview. They employed circumlocutions, so that Butler's enemies were able to claim authorship for Captain Tylor of the Twenty-ninth Massachusetts Regiment. *Butler's Book*, 256-64; Springfield *Republican*, August 22, 1873; The New York *Times*, October 21, 1883.
18. Even George Hoar admitted this contribution. Hoar, *op. cit.*, I, 332-34.
19. Winthrop, *op. cit.*, 293. Butler had appointed Winthrop Military Secretary. *The Life and Poems of Theodore Winthrop*, Edited By His Sister (New York, 1884), 288; Ellsworth Eliot Jr., *Theodore Winthrop* (New Haven, 1938), 22.
20. *Butler Cor.*, I, 93-94.
21. *Ibid.*, 125-27.
22. *Ibid.*, 127-30.

# NOTES

23. Boston Daily Evening *Transcript,* May 23, 1861.
24. Sumner said Butler had predicted the war would be over "at the second frost." Adams, *op. cit.,* II, 259.
25. Walter Clark (ed.), *Histories of the Several Regiments and Battalions from North Carolina in the Great War 1861-1865* (Raleigh, 1901), I, 83; *Battles and Leaders,* II, 148; Benson J. Lossing, *Pictorial History of the Civil War* (Philadelphia, 1866-1874), I, 504 ff.; plan in 1861 folder of Butler MSS, 1954 boxes.
26. Walter Clark, *op. cit.,* I, 69 ff., 83; Douglas Southall Freeman, *Lee's Lieutenants* (New York, 1945), I, 15, 17-18, 192 ff.
27. Marion L. Starkey, *The First Plantation* (Hampton, Va., 1936), 80-81. The First North Carolina Volunteers later made up a purse for the old lady.
28. O. R., Series I, II, 88; Lossing, *op. cit.,* I, 505 ff.
29. *Ibid.,* 504-10; *Butler Cor.,* I, 144-47; O. R., Series I, II, 86 ff.
30. *Ibid.,* 77-93; Lossing, *op. cit.,* I, 504-10; *Battles and Leaders,* II, 148; Walter Clark, *op. cit.,* I, 86-102.
31. O. R., Series I, II, 82, 90; *The Life and Poems of Theodore Winthrop,* 292-97.
32. O. R., Series I, II, 80-82. Visiting officers found the General talkative and nervous about the defeat. Charles S. Foltz, *Surgeon of the Seas* (Indianapolis, 1931), 198.
33. Walter Clark, *op. cit.,* I, 102-03. In the Virginia Convention, ex-President Tyler introduced a resolution eulogizing Magruder and Hill.
34. New York *Times,* June 12, 1861; Boston Daily Evening *Transcript,* June 19, 1861. The *Tribune* remained steadfast and fastened the blame on Pierce. New York *Tribune,* June 12-20, 1861.
35. Harding, *op. cit.,* 23.
36. Curowski, *op. cit.,* I, 58.
37. *Journal of Executive Proceedings of the Senate,* 37th Cong., 1st Sess., 558; *Butler's Book,* 275.
38. He engaged in controversy with the unhappy General Pierce and made aspersions on the New York regiments. *Butler Cor.,* I, 142-44; Boston Daily Evening *Transcript,* August 5, 1861; *Butler's Book,* 268 ff.; Parton, *op. cit.,* 142, 152.
39. O. R., Series I, II, 93; Arthur, *op. cit.,* 85.
40. *Butler Cor.,* I, 154, 175, 211. Always fond of novel expedients, he employed a balloonist to procure aerial intelligence.
41. *Ibid.,* 101-03; 123 ff., 134, 155, 156 ff; 163; O. R., Series I, II, 603, 612, 673, 706, 708, 741, 763; Russell, *op. cit.,* 406.
42. *Butler Cor.,* I, 185; Arthur, *op. cit.,* 87; James H. Matheny, "A Modern Knight Errant, Edward Dickinson Baker," in *Journal of the Illinois State Historical Society,* IX (April, 1916-January, 1917), 23-42.
43. O. R., Series I, II, 741.
44. *Butler Correspondence,* I, 180-81; *Harper's Weekly,* V (August 17, 1861).
45. *Butler Cor.,* I, 167, 179-80.
46. *Harper's Weekly,* V (August 17, 1861).
47. *Butler Cor.,* I, 185-88.
48. New York *Tribune,* August 4, 1861.

49. Roy P. Basler (ed.), *The Collected Works of Abraham Lincoln* (New Brunswick, 1953), IV, 457.
50. J. H. E. Whitney, *The Hawkins Zouaves* (New York, 1866), 39; Matthew J. Graham, *The Ninth New York Volunteers (Hawkins' Zouaves)* (New York, 1900), 55-70; Charles F. Johnson, *The Long Roll* (East Aurora, N. Y., 1911), 34 ff.
51. New York *Tribune*, August 5, 1861.
52. *Ibid.*
53. *Cong. Globe*, 37th Cong., 1st Sess., 415 ff.
54. *Butler Cor.*, I, 201-03.
55. *Journal of the Executive Proceedings of the Senate*, 37th Cong., 1st Sess., 558.
56. Basler, *op. cit.*, IV, 468; *Butler's Book*, 298. Butler gives an account of the final implementation of the order one month later. He maintains that he drew up the order, but it is probable that he confused the two incidents as the former order is in his handwriting, but the latter is not.
57. *Butler Cor.*, I, 199, 206, 210.
58. *O. R.*, Series I, IV, 568, 569 ff.; Series II, I, 763-64; Patterson, *op. cit.*, 30-32; Betts, *op. cit.*, 54 ff.; Gillie C. McCabe, *The Story of an Old Town* (Richmond, 1929), 40 ff.
59. *O. R.*, Series I, IV, 600.
60. Basler, *op. cit.*, IV, 478. On August 5, the very day of Butler's confirmation, Edwin D. Morgan had written to Lincoln: "Against the distinguished and loyal General Officer in command at Fort Monroe, I should be the last to make complaint . . . . But . . . the duty of disciplining undrilled troops could be most safely committed to an experienced army officer." He proposed General Wool.
61. *O. R.*, Series I, IV, 600.
62. *Butler Cor.*, I, 206-07.
63. *Ibid.*, 208-09, 215.
64. *Ibid.*, 218, 219, 220-21.
65. *National Intelligencer*, August 20, 1861; Moore, *op. cit.*, II, 70. The volunteers inside the Fort were excepted. Cf. Henry Warren Howe, *Passages from the Life of Henry Warren Howe* (Lowell, 1899), 29.
66. *O. R.*, Series I, IV, 602.
67. *Ibid.*, 580; *O. R.* (Navies), Series I, VI, 69; Richard S. West, Jr., *Gideon Welles* (Indianapolis and New York, 1943), 126; Gideon Welles, "Admiral Farragut and New Orleans," *Galaxy*, XII (November, 1871), 671.
68. *Butler Cor.*, 227-28; *O. R.*, Series I, 580-86; Lossing, *op. cit.*, I, 105 ff.; *The American Annual Cyclopedia*, 1861 (New York, 1862), 287 ff.
69. R. M. Thompson and R. Wainwright (eds.), *Confidential Correspondence of Gustavus Vasa Fox* (New York, 1938), I, 385. J. P. Bankhead wrote Fox that the two leaders, Stringham and Butler, "after the fight . . . had a footrace North to see who should get there first and get the most credit. Butler beat Stringham. Had they both remained, we might have had the whole coast in our possession."
70. *O. R.*, Series I, IV, 580-81.
71. *Butler's Book*, 286-88.
72. *Ibid.*; *O. R.*, Series I, IV, 604; Nicolay and Hay, *op. cit.*, V, 13.

# NOTES

73. Harding, *op. cit.*, 27; New York Weekly *Tribune*, September 7, 1861; New York *Tribune*, September 2, 1861; *Harper's Weekly*, V (September 14, 1861).
74. Russell, *op. cit.*, 518.
75. Cowley, *History of Lowell*, 180-81.
76. Within a short time, they were going to enlist enthusiastically in his volunteer regiments.
77. Harriet Beecher Stowe is a good example. Forest Wilson, *Crusader in Crinoline* (Philadelphia, 1941), 475.

CHAPTER VIII  *Preparing for The Great Expedition*
(Pages 88 to 97)

1. *Butler Cor.*, I, 337.
2. New York Weekly *Tribune*, September 14, 1861.
3. Edith Ellen Ware, *Political Opinion in Massachusetts During the Civil War and Reconstruction* (New York, 1916), 77.
4. *Butler Cor.*, I, 238; *Butler's Book*, 295-96.
5. *Butler Cor.*, I, 219-24; *O. R.*, Series III, I, 423. On August 17, the War Department granted permission to raise troops, but as the orders did not include the extensive authority he desired, he wrote a scathing letter of protest.
6. *Butler's Book*, 296-98.
7. Basler, *op. cit.*, IV, 515-16.
8. *Ibid.*, 518; 515-16; *Butler Cor.*, I, 255-56, 336; *O. R.*, Series III, I, 498, 499, 507; General Order No. 2, September 10, 1861, endorsed on September 12, 1861, Butler MSS. The final version does not contain Lincoln's proviso.
9. *O. R.*, Series III, I, 817.
10. *Butler Cor.*, I, 279-84; *Butler's Book*, 299 ff.; Thomas Hamilton Murray, *History of the Ninth Regiment, Connecticut Volunteer Infantry* (New Haven, 1903), 43; *Descriptive Brochure of General Stephen Thomas* (Randolph, Vt., 1914), 14.
11. William Schouler, *op. cit.*, I, 255; *Correspondence Between Governor Andrew and Maj. Gen. Butler* (Boston, 1862), 5-7, 11; James L. Bowen, *Massachusetts in the War, 1861-1865* (Springfield, 1889), 38-40.
12. *Butler Cor.*, I, 282, 337-38; Pearson, *op. cit.*, I, 288; *Butler's Book*, 306. The regiments were the Twenty-Sixth, Twenty-Eighth, and the Salem Light Artillery.
13. *Ibid.*, 307-08; John A. Andrew-Charles Sumner, John A. Andrew MSS, December 28, 1861.
14. *O. R.*, Series I, LI, Part I, 490.
15. *Ibid.*, Series III, I, 822.
16. The President had direct authority to raise troops only in states where the Governors were disloyal. Elsewhere, the Governors were the only legitimate source of commissions.
17. *Correspondence Between Governor Andrew and Major General Butler*, 29 ff.
18. *Butler Cor.*, I, 247, 271, 286-91.

19. William Schouler, *op. cit.*, I, 263; Pearson, *op. cit.*, I, 291; Howe, *op. cit.*, 29. The Eastern Bay State Regiment was to be commanded by Colonel French.
20. *Butler Cor.*, I, 251.
21. Butler-Andrew, October 12, 1861, Butler MSS.
22. Boston *Journal*, October 28, 1861.
23. *Correspondence Between Governor Andrew and Maj. Gen. Butler*, 34; *Butler Cor.*, I, 263.
24. Boston *Journal*, October 28, 1861.
25. *Butler Cor.*, I, 266-67.
26. William Schouler, *op. cit.*, I, 265 ff.; Pearson, *op. cit.*, I, 291.
27. *Butler Cor.*, I, 253.
28. Montgomery Blair-Butler, October 22, 1861, 1954 boxes, Butler MSS.
29. Henry Lee, Jr.-John A. Andrew, November 2, 1861, John A. Andrew MSS.
30. Henry Lee, Jr.-John A. Andrew, November 2, 5, 1861, John A. Andrew MSS.
31. Henry Lee, Jr.-John A. Andrew, November 7, 1861, John A. Andrew MSS.
32. *Butler Cor.*, I, 272-73, 274-77, 282. Andrew had offered Butler an additional Irish regiment, but the General refused it on the grounds that it would compete with the Twenty-Ninth. Cf. *Correspondence Between Governor Andrew and Maj. Gen. Butler*, 13.
33. Gideon Welles, "Admiral Farragut and New Orleans," *loc. cit.*, 674. That Butler was sent to Ship Island to get him out of the way is borne out by Attorney General Bates. Howard K. Beale (ed.), *The Diary of Edward Bates, American Historical Association Annual Report for 1930*, IV (Washington, 1933), 208. The ultimate destination was still vague and might be anywhere along the Gulf coast. Nicolay and Hay, *op. cit.*, V, 253; G. V. Fox Butler, November 14, 1861, 1954 boxes, Butler MSS.
34. Gideon Welles-G. V. Fox, July 25, 1871, Gideon Welles MSS, New York Public Library.
35. Welles, "Admiral Farragut and New Orleans," *loc. cit.*, 675 ff.; David Dixon Porter, *Incidents and Anecdotes of the Civil War* (New York, 1885), 63 ff.; West, *op. cit.*, 16 ff.; Richard S. West, Jr., The Second Admiral (New York, 1937), 11; Charles Lee Lewis, *David Glasgow Farragut* (Annapolis, 1943), II, 5-14, with a good discussion of the conflicting evidence given by Welles and Porter. Although Butler believed that he had been the originator of the New Orleans expedition (Butler-Col. Irwin, May 5, 1890, letterbooks, Butler MSS), there is no longer much doubt that Welles' account is substantially correct.
36. *Butler Cor.*, I, 279-84; *O. R.*, Series III, I, 652-56.
37. William Schouler, *op. cit.*, I, 266-68.
38. *O. R.*, Series III, I, 656; *Butler's Book*, 324.
39. Murray, *op. cit.*, 54; *Butler Cor.*, I, 294.
40. *Ibid.*, 293.
41. *O. R.*, Series III, I, 840 ff.; *Correspondence Between Governor Andrew and Maj. Gen. Butler*, 53 ff.

# NOTES

42. *O. R.*, Series III, I, 861. Butler heard that Sumner had received a box with voluminous manuscripts of evidence against the General from the Governor, with a request that Lincoln be informed. *Butler Cor.*, I, 309, 298-99.

43. *Correspondence Between Governor Andrew and Maj. Gen. Butler*, 52; *O. R.*, Series III, I, 756.

44. *Correspondence Between Governor Andrew and Maj. Gen. Butler*, 53 ff.

45. He also wrote: "I am compelled to declare . . . that the whole course of proceedings under Major General Butler in this Commonwealth seems to have been designed and adopted simply to afford means to persons of bad character to make money unscrupulously, and to encourage men whose unfitness excluded them from any appointment by me to the volunteer military service to hope for such appointment over Massachusetts troops from other authority . . ." Butler had appointed his brother Andrew commissioner of subsistence.

46. *Correspondence Between Governor Andrew and Maj. Gen. Butler*, 61.

47. *O. R.*, Series III, I, 851-52. He did, however, yield on the question of the Salem Light Artillery. *Correspondence Between Governor Andrew and Maj. Gen. Butler*, 70.

48. *Butler Cor.*, I, 315-18, 314.

49. *Ibid.*, 321-22, 330; Pearson, *op. cit.*, I, 303; *O. R.*, Series III, I, 810-11. The resulting publication was the *Correspondence Between Governor Andrew and Maj. Gen. Butler*, but to Butler's disgust, it did not contain the entire correspondence. *Butler Cor.*, I, 331.

50. *Ibid.*, 335. Charles Sumner hastened to inform Andrew that the General had not received any private telegrams from him, but he deplored the controversy. Sumner-Andrew, February 9, 1862, John A. Andrew MSS.

51. *Butler Cor.*, I, 310.

52. *O. R.*, Series III, I, 777; Bowen, *op. cit.*, 453 ff.

53. *Butler Cor.*, I, 318-19.

54. George C. Gorham, *Life and Public Services of Edwin M. Stanton* (Boston, 1899), 313; Welles, "Admiral Farragut and New Orleans," *loc. cit.*, 820. In a cabinet meeting on January 13, McClellan, hard pressed to do something with his army, said he needed men and was not at all sure whether he would let Butler go to Ship Island. Lossing, *op. cit.*, II, 355.

55. T. Harry Williams, *Lincoln and the Radicals* (Madison, 1941), 87.

56. T. Harry Williams, *Lincoln and His Generals* (New York, 1952), 50, 70.

57. *Ibid.*, 54-60; "General M. C. Meigs on the Conduct of the War," *American Historical Review*, XXVI (1921), 292 ff.

58. *Reports of the Joint Committee on the Conduct of the War*, 37th Cong., 3d Sess. (Washington, 1863), I, 75; II, 247-48; *Butler's Book*, 331-33; Williams, *Lincoln and the Radicals*, 87.

59. *Butler's Book*, 333.

60. Randall, *Lincoln, The President*, II, 55-64.

61. Gorham, *op. cit.*, 314; *Butler Cor.*, I, 323.

62. Memorandum by Benjamin F. Butler, January, 1862, Edwin M. Stanton MSS, Library of Congress, Washington, D. C.

63. Gorham, *op. cit.*, 314.

64. *O. R.*, Series I, VI, 677-78.

65. Welles, "Admiral Farragut and New Orleans," *loc. cit.*, 820. According to Welles, Butler came to tell Fox his troops were at Fortress Monroe with orders to disembark. He apparently enlisted Fox's aid to overrule McClellan's unfavorable report of January 24. On January 26, he wrote to his wife: "This wearisome business drags its slow length along, day by day . . . . Two weeks I have been waiting for a decision that should have been made in an hour by any person fit to be trusted with the affair at all . . . . Mr. Stanton has done all and more than I could ask of him . . . . After waiting day by day till Friday, I then got a report by McClellan *against* my *expedition*. By dint of hard work and personal exertion I have got that overruled." Three days later, he was able to issue sailing orders to Shepley. *Butler Cor.*, I, 330-31, 333-34. The account in *Butler's Book*, 334 ff., is vague and not very trustworthy. Cf. Willis Weaver, "A Criticism of Butler's Book," MSS. Yet Weaver does not cite Welles and is inclined to give full credence to Gorham.

66. John T. Morse (ed.), *Diary of Gideon Welles* (Boston and New York, 1911), II, 60-61. That Butler did not know of the destination before is evident in view of his preparation for other places. *O. R.*, Series I, LIII, 507.

67. *Butler Cor.*, I, 335, 345, 349.

68. Pearson, *op. cit.*, I, 305 ff. To Mrs. Andrew, Lincoln said: "Well, how does your husband and Butler get on — has the Governor commissioned these men yet?" Mrs. Andrew hesitated, but her friend, Frank Howe, replied: "We are informed, Sir, that you have commissioned them." "No," said the President, "but I am getting mad with the Governor and Butler both." A few weeks earlier, he had pleaded earnestly that the Governor "arrange somehow with General Butler to officer his two unofficered regiments." Later, these became the Thirtieth and Thirty-First, but at the time, Andrew insisted his antagonist be satisfied with the Twenty-Sixth and Twenty-Eighth. Basler, *op. cit.*, V, 96.

69. *O. R.*, Series III, I, 896.

70. *Ibid.*, 897; Schouler, *op. cit.*, I, 276; Charles Loring-John A. Andrew, February 9, 1862, John A. Andrew MSS.

71. *O. R.*, Series I, VI, 704; Series III, I, 897; *Butler Cor.*, I, 330. Charles M. Wheldon, the rejected commander of the Western Bay State Regiment, also found a place on Butler's staff. Bowen, *op. cit.*, 466.

72. Gorham, *op. cit.*, 314; *Butler's Book*, 334 ff.

73. T. Harry Williams, *Lincoln and His Generals*, 62 ff.

74. George B. McClellan, *McClellan's Own Story* (New York, 1887), 212-13; *O. R.*, Series I, V, 50.

75. *Butler Cor.*, 1, 363. Butler maintained that, in Lincoln's presence, he said to Stanton: "I am going to take New Orleans or you will never see me again," whereupon the Secretary allegedly answered: "You take New Orleans and you shall be Lieutenant General." He also remembered a report that McClellan's father-in-law had said, "I guess we have found a hole to bury this Yankee elephant in."

# NOTES

## CHAPTER IX  Off for The Father of Waters
### (Pages 98 to 106)

1. He had dissolved his law partnership a week earlier and brought his will up to date. Hand memorandum, February 17, 1862; Last Will and Testament of Benjamin F. Butler, February 20, 1862, Butler MSS. He left $140,000 to be invested for his mother; the rest, with minor exceptions, to his wife. It is obvious that he was a wealthy man before the war.
2. *Butler's Book*, 327-50; O. R. (Navies), Series I, VI, 674; *Butler Cor.*, I, 363-69; *Confidential Correspondence of Gustavus Vasa Fox*, I, 430-32.
3. "Letters of General Thomas Williams, 1862," *The American Historical Review*, XVI (1908-09), 307.
4. J. R. Salla-Richardson, January 11, 1862, Butler MSS.
5. Lossing, *op. cit.*, II, 325-26; Parton, *op. cit.*, 198 ff.; Moore, *op. cit.*, III, 449 ff. Butler disapproved of the proclamation. Butler-Major Watson, December 18, 1861, Butler MSS.
6. Murray, *op. cit.*, 72.
7. *Butler's Book*, 356-58; *Butler Cor.*, I, 392-94, 401.
8. General Lorenzo Thomas-A. J. Butler, February 6, 1862, 1954 boxes, Butler MSS.
9. O. R., Series I, VI, 706-07; Howe, *op. cit.*, 116; Thomas Williams, *op. cit.*, 308.
10. *Confidential Correspondence of Gustavus Vasa Fox*, I, 307; O. R. (Navies), Series I, XVIII, 109.
11. *Ibid.*, 90.
12. Loyall Farragut, *The Life of David Glasgow Farragut* (New York, 1882), 204.
13. Charles Lee Lewis, *David Glasgow Farragut* (Annapolis, 1943), II, 1-30.
14. O. R. (Navies), Series I, XVIII, 15-23, 252, 393.
15. Farragut, *op. cit.*, 216. A chain barred the upstream passage.
16. O. R., Series I, LIII, 517.
17. Murray, *op. cit.*, 72.
18. Thomas Williams, *op. cit.*, 307 ff.
19. J. H. Croushore (ed.), John William De Forest, *A Volunteer's Adventures*, (New Haven, 1946), 8-9; Murray, *op. cit.*, 73-84; *Butler Cor.*, I, 395-98.
20. Foltz, *op. cit.*, 215.
21. O. R., Series I, LIII, 521-22.
22. Murray, *op. cit.*, 90-95; Thomas Williams, *op. cit.*, 310.
23. Foltz, *op. cit.*, 215.
24. *Correspondence Between the War Department and General Lovell Relating to the Defense of New Orleans* (Richmond, 1863), 15, 36, 59; Lewis, *op. cit.*, II, 41-42.
25. *Correspondence Between the War Department and General Lovell Relating to the Defense of New Orleans*, 56.
26. *Ibid.*, 59; Lewis, *op. cit.*, 42.
27. O. R. (Navies), Series I, XVIII, 134-37, 152-53; *Battles and Leaders*, II, 22-55.
28. Lewis, *op. cit.*, II, 50 ff.
29. Howe, *op. cit.*, 117.
30. *Butler's Book*, 365-67.

31. *O. R.* (Navies), Series I, XVIII, 153-55; *Battles and Leaders,* II, 22-55; Lewis, *op. cit.,* II, 55-64; West, *Porter,* 133-41.
32. *O. R.,* Series I, VI, 713.
33. *Butler Cor.,* I, 422.
34. *Ibid.,* 426; *O. R.,* Series I, VI, 713.
35. *Butler Cor.,* I, 426-27; *Butler's Book,* 367-69.
36. *Ibid.;* Thomas Williams, *op. cit.,* 313-14; Farragut, *op. cit.,* 241.
37. *O. R.* (Navies), Series I, XVIII, 280.
38. *Ibid.*
39. Thomas Williams, *op. cit.,* 314; West, *Porter,* 142; *Butler Cor.,* I, 227-28. In his report, Butler made a point of the fact that the larger portion of the garrison surrendered to his pickets and that no shot had been fired at them for three days.
40. *Ibid.*
41. West, *Porter,* 135.
42. *Confidential Correspondence of Gustavus Vasa Fox,* II, 131.
43. Parton, *op. cit.,* 238, 251; Weitzel's Report, May 5, 1862, 1954 boxes, Butler MSS; William T. Meredith-Butler, May 1, 1885, 1954 boxes, Butler MSS; *O. R.,* Series I, XV, 435.
44. *Ibid.,* 461-62; *O. R.* (Navies), Series I, XVIII, 390 ff.
45. Boston *Herald,* May 5, 1889; Washington *Star,* May 6, 7, 1889, clippings in Butler MSS.
46. New York *Times,* May 7, 8, 1889.
47. *O. R.* (Navies), Series I, XVIII, 271; Porter, *op. cit.,* 47 ff.
48. Lewis, *op. cit.,* II, 76-77.
49. Horace Greeley, *The American Conflict* (Hartford, 1866), II, 81 ff. The emphasis is on Butler's role.
50. *Butler's Book,* 358 ff.; West, *Porter,* 330-31. In later years, Butler became Farragut's lawyer. Correspondence of April 29, 1866, October 3, 1870, Butler MSS.
51. *O. R.* (Navies), Series I, XVIII, 152, 158.
52. *Ibid.,* 770.
53. New Orleans *Tägliche Deutsche Zeitung,* April 27, 1862.
54. *Ibid.;* James Morris Morgan, *Recollections of a Rebel Reefer* (Boston, 1917), 75-76; *O. R.* (Navies), Series I, XVIII, 229.
55. *Ibid.,* 230-31.
56. *Ibid.,* 231-32, 771.
57. *Ibid.; Battles and Leaders,* II, 96; New Orleans *Tägliche Deutsche Zeitung,* April 27, 1862; *Butler Cor.,* I, 482-83; *Butler's Book,* 439.
58. New Orleans Daily *True Delta,* May 4, 1862; Foltz, *op. cit.,* 23; *O. R.* (Navies), Series I, XVIII, 232-33.
59. *Ibid.,* 233-37; New Orleans *Tägliche Deutsche Zeitung,* April 30, 1862; New Orleans Daily *Picayune,* April 30, 1862.
60. *O. R.* (Navies), Series I, XVIII, 771.
61. *Battles and Leaders,* II, 93.
62. *O. R.* (Navies), Series I, XVIII, 771.
63. Albert B. Paine, *A Sailor of Fortune, Personal Memoirs of Captain B. S. Osbon* (New York, 1906), 209.
64. *Butler Cor.,* I, 425-28.
65. Foltz, *op. cit.,* 234.

# NOTES

CHAPTER X  "*Picayune Butler's Come To Town*"
(Pages 107 to 121)

1. De Forest, *op. cit.*, 21-22; Howe, *op. cit.*, 120; *Battles and Leaders*, II, 16-17; Eleanor Early, *New Orleans Holiday* (New York, 1947), 158; Lyle Saxon, *Fabulous New Orleans* (New York, 1928), 251.
2. Kate Mason Rowland and Mrs. M. L. Croxwell (eds.), *The Journal of Julia Le Grand* (Richmond, 1911), 40; *Battles and Leaders*, II, 21; Thomas Ewing Dabney, "The Butler Regime in Louisiana," *The Louisiana Historical Quarterly*, XXVII (1944), 489 ff.
3. New Orleans Evening *True Delta*, May 2, 1862; Parton, *op. cit.*, 279 ff.; Thomas Williams, *op. cit.*, 315; Foltz, *op. cit.*, 234; Dabney, *op. cit.*, 495. The song about a barber went as follows:
"Picayune Butler's coming, coming
Picayune Butler's come to town
Ahoo! Ahoo! Ahoo!"
4. New York *World*, May 24, 1862; New Orleans *Tägliche Deutsche Zeitung*, May 3, 1862; Parton, *op. cit.*, 283-84. A minor variation appears in *Butler's Book*, 374.
5. Parton, *op. cit.*, 284; New York *World*, May 24, 1862. New Orleans was thrilled by the story that Soulé had refused Butler's proferred hand. *The Journal of Julia Le Grand*, 46.
6. *Butler's Book*, 374-77; Parton, *op. cit.*, 287-89.
7. *Butler Cor.*, I, 439.
8. *The Journal of Julia Le Grand*, 44; George N. Carpenter, *History of the Eighth Regiment, Vermont Voluteers, 1861-1865* (Boston, 1886), 38.
9. W. Goldswaithe-Butler, May 3, 1862, Butler MSS.
10. New Orleans Evening *True Delta*, May 2, 1862; *Butler Cor.*, I, 440.
11. *Ibid.*, 433.
12. *Ibid.*; Thomas Williams, *op. cit.*, 315; Parton, *op. cit.*, 291 ff.; *Butler's Book*, 378 ff.; Howard P. Johnson, "New Orleans Under General Butler," *Louisiana Historical Quarterly*, XXIV (1941), 469-70. Johnson calls attention to the discrepancies between Butler and Parton. According to the latter, the City Council accepted Butler's propositions only on the next day; according to the former, agreement was reached during the evening conference.
13. *Butler Cor.*, I, 440.
14. Parton, *op. cit.*, 298.
15. *Butler Cor.*, I, 432-33, 492.
16. *Ibid.*, 442, 443, 458.
17. Lincoln announced the lifting of the blockade from Port Royal, Beaufort, and New Orleans on May 13, 1862. The order went into effect as of June 1 (for New Orleans). New Orleans Daily *Picayune*, June, 1, 1862.
18. Dabney, *op. cit.*, 507; Williams, *op. cit.*, 316; Carpenter, *op. cit.*, 38.
19. George S. Denison-James Denison, July 6, 1862, Denison MSS, Library of Congress, Washington, D. C.; New Orleans Daily *True Delta*, May 31, 1862.
20. *The Journal of Julia Le Grand*, 44.
21. Foltz, *op. cit.*, 237.

22. Arthur C. Cole, *The Irrepressible Conflict, 1850-1865* (New York, 1934), 395-97; *Two Months in the Confederate States*, By an English Merchant, in Etolia S. Basso, *The World from Jackson Square* (New York, 1948), 263.
23. Carpenter, *op. cit.*, 38.
24. *Ibid.*, 39; Parton, *op. cit.*, 325.
25. B. B. Floyd-Butler, January 31, 1892, Butler MSS.
26. *Butler's Book*, 416.
27. *Ibid.*, 416 ff.; *Butler Cor.*, I, 581; II, 35.
28. He copied the order from an old English ordinance which he vaguely remembered.
29. *O. R.*, Series I, XV, 426.
30. B. A. Williams (ed.), Mary Boykin Chestnut, *A Diary From Dixie* (Boston, 1949), 224. Cf. Marion Southwood, *Beauty and Booty* (New York, 1867), expecially 109.
31. Jackson *Mississippian*, quoted in New York *Tribune*, June 14, 1862.
32. *O. R.*, Series I, X, Part II, 531; XI, Part I, 979; LII, Part II, 360.
33. *Ibid.*, Series I, XV, 743.
34. *Ibid.*, Series II, IV, 852-55.
35. Chestnut, *op. cit.*, 224.
36. *Punch*, July 5, 1862.
37. The *Saturday Review* devoted a whole article to Butler's alleged infamies. *Saturday Review*, XIV (October 18, 1862), 463-64.
38. Hansard's *Parliamentary Debates*, 3d Series, V, 167, 533, 611.
39. Jackson *Mississippian*, June 29, 1862, clipping in Butler MSS; Harding, *op. cit.*, 40; Robert Ferguson, *America During and After the War* (London, 1866), 98-100; E. Merton Coulter, *The Confederate States of America* (New Orleans, 1950), 370.
40. *O. R.* (Navies), Series I, XVIII, 773.
41. *Butler Cor.*, I, 581; II, 35; *Butler's Book*, 414-25; New York *Weekly Tribune*, July 26, 1862; Carpenter, *op. cit.*, 39.
42. Cf. New York *World*, May 30, 31, 1862.
43. Alexander K. McClure, *Recollections of a Half Century* (Salem, Mass., 1902), 385-87; Nicolay and Hay, *op. cit.*, V, 284.
44. *Butler's Book*, 421.
45. *Harper's Weekly*, July 12, August 16, 1862; New York *Tribune*, June 19, 1862. Publishing houses began to advertise "A first rate card picture of Gen. Butler" for 25 cents. *Ibid.*, June 9, 1862.
46. *Papers Relating to Foreign Affairs*, 1862, 127.
47. McClure, *op. cit.*, 385-87; Nicolay and Hay, *op. cit.*, V, 283-84.
48. *Butler Correspondence*, I, 496-97; *Harper's Weekly*, June 14, 1862.
49. *O. R.*, Series I, LIII, 526.
50. *Butler Cor.*, I, 498-99.
51. *Ibid.*; Monroe-Butler, May 16, 1862, 1954 boxes, Butler MSS.
52. Monroe-Butler, May 17, 1862, 1954 boxes, Butler MSS.
53. *Butler Cor.*, I, 499-501.
54. *Ibid.*, Parton, *op. cit.*, 336; Dabney, *op. cit.*, 512.
55. *Ibid.*
56. Edward Pollard, *The Lost Cause* (New York, 1866), 257.
57. Porter, *op. cit.*, 72-73.

# NOTES 285

58. Record of the Military Commission, May 15, 1862, Butler MSS.
59. *Butler Cor.*, I, 482-83.
60. *Butler's Book*, 439 ff.
61. *Butler Cor.*, I, 573-74.
62. Morgan Dix (ed.), *Memoirs of John Adams Dix* (New York, 1883), I, 371.
63. *Butler Cor.*, I, 574-75.
64. New Orleans *Delta*, June 8, 1862; *Battles and Leaders*, III, 582.
65. *Butler Cor.*, I, 520-21, 588 ff.; II, 1; Thomas Major-C. A. Good, October 24, 1883, letterbooks, Butler MSS.
66. Pollard, *op. cit.*, 257; Jefferson Davis, *The Rise and Fall of the Confederate Government* (New York, 1881), II, 231-32; Southwood, *op. cit.*, 107-08.
67. Johnson, *op. cit.*, 490.
68. Coulter, *op. cit.*, 72-73.
69. Pollard, *op. cit.*, 260.
70. Southwood, *op. cit.*, 107-08, maintained that a young boy, Adolphe Harper, was the culprit, but managed to leave the city before Butler could apprehend him. It is impossible to determine whether Mumford was the chief offender, but it is certain that he was one of the party which tore down the flag. Cf. Johnson, *op. cit.*, 489.
71. *O. R.*, Series II, IV, 134-36, 793, 835. The Confederate authorities maintained Butler had no right to execute the prisoner as the alleged offense occurred before the city had formally surrendered. Since the Federal fleet had the city completely at its mercy at the time, the argument seems specious.
72. James D. Richardson, *A Compilation of the Messages and Papers of the Confederacy* (Nashville, 1904), I, 269.
73. McClure, *op. cit.*, 385. He befriended Mrs. Mumford after the war, secured government jobs for her, and looked after her welfare after she was, as he put it, "reformed out" during Hayes' Administration, to make room "for reformers' nieces." *Butler's Book*, 443-46; Mary Mumford-Butler, August 19, 1866; July 7, 1870; September 1, 1876; February 19, 1877; July 2, 1877; July 17, 24, 1877; August 5, 1877; January 17, August 19, 1878; April 16, 1881, Butler MSS.
74. *Butler Cor.*, II, 189-90.
75. *Ibid.*, I, 563, 574-76.
76. *Ibid.*, I, 619; *O. R.*, Series III, II, 154 ff., 172.
77. Notices appeared in the newspapers to the effect that the subscribers denied having taken the oath. New Orleans Daily *Picayune*, August 12, 1862. For the oath, cf. Parton, *op. cit.*, 462. Parton maintained 11,723 citizens and 2,499 neutrals had taken their respective oaths by August 7; Johnson, in the Adjutant General's Office, was able to account for only 6,000. Johnson, *op. cit.*, 500.
78. Oath of allegiance, June 29, 1862, written in Butler's own hand and signed by S. Benjamin and B. F. Bryan, Butler MSS.
79. *O. R.*, Series I, XV, 899; *Butler Cor.*, 305-06.
80. *Ibid.*, 480; *Butler's Book*, 506.
81. *Butler Cor.*, I, 490-95, 504, 481.
82. New Orleans *True Delta*, May 21, 1862.
83. Southwood, *op. cit.*, 57.

84. Statements in Smith Case, May-June, 1862, Butler MSS; *Butler Cor.*, II, 14.
85. Instead of turning the kegs over to the Government, Butler kept them in his own possession. He tried to have the Government accept responsibility for the transaction but was unsuccessful. Consequently, he had to negotiate personally with Smith's attorney and was eventually forced to give up his kegs. The settlement also required Butler to pay the legal costs of the negotiations. *Ibid.*, III, 7, 476-77, 560-63, 595-96; IV, 385; V, 280, 352, 340-41, 411, 420, 434, 524, 689-91; Edwards Pierrepont, *A Review By Judge Pierrepont of Gen. Butler's Defense Before the House of Representatives in Relation to the New Orleans Gold* (New York, 1865); John K. Hackett-Butler, March 16, 1866, Butler MSS.
86. *Butler Cor.*, II, 52-53; H. A. Rathbone-Butler, June 26, 1862; Memorial Against Orders 29 and 30, filed May 30, 1862, Butler MSS.
87. *O. R.*, Series II, 616, 675; *Butler Cor.*, I, 513-14. Unionists furnished Butler with a list of leading secessionists. Memorandum of May 8, 1862, Butler MSS.
88. New York *Tribune*, June 19, 1862; *Butler Cor.*, II, 24-25; *Butler's Book*, 510 ff.; *O. R.*, Series II, IV, 151, 880-85.
89. Southwood, *op. cit.*, 148-49.
90. Ishbel Ross, *Rebel Rose* (New York, 1954), 166-67; Eugenia Levy Phillips, "A Southern Woman's Story of Her Imprisonment During the War of 1861 and 1862," Philip Phillips MSS, Library of Congress, Washington, D. C.
91. *Ibid.*; Philip Phillips, "A Summary of the Principal Events of My Life," Phillips MSS.
92. *Butler Cor.*, II, 36. The order was couched in the following terms: "It is . . . ordered that she be not 'regarded and treated as a common woman,' of whom no officer or soldier is bound to take notice, but as an uncommon, bad, and dangerous woman . . ."
93. Originally, Fidel Keller, the bookseller who had exhibited the skeleton, had been allowed social intercourse with Mrs. Phillips, but he asked to be exempted from such association. The orders concerning him were modified accordingly. *Ibid.*, II, 24. Southerners were shocked; they were sure that Keller had been made to understand that Mrs. Phillips was a prostitute. Southwood, *op. cit.*, 148-149. It is possible that Butler's severity toward the lady had something to do with the fact that she was Jewish while he was anti-Semitic. Cf. 301, n. 31, below.
94. *O. R.*, Series II, IV, 516; New Orleans *Delta*, November 20, 1862.
95. Cf. Mrs. R. L. Hunt-Salmon P. Chase, November 8, 1862, Salmon P. Chase MSS, Library of Congress, Washington, D. C.
96. *Butler Cor.*, II, 57.
97. *O. R.*, Series II, IV, 707.
98. Undated note in 1872 folder, 1954 boxes, Butler MSS.
99. *Butler Cor.*, I, 476; II, 130; Dabney, *op. cit.*, 500 ff.
100. New Orleans *Delta*, July 15, 1862; Carpenter, *op. cit.*, 44.
101. New York Weekly *Tribune*, June 24, 1862.
102. New Orleans Daily *Picayune*, September 28, 1862.
103. *Butler Cor.*, II, 475, 480. Dabney, *op. cit.*, 590.
104. *Butler Cor.*, I, 477.

**NOTES** 287

105. W. F. Leacock-Butler, September 26, 1862; Butler-William Wright, February 11, 1889, Butler MSS and letterbooks.
106. Parton, *op. cit.*, 483. It was after this incident that Butler sent north the offending divine and two others. *O. R.*, Series II, IV, 650.
107. Southwood, *op. cit.*, 111.
108. Butler-Mother Superior Santa Clara Maria, September 2, 1862, Butler MSS.
109. *Butler's Book*, 421 ff.; Washington *New National Era*, May 4, 1871, clipping in Butler MSS.
110. Johnson, *op. cit.*, 472 ff.; Dabney, *op. cit.*, 505 ff.
111. *Butler Cor.*, I, 564, II, 30; *O. R.*, Series I, XXVI, Part I, 735.
112. *Butler Cor.*, I, 456-57, 554-55.
113. *Ibid.*, II, 151.
114. *O. R.*, Series III, II, 720 ff.; 567 ff.; *Butler's Book*, 436.
115. *Ibid.*, 395 ff.; Mary Newman to her sister, May 28, 1862, Butler MSS.
116. J. Chandler Gregg, *Life in the Army* (Philadelphia, 1868), 161; Porter, *op. cit.*, 72-73; Lossing, *op. cit.*, II, 349.
117. R. K. Smith-Butler, May 5, 1862, Butler MSS; Foltz, *op. cit.*, 253.
118. *Butler's Book*, 402; George Denison-Chase, August 11, 1862, Salmon P. Chase MSS.
119. *Butler's Book*, 408; George Denison-D. C. Denison, September 25, 1862, Denison MSS.
120. Southwood, *op. cit.*, 182; New York *Times*, June 6, 1869; Springfield *Republican*, December 31, 1878; Hoar, *op. cit.*, I, 334; William M. Caskey, *Secession and Restoration in Louisiana* (New Orleans, 1938), 48.

CHAPTER XI   *"Butler Must Go"*
(Pages 122 to 134)

1. E. J. Sherman-Butler, October 10, 1891, Butler MSS.
2. Dabney, *op. cit.*, 491 ff.; Parton, *op. cit.*, 486 ff.
3. *Butler Cor.*, I, 445 ff., 465.
4. *Ibid.*, 490 ff., 521, 533, 551, 579, 585, 612, 628.
5. *Ibid.*, II, 422-23; Howe, *op. cit.*, 128-29.
6. Edward L. Tinker, *Crescent City* (New York, 1953), 94.
7. *O. R.*, Series II, V, 792.
8. W. P. Webster-Butler, October 23, 1864, Butler MSS. The letter contains information about "Jackson's" ownership of Confederate cotton bonds. Cf. Webster & Craig-William Webster, April 21, 1864, Butler MSS.
9. Howe, *op. cit.*, 128-29; Southwood, *op. cit.*, 86.
10. *Ibid.*
11. *Diary and Correspondence of Salmon P. Chase*, American Historical Association Report, 1902, II, 320.
12. Wickham Hoffman-Hamilton Fish, September 30, 1862, Hamilton Fish MSS, Library of Congress.
13. *Diary and Correspondence of Salmon P. Chase*, 320. Denison decided later that his suspicions were unfounded. *Ibid.*, 327, 329; George Denison-James Denison, November 14, 1862, Denison MSS.

14. New York *World*, December 4, 1862.
15. *Confidential Correspondence of Gustavus Vasa Fox*, II, 105.
16. Jones, *op. cit.*, I, 187.
17. Basler, *op. cit.*, V, 552-53.
18. Signed receipt, January 1, 1863, Butler MSS, 1862 box.
19. *Butler Cor.*, II, 393.
20. William N. Orcutt, "Ben Butler and the 'Stolen Spoons'," *North American Review*, CCVII (January, 1918), 67 ff.
21. *Ibid.*; *Butler Cor.*, III, 531 ff.; Merrill, *op. cit.*, 36. For a full discussion, cf. Murray M. Horowitz, "Ben Butler, Making of a Radical," unpublished doctoral dissertation, Columbia University, 1955, 89-100.
22. *Battles and Leaders*, II, 15.
23. *Butler Cor.*, I, 450-51, 474-76, 591.
24. Papers Relating to Foreign Affairs, 1862, 133, 259-60, 265; for later cases, cf. J. J. Burrowes-George Coppell, September 28, 1862; James Dacres-Lord Lyons, August 26, 1862, Butler MSS.
25. *O. R.*, Series III, II, 117, 119; Sam Ward-Salmon P. Chase, May 30, 1862, Chase MSS.
26. *Papers Relating to Foreign Affairs*, 1862, 420-23, 426-27, 625-29; *Butler Cor.*, I, 506-07.
27. *O. R.*, Series III, II, 141, Series I, XV, 471; *Papers Relating to Foreign Affairs*, 1862, 423.
28. *O. R.*, Series III, II, 115; *Butler Cor.*, I, 552-53.
29. *Ibid.*, I, 581.
30. *Ibid.*, 580; Bernard C. Steiner, *Life of Reverdy Johnson* (Baltimore, 1914), 54.
31. *Butler Cor.*, I, 595-604.
32. *O. R.*, Series III, II, 179.
33. 37th Congress, 3d Sess., *Executive Document No. 16*.
34. *Butler Cor.*, II, 98-102; Johnson-Butler, July 26, 1862, Butler MSS.
35. *O. R.*, Series III, II, 571-73. He maintained Johnson was an agent of the Confederates and that another such mission "would render the city untenable." For Johnson's angry denials, cf. Johnson-James Parton, May 17, 1864, James Parton MSS, Harvard University, Cambridge, Massachusetts.
36. *Papers Relating to Foreign Affairs*, 1862, 431-32, 634 ff., 282-83, 629. For the Administration's endorsement of Johnson's actions, cf. Seward-Johnson, September 27, 1862, Reverdy Johnson MSS, Library of Congress.
37. *The Journal of Julia Le Grand*, 52.
38. *O. R.*, Series I, XV, 612; *Butler Cor.*, II, 192-93, 274-75, 339-48, 368; Gabriel G. Tarsara-Seward, June 28, 1862, August 26, 1862, Butler MSS.
39. *O. R.*, Series III, II, 423, 567 ff., 580-82, 674, 720; *Butler Cor.*, II, 219 ff. The Acting Prussian Consul aroused Butler's special ire as he was Judah P. Benjamin's brother-in-law.
40. At various times, he was in trouble with the consuls of Great Britain, France, Russia, Prussia, Spain, Holland, Belgium, Greece, and Switzerland.
41. *O. R.*, Series III, II, 766-79.
42. *Battles and Leaders*, III, 582 ff.
43. *O. R.* (Navies), Series I, XVIII, 491.
44. *Ibid.*, 507; Thomas Williams, *op. cit.*, 317; *Butler Cor.*, I, 539 ff.

# NOTES

45. *Ibid.*, 562-63; *O. R.* (Navies), Series I, XVIII, 521.
46. *Ibid.*, 521, 543, 558, 576, 577, 579, 580, 708; Lewis, *op. cit.*, II, 434.
47. Williams, *op. cit.*, 322-23; Murray, *op. cit.*, 108 ff.; Howe, *op. cit.*, 123; *Battles and Leaders*, III, 582 ff.
48. *O. R.*, Series I, XV, 514-15; 518-19; X, Part I, 671; XVII, Part I, 26; John C. Ropes, *The Story of the Civil War* (New York, 1898), II, 384.
49. *Butler Cor.*, II, 82-83.
50. *Ibid.*, 155, 172-73; George Denison-D. C. Denison, August 10, 1862, Denison MSS. He spread word that 2,000 had routed 6,000.
51. Moore, *op. cit.*, V, 308.
52. *Battles and Leaders*, III, 583; *O. R.*, Series I, XV, 545. Of the *ca.* 2,500 men who participated on each side, the Federals suffered 383 casualties to the Confederates' 456.
53. Butler had stated that the Confederate ram *Arkansas* "hardly awaited the gallant attack of the *Essex* (Porter's vessel), but followed the example of her sister by her own destruction." *O. R.*, Series I, LIII, 531-32.
54. *Butler Cor.*, II, 147-48; West, *Porter*, 151 ff. Porter maintained that he had been unable to get prompt assistance from the army when he wanted to tow his ships, because the tows were being used for private speculation.
55. *Butler Cor.*, II, 245-47.
56. *Ibid.*, 13 ff., 400-02, 465-66; Butler-Sumner, November 15, 1862, Sumner MSS.
57. *Battles and Leaders*, III, 584.
58. *Butler Cor.*, IV, 32-38; undated memo, G. O. 91, 1862 box, Butler MSS; *Diary and Correspondence of Salmon P. Chase*, 327; George Denison-Chase, October 8, 1862, Chase MSS; George Denison- C. C. Denison, November 14, 1862, Denison MSS; Butler- J. F. Fite, December 12, 1882, letterbooks, Butler MSS; Basler *op. cit.*, V, 428-29.
59. *Harper's Weekly* was one of the magazines extremely favorable to Butler.
60. *O. R.*, Series I, XV, 439 ff.; General Weitzel-Butler, October 29, 1862, Butler MSS.
61. Cecil H. Cutts, *Life and Public Services of General John Wolcott Phelps* (Boston, 1887), 29 ff.; *Butler Cor.*, I, 509-10, 613-15; II, 125 ff.; 145 ff.; George Denison-D. C. Denison, July 29, 1862, Denison MSS.
62. New York Weekly *Tribune*, August 16, 1862; *Commonwealth*, October 11, 1862.
63. *Butler Cor.*, II, 109-10.
64. *Ibid.*, 447-50; *O. R.*, Series I, XV, 588; Parton, *op. cit.*, 492 ff.; Carpenter, *op. cit.*, 43.
65. *Butler Cor.*, II, 209-11; *Diary and Correspondence of Salmon P. Chase*, 312, 315; George Denison-James Denison, November 14, 1862, Denison MSS.
66. *Butler Cor.*, II, 131-34, 323-24; 541-43; Chase-George Denison, September 8, 1862, Denison MSS.
67. *Butler Cor.*, II, 147-48, 282-83, 503-04; New Orleans *Delta*, September 2, 1862. Thaddeus Stevens spoke of Butler's recall as a finality two months before it occurred. Thaddeus Stevens-S. Stevens, September 5, 1862, Stevens MSS, Library of Congress.
68. *Butler Cor.*, II, 248, 256-59; 271-73; 282-83, 286-87, 297, 503-04.

69. *Two Months in the Confederate States,* loc. cit., 261-62. The writer remarked: "As we were being made fast to the wharf, I noticed a Federal officer in undress push quietly through the few score staring Irishmen and Negroes . . . and slip aboard, followed by a sort of serving-man. This, I found, was no less a personage than General Butler himself who had come . . . to meet his wife . . . . I could not help looking almost with pity on that one unarmed man, for whose blood a whole nation was thirsting."
70. O. R., Series I, XV, 558, 572.
71. *Butler Cor.,* II, 570-71; Harrington, op. cit., 85-86.
72. Bonanzo-Chase, September 6, 1862; Denison-Mrs. Denison, August 25, 1862, Chase and Denison MSS.
73. Basler, op. cit., V, 462-63; Caskey, op. cit., 55-65; New Orleans *Delta,* December 4, 1862.
74. Harrington, op. cit., 86.
75. *Butler Cor.,* II, 469. So did Welles and Fox. *Confidential Correspondence of Gustavus Vasa Fox,* II, 445-47; *Diary of Gideon Welles,* I, 209-10.
76. Flower, op. cit., 362-64.
77. Thornton Kirkland Lothrop, *William Henry Seward* (Boston, 1898), 378.
78. O. R., Series I, XV, 590.
79. *Butler Cor.,* II, 469.
80. *Butler's Book,* 529 ff.
81. O. R., Series I, XV, 613; Memorandum of Conversation with General Butler, December 18, 1862, N. P. Banks MSS, Essex Institute, Salem, Massachusetts.
82. *Butler Cor.,* II, 547.
83. O. R., Series I, XV, 610.
84. *Butler Cor.,* II, 554-57.
85. His name was used to frighten children in New Orleans. Grace King, *New Orleans* (New York, 1904), 304.
86. New York *World,* December 9, 1862.
87. *Harper's Weekly,* VII (January 10, 1863), 18; New York Weekly *Tribune,* January 10, 1863; *Commonwealth,* January 10, 1863; Gurowski, op. cit., II, 65.
88. Dabney, op. cit.; Johnson, op. cit.
89. Merrill, op. cit., 38. The author presents a summary of the trial balances of Butler's fortune in the Butler MSS. According to these figures, no great increase of wealth occurred during the war. The figures are: 1862: $163,635; 1866, $201,908. In view of the substantial sum Butler left to his mother, however, it would seem that his actual fortune was greater.

**NOTES**

CHAPTER XII  *From The Mississippi to The James*
(Pages 135 to 145)

1. Basler, *op. cit.*, VI, 22; H. H. Bennett-Butler, June 6, 1884, 1954 boxes, Butler MSS. He received the message in the Narrows.
2. *The Diary of Gideon Welles*, I, 209-10. Welles agreed.
3. Jonathan W. Turner-A. J. Butler, January 15, 1863, Butler MSS; Memorandum, January 8, 1878, Butler MSS, 1954 boxes; T. C. Pease and J. G. Randall (eds.), *The Diary of Orville Hickman Browning, Illinois Historical Collections*, XX, XXII (1927-1933), I, 609-10; *Butler's Book*, 534 ff., 549 ff. Butler maintained that he refused an offer to take over Grant's command.
4. D. W. Farrington-A. J. Butler, January 15, 1863, Butler MSS; New York Weekly *Tribune*, January 10, 1863, January 17, 1863.
5. *Ibid.*, January 3, 1863; *Butler Cor.*, II, 562-63; *Butler's Book*, 547; *Commonwealth*, January 31, 1863.
6. *Ibid.*, January 17, 1863; Boston Daily *Advertiser*, January 5, 1863; Boston Daily *Journal*, January 13, 14, 1863.
7. *Cong. Globe*, 37th Cong., 3d Sess., 222-23, 236; notification of action of legislatures of Massachusetts and Ohio, January 20 and 30, 1863, Butler MSS.
8. *Commonwealth*, January 17, 1863; New York Weekly *Tribune*, January 10, 17, 1863.
9. Cowley, *History of Lowell*, 184.
10. New York *Times*, January 14, 1863; Springfield *Republican*, January 3, April 12, 1863. Even "Warrington" praised him.
11. Amasa McCoy-Thaddeus Stevens, January 19, 1863, Butler MSS. McCoy suggested that the House withhold supplies to force Lincoln to dismiss Seward and put Butler in his place. Others wanted the General in the War Department. *Butler Cor.*, II, 589-90.
12. Shaffer-Butler, January 28, 1863, Butler MSS.
13. *Butler Cor.*, II, 589-90.
14. John D. Sanborn-Butler, February 3, 1863, Butler MSS.
15. *O. R.*, Series I, LIII, 547.
16. Basler, *op. cit.*, VI, 73.
17. Williams, *Lincoln and the Radicals*, 223; New York *Times*, April 28, 1863.
18. Even the devoted Shaffer had doubts on this score. Basler, *op. cit.*, V, 428-29.
19. Lincoln had entrusted a confidential mission to New Orleans to his chiropodist, Isachar Zacharie. Zacharie's reports were not encouraging. Charles M. Segal, "Isachar Zacharie, Lincoln's Chiropodist," *Publications of the American Jewish Historical Society*, XLIII (December, 1952), 71 ff.
20. Seward-Stanton, January 14, 1863, Banks MSS.
21. Basler, *op. cit.*, VI, 100.
22. *Butler's Book*, 570. Both Chase and Sumner had written that he was to return. *Butler Cor.*, II, 570-71, 584.
23. *Ibid.*, III, 13; Beale, *op. cit.*, 76; Butler-A. J. Butler, February 18, 1863, Butler MSS.
24. Order, February 16, 1863, in Butler's handwriting; draft order of February 17, 1863, slightly different, Butler MSS.

25. *Butler Cor.*, III, 21-27, 54-64.
26. Butler-A. J. Butler, February 18, 1863, Butler MSS.
27. *Butler's Book*, 570.
28. Butler-Henry Wilson, February 22, 1863, Henry Wilson MSS, Library of Congress.
29. *Butler Cor.*, II, 271-73. He welcomed the coming of a strong man, if we are to believe his letter to his wife.
30. Williams, *Lincoln and the Radicals*, 272.
31. *Butler Cor.*, II, 563; George Denison-James Denison, January 3, 1863, Denison MSS. In a letter to Mrs. H. H. Grenough, March 4, 1863, Butler MSS, he disclaimed any intentions of running for the Presidency, on the grounds that he was much too young to retire afterwards. Yet his agent was actively seeking support in Chicago. *Butler Cor.*, III, 99-100.
32. *Ibid.*, 36, 71, 77 ff.
33. New York *Times*, April 3, 1863; Benjamin F. Butler, *Character and Results of the War, How to Prosecute and How to End It* (Philadelphia, 1863). The pamphlet was printed for "gratuitous distribution."
34. Gurowski, *op. cit.*, II, 187-88; Cowley, *History of Lowell*, 185.
35. *Butler Cor.*, II, 582; Milton E. Flower, *James Parton* (Durham, 1951), 64.
36. New York *World*, February 4, 17, April 28, 1863; Bernard A. Weisberger, *Reporters for the Union* (Boston, 1953), 262; Butler-Parton, May 5, 1863, Parton MSS.
37. Flower, *op. cit.*, 62 ff.; Parton-Butler, April 10, 1863, 1954 boxes, Butler MSS.
38. *Butler Cor.*, III, 150.
39. Parton spoke of his subject as the next President. Parton, *op. cit.*, 615.
40. Flower, *op. cit.*, 71-72.
41. Butler-Parton, December 7, 1863, Parton MSS, shows that the General was fully aware of this result. Cf. *The Diary of George Templeton Strong*, III, 379-380.
42. *Harper's Weekly*, VII (July 25, 1863), 466; Schouler, *op. cit.*, II, 422; *Commonwealth*, October 30, 1863.
43. *Ibid.*, September 16, October 16, 1863; New York *Times*, September 26, 1863; E. H. Rollins-Butler, June 25, 1863; Butler-James G. Blaine, June 22, 1863, Butler MSS; H. W. Chapin-Andrew, September 14, 1863, John A. Andrew MSS.
44. "Our General," *Atlantic Monthly*, XII (July, 1863), 103-115.
45. John D. Sanborn-Butler, October 3, 1863, September 28, 1863, Butler MSS; *Commonwealth*, July 17, 1863; *Butler Cor.*, III, 98, 118 ff.
46. In July, he came to Washington in person to try again. Edward L. Pierce, *Memoir and Letters of Charles Sumner* (Boston, 1877), IV, 142. Even Andrew was approached on his behalf. Cyrus Woodman-Andrew, April 25, 1863, John A. Andrew MSS. For other efforts, cf. J. W. Cozzens-A. J. Butler, October 6, 1863; George Denison-A. J. Butler, October 9, 1863, Butler MSS.
47. Stephen W. Allen-Butler, September 30, 1891, Butler MSS; *Butler Cor.*, II, 595 ff.
48. *Ibid.*, III, 97. Welles also thought New York might be a good place for Butler, and the radical press agreed. *The Diary of Gideon Welles*, I, 373; *Commonwealth*, July 17, 1863.

# NOTES

49. *O. R.*, Series I, XXII, Part II, 581, 604. Lincoln expressed the highest admiration for Butler but refused politely.

50. B. F. Flanders was active on Butler's behalf. J. W. Cozzens-A. J. Butler, October 6, 1863; George Denison-A. J. Butler, October 9, 1863; J. W. Cozzens-A. J. Butler, October 7, 1863, Butler MSS.

51. *Butler Cor.*, III, 118-19.

52. *Ibid.*, 139-41; *O. R.*, Series I, XXIX, Part II, 397; *Letters of John Hay* (Washington, 1908), I, 117.

53. *O. R.*, Series II, IV, 266-68.

54. William B. Hesseltine, *Civil War Prisons* (Columbus, 1930), 32 ff., 69-70. For evidence that Stanton considered the exchange disadvantageous to the North before Grant said so, cf. *Butler Cor.*, III, 198.

55. New York *Times*, November 10, 1863.

56. Ethan Allan Hitchcock, *Fifty Years in Camp and Field* (New York, 1909), 458; *O. R.*, Series II, VI, 528, 532-34.

57. *Ibid.*, 556.

58. *Ibid.*, 658. On December 12, however, the Confederates refused to accept further supplies. Butler-Stanton, Stanton MSS, December 12, 1863.

59. *O. R.*, Series II, VI, 711; Hesseltine, *op. cit.*, 210 ff.

60. To a Southern observer, Butler's appointment seemed to put the exchange "farther off than ever." Frank E. Vandiver (ed.), *The Civil War Diary of General Josiah Gorgas* (Tuscaloosa, 1947), 75.

61. Hesseltine, *op. cit.*, 69.

62. *O. R.*, Series II, VI, 752, 754.

63. *Ibid.*, 768-69.

64. *Butler's Book*, 586; J. W. Shaffer-"Colonel", December 29, 1863, Butler MSS.

65. *O. R.*, Series II, VI, 836, 867.

66. J. W. Shaffer-A. J. Butler, December 29, 1863, Butler MSS; Hesseltine, *op. cit.*, 211 ff.

67. *O. R.*, Series II, VI, 871-74, 880, 937, 944-45, 1007, 1093 ff.; Hitchcock, *op. cit.*, 459 ff. Hitchcock was so incensed that he refused to shake hands with Butler when the two met at Lincoln's funeral a year later.

68. *O. R.*, Series II, VI, 958-61, 934.

69. *Ibid.*, 986; VII, 94-95.

70. *Ibid.*, VI, 1121-22; *Butler Cor.*, IV, 44-53.

71. *Ibid.*, IV, 31.

72. *Ibid.*, 72, 83-84; *Butler's Book*, 592-93.

73. *O. R.*, Series II, VII, 101-05.

74. He wrote that all exchanges must stop. Hesseltine, *op. cit.*, 224-25; *Butler Cor.*, V, 70 ff.

75. *Butler's Book*, 599 ff. Butler was ready to demand a formal repeal of the declaration of outlawry should the Confederates accept his propositions.

76. West, *Welles*, 292 ff.; *O. R.*, Series II, VII, 915-25.

77. *Butler Cor.*, V, 281, 293, 303, 595.

78. Henry Kyd Douglas, *I Rode With Stonewall* (Chapel Hill, 1940), 268-73.

79. Louis Sigaud, *Belle Boyd* (Boston, 1947), 140-46.

## CHAPTER XIII  "Bottled Up"
(Pages 146 to 157)

1. *O. R.*, Series I, XXIV, Part III, 333.
2. Isaac Wistar, *Autobiography of Isaac Wistar* (Philadelphia, 1937), 426-29; *Butler Cor.*, III, 331, 400-01, 421; *O. R.*, Series I, XXXIII, 506, 511, 514, 518-19, 532, 553-55; LI, Part I, 1285; Part II, 810-11; *Butler's Book*, 619. Wistar and Butler blamed an escaped prisoner who had been under sentence of death for murder; yet the Confederates had obtained warning even before the escapee confirmed it.
3. He also became involved in the aftermath of Colonel Ulric Dahlgren's raid on Richmond. His informant in the Capital, Miss Elizabeth Van Lew, let him know that she had spirited away the body of the fallen raider, and he transmitted this intelligence to Admiral Dahlgren, the father. *O. R.*, Series I, XXXIII, 168, 197, 177, 180-81, 425, 649; Bruce Catton, *A Stillness at Appomattox* (Garden City, 1954), 7-18; Elizabeth Van Lew Diary, Van Lew MSS, New York Public Library.
4. Memo, January 8, 1879, letterbooks, Butler MSS. As early as December 21, 1862, the plan had been suggested to Lincoln by Generals W. B. Franklin and W. F. Smith, copy in Butler MSS.
5. Adam Badeau, *Military History of Ulysses S. Grant* (New York, 1868), II, 95-96; U. S. Grant, *Personal Memoirs of U. S. Grant* (Clevland and New York, 1952), 367.
6. *Ibid.*; *Butler's Book*, 627 ff.
7. *O. R.*, Series I, XXXIII, 794-96.
8. *Ibid.*, 885-86, 904 ff.
9. *Ibid.*, XXII, Part III, 246; Catton, *op. cit.*, 132.
10. Butler's Memo, January 8, 1879, letterbooks, Butler MSS; *The Diary of Gideon Welles*, II, 19. Welles was skeptical about the movement.
11. Andrew A. Humphreys, *The Viriginia Campaign of '64 and '65* (New York, 1883), 137 ff.
12. *O. R.*, Series I, XXXIII, 287 ff., 966; LI, Part I, 1288. In spite of Butler's nonchalance, Halleck took a dim view of the affair. He wrote: "It is useless for me to consult with General Butler on this subject, for his opinion would not change my judgement."
13. *Ibid.*, XXXIII, 1009.
14. George A. Bruce, "General Butler's Bermuda Campaign," *Papers of the Military Historical Society of Massachusetts*, IX (1912), 310 ff. Neighboring points such as Wilson's Wharf and Fort Powhatan were also occupied. *O. R.*, Series I, XXXVI, Part II, 20 ff.
15. Bruce, *op. cit.*, 313. For the Confederates' worries, cf. Mrs. Pickett, *The Heart of A Soldier* (New York, 1913), 123.
16. Bruce, *op. cit.*, 316; Alfred P. Rockwell, "The Tenth Army Corps in Virginia, May 1864," *Papers of the Military Historical Society of Massachusetts*, IX (1912), 276; A. W. Bartlett, *History of the Twelfth Regiment New Hampshire Volunteers in the War of the Rebellion* (Concord, 1897), 173; *Battles and Leaders*, IV, 114 ff.
17. Thomas L. Livermore, *Days and Events, 1860-1866* (New York and Boston, 1920), 337.

# NOTES

18. *Butler's Book,* 637-38. In his final report, Grant maintained that he had pointed out the importance of obtaining possession of Petersburg and destroying communications as far south as possible. Yet he conceded that he set Richmond as the objective. U. S. Grant, *Official Report of Lt.-Gen. U. S. Grant* (New York, 1865), 15.

19. Butler's Memo, January 8, 1879. General Gillmore denied this assertion when it appeared in print. New York *Times,* July 3, 1879.

20. *Dictionary of American Biography,* VII, 295

21. Clarence E. Macartney, *Grant and His Generals* (New York, 1954), 189 ff.; Badeau, *op. cit.,* II, 352, 463; Grant, *Personal Memoirs,* 367.

22. Gillmore wrote Butler on May 6 that he had abandoned the project of striking the railroad on his front for what he deemed "good and sufficient reasons." Smith likewise failed and blamed Gillmore. *O. R.,* Series I, XXXVI, Part II, 473 ff.

23. Rockwell, *op. cit.,* 280 ff.; Bruce, *op. cit.,* 322 ff.; *Butler Cor.,* IV, 183-187.

24. *O. R.,* Series I, XXXVI, Part II, 593-94; Livermore, *op. cit.,* 342.

25. *Butler Cor.,* IV, 181; *Butler's Book,* 645 ff.; Rockwell, *op. cit.,* 281.

26. Catton, *op. cit.,* 132-33.

27. *Battles and Leaders,* IV, 195 ff.; *O. R.,* Series I, XXXVI, Part II, 1024, 196 ff.; Humphreys, *op. cit.,* 149.

28. *Ibid.,* 112-18; *Butler Cor.,* IV, 228-29; *Battles and Leaders,* IV, 197-200; 206 ff.; Wistar, *op. cit.,* 450-456; Bartlett, *op. cit.,* 184 ff.; William F. Smith, *From Chattanooga to Petersburg Under Generals Grant and Butler* (Boston, 1893), 163; *Butler's Book,* 655 ff.; Bruce, *op. cit.,* 332 ff.

29. Butler-W. P. Darby, June 26, 1882, letterbooks, Butler MSS; *Butler's Book,* 656.

30. Grant, *Official Report,* 20.

31. Grant, *Personal Memoirs,* 426; Catton, *op. cit.,* 132-33.

32. *Butler Cor.,* IV, 262-63; *O. R.,* Series I, XXXVI, Part III, 43, 44, 177-78.

33. *Ibid.,* 77, 176, 183. Grant wrote to Halleck: "The force under General Butler is not detaining 10,000 men in Richmond, and is not even keeping the roads south of the city cut. Under these circumstances, I think it advisable to have all of it here except enough to keep a foothold at City Point." Consequently 20,000 men under Smith were ordered to Cold Harbor.

34. *Butler Cor.,* IV, 275-85; Edward Everett Hale-Sarah Butler, May 29, 1864, Butler MSS; *Butler's Book,* 671 ff.

35. *Battles and Leaders,* IV, 204, 534; Humphreys, *op. cit.,* 196-97; Mrs. Roger A. Pryor, *Reminiscences of Peace and War* (New York, 1904), 272 ff.; *O. R.,* Series I, XXXVI, 740.

36. Butler caused a devastating endorsement to be put on Gillmore's report of the affair. It characterized the Corps Commander's conduct as "dilatory and ill-judged," accused him of "direct disobedience to orders," and called his report "entirely unsatisfactory." Thereupon Gillmore demanded a court of inquiry. Heated correspondence followed, and Grant finally relieved Gillmore at his own request. *Ibid.,* XXXVI, Part II, 273 ff., 283 ff., 287 ff.; XL, Part I, 23; Part II, 120, 142, 302.

37. Sarah Butler tried to impress this necessity upon her husband. *Butler Cor.,* IV, 363-64.

38. Thomas A. Livermore, "The Failure to Take Petersburg, June 15, 1864," *Papers of the Military Historical Society of Massachusetts*, V (1906), 36 ff.

39. *O. R.*, Series I, XL, Part II, 37, 73. The signal tower was one hundred seventy-five feet high and served the intelligence-conscious General in good stead. Bartlett, *op. cit.*, 173; Frederick W. Seward, *Seward in Washington* (New York, 1891), III, 229.

40. Frank E. Peabody, "Crossing of the James and First Assault Upon Petersburg," *Papers of the Military Historical Society of Massachusetts*, V (1906), 135 ff.; Livermore, *Days and Events*, 362; Livermore, *The Failure to Take Petersburg*, 64-72; John I. Davenport-Butler, December 7, 1891, Butler MSS; Catton, *op. cit.*, 185-92; *O. R.* Series I, XL, Part II, 12, 37 ff.; 56 ff.; *Butler Cor.*, IV, 366 ff., 379 ff., 384 ff., 390 ff.

41. Smith, *From Chattanooga To Petersburg*, 23-25, 68; William F. Smith, "The Movement Against Petersburg, June, 1864," *Papers of the Military Historical Society of Massachusetts*, V (1906), 77-115. Smith also blamed Butler for exaggerating the strength of the reinforcements on the way and for informing him that the works were not strong. Yet, in view of the fact that the fortifications, though strong, were virtually unmanned, Butler had a point.

42. *O. R.*, Series I, XL, Part II, 27, 56 ff.; Part I, 303-08; Peabody, *op. cit.*, 141-45. Controversy developed later concerning the causes of the delay, which seems to have been due to bad staff work. Hancock-Butler, June 8, 1880, Butler MSS; Macartney, *op. cit.*, 207.

43. Grant, *Official Report*, 27; *Butler Cor.*, IV, 380; John I. Davenport-Butler, December 7, 1891, Butler MSS; Livermore, *The Failure to Take Petersburg*, 72, 55.

44. *Ibid.*, 72; Peabody, *op. cit.*, 143; Smith, *The Movement Against Petersburg*, 96. An attack of malaria may have rendered Smith too sick to act at the crucial moment.

45. Beauregard conceded this point. *Battles and Leaders*, IV, 540 ff.

46. Bartlett, *op. cit.*, 217; Catton, *op. cit.*, 192; Livermore, *Days and Events*, 362; Badeau, *op. cit.*, II, 352 ff.; Peabody, *op. cit.*, 135.

47. *O. R.*, Series I, XXXIV, Part I, 22; XL, Part I, 23-24; Part II, 131 ff.; John C. Ropes, "The Failure to Take Petersburg on June 16-18, 1864," *Papers of the Military Historical Society of Massachusetts*, V (1906), 177; Francis A. Osborn, "Bermuda Hundred, June 16-17, 1864," *ibid.*, 191, 201-02.

48. *O. R.*, Series I, XL, Part II, 558-59.

49. *Ibid.*, 598.

50. On July 2, 1864, he wrote to Grant: "I want to ask you how you can place a man in command of two army corps who is as helpless as a child on the field of battle, and as visionary as an opium eater in council . . ." *Ibid.*, 595.

51. *Ibid.*, Part III, 31.

52. *Ibid.*, 31, 59, 69; William D. Mallam, "The Grant-Butler Relationship," *Mississippi Valley Historical Review*, XLI (September, 1954), 262; Williams, *Lincoln and His Generals*, 321-23. After Lincoln saw the order, the language was slightly changed, the words "by order of the President" being deleted from the body of the text. Williams considers this significant, but Mallam points out that Lincoln's signature appeared on the final order. There is no evidence that the President stopped the order.

# OLD ERIE STREET BOOKSTORE
**Old-Rare-Books Bought & Sold**
2128 East 9th Street
CLEVELAND, OHIO 44115
**(216) 575-0743**

| NAME | | | | | | DATE 8-14-95 |
|---|---|---|---|---|---|---|
| ADDRESS | | | | | | |
| | | | | PHONE | | |
| SOLD BY | CASH ✓ | C.O.D. | CHARGE | ON ACCT. | MDSE. RET'D | |

| QTY. | DESCRIPTION | AMOUNT |
|---|---|---|
| 1 | Ben Butler biog. by Hans Louis Trefousse | 25 00 |
| | TAX | 1 75 |
| | TOTAL | 26 75 |

31636

*Thank You*

# NOTES

53. *Butler Cor.*, IV, 481-82.
54. After Smith's failure to take Petersburg, his relations with Butler deteriorated. Butler accused Smith of tardiness on June 21; Smith resented this and engaged in further controversy with the Army Commander concerning the use of colored troops. When Smith returned from leave, he found that Butler had prevailed and the Corps Commander was relieved. *O. R.*, Series I, XL, Part II, 301, 458-60, 489-91; Part III, 334; Smith, *From Chattanooga to Petersburg*, 28-37, 155 ff.; Grant, *Official Report*, 27; Macartney, *op. cit.*, 208 ff.
55. Smith, *From Chattanooga to Petersburg*, 60, 189.
56. *O. R.*, Series I, XL, Part III, 91, 120-22. Lincoln was not only faced with an imminent invasion of Washington, but also with the radical challenge of the Wade-Davis Bill. The dismissal of Butler and the pocket veto of that measure would have added insult to injury.
57. Mallam, *op. cit.*, 261, believes Grant realized that sending Butler to Fort Monroe would create great confusion of command. Badeau, *op. cit.*, II, 44, emphasizes political considerations. For similar views, cf. Helen Todd, *A Man Named Grant* (Boston, 1940), 230 ff.; William B. Hesseltine, *Ulysses S. Grant* (New York, 1935), 44-45.
58. *Butler Cor.*, IV, 491, 499-500. He wrote: "Permit me here to say that I desire to serve you not in this only, but in all things. My future is not in the army, yours is. Our paths can never cross. Therefore, amid all the selfishness of life, I can see no reason why I cannot always subscribe myself, as I do now, Most truly your friend, Benj. F. Butler."
59. *O. R.*, Series I, XL, Part III, 114.
60. *Butler Cor.*, IV, 484.
61. Smith, *From Chattanooga to Petersburg*, 60, 174, 178 ff. Unburdening himself to Senator Foote of Vermont, he accused Butler of blackmail. The Senator published the letter.
62. Macartney, *op. cit.*, 219.
63. *O. R.*, Series I, XXXVI, Part II, 282-92.
64. *Ibid.*, XL, Part III, 355, 361. Butler also received an additional corps, the XIX. The XVIII Corps was later given to General Weitzel.
65. George R. Agassiz (ed.), Theodore Lyman, *Meade's Headquarters, 1863-1865* (Boston, 1922), 192.
66. Badeau, *op. cit.*, II, 505. He did this willingly.
67. *Butler's Book*, 717 ff.
68. George A. Bruce, "Petersburg, June 15 — Fort Harrison, September 29: A Comparison," *Papers of the Military Historical Society of Massachusetts*, XIV (1917), 89 ff.; Memorandum, January 29, 1879, letterbook, Butler MSS.
69. Jones, *op. cit.*, II, 295; Bruce, *op. cit.*, 96-98.
70. *O. R.*, Series I, LII, Part II, 48-49.
71. *Ibid.*, Part III, 65; *Butler's Book*, 730-43.
72. Badeau, *op. cit.*, III, 115; Grant, *Personal Memoirs*, 418; *O. R.*, Series I, LII, Part III, 331, 390-99.

CHAPTER XIV  *The Election of 1864*
(Pages 158 to 165)

1. Harding, op. cit., 79.
2. Gurowski, op. cit., III, 86; *Butler Cor.*, III, 348-49.
3. The Republicans of Rockingham, N. H., passed resolutions to that effect. Butler was warned not to accept lest for four years he be "dumb and inert as an oyster." Portsmouth, N. H., *Journal*, January 16, 1864; J. A. Griffin-Butler, January 20, 1864, Butler MSS.
4. Butler-A. T. Rice, August 19, 1885, letterbooks, Butler MSS; *Butler's Book*, 631-33; Benjamin F. Butler, "Vice Presidential Politics in '64," *North American Review*, CXLI (October, 1885), 331-35.
5. William Roscoe Thayer, *The Life and Letters of John Hay* (Boston and New York, 1915), I, 144.
6. Basler, op. cit., VII, 207; J. W. Shaffer-Butler, February 27, 1864, Butler MSS.
7. *Butler Cor.*, III, 515.
8. Butler, "Vice Presidential Politics in '64, loc. cit.; Alexander K. McClure, *Abraham Lincoln and Men of War Times* (Philadelphia, 1892), 118. *Butler's Book*, 633-35, including Cameron's testimony.
9. *Butler's Book*, 633-35.
10. Louis Taylor Merrill, "General Benjamin F. Butler in the Presidential Campaign of 1864," *Mississippi Valley Historical Review*, XXXIII (March, 1947), 551; William F. Zornow, *Lincoln and the Party Divided* (Norman, Okla., 1954), 70-72. Because of the lack of contemporary evidence — neither Butler, nor McClure, nor Cameron wrote about the incident until many years had passed — Dr. Horowitz has questioned it. Horowitz, op. cit., 230 ff.
11. J. D. Sanborn-Butler, February 28, 1864; Williams, *Lincoln and the Radicals*, 306 ff.
12. *Commonwealth*, March 25, 1864.
13. Zornow, op. cit., 66.
14. Isaac Morse-Butler, March 22, 1864; N. T. Spear-Butler, March 21, 1864, Butler MSS.
15. New York *Tribune*, April 15, 1864.
16. J. K. Herbert-Butler, March 26, 1864, Butler MSS; *Butler Cor.*, IV, 66-67, 292.
17. One enthusiastic supporter had even composed a "National Song," entitled *The Union and Butler*. Sung to the tune of *The Red, White and Blue*, it contained four fulsome stanzas, starting:

> Columbia, though under thy altars
> Rebellion's great earthquake is rolled
> Yet from the bright struggle is tossing
> The purest, the brightest of gold:
> And here shines an ingot of glory —
> Our Butler all fearless and true —
> The patriot, hero, and statesman,
> Beneath the old Red, White and Blue.

**NOTES** 299

The song was instigated by N. T. Spear. N. T. Spear-Butler, March 21, 1864, Butler MSS. It appeared in the New York *Courier,* April 18, 1864.
18. Benjamin P. Thomas, *Abraham Lincoln* (New York, 1952), 410-411; Williams, *Lincoln and the Radicals,* 310-311.
19. H. C. Gardiner-Butler, March 28, 1864, Butler MSS.
20. Williams, *Lincoln and the Radicals,* 314-15.
21. *Butler Cor.,* IV, 520-21; *The Diary of George Templeton Strong,* III, 323.
22. Weisberger, *op. cit.,* 203.
23. New York Evening *Post,* May 24, 1864; Harding, *op cit.,* 83; *Butler Cor.,* IV, 272-74, 314-18.
24. John Clark-Butler, May 27, 1864, Butler MSS.
25. *Commonwealth,* June 17, 1864; *O. R.,* Series I, XXXVI, Part III, 565-66.
26. J. W. Shaffer-Butler, June 5, 1864, Butler MSS.
27. *Butler Cor.,* IV, 337.
28. *O. R.,* Series I, XXXVI, Part III, 704.
29. Williams, *Lincoln and the Radicals,* 316-17, 323.
30. *Butler Cor.,* IV, 464.
31. *Ibid.,* 510-12.
32. *Ibid.,* 494, 512-13, 534-36; V, 67-68; J. B. Ashley-Butler, August 5, 1864; J. W. Shaffer-Butler, August 14, 1864, Butler MSS.
33. Williams, *Lincoln and the Radicals,* 324-25; Sandburg, *op. cit.,* III, 203; Henry L. Stoddard, *Horace Greeley* (New York, 1946), 227; Zornow, *op. cit.,* 114-15.
34. *Butler Cor.,* V, 47-48, 74-75, 109-10.
35. *Ibid.,* 85.
36. *O. R.,* Series I, XLII, Part II, 498; Sandburg, *op. cit.,* III, 203.
37. J. W. Shaffer-Butler, August 14, 1864, Butler MSS.
38. *Butler Cor.,* V, 116-19.
39. *Ibid.,* 134-35; J. K. Herbert-Butler, September 13, 1864, Butler MSS; *Spirit of the Times,* September 17, 1864. Efforts to get Butler a place in the cabinet predated the failure of the Cincinnati Convention. *Butler Cor.,* V, 120-21.
40. Williams, *Lincoln and the Radicals,* 330-33; Benjamin Wade-Zachariah Chandler, October 2, 1864, Zachariah Chandler MSS.
41. *Butler Cor.,* IV, 503-04; V, 151, 269, 277-78, 300-01, 305-06; Henry J. Raymond-Butler, October 21, 1864, Butler MSS.
42. Nicolay and Hay, *op. cit.,* IX, 373-375.
43. *O. R.,* Series I, XLIII, Part II, 532; XLII, Part III, 489.
44. *Ibid.;* New York *World,* November 7, 1864; *Butler's Book,* 756, 758. He only got 3,100 men. *Butler Cor.,* V, 311.
45. *Butler's Book,* 753-54.
46. James D. Horan, *Confederate Agent* (New York, 1954), 89, 166 ff., 208 ff.
47. Badeau, *op. cit.,* III, 177.
48. *O. R.,* Series I, XLIII, Part II, 535, 549, 550, 558, 567.
49. *Ibid.,* XLII, Part III, 470; *Butler Cor.,* V, 320, 326, 332; New York *Times,* November 1, 1864.

50. *O. R.*, Series I, XLIII, Part II, 549, 568; Butler-Stanton, November 5, 1864, Stanton MSS. Butler proposed a specific order requiring the militia officers to report to him. Lincoln, however, thought it wise to avoid trouble with the militia.
51. *Ibid.*, 550.
52. *Butler's Book*, 757-58.
53. *Ibid.*, 762-68; *Butler Cor.*, V, 326-29; *O. R.*, Series I, XLIII, Part II, 933; Horan, *op. cit.*, 89, 210-23. The firebugs, too, failed to carry out their scheme. Much to their surprise, they found themselves in the same hotel with the General. Only after he had left, they started a few conflagrations.
54. New York *Herald*, November 8, 1864; *The Diary of George Templeton Strong*, III, 509.
55. New York *World*, November 8, 1864.
56. *Ibid.*, November 7, 1864; *Butler's Book*, 756, 761.
57. *Butler Cor.*, V, 519-20; *Butler's Book*, 759; George H. Gordon, *A War Diary of Events in the War of the Great Rebellion* (Boston, 1882), 355.
58. New York *Tribune*, November 9, 1864.
59. *Ibid.*; *Commonwealth*, November 12, 1864; *Butler Cor.*, V, 346-47.
60. *Ibid.*, 337; *Commonwealth*, November 12, 1864; New York *Tribune*, November 15, 1864; *Butler's Book*, 773.
61. *Butler Cor.*, V, 330, 357.

## CHAPTER XV  The Downfall of A Political General
(Pages 166 to 177)

1. Gordon, *op. cit.*, 365; Boston Daily *Advertiser*, October 17, 1868; *The Diary of Gideon Welles*, I, 336; II, 56-57; Susan Leigh Blackford, *Reminiscences of Lee's Army* (New York, 1947), 251-53; *Butler Cor.*, III, 171, 428 ff., 506; V, 576 ff., 582-83; *Trade With Rebellious States*, House Report No. 24, 38th Cong., 2d Sess. The most notorious cases involved the trading permits given to the groups who operated the *Philadelphia* and the *Princeton*, both engaged in contraband trade. Mallam, *op. cit.*, 266-67. Cf. *Butler Cor.*, III, 512-13; IV, 474-75, 489-90, 493 ff., 515, 523, 526-27; V, 149, 502-04.
2. *The Diary of Gideon Welles*, II, 81.
3. *Butler's Book*, 413; *O. R.*, Series I, XL, Part III, 337.
4. *Commonwealth*, January 7, 1865.
5. Norfolk *Old Dominion*, March 1, 1864.
6. Some were sent to Fort Hatteras, others to local jails, where their punishment included cleaning the streets in prison garb. S. O. No. 44, February 25, 1864; S. O. No. 65, March 5, 1864; Examination of Reverend D. Armstrong, February 24, 1864, Butler MSS; *Butler Cor.*, IV, 54-56. Cf. Nicolay and Hay, *op. cit.*, VI, 334, for Lincoln's reversal of one of the sentences.
7. Norfolk *Old Dominion*, September 24, 1864.
8. *Butler Cor.*, IV, 159-60, 306-10; Francis H. Peirpont, *Letter of Governor Peirpont to His Excellency the President and the Honorable Congress of the United States* . . . (Washington, 1864), 83-89.
9. *Butler's Book*, 843; Gordon, *op. cit.*, 375; Charles H. Ambler, *Francis H. Pierpont* (Chapel Hill, 1937), 232-33; *Butler Cor.*, III, 450-460.

# NOTES

10. Thomas J. Wertenbaker, *Norfolk* (Durham, 1931), 250; *Butler Cor.*, III, 282-84, 321-24.
11. Peirpont, *op. cit.*, 27. The oyster trade was also licensed and gave rise to complaints. Joseph Segar-J. W. Shaffer, February 13, 1864, Butler MSS.
12. *Butler Cor.*, IV, 532, 567; Captain Carney's statement, July 22, 1864; Casaran Interrogation, July 30, 1864, Butler MSS.
13. Norfolk *Old Dominion*, February 13, 1865, May 5, 1864; Gordon, *op. cit.*, 400.
14. Ambler, *op. cit.*, 231-35; Nicolay and Hay, *op. cit.*, IX, 438-45; William Reynold Thacher, "The Pierpont Government in Virginia," M. A. Dissertation, University of Chicago, 1916.
15. *Butler Cor.*, III, 180-81.
16. Basler, *op. cit.*, VII, 103, 135.
17. *Ibid.*, VII, 487; Ambler, *op. cit.*, 219-30, 247.
18. Basler, *op. cit.*, VII, 135.
19. *Butler Cor.*, III, 450-60.
20. Peirpont, *op. cit.*
21. *Butler Cor.*, IV, 586-90; Norfolk *New Regime*, June 25, 1864.
22. Beale, *op. cit.*, 350, 358-59; *The Diary of Gideon Welles*, II, 81.
23. Edward K. Snead-Butler, August 2, 1864, Butler MSS; Order, July 31, 1864, Parton MSS; *Butler Cor.*, IV, 567-74, 591.
24. *Ibid.*, 576-86.
25. Basler, *op. cit.*, VII, 487-88.
26. *Butler Cor.*, V, 351-52, 443-44; Pierpont's message, December 6, 1864, Butler MSS.
27. Basler, *op. cit.*, VIII, 174, 186.
28. Ambler, *op. cit.*, 238 ff.
29. Henry N. Hudson, *A Chaplain's Campaign with Gen. Butler* (New York, 1865); *Official Documents Relating To A "Chaplain's Campaign (NOT) with General Butler," But in New York* (Lowell, 1865).
30. William H. Kent of the New York *Tribune* had blamed General Hancock for the failure to take Petersburg on June 15, whereupon he was expelled from the Union lines. Butler helped him and succeeded in having him reinstated. Weisberger, *op. cit.*, 180; Smith, *op. cit.*, 166; *O. R.*, Series I, XLII, Part III, 203 ff.
31. He also insulted the Jews by publishing a telegram stating that he had "captured 150 rebels, 90 mules, 60 contrabands and 4 Jews." Max J. Kohler, *The Board of Delegates of American Israelites, 1859-1878* (New York, 1925), 117 ff.
32. Badeau, *op. cit.*, II, 355; Agassiz, *op. cit.*, 194; Gordon, *op. cit.*, 357-58; Macartney, *op. cit.*, 177; *Butler Cor.*, IV, 462.
33. *Butler's Book*, 747-51; Bartlett, *op. cit.*, 255; Morgan, *op. cit.*, 212-13; *Harper's Weekly*, XXX (January 21, 1865), 531.
34. Lossing, *op. cit.*, III, 474-75; *O. R.*, Series I, XXXVI, Part III, 425-26; XLII, Part II, 624, 731.
35. *Report of the Joint Committee on the Conduct of the War*, 38th Cong., 2d Session, Senate Report No. 142 (Washington, 1865), II, 5, (Cited as *JCCW*); Butler-Horace Greeley, December 13, 1864, Horace Greeley MSS, New York Public Library.

36. *JCCW*, II, 5.
37. West, *Welles*, 298-300. Welles was dubious, but Fox was enthusiastic. *The Diary of Gideon Welles*, II, 209.
38. Badeau, *op. cit.*, III, 307 ff.
39. Porter, *op. cit.*, 262-63.
40. O. R. (Navies), Series I, XI, 215-16.
41. Porter, *op. cit.*, 262-63, 267-68.
42. O. R., Series I, XLII, Part III, 750-760; XLIV, 611.
43. *Ibid.*, XLII, Part III, 799, 835.
44. *Ibid.*, XLVI, Part II, 9; *JCCW*, II, 6; *Butler's Book*, 783-84.
45. *Ibid.*, 785-86; *Butler Cor.*, V, 381.
46. O. R. (Navies), Series I, XI, 746.
47. O. R., Series I, XLII, Part I, 964; Part III, 1072.
48. O. R. (Navies), Series I, XI, 225 ff., 253, 301; *Butler Cor.*, V, 442-43; William Lamb, "Defence of Fort Fisher," *Papers of the Military Historical Society of Massachusetts*, IX, 362.
49. *Ibid.*, 366-69; *Butler Cor.*, V, 436-38, 441-43, 507-08.
50. O. R., Series I, XLII, Part III, 1087.
51. *Ibid.*, 1098; XLVI, Part II, 20; O. R. (Navies), Series I, XI, 404.
52. At least he said so to the Committee on the Conduct of the War. *JCCW*, II, 17.
53. *Butler Cor.*, V, 442-43, 460-65.
54. O. R., Series I, XLVI, Part II, 4.
55. *Ibid.*, 3-4.
56. His willingness to have the army cooperate with the Admiral a second time would seem to indicate that he had no notion of Porter's strictures upon him. Cf. West, *Porter*, 271 ff.
57. Lloyd Lewis, *Sherman* (New York, 1932), 477-78.
58. O. R., Series I, XLVI, Part II, 9.
59. *Ibid.*, 29.
60. *Ibid.*, XLII, Part I, 970.
61. Lincoln thought Butler was to blame. *The Diary of Gideon Welles*, II, 215-17.
62. O. R., Series I, XLVI, Part II, 70.
63. For a discussion of the reasons leading to the recall, cf. Mallam, *op. cit.*, 266.
64. Adelbert Ames, "The Capture of Fort Fisher, January 15, 1865," *Papers of the Military Historical Society of Massachusetts*, IX, 399-400.
65. *Butler Cor.*, V, 471-72, 476, 478, 485-86.
66. *La Crosse Democrat*, January 19, 1865.
67. Gordon, *op. cit.*, 369-73.
68. O. R., Series I, XLVI, Part II, 120; Williams, *Lincoln and the Radicals*, 366.
69. Butler maintained not Grant but Meade was the intended victim. Butler-G. Weitzel, February 18, 1865, Butler MSS. The country failed to see the distinction.
70. Williams, *Lincoln and the Radicals*, 366-68; *JCCW*, II, 3 ff.; Zachariah Chandler-Mrs. Chandler, January 24, 1865, Zachariah Chandler MSS.

# NOTES

71. W. T. Sherman, *Memoirs of General W. T. Sherman* (New York, 1891), II, 242.
72. George W. Julian, *Political Recollections* (Chicago, 1884), 249; Williams, *Lincoln and the Radicals*, 369; JCCW, II, i-viii. The chief differences between the two expeditions were the following: Sherman had advanced further in North Carolina, Terry had more troops than Butler, and the fort was attacked simultaneously from north and south. Butler did his utmost to convince the Committee of the decisive nature of these facts and sent additional evidence during the spring of 1865.
73. *Cong. Globe*, 38th Cong., 2d Sess., 146, 375-77, 393-99.
74. Benjamin F. Butler, *General Butler at Home* (Lowell, 1865), 6-11; Cowley, *History of Lowell*, 193-94; New York *Times*, January 30, 1865.
75. *Commonwealth*, February 4, 1865.
76. Gordon, *op. cit.*, 375 ff. This inquiry had started earlier under General Ord's chairmanship. Extensive testimony concerning contraband trade was taken, but although the board tried to implicate the General, it was unable to find anything. Butler's supporters in Norfolk complained about its efforts to harass them. Kensel-Butler, February 6, 1865, Clark-Butler, February 17, 1865, Butler MSS; *Butler Cor.*, V, 552-53, 557-59, 587-91, 632-33.
77. *O. R.*, Series I, XLVII, Part II, 537. He cited Butler's farewell order and the Lowell speech as the principal reasons.
78. *Butler's Book*, 902-08. For Butler's harsh reconstruction views at this time, cf. *Commonwealth*, April 15, 1865 with the General's speech at Willard's Hotel.
79. *O. R.*, Series I, XLVII, Part II, 537; Basler, *op. cit.*, VIII, 195. Butler also asked Sumner to help him procure an appointment as head of the Freedmen's Bureau. Butler-Sumner, February 5, 1865, Sumner MSS. For other efforts, cf. *Butler Cor.*, V, 559-60, 593; C. F. Blake-John A. Andrew, November 18, 1864, John A. Andrew MSS; Merrill, *op. cit.*, 46.
80. *Trade With Rebellious States*, 38th Cong., 2d Sess., House Report No. 24, 1.

CHAPTER XVI  *Return to Active Politics*
(Pages 178 to 188)

1. Cf. Blaine, *op. cit.*, II, 289.
2. *Commonwealth*, April 15, 1865. As early as December 20, 1864, he had written to Wendell Phillips that every effort should be made to confiscate "rebel" property. *Butler Cor.*, V, 401-04.
3. *Ibid.*, 589; *Butler's Book*, 904-07; Gordon, *op. cit.*, 401.
4. *Butler Cor.*, V, 657.
5. New York *Times*, April 16, 1865; New York *Herald*, April 16, 1865.
6. *Butler Cor.*, V, 593-94.
7. George W. Julian MSS Diary, April 15, 1865, cited in Claude G. Bowers, *The Tragic Era* (Cambridge, 1929), 6.
8. *Commonwealth*, April 22, 1865.
9. Pierce, *op. cit.*, IV, 420; *Butler Cor.*, V, 593 ff.
10. *Ibid.*, 602-05. After Davis' capture, Butler advocated a trial by military commission. *Butler's Book*, 916-18.

11. Zachariah Chandler-Mrs. Chandler, April 23, 1865, Zachariah Chandler MSS; Theophilus Fiske-Andrew Johnson, April 20, 1865; H. S. Brown-Andrew Johnson, April 20, 1865, Andrew Johnson MSS, Library of Congress; J. C. Kinsman-Butler, April 19, 1865, Butler MSS; George Boutwell-Andrew Johnson, April 20, 1865, Butler MSS, 1954 boxes; *Butler Cor.*, V, 641.
12. *Ibid.*, 594-95.
13. J. W. Shaffer-Butler, May 14, 1865, 1954 boxes, Butler MSS.
14. New York *Times*, May 2, 1865.
15. *Butler Cor.*, V, 641-42; *Commonwealth*, June 24, 1865.
16. New York *Times*, June 19, 1865.
17. *Butler's Book*, 916-18; *The Diary of Gideon Welles*, II, 348-49.
18. *Butler Cor.*, V, 271.
19. Butler-D. W. C. Farrington, April 27, 1876, letterbooks, Butler MSS.
20. Statement of Assets and Liabilities of Benjamin F. Butler, January 1, 1868, Butler MSS. The total sum listed is $514,399.04 (assets). The Butler MSS contain extensive correspondence concerning the ventures mentioned.
21. *Commonwealth*, September 23, 1865.
22. *Butler's Book*, 908; New York *Times*, May 2, 1865.
23. Butler-Stevens, November 20, 1865, Thaddeus Stevens MSS, Library of Congress.
24. Butler-Johnson, October 20, 1865; J. C. Kelton-Butler, December 4, 1865, Butler MSS. He had tendered his resignation during the summer, but it was not accepted then. Butler maintained he retained his commission from May till November at the President's request so that he might play a role in Davis' trial by military commission, should the Confederate President be subjected to such an ordeal. *Butler Cor.*, V, 684.
25. Grant, *Official Report of Lt.-Gen. U. S. Grant*.
26. A campaign booklet used against Butler in 1868 is a good example of the use to which the report was put. James McLaughlin, *The American Cyclops, The Hero of New Orleans and Spoiler of Silver Spoons* (Baltimore, 1868), 1-4.
27. Butler-Parton, January 15, 26, February 10, 1866, Parton MSS.
28. Butler-Grant, January 29, 1866, Butler MSS.
29. Butler-Rush C. Hawkins, May 1, 1866, Butler MSS.
30. *Commonwealth*, March 24, 1866; Charles Eldridge-Butler, March 26, 1866, Parton MSS.
31. Samuel Klans (ed.), *The Milligan Case* (New York, 1929); Missouri *Republican*, March 18, 1866; Pease and Randall, *The Diary of Orville Hickman Browning*, II, 65; Samuel S. Cox, *Three Decades of Federal Legislation* (Providence, 1885), 230.
32. Boutwell so informed him. George Boutwell-Butler, December 29, 1865, 1954 boxes, Butler MSS.
33. Merrill, *op. cit.*, 61, believes his hesitation was due to his fear that Grant might benefit in some way.
34. Butler-Andrew Johnson, February 2, 1866, Butler MSS; New York *Herald*, April 30, 1866.
35. Benjamin B. Kendrick, *The Journal of the Joint Committee of Fifteen On Reconstruction, Columbia University Studies in History, Economics and Public Law*, LXII (1914) 252-54, 296-301.
36. New York *Herald*, April 25, 30, 1866.

# NOTES

37. *Butler Cor.*, V, 704-05.
38. Howard K. Beale, *The Critical Year* (New York, 1930), 197.
39. For the President's attitude, cf. Lloyd Paul Stryker, *Andrew Johnson* (New York, 1936), 269.
40. *Commonwealth*, May 19, 1866; New York *Herald*, May 12, 1866; cf. Benjamin F. Butler, *The Status of the Insurgent States Upon the Cessation of Hostilities, A Speech Delivered by General Benjamin F. Butler Before the Legislature of Pennsylvania, April 11, 1866*. (1866).
41. He also mended his relations with Stanton, the Radicals' representative in the cabinet. *Commonwealth*, March 24, 1866.
42. According to the New York *Herald*, he called the General a "humbug," and referred to him as weak and superficial. New York *Herald*, July 11, 1867. Cf. *Cong. Globe*, 40th Cong., 1st Sess., 560.
43. J. F. Manahan-Butler, May 23, 1866, Butler MSS.
44. Degree, July 4, 1866, Butler MSS.
45. William H. Crook, *Through Five Administrations* (New York, 1910), 108-09.
46. Boston Daily *Advertiser*, September 4, 1866; Philip S. Foner, *The Life and Writings of Frederick Douglass* (New York, 1955), IV, 26.
47. New York *Herald*, August 30, 1866, October 5, 1866; St. Louis *Republican*, October 16, 1866.
48. Blaine, *op. cit.*, II, 289; Butler-James Garfield, September 30, 1866, James A. Garfield MSS, VII, 315, Library of Congress; J. J. Stewart-Butler, September 9, 1866, Butler MSS; Merrill, *op. cit.*, 78.
49. New York *Times*, September 27, 1866.
50. Chicago *Tribune*, October 18, 1866; New York *Herald*, October 8, 1866. He called for impeachment at Cincinnati on October 7; but there were reports that he had tried to have an impeachment plank inserted in the resolutions adopted at Pittsburgh. *Ibid.*, October 5, 1866.
51. C. P. Jacobs-Butler, August 1, 1866; G. W. Julian-Butler, September 9, 1866; Lyman Trumbull-Butler, August 29, 1866, all but last 1954 boxes, Butler MSS.
52. Butler-Goldwin Smith, September 23, 1866, 1954 boxes, Butler MSS; Boston Daily *Advertiser*, October 12, 1866; *Commonwealth*, September 15, October 13, 1866; Merrill, *op. cit.*, 71.
53. Milwaukee *Sentinel*, October 22, 1866.
54. New York *Herald*, October 6, 1866.
55. For his interest in labor, cf. *Butler Cor.*, V, 676.
56. W. E. Chandler-Butler, June 4, 1866, 1954 boxes, Butler MSS.
57. *Adjutant Gen. Schouler's Letter on the Nomination of Gen. Benj. F. Butler*, Lynn, October 25, 1866, Butler MSS; cf. the objections of P. Waters, A. G. Browne, J. O. Safford, Boston Daily *Advertiser*, October 10, 1866.
58. New York *Times*, November 4, 1866.
59. Boston Daily *Advertiser*, December 6, 1866; *Commonwealth*, December 8, 1866. The returns were: Butler, 9,021; Northend, 2,838.

## CHAPTER XVII  Radical of Radicals
## (Pages 189 to 204)

1. New York *Herald,* November 25, 1866.
2. J. W. Shaffer-Butler, December 16, 1866, Butler MSS.
3. *Commonwealth,* January 26, 1867; Boston Daily *Advertiser,* February 14, 1867. He addressed the Legislature of Maine on February 13.
4. *Commonwealth,* December 29, 1866.
5. David Miller DeWitt, *The Impeachment of Andrew Johnson* (New York, 1903), 152-157.
6. George Fort Milton, *The Age of Hate* (New York, 1930), 426-27.
7. Boston Daily *Advertiser,* March 5, 1867.
8. *The Diary of Gideon Welles,* II, 619-20.
9. *Commonwealth,* March 2, 1867.
10. *Ibid.,* May 4, 25, 1867; *Cong. Globe,* 40th Cong., 1st Sess., 21; DeWitt, *op. cit.,* 209-10; Milton, *Age of Hate,* 405.
11. Blaine, *op. cit.,* II, 289; Hoar, *op. cit.,* II, 269-70.
12. *Cong. Globe,* 40th Cong., 1st Sess., 256-64, 362-64; Merrill, *op. cit.,* 105 ff.
13. Butler-J. W. Shaffer, April 8, 1867, Butler MSS.
14. *Commonwealth,* July 13, 1867; DeWitt, *op. cit.,* 237, 290.
15. Butler MSS, July-September, 1867.
16. Pease and Randall, *The Diary of Orville Hickman Browning,* II, 152-53; Boston Daily *Advertiser,* August 12, 1867; DeWitt, *op. cit.,* 280.
17. *Commonwealth,* August 17, 1867.
18. DeWitt, *op. cit.,* 298.
19. G. B. Alley-Sumner, April 21, 1867, Sumner MSS.
20. The Army Appropriation Act is a good indication. Cf. Milton, *The Age of Hate,* 375; J. B. Kinsman-Butler, July 7, 1867, Butler MSS.
21. *The Diary of Gideon Welles,* III, 81-82.
22. *Commonwealth,* March 23, 1867.
23. A. D. Staight-Butler, July 13, 1867, Butler MSS.
24. Butler-J. R. Young, August 5, 1867, J. R. Young MSS, Library of Congress.
25. Boston Daily *Advertiser,* September 4, 1867.
26. Merrill, *op. cit.,* 124. He had been doing so for some time. George Suckley-Butler, January 29, 1866; William Brotherhead to Butler, April 4, 1867, Butler MSS.
27. Cf. the long disquisitions in the 1851 and 1853 folders of the 1954 boxes, Butler MSS.
28. Boston Daily *Advertiser,* September 14, 18; October 3, 5, 19, 23, 1867; Merrill, *op. cit.,* 130-32.
29. *Harper's Weekly,* XI (October 12, 1867), 643; *Commonwealth,* October 12, 1867.
30. *Butler's Book,* 931-54; *Cong. Globe,* 40th Cong., 1st Sess., Appendix, 29 ff. He always contended that his position could not be compared with that of George H. Pendleton. The Ohioan wanted to pay the entire debt in greenbacks, while Butler merely desired to pay in paper money that part which could be discharged legally in that manner. In effect, the difference was not great.

## NOTES

31. Jay Cooke-Butler, November 5, 1867, Butler MSS.
32. *Commonwealth*, December 14, 1867.
33. *Cong. Globe*, 40th Cong., 2d Sess., 1391-93.
34. Robert W. Winston, *Andrew Johnson* (New York, 1928), 424 ff.; Milton, *The Age of Hate*, 518.
35. New York *Times*, March 4, 1868.
36. Thaddeus Stevens-Butler, February 28, 1868, 1954 boxes, Butler MSS.
37. James D. Richardson, *A Compilation of the Messages and Papers of the Presidents*, 1789-1897 (Washington, 1896-1909), VI, 531 ff.
38. *Cong. Globe*, 40th Cong., 2d Sess., 1638.
39. *Ibid.*, 1615, 1618-19.
40. *Butler's Book*, 927-28.
41. Journal of the Proceedings of the Honorable Managers of the House of Representatives in the Matter of the Impeachment of Andrew Johnson, President of the United States, March 3, 1868, Butler MSS; *Commonwealth*, March 7, 1868; Georges Clemenceau, *American Reconstruction* (New York, 1928), 162.
42. *Ibid.*, 163; *Commonwealth*, March 7, 1868.
43. DeWitt, *op. cit.*, 395-97; *Impeachment Trial* (Washington, 1868), 8 ff.
44. *Butler's Book*, 929.
45. *Ibid.*; *Impeachment Trial*, 29-41; New York *Times*, March 31, 1868; M. A. De Wolfe Howe, *Portrait of an Independent, Moorfield Storey* (Boston and New York, 1932), 87, 99.
46. *Impeachment Trial*, 53 ff.
47. Boston Daily *Advertiser*, April 8, 1868.
48. Stryker, *op. cit.*, 596-98.
49. E. G. Ross, *History of the Impeachment of Andrew Johnson* (Santa Fe, 1896), 58-60.
50. The Court upheld the President's right of independent removal in Myers v. U. S., 272 U. S. 52 (1926).
51. *Harper's Weekly*, XII (March 21, 1868), 179; Boston Daily *Advertiser*, March 4, 1868.
52. *Impeachment Trial*, 59-63.
53. *Ibid.*, 98-121.
54. *Ibid.*, 75.
55. *Ibid.*, 53-124.
56. *Ibid.*, 125-36; Clemenceau, *op. cit.*, 174-76.
57. *Butler's Book*, 930.
58. *Impeachment Trial*, 136-238.
59. Howe, *op. cit.*, 91; Chester L. Barrows, *William M. Evarts* (Chapel Hill, 1941), 147.
60. Stryker, *op. cit.*, 653-54, 664-5; *The Diary of Gideon Welles*, III, 333. He went so far as to display literally the bloody shirt of a Southern victim of the Klan in the Senate Chamber. Stanley F. Horn, *The Invisible Empire* (Boston, 1939); Robert S. Holzman, *Stormy Ben Butler* (New York, 1954), 180.
61. *Cong. Globe*, 40th Cong., 2d Sess., 2333 ff., 2347; *Impeachment Trial*, 170-74.
62. *Ibid.*, 247-406.

63. *Ibid.*, 295 ff., 335-41, 350; Crook, *op. cit.*, 122-23; Butler-J. W. Shaffer, Andrew Johnson MSS, March 9, 1868.
64. Merrill, *op. cit.*, 173; DeWitt, *op. cit.*, 515.
65. Ross, *op. cit.*, 129-133.
66. Butler-J. R. Young, May 12, 1868, J. R. Young MSS.
67. New York *Tribune*, May 15, 1868.
68. Stryker, *op. cit.*, 711; Francis Fessenden, *Life and Public Services of William Pitt Fessenden* (Boston, 1907), II, 165, 207.
69. DeWitt, *op. cit.*, 521.
70. George Wilkes-Butler, May 27, 1868, Butler MSS.
71. Adam Badeau, *Grant in Peace* (Hartford, 1887), 136-37. Cf. John B. Alley-Butler, May 2, 1868, Butler MSS.
72. E. M. Stanton-J. R. Young, May 13, 1868; Simon Cameron-J. R. Young, May 13, 1868, J. R. Young MSS.
73. *Impeachment Trial*, 409 ff.; Ross, *op. cit.*, 136-39; Milton, *The Age of Hate*, 607-10.
74. Butler-J. R. Young, May 16, 1868, J. R. Young MSS.
75. Boston Daily *Advertiser*, May 19, 20, 26, 1868; *The Diary of Gideon Welles*, III, 362; 366-68; Butler MSS, May-June, 1868. Woolley refused the subpoena on the ground that it had been issued on the Sabbath, only to be incarcerated and dragged before the House. *Cong. Globe*, 40th Cong., 2d Sess., 2525-37, 2585 ff., 2588, 2651 ff., 2678, 2702 ff., 2937 ff.
76. Ross, *op. cit.*, 142-43; William Salter, *The Life of James Grimes* (New York, 1876), 357. Henderson refused to appear before the committee on the grounds that the summons constituted an insult to the dignity of the Senate. Henderson-Butler, May 19, 1868, Butler MSS.
77. Ross, *op. cit.*, 153; George Wilkes-Butler, May 20, 23, 1868, Butler MSS.
78. *Impeachment Trial*, 415.
79. M. H. Alberger-Butler, June 1, 1868; Boston Daily *Advertiser*, July 1, 1868; House *Report* No. 75, 40th Cong., 2d Sess. (Washington, 1868); Salter, *op. cit.*, 361.
80. The following authorities believe Butler's tactics harmed the trial: Winston, *op. cit.*, 453; Ellis P. Oberholtzer, *A History of the United States Since the Civil War* (New York, 1922), II, 138; James Ford Rhodes, *History of the United States* (New York, 1910), VI, 135.
81. *Harper's Weekly*, XII (May 2, 1868), 274; New York *Times*, March 4, 5, 1868; Henderson-Butler, May 19, 1868, Butler MSS.

**NOTES**

CHAPTER XVIII   *Grant's Lieutenant*
(Pages 205 to 216)

1. E. J. Sherman-Butler, December 26, 1867, Butler MSS.
2. Butler-E. J. Sherman, December 27, 1867, Butler MSS.
3. A. L. Chettame-Elihu Washburne, January 22, 1868; George H. Gordon-Washburne, February 1, 1868, Elihu Washburne MSS, Library of Congress; *Cong. Globe*, 40th Cong., 2d Sess., 1282.
4. Continual warnings arrived from Essex, not only about Grant's growing popularity, but also about movements to unseat Butler. S. P. Cummings-Butler, February 24, 1868, March 16, 1868; G. Cluseret-Butler, March 12, 1868, Butler MSS.
5. George Wilkes-Butler, April 14, 1868, Butler MSS.
6. Butler-George Wilkes, May 2, 1868, Butler MSS.
7. George Wilkes-Grant, May 6, 1868, Butler MSS.
8. Grant-George Wilkes, June 19, 1868, Butler MSS.
9. George Wilkes-Butler, June 20, 1868, Butler MSS.
10. Boston Daily *Advertiser*, June 22, 1868.
11. George Wilkes-Butler, June 23, 1868, Butler MSS.
12. Boston Daily *Advertiser*, June 25, 1868.
13. *Ibid.*, August 10, 1868.
14. Butler-N. G. Upham, July 8, 1868, Butler MSS.
15. New York *Times*, September 24, 27; October 6, 7, 1868; Boston Daily *Advertiser*, September 18, 19, 21, 29; October 3, 6, 1868.
16. Memorandum of Conversation Between W. W. Lander of Salem and B. F. Butler, September 15, 1870, Butler MSS.
17. Boston Daily *Advertiser*, October 6, 27, 1868.
18. Memorandum of Conversation Between W. W. Lander of Salem and B. F. Butler, September 15, 1870, Butler MSS; Boston Daily *Advertiser*, October 16, 17, 27, 31, November 2, 1868; *Commonwealth*, October 31, 1868.
19. Simon Cameron-J. R. Young, September 17, 1868, J. R. Young MSS; Simon Cameron-Butler, August 28, 1868; Theodore Tilton-Butler, September 4, 10, 1868, 1954 boxes, Butler MSS.
20. Worthington C. Ford (ed.), *Letters of Henry Adams* (Boston and New York, 1930), 146-47.
21. *Commonwealth*, October 3, 12, 24, 1868; November 14, 1868; New York *Times*, October 24, 1868.
22. Mary E. Tucker, *Life of Mark M. Pomeroy* (New York, 1868), 168. "Look at your pet, Ben Butler, better known as the spoon thief and woman insulter of America," cried Pomeroy, while audiences hooted, "Spoons, spoons." He also owned a minature statue of Butler with a spoon in the mouth. Cf. Pomeroy, *op. cit.*
23. New York *Times*, October 24, 1868; W. E. Chandler-Elihu Washburne, Washburne MSS, November 7, 1868. For Butler's answers to Gordon, cf. Boston Daily Evening *Traveller*, October 26, 1868. The epithets are in McLaughlin, *op. cit.*, 1-4.
24. *Butler's Book*, 922.
25. *Ibid.* The pithy expression is lacking in the printed version of *Speech of Richard H. Dana, Jr., at Middleton in the Fifth District, October 26, 1868* (1868). Cf. Richard H. Dana 3d (ed.), *Richard Henry Dana, Jr.* (Boston, 1910), 445.

26. *Commonwealth,* November 7, 1868.
27. W. P. Phillips-Sumner, November 10, 1868, Sumner MSS.
28. Butler-Mrs. J. E. Rantoul, January 22, 1869, Butler MSS; Merrill, *op. cit.,* 229.
29. Butler proposed to abolish the legation in Santiago altogether. Boston *Transcript,* January 15, 1869; *Cong. Globe,* 40th Cong., 3d Sess., 218 ff.; J. Kilpatrick-Elihu Washburne, January 10, 1869, Elihu Washburne MSS.
30. Butler-E. J. Sherman, December 10, 1868, Butler MSS.
31. *Cong. Globe,* 40th Cong., 3d Sess., 16; Clemenceau, *op. cit.,* 267; Mallam, *op. cit.,* 272; Hesseltine, *Grant,* 152-53.
32. As late as March, 1869, Senator Doolittle told Welles that Butler had referred to Grant as follows: "He is stupidly dull and ignorant and no more comprehends his duty or his power under the Constitution than that dog" (pointing to a small dog). *The Diary of Gideon Welles,* III, 564-65.
33. Butler-E. J. Sherman, December 25, 1868, Butler MSS; Merrill, *op. cit.,* 234.
34. Boston Daily *Advertiser,* January 2, 1869; Welles was intrigued and Grant refused to appear. *The Diary of Gideon Welles,* III, 495; Clemenceau, *op. cit.,* 266.
35. *Commonwealth,* February 27, 1869.
36. Hesseltine, *Grant,* 155-56; Allan Nevins, *Hamilton Fish* (New York, 1936), 585.
37. Hoar, *op. cit.,* I, 361; Rhodes, *op. cit.,* VII, 23-24; Mallam, *op. cit.,* 270. Hoar averred that he asked Grant whether the rumors of blackmail were true, whereupon the General gave no answer but puffed vigorously on his cigar. However, Mallam points out that Grant habitually lapsed into silence when displeased.
38. Blaine, *op. cit.,* II, 449-55; New York *Times,* April 2, 1869; Hesseltine, *Grant,* 152-59.
39. *The Diary of Gideon Welles,* III, 567-68.
40. *The Nation,* IX (December, 1869), 497; *Cong. Globe,* 41st Cong., 2d Sess., 21; 3d Sess., 65; 42d Cong., 2d Sess., 3410 ff. The Act was finally repealed in 1887 and declared unconstitutional in 1926.
41. Nevins, *Fish,* 261-278, 309-34.
42. *Independence of Cuba, Speech of Hon. Benjamin F. Butler of Massachusetts, Delivered in the House of Representatives, June 15, 1870* (Washington, 1870).
43. Blaine, *op. cit.,* II, 335-37.
44. Capt. B. W. Perkins' claim arose because of a cancelled Crimean War contract. Harrington, *Banks,* 182.
45. *Cong. Globe,* 40th Cong., 2d Sess., Appendix, 400-03.
46. J. W. Fabens-Butler, January 11, 1869, Butler MSS; J. W. Fabens-C. K. Garrison, quoted by Nevins, *Fish,* 258-59.
47. Pierce, *op. cit.,* IV, 453; Hesseltine, *Grant,* 203; Joseph E. Cove, "The Political Career of Benjamin F. Butler After 1870," M. A. thesis, Clark University, 1929, 49.
48. Andrew D. White, *Autobiography of Andrew D. White* (New York, 1905), I, 487.

49. Butler-Sumner, April 16, 1871, Sumner MSS; Sumner-Butler, April 17, 1871, Butler MSS. His son-in-law, Senator Ames, voted steadily for Sumner's removal. Nevins, *Fish*, 492.
50. Sumner-E. L. Pierce, December 15, 1870, Sumner MSS.
51. Hesseltine, *Grant*, 209-10.
52. Butler-Sumner, July 3, 1869, Butler MSS; Merrill, *op. cit.*, 206.
53. Butler MSS, 1869-1877, for appointments. Grant later praised the General. "I have always regretted the censure that unwittingly came upon Butler . . . ," he said, "and my report was the cause. I said that the General was 'bottled up' and used the phrase without meaning to annoy the General, or give his enemies a weapon. I like Butler, and have always found him not only, as all the world knows, a man of great ability, but a patriotic man, and a man of courage, honor, and sincere convictions." John Russell Young, *Around the World With General Grant* (New York, 1879), II, 304.
54. *The Nation*, X (February, 1870), 66; New York *Times*, January 7, 27, 29, 1870; Boston *Transcript*, February 28, 1870; Cove, *op. cit.*, 39-40.
55. Mallam, *op. cit.*, 271.
56. *Independence of Cuba, Speech . . . June 15, 1870*; Nevins, *Fish*, 386.
57. New York *Standard*, May 1, 1870-July 10, 1872; Butler-J. R. Young, February 27, March 12, April 11, November 27, 1870, J. R. Young MSS; Confidential Statement to General Butler, September, 1870, Butler MSS; J. R. Young-Butler, March 21, June 22, September 18, December 22, 1871; July 10, 1872, Butler MSS.
58. Butler-Sarah Butler, February 26, 1870, Butler MSS.
59. Butler MSS for the period; Springfield *Republican*, March 2, 1871; Hoar, *op. cit.*, I, 356; Cove, *op. cit.*, 37-38; Pierce, *op. cit.*, IV, 498.
60. Edward Preston Usher, *A Memorial Sketch of Roland Greene Usher* (Boston, 1895), 23, ff.; E. J. Sherman-Butler, March 7, 1871; J. W. Shatter-Butler, May 7, 1870, Butler MSS; Springfield *Republican*, April 24, 1872.
61. *Commonwealth*, July 10, 1869; J. M. Parker-Butler, March 28, 1872; Butler MSS; George Wilkes-Butler, February 4, 1870, Zachariah Chandler MSS.
62. Mallam, *op. cit.*, 274-76.
63. Boston Daily *Traveller*, August 20, 1869.
64. *Commonwealth*, February 12, 27, 1869.
65. *Ibid.*, July 23, 1870; New York *Times*, July 23, 1870.
66. *Commonwealth*, December 26, 1868.
67. New York *Herald*, March 2, 1869; Robert Selph Henry, *The Story of Reconstruction* (New York, 1938), 376.
68. *Cong. Globe*, 41st Cong., 1st Sess., 253, 625; 2d Sess., Appendix, 576; 3d Sess., 710; 42d Cong., 1st Sess., 441 ff.; Butler-M. C. Johnson, January 13, 1868, Butler MSS; Springfield *Republican*, March 17, 1871.
69. *Butler's Book*, 733.
70. He appointed a colored cadet to West Point, established a scholarship for the sons of veterans of both races, and befriended Negro leaders. Boston Daily *Traveller*, March 8, 1870; *Butler Cor.*, V, 547; Frederick Douglass, *Life and Times of Frederick Douglass* (Boston, 1881), 398; Butler-B. K. Bruce, January 1, 1876, Butler MSS. He wrote a speech for the Mississippi Senator.

71. Mildred Thompson, *Reconstruction in Georgia*, Columbia University Studies in History, Economics, and Public Law, LXIV, I (1915), 255 ff.
72. *Cong. Globe*, 40th Cong., 3d Sess., 1056 ff.; *Boston Daily Advertiser*, February 11, 1869.
73. *Ibid.;* New York *Times*, February 11, 1869. Senator Garrett Davis introduced an unsuccessful resolution of censure in the Senate, while Bingham and Garfield took issue with Butler in the House. *Cong. Globe*, 40th Cong., 3d Sess., 1069, 1097 ff.
74. Nevins, *Fish*, 290-91.
75. *Boston Daily Advertiser*, March 16, 1869; Blaine-Butler, March 12, 1869, Butler MSS. According to Hoar, *op. cit.*, I, 201-02, Butler supported Blaine against Dawes in their contest for Speaker in order to obtain the Chairmanship of the Committee of Appropriations. He went to Blaine to press his claims for the reward, but the Speaker jumped out of the window, went to the House, and announced Dawes as Chairman. Blaine denied the story, but Butler was dissatisfied with his committee assignments. Cf. Springfield *Republican*, April 20, 1871.
76. *Cong. Globe*, 41th Cong., 1st Sess., 164, 253, 633, 699; 283 ff., 398, 425; 2d Sess., 97, 716, 1013, 1969 ff. 2291 ff.; Henry, *op. cit.*, 376, 389-93. He did, however, yield to the President by allowing Virginia to vote separately on the disenfranchisement clauses in her constitution.
77. *Ibid.*, 394; *Cong. Globe*, 41st Cong., 1st Sess., 278, 591-606; 2d Sess., 1701 ff., 1765 ff., 1969 ff., Appendix, 576 ff.; Rufus Bullock-Butler, July 23, 1870, Butler MSS, acknowledging Georgia radicals' debt to Butler.
78. Hoar, *op. cit.*, I, 204-05; *Cong. Globe*, 42d Cong., 1st Sess., 116 ff.; Springfield *Republican*, March 16, 17, 1871.
79. *The Ku Klux Outrages in the South, The Work of the Democratic Party, Speech of Hon. Benjamin F. Butler, Delivered in the House of Representatives, April 4, 1871;* New York *Times*, March 31, 1871; Boston *Times*, March 31, 1871.
80. Blaine, *op. cit.*, II, 469; Hoar, *op. cit.*, I, 205.
81. Springfield *Republican*, April 7, 15, May 9, 1871.
82. Rhodes, *op. cit.*, VI, 430-31.
83. New York *Tribune*, November 27, 1869.
84. New York *Times*, December 16, 1869.
85. Blaine, *op. cit.*, II, 512; Cox, *op. cit.*, 595 ff.; Rhodes, *op. cit.*, VI, 436-40.
86. Nevins, *Fish*, 740 ff.

**NOTES** 313

CHAPTER XIX   Enfant Terrible *of The Republican Party*
(Pages 217 to 233)

1. Hoar, *op. cit.*, I, 329-30; 347-48.
2. *Ibid.*, 334; Julian, *op. cit.*, 363. Butler's flair for the unusual led him, at least on one occasion, to receive his political co-workers in his underwear. Mrs. Hope Hammond-Henry F. Graf, January 18, 1955, courtesy of Professor Graf.
3. Merrill believes his espousal of inflation was the principal cause of his troubles with the conservatives. Merrill, *op. cit.*, 130. Butler partially agreed. Butler-F. P. Wood, February 25, 1878, Butler MSS, letterbooks.
4. Ford, *op. cit.*, 149; *The Nation*, VIII (January 21, 1869), 42; *The Diary of Gideon Welles*, III, 506.
5. *Cong. Globe*, 40th Cong., 3d Sess., 303 ff.
6. New York *Times*, January 13, 1869.
7. Cove, *op. cit.*, 107 ff.; Rhodes, *op. cit.*, VI, 241-42; *Commonwealth*, February 26, 1870; Springfield *Republican*, March 24, April 16, 24, 1874.
8. New York *Times*, May 6, 1870.
9. *Ibid.*, July 6, 1878. Butler saw Grant early in May; on May 19, the President ruled that the standard of wages be left unchanged, the reduction of hours notwithstanding. *Ibid.*, May 12, 1869.
10. Springfield *Republican*, June 24, 1871.
11. Paxton Hibben, *Henry Ward Beecher* (New York, 1927), 268; Cove, *op. cit.*, 51-52; New York *Herald*, January 25, 1872; Victoria Woodhull-Butler, February 26, 1871; Susan B. Anthony-Butler, December 9, 1872, April 27, 1873, Butler MSS; Rochester Evening *Express*, February 26, 1874. Butler presented to Congress the petition of 35,000 advocated by Victoria Woodhull and Elizabeth Cady Stanton. He also befriended Susan B. Anthony and gave her legal advice after she had defied the law by voting in Rochester.
12. New York *Times*, June 15, 1874; Springfield *Republican*, March 18, 1871; William Harlan Hale, *Horace Greeley* (New York, 1950), 325-36.
13. He was instrumental in depriving William Schouler and "Warrington" of their positions and used his influence to defeat R. H. Dana's nomination for the London legation.
14. Cf. Merrill, *op. cit.*, 237-38.
15. *Cong. Globe*, 42d Cong., 2d Sess., Appendix, 267.
16. For example, *ibid.*, 42d Cong., 2d Sess., 237, 2351; Butler-F. A. Sawyer, December 14, 1873, Butler MSS. He also played a prominent role in killing the modest beginnings of Grant's civil service reform program by discontinuing appropriations for the Civil Service Commission. *Cong. Rec.*, 43d Cong., 1st Sess., II, 4891.
17. Springfield *Republican*, April 27, 1878. His legal services for the Union Pacific Railroad and the blackmailer Jayne are good examples.
18. *Commonwealth*, January 8, 1870; Boston *Post*, September 20, 1870.
19. *Report on the National Asylum*, House Military Affairs Committee, 41st Cong., 3d Sess., Report No. 45 (Washington, 1871); Patterson, *Memories of Fort Monroe and Vicinity*, 57.
20. *Cong. Globe*, 41st Cong., 3d Sess., 1900.

21. Boston *Post*, September 20, 1870. In spite of his denials, by 1883, he did hold stock in the company. He collected a $5,000 dividend in 1884. Butler-O. D. Barrett, December 27, 1883, February 27, 1884, letterbooks, Butler MSS.

22. *Report on the National Asylum*. Charges concerning the Home continued to plague the General until the time of his death. An entire box of the MSS is devoted to the affairs of the institution, and he tried hard to prove that he faithfully accounted for every penny of its funds. Yet at the time of his death, a suit was pending against him for the recovery of some money on behalf of the Government. His executors settled the case out of court for $18,000. Butler was convinced that he had been wronged because the controversy involved largely a matter of bookkeeping. Even the hostile New York *Times*, September 25, 1887, thought it unlikely that he would steal from veterans; yet the responsibility for mingling his private funds with those of the institution is clearly his, and he laid himself open to the charge of appropriating the interest. J. G. Carlisle-R. Olney, January 27, 1894, Butler MSS; Adelbert Ames, "The National Home for Disabled Volunteer Soldiers," February 16, 1914, 1954 boxes, Butler MSS.

23. *Cong. Globe*, 41st Cong., 3d Sess., 1510 ff.; 1900; 42d Cong., 1st Sess., 835-42, 493 ff., 672; Boston *Times*, March 31, 1871.

24. New York *Times*, May 8, 1881, July 21, 1872; Boston Daily *Advertiser*, July 29, 1868. The Smith suit was an exception.

25. Butler also had close connections with the principal figures involved in the District Ring, a group which undertook the paving of the streets of Washington. He was accused of wrong-doing; however, he negotiated for a contract for the paving of Pennsylvania Avenue long after the scandals had been aired. Matthew Josephson, *The Politicos, 1865-1896* (New York, 1938), 125-26; Butler-Jonas French, March 31, 1877, letterbooks, Butler MSS.

26. Worcester Evening *Gazette*, December 7, 1870; Cincinnati *Catholic Telegraph*, February 17, 1871; *Butler's Book*, 320.

27. Butler-Hamilton Fish, September 25, 1870, Fish MSS; *Letter By Benjamin F. Butler to Hon. A. Ames, U. S. Senate* (Lowell, 1871). Ceaselessly agitating the fishermen's wrongs, he nevertheless insisted that annexation should follow, not precede, reciprocity with Canada.

28. Butler-Hamilton Fish, September 25, 1870, Fish MSS.

29. Boston Daily *Advertiser*, April 29, 1869; New York *Times*, May 25, 1869, November 4, 1870; *Commonwealth*, November 12, 26, 1870.

30. Benjamin F. Butler, *The Treaty of Washington, An Analysis of Its Provisions. Our Losses, England's Gains. Address at the Music Hall in Philadelphia, October 16, 1871* (Boston, 1871); Nevins, *Fish*, 528.

31. Butler-Governor Onslow Stearns, February 2, 1870, Butler MSS; "Warrington," in *Commonwealth*, December 3, 1870.

32. John C. Hanner-Hamilton Fish, October 5, 1870, Fish MSS; Governor J. M. Ashley of Montana-Butler, April 17, 1870, Butler MSS. There was even talk of alleged Presidential ambitions. *The Nation*, X (March 3, 1870), 130.

33. Robinson, *op. cit.*, 130-31.

34. *Commonwealth*, November 26, 1870.

35. Boston *Journal*, March 15, 1871; Hoar, *op. cit.*, I, 348; Merrill, *op. cit.*, 238; Ware, *op. cit.*, 188; John F. Rich-Butler, August 13, 1871, Butler MSS.

36. Ware, *op. cit.*, 188-93.
37. Springfield *Republican*, March 18, 1871.
38. "Gubernatorial Canvass in Massachusetts," 1871 Misc. Box, Butler MSS.
39. Boston Sunday Morning *Chronicle*, July 16, 1871. The allegation was that Butler had promised the Doctor a seat in Congress in return for support for the governorship.
40. Springfield *Republican*, July 31, 1871.
41. *Ibid.*, August 24, 1871, with an article about his career, entitled, "The Great Fizzler."
42. Benjamin F. Butler, *Address at Springfield, August 24, 1871* (Boston, 1871); New York *Times*, August 25, 1871.
43. *Ibid.*, September 9, 1871; Robinson, *op. cit.*, 134; Springfield *Republican*, August 31, 1871.
44. Wendell Phillips, *The People Coming to Power, Speech . . . at the Salisbury Beach Gathering, September 13, 1871* (Boston, 1871).
45. "Gubernatorial Canvass in Massachusetts," *loc. cit.*
46. Boston *Journal*, September 19, 1871; Pierce, *op. cit.*, IV, 494-95; Sumner Scrapbook, September 1871, Sumner MSS; Butler-Sumner, October 2, 1871, Sumner MSS.
47. Robinson, *op. cit.*, 132-33, 443 ff.
48. Ware, *op. cit.*, 192-93; Cove, *op. cit.*, 27; Springfield *Republican*, September 25, 26, 27, 1871. There was talk of 500 delegates for Butler, 350 for Washburn, and 250 for Rice and Loring combined.
49. New York *Times*, September 28, 1871; Hoar, *op. cit.*, I, 348-49. The vote was 643-464.
50. Parton-Butler, June 18, 1871; Horace Porter-Butler, June 25, 1871, Butler MSS. Strangely enough, his enemies accused him of fishing for the anti-Grant nomination himself. Thurlow Weed-Hamilton Fish, November 23, 1871, Fish MSS.
51. Butler-Mrs. Butler, June 8, 1872, Butler MSS.
52. Butler-J. B. Alley, August 12, 1872, Butler MSS.
53. He absented himself from the Philadelphia Convention which nominated Grant. As he wrote to his wife, "You observe that I have not been to Philadelphia. I go with my party but I do not see that I am called upon to throw up my hat even if it is an old one for either the 'Galena James' or the 'Natick Cobbler'!" Butler-Mrs. Butler, June 8, 1872, Butler MSS.
54. Springfield *Republican*, August 22, September 12, October 18, November 4, 6, 1872; *The Nation*, XV (September 26, 1872), 194. The vote for Butler was 10,663 to Thompson's 5,693.
55. *Cong. Globe*, 42d Cong., 3d Sess., 1651, Appendix, 176 ff. He also denied the right to punish members for acts committed in the past and prepared a report against the impeachment of the Vice President. Ames and Brooks were censured, but not expelled.
56. Butler-J. R. Young, January 19, 1873; J. R. Young MSS; Springfield *Republican*, December 21, 30, 1871.
57. *Ibid.*, January 28, February 14, 1873. An effort was made to link Butler to the scandal through his private secretary, George B. Conlam, but not even the *Republican* gave credence to the charge. *Ibid.*, February 3, 1873.
58. William S. Robinson, *The Salary Grab* (Boston, 1873); Cove, *op. cit.*, 60 ff. For Butler's defense, cf. New York *Times*, August 27, 1873.

59. *The Nation,* XVI (June 26, 1873), 426.
60. Jonas French-Butler, January 21, 1873; J. H. Chadwick-Butler, February 6, 1873; G. D. Whittle-Butler, February 12, 1873; Fred Wilcomb-Butler, February 14, 1873, Butler MSS; Springfield *Republican,* January 1, 2, March 11, 12, 13, 1873. Dawes was the leading alternate candidate. Butler was anxious to get Boutwell into the Senate and his friend W. A. Richardson into the Treasury.
61. *Ibid.,* March 7, 19, 20, 1873.
62. New York *Times,* April 22, July 5, 1873; Ware, *op. cit.,* 194; Springfield *Republican,* June 17, 1873.
63. His erratic voting record on the Northern Pacific Railroad Bill is a case in point. He finally supported it. Oberholtzer, *op. cit.,* II, 179. Moreover, he maintained friendly relations with Jay Gould who contributed $1,000 to the 1873 Butler campaign chest. Jay Gould-Butler, June 26, 1873, Butler MSS.
64. Robinson, *"Warrington" Pen Portraits,* 143; Hoar, *op. cit.,* I, 349; Springfield *Republican,* August 26, 1873. They met at Boston's Hamilton Hall.
65. *Ibid.,* August 16, 1873, August 22, 1873; Hoar, *op. cit.,* I, 349-53.
66. Robinson, *"Warrington" Pen Portraits,* 141-44; Robinson, *The Salary Grab.*
67. *Merrimac Valley Visitor,* July 19, 1873; *The Salaries of Public Officials, Letter of General Butler, of Massachusetts* (Boston, 1873); New York *Times,* August 27, 1873; Springfield *Republican,* August 9, 1873, August 22, 27, September 1, 2, 1873.
68. *Ibid.,* September 8, 9, 10, 11, 1873; Cove, *op. cit.,* 85-90. On the critical motion, the vote was 584-539. For the ten hour bill, cf. Marion Cahill, *Shorter Hours* (New York, 1932), 107.
69. Springfield *Republican,* December 2, 1873, January 14, 1874.
70. *Ibid.,* February 23, 1874; Boutwell, *op. cit.,* II, 283.
71. Pierce, *op. cit.,* IV, 589; Albert B. Hart, *Commonwealth History of Massachusetts,* IV, 599; Springfield *Republican,* February 19-27, 1874; Hoar, *op. cit.,* I, 210-11.
72. Boutwell, *op. cit.,* II, 283-84. Butler threatened to spend $500,000 to defeat Boutwell's reelection.
73. Boston *Journal of Commerce,* March 7, 1874; New York *Times,* February 21, 28, 1874.
74. Fuess, *Cushing,* II, 366 ff. Butler had urged Cushing's appointment.
75. Cove, *op. cit.,* 55 ff.; W. E. Woodward, *Meet General Grant* (New York, 1946), 419; Nevins, *Fish,* 708; *Gen. Benjamin F. Butler's True Record* (Boston, 1879), 25-26.
76. Springfield *Republican,* May 27, 1874.
77. New York *Times,* June 20, 1874; *Cong. Record,* 43d Cong., 1st Sess., II, 5220-28.
78. Young, *op. cit.,* I, 153; Robert G. Caldwell, *James A. Garfield* (New York, 1931), 315; Moorfield Storey and Edward Emerson, *Ebenezer Rockwood Hoar* (Boston & New York, 1911), 253; Butler-Sarah Butler, April 24, 1874, Butler MSS.
79. J. B. Smith-Butler, February 4, 1874; G. F. Moore-Butler, March 5, 1874, Butler MSS.

80. Jonas French-Butler, March 25, April 3, 1874; C. H. Chadwick-Butler, April 4, 9, 1874, Butler MSS; New York *Times*, March 14, 18, April 1, 2, 18, 1874; *The Diary of George Templeton Strong*, IV, 522; Hoar, *op. cit.*, I, 227.
81. Butler-Sarah Butler, April 24, 1874, Butler MSS.
82. Springfield *Republican*, May 15, 16, July 24, 1874; New York *Times*, May 25, 1874.
83. Springfield *Republican*, July 9, 1874.
84. After trying to keep the scandal from the public, Butler became the legal counsel of Francis T. Moulton, Beecher's and Tilton's "mutual friend." As in the impeachment trial, he again opposed Evarts. Paxton Hibben, *op. cit.*, 264, 302, 383. Butler MSS, 1875, 1876.
85. Springfield *Republican*, September 9, October 1, 7, 13, 1874.
86. New York *Times*, September 13, 1874.
87. Springfield *Republican*, September 21, 1874.
88. Clark & Jones-Butler, October 22, 23, 1874, Butler MSS.
89. New York *Times*, November 4, 5, 1874. Butler received 7,747 to Thompson's 8,716 votes.
90. Butler-Benjamin Pitman, letterbooks, February 2, 1876, Butler MSS.
91. Wirt Armistead Cate, *Lucius Q. C. Lamar* (Chapel Hill, 1935), 189-91; Rhodes, *op. cit.*, VII, 89-90.
92. *Cong. Rec.*, 43d Cong., 2d Sess., III, 886 ff., 938 ff., 985 ff., 1006 ff. John Young Brown of Kentucky said: "If I were . . . to describe that which is pusillanimous in war, inhuman in peace, forbidden in morals, and infamous in politics, I would call it Butlerizing." Terrific excitement accompanied these outbursts and Brown was censured.
93. Rhodes, *op. cit.*, VII, 89-90. He was less successful with a new Force Bill, which passed the House too late to be considered in the Senate. Cate, *op. cit.*, 184-85; Henry, *op. cit.*, 541; *Cong. Rec.*, 43d Cong., 2d Sess., III, 1906. He also engaged in a new spat with Speaker Blaine. Springfield *Republican*, March 1, 1875.
94. Herman Ward-Butler, March 8, 1875; Joshua Nickerson-Butler, June 21, 1875, Butler MSS; Springfield *Republican*, March 12, 1875.
95. Butler-C. C. Merritt, September 8, 1875; Butler-C. L. Fiske, September 10, 1875, Butler MSS.
96. Springfield *Republican*, July 9, October 15, 1875.
97. "Memorandum of Conversation with Senator Dawes, December 30, 1885," Richard Henry Dana MSS, *Massachusetts Historical Society*, Boston; C. B. Curtis-Simon Cameron, March 27, 1876, Cameron MSS, Library of Congress; Butler-W. A. Simmons, March 18, 1876; Butler-Bruce, March 21, 1876; Butler-R. Conkling, March 21, 1876, letterbooks, Butler MSS.
98. Death Certificate, April 8, 1876, Butler MSS. It was a thyroid tumor.
99. Bowers, *op. cit.*, 453; Butler-A. Ames, December, 1875-March, 1876, Butler MSS.
100. Butler-Adelbert Ames, February 25, March 25, April 1, 1876; Death Certificate, April 8, 1876, Butler MSS; Butler-J. R. Young, April 15, 1876, J. R. Young MSS. To make things worse, his enemies picked this very time to abolish the grade of Major General in the Massachusetts Militia. New York *Times*, May 7, 1876.
101. *Butler's Book*, 925; Butler-W. H. P. Wright, March 31, 1876, letterbooks, Butler MSS.

102. G. A. Smith-Butler, May 2, 1876; Butler-N. C. Munson, W. H. P. Wright-Butler, June 25, 1876, Butler MSS.
103. W. A. Simmons-Butler, August 2, 1876. Simmons' postscript was as follows: "Anything to win and for this reason I said you were 'OK' on all the platform, so don't say anything on currency while the fight progresses. After we win, you are not responsible for what I say." Butler MSS.
104. Boston Daily *Advertiser,* August 22, 23, 1876. On August 5, he had written an acceptance letter to various citizens asking him to run. Letterbooks, Butler MSS.
105. *Ibid.*
106. Boston *Advertiser,* September 14, 1876.
107. *Ibid.,* October 5, 1876; Hoar, *op. cit.,* I, 355. Judge Hoar entered the campaign with a strong letter against Butler.
108. Benjamin F. Butler, *Letter to Hon. E. R. Hoar* (Lowell, 1876).
109. Boston *Advertiser,* November 2, 1876; J. M. Forbes pledge, November 4, 1876, Amos Lawrence MSS, *Massachusetts Historical Society.*
110. Handbill in Butler MSS; Frederick Douglass, Jr.-Butler, October 14, 1876, Butler MSS; New York *Times,* August 22, 1876; Washington *National Republican,* October 30, 1876; Storey, *op. cit.,* 352-55.
111. The vote was: Butler, 12,000; Tarbox, 9,379; Hoar, 1,696.
112. This was clearly shown as early as 1872, when Governor Washburn made some of Butler's demands his own. George A. Shaw-Butler, January 5, 1872, Butler MSS.

## CHAPTER XX  *Return To The Democrats*
(Pages 234 to 243)

1. *Butler's Book,* 446, 967; Butler-R. Conkling, November 26, 1876; Butler-T. B. Ross, October 10, 1876; Butler-J. A. Berryman, December 9, 1876; Butler-Somerby, February 12, 1877, letterbooks, Butler MSS. Hayes reciprocated. Charles R. Williams (ed.), *Diary and Letters of Rutherford B. Hayes* (Columbus, 1924), III, 269, 271.
2. Butler-Roscoe Conkling, November 26, 1876, letterbooks, Butler MSS.
3. New York *Times,* December 24, 1876.
4. Butler-W. E. Chandler, January 4, 1877, letterbooks, Butler MSS.
5. Hoar, *op. cit.,* II, 1-6; Boutwell, *op. cit.,* II, 284; Butler-Boutwell, December 29, 1876, January 9, 1877, letterbooks, Butler MSS; Springfield *Republican,* January 8, 20, 13, 25, 1877; Story, *op. cit.,* 260-61.
6. C. Vann Woodward, *Reunion and Reaction* (Boston, 1951), 22 ff.
7. New York *Times,* March 10, 1877.
8. Barrows, *op. cit.,* 312; Springfield *Republican,* March 8, 1877. Devens was a Massachusetts opponent.
9. Hamilton Fish-Butler, July 23, 1872, letterbooks, IV, 823, Fish MSS; George Butler-Butler, August 3, 1871, Butler MSS; Butler-George Butler, February 2, 1876, Butler MSS; Springfield *Republican,* May 3, 5, 11, 1877.
10. Butler-Roscoe Conkling, April 26, 1877; Butler-Blanche Butler Ames, March 21, 1877, letterbooks, Butler MSS.

11. New York *Times*, May 29, 30; June 6, 7, 1877. Butler replied as follows to McVeagh's insinuations concerning New Orleans: "A half dozen dirty newspapers have been enabled to preserve themselves from bankruptcy for the last dozen years by printing the assertions about me which you only insinuate. Every man has his own taste in choosing his way to acquire money, but if I were obliged to choose one of two ways either to 'appropriate it as military commandant' or to marry into a family where I was neither wanted nor by which I should be respected, 'to get money to spare,' I certainly should choose the former . . ."

12. Baltimore *Gazette*, December 23, 1877; New York *Times*, December 24, 1877.

13. *Ibid.*, December 30, 1877.

14. Springfield *Republican*, November 1, 1877. The Act of 1875 had provided for the resumption of specie payments on January 1, 1879; a section of the Bland Bill provided for its repeal.

15. Chicago *Times*, April 20, 1877.

16. *Cong. Rec.*, 45th Cong., 2d Sess., 1250, 1350-57, 1420; Cove, *op. cit.*, 121 ff. At the close of the oration, he engaged in a tiff with Representative Chittenden of New York, with whom he later arranged for a test case concerning the constitutionality of the greenback. The Supreme Court upheld him. Butler-Chittenden, February 13, 1879; Butler-George Bancroft, April 11, 1884, letterbooks, Butler MSS. For the case, cf. *Julliard v. Greenman*, 110 U. S. 421 (1884).

17. Hoar, *op. cit.*, I, 363.

18. Storey, *op. cit.*, 265.

19. He kept in close touch with the new National Party organized at Toledo that year. Solon J. Buck, *The Agrarian Crusade* (New Haven, 1919), 88-90; Marcus Hanlon-Butler, March 11, 1878; Butler-L. R. Train, March 23, 1878, Butler-Luther Day, April 11, 1878, Butler MSS and letterbooks.

20. *Cong. Rec.*, 45th Cong., 2d Sess., 2084 ff.; Springfield *Republican*, March 29, 30, April 6, 1878. Secretly, he had also supported the Democratic candidate for mayor in Boston in December, 1877. J. H. Chadwick-Butler, December 4, 1877; G. W. Copeland-Butler, December 6, 1877, Butler MSS.

21. *Cong. Rec.*, 45th Cong., 2d Sess., 2310 ff., 2341 ff.; clipping from Scranton Sunday Morning *Free Press* and letters from Irish correspondents, Butler MSS. 1878.

22. "Presidential Election Investigation," *House Miscellaneous* Documents, 45 Cong., 3d Sess., Doc. No. 31 (Washington, 1879); Blaine, *op. cit.*, II, 589-90.

23. *Ibid.*, 590; Leon Burr Richardson, *William E. Chandler, Republican* (New York, 1940), 227 ff. Washington *Post*, October 3, 1878. He opposed the dispatches' investigation. *Cong. Rec.*, 45th Cong., 3d Sess., 609 ff.

24. *Cong. Rec.*, 45th Cong., 2d Sess., 4825-27.

25. New York *Times*, March 1, 1879.

26. The railroad had not paid the interest on the subsidies it had received from the government. Josephson, *op. cit.*, 268.

27. *Cong. Rec.*, 45th Cong., 2d Sess., 2779. He was responding to his friend, Jay Gould's entreaties, although he put his opposition on moral grounds — confiscation of private property, the debt of the nation to the railroads for tying the country together. Jay Gould-Butler, April 9, 1878, Butler MSS.

28. *Cong. Rec.*, 45th Cong., 2d Sess., 3323, 3631-35, 4380; Washington Sunday *Chronicle*, March 25, 1878.
29. New York *Times*, July 6, 12, 1878.
30. *Ibid.*, July 16, 1878; William D. Northend-Butler, July 16, 1878; A. J. Hall-Butler, July 18, 1878; Butler-Randall, July 16, 23, 1878, Butler MSS and letterbooks.
31. George Lowell Austin, *The History of Massachusetts* (Boston, 1885), 578; Albany Evening *Journal*, August 10, 1878.
32. Boston *Journal*, August 29, 1878.
33. Springfield *Republican*, September 12, 1878.
34. *Ibid.*, August 30-September 17, 1878.
35. Austin, *op. cit.*, 512.
36. Springfield *Republican*, September 17, 18, 26, 1878; Solomon F. Griffin, *People and Politics* (Boston 1923), 187-91; Cove, *op. cit.*, 147 ff.
37. Boston *Post, Journal, Herald*; New York *Times, World, Tribune*, September 18, 1878; other papers quoted in Springfield *Republican*, September 19, 1878.
38. *Ibid.*, October 1, 7, 12, 24; Boston *Advertiser*, October 14, 1878; Boston *Transcript*, September 26, 1878; J. M. Coburn-Butler, October 3, 1878. His enormous fee in the Farragut prize case was constantly attacked. A. A. Dodge-Butler, October 18, 1878, with handbill, Butler MSS. It read as follows: "All citizens . . . who wish to see the Old Bay State disgraced, who wish to put a liar and a plunderer of the sailors' money in the Governor's chair, all men of both parties who approve of a man who has gone back on both parties, and who has never kept his promises will please vote for the man who was Bottled Up at Bermuda Hundred and kept shop for rebel customers."
39. Boston Daily Evening *Traveller*, September 30, 1878; Boston *Globe*, October 24, 1878.
40. Springfield *Republican*, September 26, 1878.
41. Williams, *Hayes Diary*, III, 508; Hart, *op. cit.*, III, 602-03. The vote was: Talbot, 134,725; Butler, 109,435; Abbott, 10,162. This compares with the following figures for 1877: Rice (R), 91,255; Gaston (D), 73,185.
42. Springfield *Republican*, January 20, 31, April 25, 1879. In 1879, Talbot endorsed many of Butler's ideas. New Bedford *Signal*, February 15, 1879; Butler-Talbot, January 5, 1879, letterbooks, Butler MSS.
43. New York *Times*, November 14, 1878.
44. *Butler's Book*, 985 ff.; special boxes in Butler MSS. Thomas A. Edison was one of his clients.
45. Benjamin F. Butler, "The Story of the *America*," *Harper's Monthly*, LXXI (June, 1885), 304-08.
46. James Parton-Mrs. Parton, August 15, 1882, Parton MSS.
47. Boston *Herald*, March 21, 1874; Springfield *Republican*, June 20, 1879.
48. *Ibid.*, February 13, 1879.
49. *Butler's Book*, 80. He maintained he did not want his son mistreated by the regulars as he had been; for he was sure that there would be another war, preferably with England.
50. Giraud Chester, *Embattled Maiden, The Life of Anna Dickinson* (New York, 1951), 112-13, 195-97; Butler-Anna Dickinson, October 24, 1873, June

2, July 11, August 29, 1874, October 1, 1875, July 19, 22, 25, 1878, Dickinson MSS, Library of Congress.

51. *Cong. Rec.*, 45th Cong., 3d Sess., 469, 609 ff., 1331 ff.; Appendix, 216-17.

52. Springfield *Republican*, November 15, December 13, 1878.

53. T. A. Bland, *Life of Benjamin F. Butler* (Boston, 1879).

54. *Butler's Record* (1879). Among other things, the pamphlet contained an unfavorable comparison of the wages paid by Talbot's mill with those paid by the Middlesex Mill. *Ibid.*, 8. Moorfield Storey was the author of the anonymous publication.

55. Springfield *Republican*, October 8, 1879.

56. New York *Times*, September 18, 1879.

57. Boston *Herald*, November 5, 1879; Springfield *Republican*, November 5, 1879. The vote was: Long, 122,751; Butler, 109,149; Adams, 9,989. Cove, *op. cit.*, 159 ff.

58. Newburyport *Herald*, February 24, 1880; Springfield *Republican*, June 23, 24, 1880.

59. *Ibid.*, June 19, 1880.

60. *Ibid.*, July 30, August 30, 1880.

61. W. E. Chandler wrote him: "Of all the foolish reasons a man ever gave for leaving one party and joining another yours are the worst." W. E. Chandler-Butler, September 4, 1880, Butler MSS. Cf. Providence *Journal*, August 23, 1880. In spite of misgivings, the Democratic National Committee welcomed him. W. H. Barnum-Butler, August 31, 1880, Butler MSS. He campaigned for the party thereafter.

62. Springfield *Republican*, September 2, 1880.

CHAPTER XXI  *Climax and Anti-Climax*
(Pages 244 to 256)

1. Butler-Blanche Ames, March 17, 1881, letterbooks, Butler MSS; Parton-Mrs. Parton, August 15, 1882, Parton MSS; Flower, *op. cit.*, 182-83.

2. Griffin, *op. cit.*, 242 ff.; Hoar, *op. cit.*, II, 117.

3. Butler-Clarke, September 10, 1882, letterbooks, Butler MSS.

4. *Ibid.*; Butler-General Sutton, April 12, 1882, letterbooks, Butler MSS. The Greenback-Labor party nominated him as early as August 18, in spite of opposition. Some Greenbackers took offense at his remarks that since paper money had risen to par, the party was dead. Boston Daily *Advertiser*, August 19, 1882.

5. *Butler's Book*, 79-81.

6. Boston Daily *Advertiser*, September 20, 1882; October 9, 1882.

7. Griffin, *op. cit.*, 163 ff., 242 ff.; Hoar, *op. cit.*, I, 345-46. Butler's triumph was complete when his candidate was elected Mayor of Boston early in December. The figures for the gubernatorial election were: Butler, 133,946; Bishop, 119,997. Even the Lieutenant Governor-elect was a Republican.

8. *Butler's Book*, 969.

9. Springfield *Republican*, January 4, 5, 1883.

10. *Ibid.*, Griffin, *op. cit.*, 244-45; *Address of His Excellency Benjamin F. Butler to the Two Branches of the Legislature of Massachusetts, January 4, 1883* (Boston, 1883).
11. Austin, *op. cit.*, 579; Haverhill *Bulletin*, August 4, 1883. Vetoes in Butler MSS.
12. Austin, *op. cit.*, 582-83.
13. *The Nation*, XXXVI (April 5, 1883), 286.
14. *The Record of Benjamin F. Butler* (Boston, 1883), 33; Boston Evening *Transcript*, June 9, 12, 1883.
15. *Butler's Book*, 969-74; Boston Evening *Journal*, April 2, 6, 1883.
16. Springfield *Republican*, February 15, March 23, 27, April 12, 1883. He finally appointed John K. Tarbox, his old Lowell opponent, to the post. *Butler's Book*, 975.
17. Hart, *op. cit.*, IV, 604 ff.; Springfield *Republican*, February 1, 13; March 1, 21, 28; April 5, 1883; Boston Evening *Transcript*, April 26, 1883; Boston Evening *Journal*, May 27, 1883.
18. *Ibid.*, March 12, 1883; *The Record of Benjamin F. Butler*, 20.
19. *Butler's Book*, 969.
20. He recognized this himself and wrote: "I took my seat and gave the legislature an address in which I advocated many democratic measures. Many of them have since been adopted by the Republican party in order to hold their power." *Ibid.*; Cf. Hart, *op. cit.*, IV, 604.
21. Commonwealth of Massachusetts, House Report No. 300, *Report of the Hearings Before the Joint Standing Committee on Public Charitable Institutions . . . and the Special Charges of the Mismanagement of the State Almshouse at Tewksbury* (Boston, 1883).
22. *Butler's Book*, 974; Springfield *Republican*, February 10, 13, 25, 1883.
23. *Ibid.*, April 12, 1883.
24. Howe, *op. cit.*, 166-67; Hoar, *op. cit.*, I, 300-01.
25. Edward Sandford Martin, *The Life of Joseph Hodges Choate* (New York, 1920), I, 355-61; Griffin, *op. cit.*, 249-50.
26. Bliss Perry, *And Gladly Teach* (Boston and New York, 1935), 83.
27. William Endicott-Amos Lawrence, J. M. Forbes, S. C. Coble and Henry Lee, July 10, 1883; Henry Lee-Amos Lawrence, August 16, 1883, Amos Lawrence MSS.
28. Howe, *op. cit.*, 147. He wrote another pamphlet called *The Record of Benjamin F. Butler*.
29. Hoar, *op. cit.*, I, 356; Cove, *op. cit.*, 180 ff.
30. John A. Garraty, *Henry Cabot Lodge* (New York, 1953), 70-74; Austin, *op. cit.*, 583; Griffin, *op. cit.*, 250.
31. Boston *Traveller*, August, 1883; *The Nation*, October 13, 25, 1883.
32. Springfield *Republican*, September-November, 1883.
33. *Argument Before the Tewkesbury Investigation Committee by Governor Benj. F. Butler Upon Facts Disclosed During the Recent Investigation, July 15, 1883* (1883).
34. Haverhill Weekly *Bulletin*, September 29, 1883. The Democrats replied:

> And must Ben Butler go?
> And shall Ben Butler go?
> No! Fifteen times 10,000 men
> Shall rise and answer, No!

# NOTES

This caused the Republicans to answer in turn:

> And must Ben Butler stay?
> And shall Ben Butler stay?
> No! Sixteen times 10,000 men
> Shall rise and answer, Nay!

*Ibid.*, November 10, 1883.

35. The vote was: Robinson: 159,084; Butler: 150,351. Only 282,512 had voted in 1880.

> And George D.
> Robinson, he
> Was one too many for
> Benjamin B.,

wrote the Springfield *Republican*, November 7, 1883.

36. Butler-Otis P. Lord, November 7, 1883; Butler-Jonas B. French, November 12, 1883, letterbooks, Butler MSS.

37. W. J. A. Montgomery-Butler, January 1, 1884; C. S. Hampton-Noah Plympton, February 27, May 5, 1884, 1954 boxes, Butler MSS; P. H. Coney-Butler, January 8, 1884; Roger Pryor-Butler, January 30, 31, 1884, Butler MSS.

38. St. Louis *Republican*, January 16, 1884; *The Nation*, December 13, 1883; New York *Times*, December 22, January 12, 1884, January 28, 1884; W. H. Shupe-B. F. Shiveley, April 7, 1884, 1954 boxes, Butler MSS.

39. New York *Times*, January 28, 1884.

40. Butler-B. F. Shiveley, March 13, 1884; Butler-L. H. Perkins, March 24, 1884, letterbooks, Butler MSS.

41. W. J. A. Montgomery-Butler, January 1, 1884; W. H. Shupe-Butler, January 1, 1884; J. S. Haseltine-Butler, January 6, 1884; H. E. Brown-T. E. Major, February 27, 1884; John Looney-Butler, February 8, 1884; C. S. Hampton-Noah Plympton, February 27, 1884; W. H. Shupe-Butler, March 24, 1884, May 1, 1884; Butler-W. H. Shupe, April 26, 1884; C. S. Hampton-Noah Plympton, May 5, 1884, 1954 boxes, Butler MSS.

42. *Argument of Benjamin F. Butler Before the Committee on Commerce of the House of Representatives for an Investigation of the Monopoly of the Standard Oil Company and Its Confederates* (Washington, 1880).

43. W. H. Shupe-B. F. Shiveley, April 7, 1884, 1954 boxes, Butler MSS. Those who were more idealistic walked out. J. A. George-Butler, May 21, 1884, 1954 boxes, Butler MSS.

44. Fred E. Haynes, *Third Party Movements Since the Civil War* (Iowa City, 1916), 148-49. A. M. West of Alabama was his running mate.

45. Springfield *Republican*, May 17, 29, 1884.

46. Butler-Samuel Randall, January 25, 1884; Butler-John Kelly, May 8, 1884; Butler-Ernest Eaton, April 4, 1884, letterbooks, Butler MSS; John Kelly-Butler, June 11, 1884; Roger Pryor-Butler, March 17, 1884, 1954 boxes, Butler MSS. Cf. Detroit Evening *Journal*, May 24, 1884.

47. Roger Pryor-Butler, March 17, 1884, May 31, June 10, 1884; Noah Plympton-Butler, June 24, 1884, Butler MSS. Roger Pryor was a former Confederate General who had settled in New York. He was a friend of Butler's and conducted negotiations on his behalf in the City.

48. Noah Plympton-Butler, June 20, 24, 1884, 1954 boxes, Butler MSS. Plympton acted as Butler's advance agent.
49. Springfield *Republican,* July 7-10, 1884; C. W. Hudson, *Random Recollections of an Old Political Reporter* (New York, 1911), 171.
50. *Ibid.*; *Official Proceedings of the National Democratic Convention* (New York, 1884), 43, 84, 195, 203, 218, 206-11; Allan Nevins, *Grover Cleveland* (New York, 1948), 150 ff.
51. William A. Simmons strongly advised him to do so. W. A. Simmons-Butler, July 23, 1884, Butler MSS, 1954 boxes.
52. Butler-Henry Barnard, July 21, 1884, letterbooks, Butler MSS; *Butler's Book,* 982.
53. F. M. Fogg-Butler, July 15, 1884; W. T. Fuller-W. H. Shupe, July 18, 1884; T. E. Major-Butler, July 16, 1884; J. W. Begole-Butler, July 13, 1884, 1954 boxes, Butler MSS.
54. W. Litchman-Butler, July 12, 1884, 1954 boxes, Butler MSS; Butler-Noah Plympton, December 3, 1891, letterbooks, Butler MSS.
55. Butler-J. F. Henry, July 29, 1884, letterbooks, Butler MSS.
56. *The Nation,* IXI, (August 21, 1884), 148; *Harper's Weekly,* XXVIII (October 25, 1884), 697; Leon Burr Richardson, *William E. Chandler* (New York, 1940), 351-52.
57. New York *Sun,* August 6, 1884. After Cleveland had published his letter of acceptance, Butler came out with a lengthy "Address to Constituents," in which he stressed his tariff, labor, anti-monopoly, and greenback views. *Ibid.,* August 19, 1884.
58. J. B. O'Reilley-Butler, July 26, 1884; Noah Plympton-Butler, December 3, 1891; Butler-Charles Dana, August 6, 1884, 1954 boxes, Butler MSS. According to Plympton, a seat in the cabinet, a foreign mission, and the patronage of New England were under discussion, but Butler refused for principle's sake. Collateral evidence is completely lacking. Cf. Buffalo *Times,* August 23, 1896.
59. *Harper's Weekly,* XXVIII (October 25, 1884), 697.
60. Richardson, *op. cit.,* 351-52; New York *Times,* October 27, 1884.
61. On September 24, 1884, Butler wrote to M. A. Clancey: "I want you to take the enclosed letter and read it to Mr. Chandler and then bring it back to me." The enclosed letter to Chandler follows: "My dear Chandler: I am anxious to have a communication made to you and I have sent Mr. Clancey in whom you have the most implicit confidence . . . . Now before the first day of October we should have at least $25,000 beyond what was understood, i.e., $5,000 a week . . . . Will you see to it that this is done?"
62. W. D. Fuller-W. H. Shupe, August 21, 22, 1884, Butler MSS, 1954 boxes; C. S. Hampton-Plympton, September 23, 1884; T. E. Major-Butler, October 8, 1884; Butler MSS, 1954 boxes; Solon J. Buck, *The Agrarian Crusade* (New Haven, 1919), 98.
63. He hoped to poll enough votes to throw the state to Blaine. Butler-W. E. Chandler, September 24, Butler MSS.
64. For evidence of Butler's support of *Father Columbia's Paper,* Butler MSS, February, 1884. Dana had broken with Cleveland because he could not prevail upon the Governor to appoint a friend to his staff. Nevins, *Cleveland,* 148, 171.
65. New York *Times,* October 15-17, 1884.

**NOTES** 325

66. Buck, *op. cit.*, 96-98.
67. New York *Times*, October 19, 20, 21, 1884.
68. *Butler's Book*, 984; Thomas H. Sherman, *Twenty Years With James G. Blaine* (New York, 1928), 96-97.
69. Bill for $2,972.25 to Anarchists Defense Committe, December 19, 1887; Butler-W. P. Black, March 1, 1888, letterbooks, Butler MSS. Gregory Weinstein, *The Ardent Eighties* (New York, 1929), 156-57. The strikers at Homestead in 1892 also received his sympathy. Butler-N. Glover, October 18, 1892, Butler MSS, letterbooks.
70. New York *Times*, September 1, 1888.
71. *Butler's Book*, 984; New York *Times*, October 30, November 14, 1888; B. A. Morrison-Butler, October 12, 1888; Butler-Elija Halford, December 5, 1889, Butler MSS, letterbooks and 1954 boxes; Butler-Benjamin Harrison, January 28, 1889, Harrison MSS, Library of Congress.
72. Butler-Weaver, November 3, 1892, letterbooks, Butler MSS.
73. *Commonwealth*, December 10, 17, 1870; West, *Porter*, 328.
74. David D. Porter, "The Opening of the Lower Mississippi, April, 1862," *Century*, XXIX (April, 1885), 922-52.
75. New York *Times*, May 1-8, 1889; Boston *Herald*, May 5, 1889; Washington *Star*, May 6, 7, 1889; New York *World*, May 5, 1889; West, *Porter*, 341 ff., xii.
76. New York *Sun*, October 23, 1889; New York *Times*, February 17, 1891.
77. *Ibid.*, December 24, 1890.
78. New York *Sun*, April 23, 1891; Philadelphia *Record*, April 21, 1891; Washington *Post*, April 23, 1891; messages in Butler MSS.
79. New York *Times*, June 9, 1891.
80. Weinstein, *op. cit.*, 156-57; New York *World*, December 1, 1891; New York *Times*, December 2, 1891.
81. Butler-Miss Cirode, September 10, 1890, letterbooks, Butler MSS; Butler-Blanche Ames, February 24, 1890, letterbooks, Butler MSS. The operation was intended to restore his failing eyesight, not, as he put it, "to improve my looks," for, he wrote to his daughter, "I have gone through life pleased that I was the homeliest man on earth."
82. Charles Foster-Butler, March 7, 1891, Butler MSS.
83. Butler-John Jay, September 8, 1892, letterbooks, Butler MSS.
84. Brooklyn Daily *Standard Union*, January 11, 1893; New York *Times*, January 11, 12, 1893.
85. Orcutt, "Ben Butler and the 'Stolen Spoons,'" *loc. cit.*, 66-67; New York *Post*, April 13, 1896; Boston *Post*, March 26, 1902; Howe, *op. cit.*, 145, 292-93; Adelbert Ames, Jr.-Moorfield Storey, February 16, 1914, copy in author's possession by courtesy of Mrs. Andrew Marshall.

# Bibliography

*Unpublished Material*

John A. Andrew MSS, Massachusetts Historical Society, Boston.
John F. Andrew MSS, Massachusetts Historical Society.
George Bancroft MSS, Massachusetts Historical Society.
Nathaniel P. Banks MSS, Essex Institute, Salem, Massachusetts.
Benjamin F. Butler MSS, Library of Congress, Washington.
James Butler MSS, Thomas F. Madigan Collection, New York Public Library, New York.
Simon Cameron MSS, Library of Congress.
William E. Chandler MSS, Library of Congress.
Zachariah Chandler MSS, Library of Congress.
Salmon P. Chase MSS, Library of Congress.
Grover Cleveland MSS, Library of Congress.
Caleb Cushing MSS, Library of Congress.
George S. Denison MSS, Library of Congress.
Anna Dickinson MSS, Library of Congress.
Stephen A. Douglas MSS, University of Chicago.
Edward Everett MSS, Massachusetts Historical Society.
Hamilton Fish MSS, Library of Congress.
James A. Garfield MSS, Library of Congress.
Horace Greeley MSS, New York Public Library.
Philip Woodruff Holmes MSS, New York Public Library.
Andrew Johnson MSS, Library of Congress.
Reverdy Johnson MSS, Library of Congress.
Amos Lawrence MSS, Massachusetts Historical Society.
James Parton MSS, Harvard University, Cambridge.
Philip Phillips MSS, Library of Congress.
Lemuel Shaw MSS, Massachusetts Historical Society.
Edwin M. Stanton MSS, Library of Congress.
Thaddeus Stevens MSS, Library of Congress.
Charles Sumner MSS, Harvard University.
Lyman Trumbull MSS, Library of Congress.
Elizabeth Van Lew MSS, New York Public Library.

Elihu B. Washburne MSS, Library of Congress.
Gideon Welles MSS, New York Public Library.
Henry Wilson MSS, Library of Congress.
James R. Young MSS, Library of Congress.

*Newspapers and Periodicals*

Baltimore:
- *American*
- *Gazette*
- *South*

Boston:
- *Advertiser*
- *Atlantic Monthly*
- *Bee*
- *Commonwealth*
- *Herald*
- *Harper's Monthly*
- *Harper's Weekly*
- *Journal*
- *Post*
- *Times*
- *Transcript*
- *Traveller*

Haverhill Weekly *Bulletin*

London:
- *Times*
- *Saturday Review*

Lowell:
- *Advertiser*
- *American*
- *Journal & Courier*
- *Vox Populi*

Newburyport Daily *Herald*

New Orleans:
- *Delta*
- *Deutsche Zeitung*
- *Picayune*
- *True Delta*

New York:
- *Herald*
- *Post*
- *Standard*
- *Sun*
- *Times*
- *Tribune*
- *World*

Norfolk:
- *New Regime*
- *Old Dominion*

Springfield *Republican*

Washington:
- *Chronicle*
- *National Intelligencer*
- *National Republican*
- *Post*

## Other Sources

ADAMS, CHARLES FRANCIS. *Charles Francis Adams.* Boston and New York, 1900.

ADAMS, CHARLES FRANCIS. *Richard Henry Dana.* 2 vols. Boston and New York, 1890.

AGASSIZ, GEORGE R. (ed). THEODORE LYMAN, *Meade's Headquarters, 1863-1865.* Boston, 1922.

AMBLER, CHARLES H. *Francis H. Pierpont.* Chapel Hill, 1937.

*The American Annual Cyclopedia.* Annually, New York.

AMES, BLANCHE BUTLER. *The Butler Ancestry of Gen. Benjamin Franklin Butler.* Lowell, 1895.

ANDERSON, GODFREY TRYGGVE. The Slavery Issue as a Factor in Massachusetts Politics From the Compromise of 1850 to the Outbreak of the Civil War. Unpublished doctoral dissertation, University of Chicago, 1944.

ARTHUR, ROBERT. *The History of Fort Monroe.* Fort Monroe, 1930.

ASBURY, HERBERT. *The French Quarter.* New York, 1951.

AUCHAMPAUGH, PHILIP GERALD. *James Buchanan and His Cabinet on the Eve of Secession.* Lancaster, 1926.

AUSTIN, GEORGE LOWELL. *The History of Massachusetts, From the Landing of the Pilgrims to the Present Time.* Boston, 1885.

BADEAU, ADAM. *Grant in Peace.* Hartford, 1887.

BADEAU, ADAM. *Military History of Ulysses S. Grant.* 3 vols. New York, 1868.

BARNARD, HARRY. *Rutherford B. Hayes and His America.* New York, 1954.

BARROWS, CHESTER. *William M. Evarts.* Chapel Hill, 1941.

BARTLETT, A. W. *History of the Twelfth Regiment New Hampshire Volunteers in the War of the Rebellion.* Concord, 1897.

BASLER, ROY P. (ed.). *The Collected Works of Abraham Lincoln.* 9 vols. New Brunswick, 1953.

*Battles and Leaders.* See Buel, Clarence.

BEALE, HOWARD K. *The Critical Year: A Study of Andrew Johnson and Reconstruction.* New York, 1930.

BEALE, HOWARD K. (ed.). *The Diary of Edward Bates.* American Historical Association Annual Report for 1930, vol. IV, Washington, 1933.

# BIBLIOGRAPHY

BETTS, CHARLES W. *Visitor's Handbook of Old Point Comfort and Vicinity.* Hampton, 1885.

BLAINE, JAMES G. *Twenty Years of Congress.* 2 vols. Norwich, Conn., 1884.

BLAND, T. A. *Life of Benjamin F. Butler.* Boston, 1879.

BOUTWELL, GEORGE S. *Reminiscences of Sixty Years in Public Affairs.* 2 vols. New York, 1902.

BOWEN, JAMES L. *Massachusetts in the War, 1861-1865.* Springfield, 1889.

BOWERS, CLAUDE G. *The Tragic Era.* Cambridge, 1929.

BRADFORD, GAMALIEL. *Damaged Souls.* Boston and New York, 1922.

BRADFORD, GAMALIEL. *Wives.* New York, 1925.

BROWNING, ORVILLE H. See Pease.

BUCK, SOLON J. *The Agrarian Crusade.* New Haven, 1919.

BUEL, CLARENCE, and JOHNSON, ROBERT, (eds.). *Battles and Leaders of the Civil War.* 4 vols. New York, 1887-1888.

BURTON, H. W. *The History of Norfolk, Virginia.* Norfolk, 1877.

BUTLER, BENJAMIN FRANKLIN. *Address . . . to the Two Branches of the Legislature of Massachusetts,* January 4, 1883. Boston, 1883.

—— *Address at the Request of the Board of Trade of New York, October 14, 1875.* New York, 1875.

—— *Argument . . . Before the Committee of the House of Representatives for an Investigation of the Standard Oil Company.* Washington, 1880.

—— *Argument Before the Tewkesbury Investigation Committee . . . Upon Facts Disclosed During the Recent Investigation, July 15, 1883.* 1883.

—— *Butler's Book. Autobiography and Personal Reminiscences of Major General Benjamin F. Butler.* Boston, 1892.

—— *Character and Results of the War.* Philadelphia, 1863.

—— *Independence of Cuba. Speech . . . Delivered in the House of Representatives June 15, 1870.* Washington, 1870.

—— *Ku-Klux Outrages in the South, the Work of the Democratic Party . . . Speech of Hon. Benj. F. Butler in the House of Representatives April 4, 1871.* 1871.

—— *Letter to Hon. E. R. Hoar.* Lowell, 1876.

—— *The Necessity of Rewards for Detection of Crime. Speech Upon the Frauds on the Revenues of the Government, and Reply to Personal Attacks Upon Himself, Delivered in the House of Representatives, June 19, 1874.* Washington, 1874.

—— *Reforms in the Commonwealth through the Republican Party Imperative . . . Address . . . at Springfield, August 24, 1871.* Boston, 1871.

—— *The Salaries of Public Officers.* Boston, 1873.

—— *The Status of the Insurgent States Upon the Cessation of Hostilities. A Speech . . . Before the Legislature of Pennsylvania, April 11, 1866.* 1866.

—— *The Treaty of Washington . . . Address . . . at Music Hall, Philadelphia, October 16, 1871.* Boston, 1871.

—— *The Treaty of Washington . . . Letter . . . to Hon. A. Ames, U. S Senate.* Lowell, 1871.

—— "Vice-Presidential Politics in '64." *North American Review,* vol. CXLI, October, 1885.

*Butler Correspondence.* See Marshall.

*Major General Butler At Home.* Lowell, 1865.

*Butler's Record.* 1879 and 1883.

*Gen. Benjamin F. Butler's True Record.* 1879 and 1883.

*Life and Public Services of Major General Butler.* Philadelphia, 1864.

CAHILL, MARION. *Shorter Hours.* New York, 1932.

CALDWELL, ROBERT G. *James A. Garfield.* New York, 1931.

CARNEGIE, ANDREW. *Autobiography.* Boston, 1920.

CARPENTER, GEORGE N. *History of the Eighth Vermont Volunteers, 1861-1865.* Boston, 1886.

CASKEY, WILLIE MALVIN. *Secession and Restoration in Louisiana.* Baton Rouge, 1938.

CATE, WIRT ARMISTEAD. *Lucius Q. C. Lamar.* Chapel Hill, 1935.

CATTON, BRUCE. *A Stillness at Appomattox.* Garden City, 1954.

CHESTER, GIRAUD. *Embattled Maiden, The Life of Anna Dickinson.* New York, 1951.

CHESTNUT, MARY BOYKIN. See Williams.

CLARK, EDWARD H. G. *General Butler.* 1884.

# BIBLIOGRAPHY

CLARK, EMMONS. *History of the Seventh Regiment of New York, 1806-1889.* 2 vols. New York, 1890.

CLARK, WALTER (ed.). *Histories of the Several Regiments and Battalions from North Carolina in the Great War, 1861-1865.* 4 vols. Raleigh, 1901.

CLEMENCEAU, GEORGES. *American Reconstruction, 1865-1870.* New York, 1928.

COGSWELL, ELLIOTT C. *History of Nottingham, Deerfield, and Northwood.* Manchester, N. H., 1876.

COLE, ARTHUR C. *The Irrepressible Conflict, 1850-1865. A History of American Life,* vol. VII. New York, 1934.

CONKLIN, EDWARD P. *Middlesex County and Its People.* 5 vols. New York, 1927.

COOLIDGE, JOHN. *Mill and Mansion.* New York, 1942.

*Correspondence Between Gov. Andrew and Maj. Gen. Butler.* Boston, 1862.

COULTER, E. MERTON. *The Confederate States of America. A History of the South,* vol. VII. Baton Rouge, 1950.

COVE, JOSEPH. The Political Career of Benjamin Franklin Butler After 1870. Unpublished MA thesis, Clark University, Worcester, 1929.

COWLEY, CHARLES. *History of Lowell.* 2d ed. Boston, 1868.

COWLEY, CHARLES. *History of the Ten Hours Movement,* in *Lowell, A City of Spindles.* Lowell, 1900.

COX, SAMUEL. *Three Decades of Federal Legislation.* Providence, 1886.

CROFFUT, W. A. (ed.), HITCHCOCK, ETHAN ALLEN. *Fifty Years in Camp and Field.* New York, 1909.

CROFFUT, W. A. and MORRIS, JOHN M. *The Military and Civil History of Connecticut During the War of 1861-1865.* New York, 1868.

CROOK, WILLIAM H. *Through Five Administrations.* New York, 1910.

DABNEY, THOMAS EWING. "The Butler Regime in Louisiana." *The Louisiana Historical Quarterly,* vol. XXVII (1944).

DANA, RICHARD HENRY 3d (ed.). *Richard Henry Dana, Jr.* Boston, 1910.

DAVENPORT, JOHN I. (ed). *Official Documents Relating to A "Chaplain's Campaign (NOT) With General Butler," But in New York.* Lowell, 1865.

DAVIS, JEFFERSON. *The Rise and Fall of the Confederate Government.* 2 vols. New York, 1881.

DAVIS, VARINA HOWELL. *Jefferson Davis, A Memoir.* 2 vols. New York, 1890.

DEMOCRATIC PARTY. *Official Proceedings of the Democratic National Convention.* 1852, 1856, 1860, 1884.

DEWITT, DAVID MILLER. *The Impeachment and Trial of Andrew Johnson.* New York, 1903.

DIX, MORGAN (ed.). *Memoirs of John Adams Dix.* 2 vols. New York, 1883.

DONALD, DAVID (ed.). *Inside Lincoln's Cabinet. The Civil War Diaries of Salmon P. Chase.* New York, 1954.

DOUGLASS, FREDERICK. *Life and Times of Frederick Douglass, Written By Himself.* Boston, 1881.

EARLY, ELEANOR. *New Orleans Holiday.* New York, 1947.

ELIOT, ELLSWORTH JR. *Theodore Winthrop.* New Haven, 1938.

FARRAGUT, LOYALL. *The Life of David Glasgow Farragut.* New York, 1882.

FESSENDEN, FRANCIS. *Life and Public Services of William Pitt Fessenden.* 2 vols. Boston, 1907.

FLOWER, FRANK ABIAL. *Edwin McMasters Stanton.* New York, 1904.

FLOWER, MILTON. *James Parton, The Father of Modern Biography.* Durham, 1951.

FOLTZ, CHARLES S. *Surgeon of the Seas.* Indianapolis, 1931.

FONER, PHILIP S. *Frederick Douglass, Life and Writings.* New York, 1955.

FORBES, J. MURRAY. See Hughes.

FORD, WORTHINGTON CHAUNCEY (ed.). *Letters of Henry Adams, 1858-1891.* Boston and New York, 1930.

FOX, GUSTAVUS VASA. See Thompson.

FREEMAN, DOUGLAS SOUTHALL. *R. E. Lee.* 4 vols. New York, 1936.

FREEMAN, DOUGLAS SOUTHALL. *Lee's Lieutenants.* 3 vols. New York, 1945.

# BIBLIOGRAPHY

FREY, JACOB. *Reminiscences of Baltimore.* Baltimore, 1893.

FUESS, CLAUDE M. *The Life of Caleb Cushing.* 2 vols. New York, 1923.

FUESS, CLAUDE M. *Rufus Choate, the Wizard of the Law.* New York, 1928.

GORDON, GEORGE H. *A War Diary of Events in the War of the Great Rebellion, 1863-1865.* Boston, 1882.

GORGAS, JOSIAH. See Vandiver.

GORHAM, GEORGE C. *Life and Public Services of Edwin M. Stanton.* Boston, 1899.

GOULD, LEVI S. *Ancient Middlesex with Brief Biographical Sketches of the Men Who Have Served the County Officially Since Its Settlement.* Somerville, Mass., 1905.

GRAHAM, MATTHEW J. *The Ninth Regiment New York Volunteers (Hawkins' Zouaves).* New York, 1900.

GRANT, U. S. *Official Report of Lt.-Gen. U. S. Grant.* New York, 1865.

GRANT, U. S. *Personal Memoirs of U. S. Grant.* 2 vols. New York, 1885.

GRAY, JOHN CHIPMAN, and ROPES, JOHN CODMAN. *War Letters, 1862-1865.* Boston, 1927.

GRAY, WOOD. *The Hidden Civil War, The Story of the Copperheads.* New York, 1942.

GREGG, J. CHANDLER. *Life in the Army.* Philadelphia, 1868.

GRIFFIN, J. Q. A. *A Portrait of Benjamin F. Butler By A Housepainter.* 1859.

GRIFFIN, SOLOMON BULKLEY. *People and Politics Observed by a Massachusetts Editor.* Boston, 1923.

GRISWOLD, LATTA (ed.). MARY CLARK STURTEVANT, *Thomas March Clark, Fifth Bishop of Rhode Island.* Milwaukee, 1927.

GUROWSKI, ADAM. *Diary.* 3 vols. Boston, 1862, New York, 1864.

HALL, CLAYTON COLMAN. *Baltimore, Its History and Its People.* New York, 1912.

HALSTEAD, MURAT. *Caucuses of 1860. A History of the National Political Conventions of the Current Presidential Campaign.* Columbus, 1860.

HANDLIN, OSCAR and MARY FLUG. *Commonwealth, A Study of the Role of Government in the American Economy: Massachusetts, 1774-1861.* New York, 1947.

HANSON, JOHN W. *Historical Sketch of the Old Sixth Regiment of Massachusetts Volunteers During Its Three Campaigns in 1861, 1862, 1863, and 1864.* Boston, 1866.

HARDING, WILLIAM KNOTT. Contemporary Opinion of General Benjamin F. Butler During the Civil War. Unpublished MA thesis, University of Wisconsin, 1929.

HARRINGTON, FRED HARVEY. *Fighting Politician, Major General N. P. Banks.* Philadelphia, 1948.

HART, ALBERT B. (ed.). *Commonwealth History of Massachusetts.* Vol. IV. New York, 1930.

HASKELL, GEORGE. *A Narrative of the Life, Experience, and Work of an American Citizen.* Ipswich, Mass., 1896.

*Letters of John Hay and Extracts from Diary.* 3 vols. Washington, 1908.

HAYNES, FRED E. *Third Party Movements Since the Civil War with Special Reference to Iowa.* Iowa City, 1916.

HEADLEY, C. P. *Massachusetts in the Rebellion.* Boston, 1866.

HENRY, ROBERT SELPH. *The Story of Reconstruction.* Indianapolis, 1938.

HESSELTINE, WILLIAM BEST. *Civil War Prisons, A Study in War Psychology.* Columbus, 1930.

HESSELTINE, WILLIAM BEST. *Ulysses S. Grant, Politician.* New York, 1935.

HIBBEN, PAXTON. *Henry Ward Beecher.* New York, 1942.

HITCHCOCK, ETHAN ALLEN. See Croffut.

HOAR, GEORGE F. *Autobiography of Seventy Years.* 2 vols. New York, 1903.

HOLZMAN, ROBERT S. *Stormy Ben Butler.* New York, 1954.

HORAN, JAMES D. *Confederate Agent.* New York, 1954.

HOROWITZ, MURRAY M. "Ben Butler, Making of A Radical." Unpublished doctoral dissertation, Columbia University, 1955.

HORN, STANLEY F. *The Invisible Empire.* Boston, 1939.

HOWARD, CECIL H. C. *Life and Public Services of General John Wolcott Phelps.* Brattleboro, Vt., 1887.

# BIBLIOGRAPHY

Howe, M. A. De Wolfe. *Portrait of An Independent, Moorfield Storey, 1845-1929.* Boston and New York, 1932.

Howe, Henry Warren. *Passages from the Life of Henry Warren Howe, Consisting of Diary and Letters Written During the Civil War, 1861-1865.* Lowell, 1899.

Hudson, H. N. *A Chaplain's Campaign With Gen. Butler.* New York, 1865. 2d ed. with title *General Butler's Campaign on the Hudson,* (Boston, 1883).

Hudson, William C. *Random Recollections of an Old Political Reporter.* New York, 1911.

Hughes, Sarah Forbes (ed.). *Letters and Recollections of John Murray Forbes.* 2 vols. Boston, 1899.

Humphreys, Andrew A. *The Virginia Campaign of '64 and '65.* New York, 1883.

Hurd, D. Hamilton (compiler). *History of Middlesex County, Massachusetts.* 3 vols. Philadelphia, 1890.

Johnson, Howard P. "New Orleans under General Butler." *The Louisiana Historical Quarterly,* vol. XXIV, 1941.

Johnson, Charles F. *The Long Roll.* East Aurora, N. Y., 1911.

Josephson, Hannah. *The Golden Threads.* New York, 1949.

Josephson, Matthew. *The Politicos, 1865-1896.* New York, 1938.

Julian, George W. *Political Recollections.* Chicago, 1884.

Kendall, John Smith. *History of New Orleans.* 3 vols. Chicago and New York, 1922.

Kendrick, Benjamin B. *The Journal of the Joint Committee of Fifteen on Reconstruction. Columbia University Studies in History, Economics, and Public Law,* LXII, 1914.

King, Grace. *New Orleans, The Place and the People.* New York, 1904.

King, Horatio. *Turning on the Light, A Dispassionate Survey of President Buchanan's Administration From 1860 to Its Close.* Philadelphia, 1895.

Kohler, Max J. *The Board of Delegates of American Israelites, 1859-1878.* New York, 1925.

Le Grand, Julia. See Rowland.

Lewis, Lloyd. *Sherman, Fighting Prophet.* New York, 1932.

Lincoln, Abraham. See Basler.

LIVERMORE, THOMAS L. *Days and Events, 1860-1866.* Boston and New York, 1920.

LONGSTREET, JAMES. *From Manassas to Appomattox.* Philadelphia, 1896.

LOSSING, BENSON J. *Pictorial History of the Civil War.* 3 vols. Philadelphia, 1874.

LOTHROP, THORNTON KIRKLAND. *William Henry Seward.* Boston and New York, 1898.

LOVELL, MANSFIELD. *Correspondence between the War Department and General Lovell Relating to the Defense of New Orleans.* Richmond, 1863.

LOWELL HISTORICAL SOCIETY, *Contributions.* 6 vols. Lowell, 1879. New Series, 2 vols., Lowell, 1926.

*Proceedings in the City of Lowell At the Semi-Centennial Celebration of the Incorporation of the Town of Lowell, March 1, 1876.* Lowell, 1876.

LYMAN, THEODORE. See Agassiz.

MCCABE, GILLIE CARIE. *The Story of an Old Town, Hampton, Virginia.* Richmond, 1929.

MCCABE, JAMES DABNEY. *Behind the Scenes in Washington.* Washington, 1873.

MACARTNEY, CLARENCE EDWARD. *Grant and His Generals.* New York, 1953.

MCCLELLAN, GEORGE B. *George B. McClellan's Own Story.* New York, 1887.

MCCLURE, ALEXANDER K. *Abraham Lincoln and Men of War-Times.* Philadelphia, 1892.

MCCLURE, ALEXANDER K. *Colonel Alexander K. McClure's Recollections of Half A Century.* Salem, 1902.

MACDONALD, ALLAN. "Lowell: A Commercial Utopia." *The New England Quarterly,* vol. X, 1937.

MCLAUGHLIN, JAMES FAIRFAX. *The American Cyclops, The Hero of New Orleans and Spoiler of Silver Spoons.* Baltimore, 1868.

MALLAM, WILLIAM D. "Benjamin Franklin Butler, Machine Congressman and Politician." Unpublished doctoral dissertation, University of Minnesota, 1941.

MALLAM, WILLIAM D. "The Grant-Butler Relationship." *The Mississippi Valley Historical Review,* vol. XLI, 1954.

## BIBLIOGRAPHY

MARSHALL, JESSIE AMES (compiler). *Private and Official Correspondence of Gen. Benjamin F. Butler During the Period of the Civil War.* 5 vols. Norwood, Mass., 1917.

MARTIN, EDWARD SANDFORD. *The Life of Joseph Hodges Choate, As Gathered Chiefly from His Letters.* 2 vols. New York, 1920.

MASSACHUSETTS. House Report No. 300. *Report of Hearings Before the Joint Standing Committee on Public Charitable Institutions . . . to Investigate . . . the State Almshouse at Tewkesbury.* Boston, 1883.

MASSACHUSETTS. *Journal of the Constitutional Convention of the Commonwealth of Massachusetts Begun and Held in Boston, on the Fourth Day of May, 1853.* Boston, 1853.

MASSACHUSETTS. Military Historical Society of Massachusetts, *Papers of the Military Historical Society of Massachusetts.* Vols. V, IX, XIV, 1906, 1912, 1917.

MERRILL, LOUIS TAYLOR. *General Butler and the Campaign of 1868.* Chicago, 1937.

MERRILL, LOUIS TAYLOR. "General Benjamin F. Butler As a Radical Leader During the Administration of President Andrew Johnson." Unpublished doctoral dissertation, University of Chicago, 1936.

MERRILL, LOUIS TAYLOR. "General Benjamin F. Butler in the Presidential Campaign of 1864." *The Mississippi Valley Historical Review*, vol. XXXIII, 1947.

MILES, HENRY A. *Lowell, As It Was And As It Is.* Lowell, 1846.

MILTON, GEORGE FORT. *The Age of Hate, Andrew Johnson and the Radicals.* New York, 1930.

MILTON, GEORGE FORT. *The Eve of the Conflict, Stephen A. Douglas and the Needless War.* New York, 1934.

MOORE, JOHN BASSETT (ed.). *The Works of James Buchanan.* 12 vols. Philadelphia, 1910.

MORGAN, JAMES MORRIS. *Recollections of A Rebel Reefer.* Boston and New York, 1917.

MORSE, JOHN T., JR. (ed.). *Diary of Gideon Welles.* 3 vols. Boston and New York, 1911.

MURRAY, THOMAS HAMILTON. *History of the Ninth Regiment, Connecticut Volunteer Infantry, "The Irish Regiment" in the War of the Rebellion, 1861-1865.* New Haven, 1903.

NASON, GEORGE W. *History and Complete Roster of the Massachusetts Regiment, Minute Men of '61* . . . Boston, 1910.

NEVINS, ALLAN, and THOMAS, MILTON HALSEY (eds.). *The Diary of George Templeton Strong.* 4 vols. New York, 1952.

NEVINS, ALLAN. *The Emergence of Lincoln.* 2 vols. New York, 1950.

NEVINS, ALLAN. *Grover Cleveland.* New York, 1948.

NEVINS, ALLAN. *Hamilton Fish.* New York, 1936.

NEVINS, ALLAN. *The Ordeal of the Union.* New York, 1947. 2 vols.

NICHOLS, ROY FRANK. *The Democratic Machine, 1850-1854.* New York, 1923.

NICHOLS, ROY FRANK. *The Disruption of the American Democracy.* New York, 1948.

NICOLAY, JOHN G. and HAY, JOHN. *Abraham Lincoln, A History.* 10 vols. New York, 1914.

NYE, RUSSELL B. *George Bancroft: Brahmin Rebel.* New York, 1944.

OBERHOLTZER, ELLIS PAXSON. *A History of the United States Since the Civil War.* 5 vols. New York, 1922.

*Official Records.* See *The War of the Rebellion.*

*Official Report of the Debates and Proceedings in the State Convention Assembled May 4, 1853, To Revise and Amend the Constitution of the Commonwealth of Massachusetts.* 3 vols. Boston, 1853.

ORCUTT, WILLIAM N. "Ben Butler and the 'Stolen Spoons.'" *North American Review,* vol. CCVII, 1918.

PAINE, ALBERT BIGELOW. *A Sailor of Fortune. Personal Memoirs of Captain B. S. Osbon.* New York, 1906.

PALFREY, JOHN GORMAN. *Remarks on the Proposed State Constitution By a Free-Soiler From the Start.* Boston, 1853.

PARTON, JAMES. *General Butler in New Orleans.* New York, 1864.

PATTERSON, H. K. W. *War Memories of Fort Monroe and Vicinity.* Fort Monroe, 1885.

PAUL, JAMES C. N. *Rift in the Democracy.* Philadelphia, 1951.

PEARSON, HENRY GREENLEAF. *The Life of John A. Andrew.* 2 vols. Boston and New York, 1904.

PEASE, THEODORE CALVIN and RANDALL, JAMES G. (eds.). *The Diary of Orville Hickman Browning. Collections of the Illinois State Historical Library,* vols XX, XXII, 1927-1933.

# BIBLIOGRAPHY

PEIRPONT, F. H. *Letter of Governor Peirpont to His Excellency the President and the Honorable Congress of the United States on the Subject of the Abuse of Military Power in the Command of General Butler in Virginia and North Carolina.* Washington, 1864.

PERRY, BLISS. *And Gladly Teach.* Boston and New York, 1935.

PHILLIPS, WENDELL. *The People Coming to Power. Speech . . . At the Salisbury Beach Gathering, September 13, 1871.* Boston, 1871.

PICKETT, MRS. GEORGE E. *The Heart of a Soldier, As Revealed in the Intimate Letters of Genl. George E. Pickett, C. S. A.* New York, 1913.

PIERCE, EDWARD L. *Memoir and Letters of Charles Sumner.* 4 vols. Boston, 1877.

PIERREPONT, EDWARDS. *A Review by Judge Pierrepont of Gen. Butler's Defense Before the House of Representatives, in Relation to the New Orleans Gold.* New York, 1865.

POLLARD, EDWARD. *The Lost Cause.* New York, 1866.

POMEROY, MARCUS M. *Life and Public Services of Benjamin F. Butler, Major-General in the Army and Leader of the Republican Party.* New York, 1868.

PORTER, DAVID DIXON. *Incidents and Anecdotes of the Civil War.* New York, 1885.

PORTER, DAVID DIXON. "The Opening of the Lower Mississippi, April 1862," *Century,* vol. XXIX, 1885.

PRATT, FLETCHER. *Stanton, Lincoln's Secretary of War.* New York, 1953.

PRYOR, MRS. ROGER A. *Reminiscences of Peace and War.* New York, 1904.

QUARLES, BENJAMIN. *The Negro in the Civil War.* Boston, 1953.

RADCLIFFE, GEORGE L. P. *Governor Thomas H. Hicks of Maryland and the Civil War. Johns Hopkins University Studies in Historical and Political Science,* Series XIX, Nos. 11-12, 1901.

RANDALL, JAMES G. *Lincoln, The President.* 3 vols. New York, 1946-1952.

*The Record of Benjamin Franklin Butler Since His Election As Governor of Massachusetts.* Boston, 1883.

RHODES, JAMES FORD. *History of the United States from the Compromise of 1850 to the McKinley-Bryan Campaign of 1896.* 8 vols. New York, 1920.

RICHARDSON, JAMES D. *A Compilation of the Messages and Papers of the Confederacy.* 2 vols. Nashville, 1904.

RICHARDSON, JAMES D. *A compilation of the Messages and Papers of the Presidents, 1789-1897.* 10 vols. Washington, 1896-1899.

RICHARDSON, LEON BURR. *William E. Chandler, Republican.* New York, 1940.

RILEY, ELIHU S. "The Ancient City," *A History of Annapolis in Maryland, 1649-1887.* Annapolis, 1887.

ROBINSON, WILLIAM S. *The Salary Grab.* Boston, 1873.

ROBINSON, MRS. WILLIAM S. *"Warrington" Pen-Portraits, A Collection of Personal and Political Reminiscences from 1848-1876.* Boston, 1877.

Ross, EDMUND G. *History of the Impeachment of Andrew Johnson.* Santa Fe, N. M., 1896.

Ross, ISHBEL. *Rebel Rose.* New York, 1954.

ROWLAND, KATE MASON, and CROXWELL, MRS. M. L. (eds.). *The Journal of Julia Le Grand.* Richmond, 1911.

RUSSELL, WILLIAM HOWARD. *My Diary North and South.* Boston, 1863.

SANDBURG, CARL. *Abraham Lincoln, The War Years.* 4 vols. New York, 1939.

SALTER, WILLIAM. *The Life of James W. Grimes.* New York, 1876.

SAXON, LYLE. *Fabulous New Orleans.* New York, 1928.

SCOTT, HENRY W. *Distinguished American Lawyers.* New York, 1891.

SCHOULER, JAMES. "The Massachusetts Convention of 1853." *Proceedings of the Massachusetts Historical Society,* 2d Series, vol. XVIII, 1903-1904.

SCHOULER, WILLIAM. *A History of Massachusetts in the Civil War.* 2 vols. Boston, 1868.

SCHURZ, CARL. *The Reminiscences of Carl Schurz.* 3 vols. New York, 1909.

SEGAL, CHARLES M. "Isachar Zacharie, Lincoln's Chiropodist." *Publications of the American Jewish Historical Society,* XLIII, 1952.

# BIBLIOGRAPHY

SEWARD, FREDERICK W. *Seward at Washington.* 3 vols. New York, 1891.

SHERMAN, THOMAS H. *Twenty Years with James G. Blaine.* New York, 1928.

SHERMAN, W. T. *Memoirs of Gen. W. T. Sherman.* 4th ed. New York, 1891.

SHERWIN, OSCAR. Prophet of Liberty. A Biography of Wendell Phillips. Unpublished doctoral dissertation, New York University, 1940.

SIGAUD, LOUIS A. *Belle Boyd, Confederate Spy.* Richmond, 1944.

SMITH, WILLIAM ERNEST. *The Francis Preston Blair Family in Politics.* 2 vols. New York, 1933.

SMITH, WILLIAM FARRAR. *From Chattanooga to Petersburg Under Generals Grant and Butler.* Boston and New York, 1893.

SOLEY, JAMES R. *Historical Sketch of the U. S. Naval Academy.* Washington, 1876.

SOUTHWOOD, MARION. *Beauty and Booty.* New York, 1867.

STARKEY, MARION L. *The First Plantation. A History of Hampton and Elizabeth City County, Virginia, 1607-1887.* Hampton, 1936.

STEINER, BERNARD CHRISTIAN. *Life of Reverdy Johnson.* Baltimore, 1914.

STEVENS, WILLIAM OLIVER. *Annapolis, Anne Arundel's Town.* New York, 1937.

STILLMAN, WILLIAM JAMES. *The Autobiography of a Journalist.* 2 vols. Boston and New York, 1901.

STODDARD, HENRY LUTHER. *Horace Greeley.* New York, 1946.

STRONG, GEORGE TEMPLETON. See Nevins.

STRYKER, LLOYD PAUL. *Andrew Johnson, A Study in Courage.* New York, 1929.

SWIGGETT, HOWARD (ed.). J. B. JONES. *A Rebel War Clerk's Diary.* New York, 1935.

SWINTON, WILLIAM. *History of the Seventh Regiment, National Guard, State of New York, During the War of the Rebellion.* New York and Boston, 1870.

THACHER, WILLIAM REYNOLDS. *The Pierpont Government in Virginia.* Unpublished MA dissertation, University of Chicago, 1916.

THOMPSON, C. MILDRED. *Reconstruction in Georgia. Columbia University Studies in History, Economics and Public Law*, LXIV, I, 1915.

THOMPSON, ROBERT MEANS and RICHARD WAINWRIGHT, (eds.). *Confidential Correspondence of Gustavus Vasa Fox*. 2 vols. New York, 1938.

TODD, HELEN. *A Man Named Grant*. Boston, 1940.

TUCKER, MARY E. *Life of Mark M. Pomeroy* . . . New York, 1868.

UNITED STATES, CONGRESS. *Papers Relating to Foreign Affairs*, 1862, 37th Congress, 3d Session.

UNITED STATES, CONGRESS. House of Representatives, Military Affairs Committee, 41st Congress, 3d Session. *House Report No. 45. Report on the National Asylum*. Washington, 1871.

UNITED STATES, CONGRESS. House of Representatives. 38th Congress, 2nd Session. *House Report No. 24. Trade With Rebellious States*.

UNITED STATES, CONGRESS, SENATE. 38th Congress, 2nd Session. *Report No. 142. Report of the Joint Committee on the Conduct of the War*. Washington, 1865.

USHER, EDWARD PRESTON. *A Memorial Sketch of Roland Greene Usher, 1823-1895*. Boston, 1895.

VANDIVER, FRANK E. (ed.). *The Civil War Diary of General Josiah Gorgas*. Tuscaloosa, 1947.

*The War of the Rebellion: . . . Official Records of the Union and Confederate Armies*. 128 vols. Washington, 1880-1901.
*Official Records of the Union and Confederate Navies in the War of the Rebellion*. 26 vols. Washington, 1894-1922.

WARE, EDITH ELLEN. *Political Opinion in Massachusetts During Civil War and Reconstruction. Columbia University Studies in History, Economics and Public Law*, vol. LXXIV, II, 1916.

WATSON, B. F. *An Oration Delivered at Huntington Hall, Lowell, Massachusetts . . . . April 19, 1886*. New York, 1886.

WEINSTEIN, GREGORY. *The Ardent Eighties, Reminiscences of an Interesting Decade*. New York, 1929.

WEISBERGER, BERNARD A. *Reporters for the Union*. Boston, 1953.

WELLES, GIDEON. "Admiral Farragut and New Orleans, With an Account of the Origin and the First Three Naval Expeditions of the War." *Galaxy*, vol. XII, 1871.

# BIBLIOGRAPHY

WELLES, GIDEON. *Diary.* See Morse.

WERTENBAKER, THOMAS J. *Norfolk, Historic Southern Port.* Durham, 1931.

WEST, RICHARD S., JR. *Gideon Welles.* Indianapolis, 1943.

WEST, RICHARD S., JR. *The Second Admiral, The Life of David Dixon Porter, 1812-1891.* New York, 1937.

WHITE, ANDREW DICKSON. *Autobiography of Andrew Dickson White.* 2 vols. New York, 1905.

WHITNEY, J. H. E. *The Hawkins Zouaves (Ninth New York Volunteers), Their Battles and Marches.* New York, 1866.

WHITTEMORE, EDWIN CAREY. *The Centennial History of Waterville.* Waterville, Me., 1902.

WILLIAMS, BEN AMES (ed.). CHESTNUT, MARY BOYKIN. *A Diary From Dixie.* Boston, 1949.

WILLIAMS, CHARLES RICHARD (ed.). *Diary and Letters of Rutherford Birchard Hayes.* 5 vols. Columbus, Ohio, 1924.

WILLIAMS, KENNETH P. *Lincoln Finds a General: A Military Study of the Civil War.* 3 vols. New York, 1949-1952.

WILLIAMS, T. HARRY. *Lincoln and His Generals.* New York, 1952.

WILLIAMS, T. HARRY. *Lincoln and the Radicals.* Madison, 1941.

WILLIAMS, THOMAS. "Letters of General Thomas Williams, 1862." *American Historical Review,* vol. XIV, 1908-1909.

WILSON, FOREST. *Crusader in Crinoline. The Life of Harriet Beecher Stowe.* Philadelphia, 1941.

WILSON, HENRY. *History of the Rise and Fall of the Slave Power in America.* 3 vols. Boston, 1872.

WINSTON, ROBERT W. *Andrew Johnson, Plebeian and Patriot.* New York, 1928.

WINTHROP, THEODORE. *Life in the Open Air and Other Papers.* New York, 1876.

WINTHROP, THEODORE. *The Life and Poems of Theodore Winthrop.* Edited by his sister. New York, 1884.

WISTAR, ISAAC JONES. *Autobiography of Isaac Jones Wistar, 1827-1905.* Philadelphia, 1937.

WOODWARD, C. VANN. *Reunion and Reaction.* Boston, 1951.

WOODWARD, W. E. *Meet General Grant.* New York, 1928.

WYMAN, LILLIE BUFFUM CHASE. *American Chivalry.* Boston, 1913.

YOUNG, JOHN RUSSELL. *Around the World with General Grant.* 2 vols. New York, 1879.

ZORNOW, WILLIAM FRANK. *Lincoln and the Party Divided.* Norman, Okla., 1954.

# Index

Abbott, J. C., 46, 47
Abbott, Josiah G., help of, 31; nomination of, 240
Abolitionists, condemnation of, 27; press and, 118
Academy of Music (New York), speech at, 138
Adams, Henry, 207
Adams, John Q., 29
Adams, John Q., Jr., 242
*Advertiser* (Boston), and reconciliation with Grant, 206; attacks of, 222
*Advertiser* (Lowell), 30, 31, 36, 47
Alaska, purchase of, 210
Alexandria, Egypt, U. S. consul at, 212
Alta Vela, 201
*America* (yacht), 241
Ames, Adelbert, marriage of, 212; impeachment of, 231; family of, 242; votes against Sumner, 311 (n. 49)
Ames, Blanche Butler, birth of, 28; education of, 54; in New York, 165; marriage of, 212; mentioned, 242
Ames, Oakes, 225
Amnesty, for Confederates, and compromise plans, 184; act for, 215-216; mentioned, 181
Anarchists, defense of, 254
Anderson, Robert, 60
Andersonville Prison, 141
Andrew, John A., victory of, 58; description of, 62; appoints Butler, 63-64, 270 (n. 78, 79); quarrels with Butler about offer to Hicks, 72; quarrels about recruiting, 90-97, 280 (n. 68); Butler's letter to, 91; Butler's support of, 1864, 163; Butler's hatred for, 269 (n. 67); quoted, 279 (n. 45); recognizes Salem Light Artillery, 279 (n. 47); approached on Butler's behalf, 292 (n. 46)
Andrew, John W., 117
Annapolis, Maryland, seizure of, 66-69; Department of, 71; mentioned, 70, 73
Annapolis & Elk Ridge Railroad, 70
Annapolis Junction, 70
Annexation of territory, Butler's belief in, 210
Anthony, Susan B., 313 (n. 11)
Anti-Monopoly party, 250, 252
Appomattox C. H., effect of surrender at, 179
Appomattox River, 147, 149
Aristocracy, Butler's dislike for, 20, 30-31, 110, 193, 217ff., 248; Southern, 136. *See also* Brahmins.
*Arkansas* (ram), 289 (n. 53)
Army Appropriation Act, 1867, 190; 306 (n. 20); 1878, 239
Arthur, Chester, troubles of administration of, 244
Ashley, James M., 190, 191, 192
*Atlantic* Monthly, reviews Butler's career, 139
Ayer, James C., 20

Babcock, Rufus, 21
Bailey, Theodorus, 105
Balcolm, George, 19, 20
Balls Bluff, engagement at, 91
Balloon ascent, ordered by Butler, 275 (n. 40)
Baltimore, Democratic conventions in: 1848, 32; 1852, 40; 1860, 56, 57; mob in, 65, 67, 73; seizure of, 72-76; Union convention in,

345

161; mentioned, 54, 70, 126, 157, 163, 273 (n. 63)
Baltimore & Ohio Railroad, 73
Bancroft, George, 31
Bank of Louisiana, 125
Bank of Mutual Redemption, 63
Bankers, Butler's treatment of, in New Orleans, 116-117
Bankhead, J. P., quoted, 276 (n. 69)
Bankruptcy law, Butler's interest in, 27
Banks, Nathaniel P., and coalition, 35; in Constitutional Convention, 38; joins Republican party, 42; at militia encampment, 49; reelected, 50, 266 (n. 52); supersedes Butler, 133; problem of replacement of, 136-138; elected Speaker of Assembly, 262 (n. 8); mentioned, 140, 146, 147
Barnard, John G., 151
Barnburners, 32
Barron, Samuel, 85
Barton, Clara, 248
Bates, Edward, supports Pierpont, 168, 169; and Butler's assignment to Ship Island, 278 (n. 33)
Baton Rouge, military engagements at, 129, 130, 289 (n. 52); capture of, 128
Bayard, Thomas F., 251
Bay View, 212
Beach, Erastus, 47, 58
Beaufort, South Carolina, 171, 283 (n. 17)
Beauregard, Pierre G. T., offer of safe conduct to, 114; treatment of wife of, 118; defeats Butler, 150; and Petersburg defenses, 296 (n. 45)
Beecher, Henry W., proposes Butler for President, 165; trial of, 230, 317 (n. 84); mentioned, 165
Begole, Josiah W., 253
Bell, Joseph M., 114
Belvedere, 27, 52
Benjamin, Judah P., Lovell's correspondence with, 101; relatives of, 116, 288 (n. 39)

Bermuda Hundred, military operations at, 148, 150, 153
Berwick Bay, capture of, 130
Big Bethel, engagement at, 80-81, 82, 253
Biloxi, Mississippi, 99, 100
Bingham, John, quarrels with Butler, 191-192, 312 (n. 73); and impeachment of Johnson, 194, 196, 201; and Crédit Mobilier, 225
Birney, William, 155
Bishop, Robert R., 245
Black Codes, 182
Blaine, James G., altercations with Butler of, 194, 215, 312 (n. 75), 317 (n. 93); and Hayes, 236; nominated in 1884, 252; secret help to, 252-253; defeat of, 253; mentioned, 217
Blair, Montgomery, Butler's relations with, 80, 82, 83, 84, 86, 92, 126; family of and Johnson, 180
Bland, T. A., biography by, 242
Bland-Allison Act, 237
Bliss, George, 38
Blockade, lifting of, 109, 110, 283 (n. 17)
Bloody Shirt, use of, 230, 232, 253; origin of term, 307 (n. 60)
Booth, John W., diary of, 191; mentioned, 178, 192
Boott, Kirk, 18
Border states, problem of, 78
Boston, Massachusetts, Butler's office in, 28, 34; Constitutional Convention in, 38-39; Collector of, 47, 53, 227-228; and outbreak of war, 62-63; delay of troops in, 95; quartermaster at, 122; post office in, 220; disputed election in, 237; Kearney's visit to, 240; mayoralty elections in, 242, 321 (n. 7); statue in, 256
Bounty, question of payment of, 91, 94
Boutwell, George, and coalition, 35, 38; joins Republican party, 42; defends Butler, 176; and impeachment of Johnson, 196, 201; Butler's relations with, 211, 316 (n.

# INDEX

60), 316 (n. 72); Butler's reliance on, 226; and Simmons appointment, 228, 235; defeated, 235; mentioned, 187, 231, 262 (n. 8); 304, (n. 32)

Bowles, Samuel, 224

Boyd, Belle, 145

Bradford, Gamaliel, 259 (n. 44)

Brahmins, Butler's dislike for, 193; Butler's clashes with, 217 ff., in Democratic party, 239, 240; hatred for Butler of, 245, 248; oppose statue to Butler, 256. *See also* Aristocracy

Breckinridge, John C., Butler's support of, 57 ff.; at Battle of Baton Rouge, 129-130; supporters of, 256; mentioned, 63

Brooks, James, attacks Butler, 176; row with, 201; and Crédit Mobilier, 225

Brooks, Preston, 47, 265 (n. 32)

Brown, John, raid of, 50; meeting in support of, 90; mentioned, 10, 62, 93

Brown, John Y., Butler's row with, 8-10, 217

Browne, A. G., 187

Bruce, Blanche K., helped by Butler, 311 (n. 70)

Buchanan, James, nomination of, 43-44; Butler's relations with, 46, 47, 48, 49; rift with Douglas of, 46 ff.; supports Butler, 58; and secession, 59 ff.; Butler's advice to, 60, 269 (n. 57)

Bull Run, Battle of, 82

Bunting, Butler's interest in, 181

Burchard, Samuel D., 253

Burlingame, Anson, 38, 265 (n. 32)

Burnham, Hiram, 156

Burnside, Ambrose B., 135

Business ventures, Butler's, 27, 52, 181

Butler, Andrew Jackson, youth of, 17; removes to West, 23; sent to Washington, 80; failure of appointment of in Senate, 99; speculations of, 123, 132, 287 (n. 8); and Mexican War, 261 (n. 48); appointment of, 279 (n. 45)

Butler, Benjamin Franklin, description of, 7, 10-11; 18, 22, 34, 155-156, 241, 255; youth of, 17 ff.; ancestry of, 17; marriage of, 24; education of, 18-24; law practice of, 25 ff.; early politics of, 29 ff.; and coalition, 34-41; as Hunker, 42 ff.; and election of 1860, 53-58; and secession, 58-64; marches to Washington, 65-70; commands Department of Annapolis, 71-75; at Fort Monroe, 77 ff.; recruits troops, 88-97; assigned to Gulf, 93-97; sails to New Orleans, 97 ff.; administration of New Orleans by, 107-134; efforts to regain command by, 135-140; and exchange of prisoners, 140-145; 1864 campaigns of, 146-157; attempted removal of, 153-155; and election of 1864, 158-165; assigned to New York, 163-165; administration of Department of Virginia and North Carolina by, 166-169; and Fort Fisher expedition, 170-173; removal of, 173-177; reconstruction policies of, 178 ff.; and Johnson's impeachment, 186, 189, 194 ff.; defeats Dana, 207-209; and Grant administration, 208 ff.; financial views of, 46, 193-194, 218; ambition for governorship of, 222 ff.; and Crédit Mobilier, 255; and Simmons appointment, 227-228; defends Sanborn, 228-229; renewed attempts at governorship by, 239-241, 242-243, 244-245; as Governor of Massachusetts, 245-249; seeks Presidency, 250-253; old age of, 253 ff.; death of, 255; statue to, 256

Butler, Ben Israel, 28, 242, 244

Butler, Charlotte, in Deerfield and Lowell, 17-22; and Mexican War, 261 (n. 48); death of, 244; bequests to, 281 (n. 1)

Butler, George, 212, 236

Butler, John, career of, 17; politics of, 20; rumors about death of, 37, 223, 257 (n. 2), 262 (n. 22)
Butler, Paul, 28, 242
Butler, Sarah, marriage of, 24; family of, 28; in 1862, 98, 108, 132; and campaign of 1864, 162, 165; bequest to, 281 (n. 1); and Grant, 211; death of, 231, 242, 244; mentioned, 290 (n. 69)
Butler, Zephania, 17
*Butler's Book*, writing of, 254-255
Butterfield, Daniel, 165

Cabinet, possible position for Butler in, 137, 138, 158, 176, 179, 184, 202, 221, 291 (n. 11), 299 (n. 39), 324 (n. 58)
California, Butler's trip to, 243
Cameron, Simon, and Hicks, 67; and Butler, 73, 76; visits Fortress Monroe, 82, 159-160; 298 (n. 10); and fugitive slaves, 82-83; and recruiting controversy, 89, 94; resignation of, 96; and Butler's removal, 137; mentioned, 63
Canada, Confederate agents in, 164; fishery controversy with, 221; demand for annexation of, 221, 254; 314 (n. 27)
Cape Anne Granite Company, 220
Cape Fear River, 171
Cape Hatteras, *see* Hatteras
Carey, John B., 79, 274 (n. 11, 17)
Carnegie, Andrew, 272 (n. 29)
Carney, James G., 63, 270 (n. 79)
Carpenter, George M., ejects Butler from court room, 255
Case, Eliphalet, 30
Cass, A. J., 265 (n. 15)
Cass, Lewis, 32
Catholics, Butler and, 30; and proposed constitution, 39; agitation against, 40, 42 ff.. *See also* Irish
Chadwick, J. H., 212
Chancellorsville, Battle of, 138
Chandler, William E., Simmons' interview with, 232; and election of 1884, 252, 324 (n. 61); and Butler's return to Democratic party, 321 (n. 61)
Chandler, Zachariah, Butler and, 95; and election of 1864, 162; on Committee on Conduct of War, 175; approached by Herbert, 179
Charitable institutions, Butler's attacks on, 246, 247 ff.
Charleston, Massachusetts, convent at, 38
Charleston, South Carolina, Democratic convention in, 53-55, 57; Cushing in, 59; forts at, 59-60, 62; plans for conquest of, 139; mentioned, 86, 176
Chase, Salmon P., supports Butler, 76, 132; Presidential boom for, 159-160
Chattanooga, Battle of, General Smith at, 149
Chestnut, Mary B., on Order No. 28, 111
Chicago, 1884 convention in, 251
Child, Linus, and ten-hour movement, 36
Child labor, early laws against, 22; Butler's stand against, 246, 247
Chinese, Kearney's attacks on, 240; Butler's hostility to, 242
Chittenden, Simeon B., and Greenback case, 319 (n. 16)
Choate, Rufus, in campaign of 1856, 44-45; Butler urges nomination of, 47; quoted, 265 (n. 17); mentioned, 38, 52
Cilley, Abigail, 17
Cincinnati, 1856 convention in, 43-44; platform of, 54; radical convention in, 161; speech at, 305 (n. 50); mentioned, 24
Cipher dispatches, 238
City Point, Virginia, prisoner exchange at, 141; seizure of, 148, 149; mentioned, 150, 295 (n. 33)
Civil Rights Act, 1866, 183, 185; 1875, 7-10, 230-231
Civil Service Reform, Butler's opposition to, 220, 313 (n. 16); Hayes and, 235, 236; Butler's endorsement of, 245

# INDEX

Claflin, William, retirement of, 224
Clark, Thomas N., at Lowell High School, 19
Clay, Henry, 29, 31
Clergymen, Butler's treatment of in New Orleans and Norfolk, 119, 167; hostility of, 246
Cleveland, Grover, and election of 1884, 250-253, 324 (n. 64)
Coalition, Butler and, 34-41
Cochrane, John, and interviews with Buchanan, 269 (n. 57)
Cockeysville, Maryland, troops halted at, 67
Colby, see Waterville
Cold Harbor, engagement at, 151, 152, 295 (n. 33)
Colfax, Schuyler, and reconciliation with Grant, 206; election of, 213; and Crédit Mobilier, 225; mentioned, 190
Commune, Butler's defense of, 219
Compromise of 1850, 35, 39
Comstock, C. B., and Fort Fisher expedition, 172, 173
Concord, Massachusetts, prison at, 248; 1850 county conventions at, 262 (n. 7)
Conduct of the War, Joint Committee on, 95, 137, 139, 175, 303 (n. 72)
Confederate States of America, formation of, 61; prospects of, 77; hatred for Butler in, 111, 112, 115, 134, 136, 142; agents of, in New York, 163-164; proposed ultimatum to, 165
Confiscation Acts, 83, 122, 123, 131
Conkling, Roscoe, 219, 226
Conover, Sanford, perjured testimony of, 192
Conservatives, struggles of Butler with, 217-233; 235, 240, 243. See also Brahmins
*Constitution*, U. S. S., rescue of, 66
Constitutional Convention, 1853, see Massachusetts
Consuls, clashes of, with Butler, 125-127, 130; mentioned 88
"Contrabands," origin of phrase, 79 ff., 274 (n. 17); mentioned, 130, 157
Convents, investigation of, 43
Cooke, Jay, deplores Butler's financial notions, 194
Coppel, George, clashes with Butler, 125
Copperheads, denunciation of, 136, Butler and plots of, 163.
Corinth, Mississippi, 128-129
Corporations, at Lowell, description of, 18; politics of, 29; Butler's attacks on, 32, 35-37; reduction of hours in, 38; mentioned, 25
Corruption, charges of, against Butler, 122-124, 130, 134, 137, 166-167, 174, 176, 207, 220-221, 226, 228-229, 230, 279 (n. 45), 320 (n. 38)
Cotton, importation of, into New Orleans, 110, 120; speculation in, 122; in western Louisiana, 130; proposed tax on, 136
*Courier* (Lowell), 25, 36-37, 41, 62
Couturié, Amadie, 125, 127
Covas & Negroponte, funds of, 127
Cox, Samuel S., 217-218
Crapo, William, 244, 245
Crédit Mobilier, Butler and, 225
Crosby, Nathan, 26
Cuba, question of recognition of insurgents in, 211
Currency, state of, in New Orleans, 107; regulations concerning, 109, 116 ff. See also finance, inflation, greenbacks
Curtis, Benjamin R., defends Johnson, 199, 200
Curtis, George W., 234
Cushing, Caleb, and Butler's application to West Point, 20; candidacy of, 31; and Free Soilers, 35; and Constitutional Convention, 38; and coalition, 39-41; friendship of, 45; in Massachusetts assembly, 48; and election of 1860, 53 ff.; rejection of, 63; nomination of, for Chief Justice, 228; death of, 244; mentioned, 257 (n. 2), 270 (n. 76)

Dahlgren, Ulric, recovery of body of, 294 (n. 3)
Dana, Charles A., supports Butler, 253
Dana, Richard H., in Constitutional Convention, 38; runs against Butler, 207-208; diplomatic appointment of, 231, 313 (n. 13); quoted, 263 (n. 32); mentioned, 210, 213
Davis, Garrett, asks for investigation of Butler, 161; row with, 217; introduces resolution of censure, 312 (n. 73)
Davis, Henry Winter, 179
Davis, Jefferson, appoints Butler, 45; visits New England, 47; Butler's interviews with, 53; Butler's votes for, 10, 53-54, 55, 176, 191; assumes Presidency of Confederacy, 61; and G. O. No. 28, 111; outlaws Butler, 10, 115, 136; and Butler's recall, 135; and prisoner exchange, 143; and Beauregard, 150; prospective punishment of, 181, 185, 303 (n. 10), 304 (n. 24); mentioned, 105, 119
Davis, William T., writes character sketch of Butler, 266 (n. 44)
Dawes, Henry, Butler's reply to, 211, in 1871, 224; defeat of, 229; committee assignments to, 312 (n. 75); mentioned, 217, 221
Dean, Benjamin, Butler's support of, 237
Deep Bottom, bridgehead at, 156
Deerfield, New Hampshire, Butler's birth in, 17; rumors in, 262 (n. 22)
Deming, Henry, 90
Democratic party, in Massachusetts, 29 ff., 42 ff., 52 ff., 55 ff., 63; conventions of: 1848, 32; 1852, 40; 1856, 43; 1860, 53 ff.; 1884, 251; Butler's refusal to run on 1861 ticket of, 88; Lincoln and, 89; gains of, 118; hostility to Butler of, 134; in South, 212; Butler's 1876 raid upon, 233; Butler's return to, 237 ff. *See also* elections
Denison, George, 123

Devens, Charles, appointment of, 235
Dexter, Eliza, 24
Dickinson, Anna, Butler's relations with, 242
Dictatorship, rumors of, during Civil War, 138
District Ring, Butler and, 314 (n. 25)
Dix, John A., occupies Eastern Shore, 88; patriotic statement of, 114; and prisoner exchange, 140; in 1864, 163 ff.; mentioned, 89
Donaldsonville, bombardment of, 119; capture of, 130
Doolittle, James R., 310 (n. 32)
Douglas, Stephen A., and Kansas-Nebraska Act, 42, 43; candidacy of, 44, 52 ff.; breaks with Buchanan, 46 ff.; and Butler, 44, 46, 49, 51, 52 ff.; defeated, 1860, 58
Douglass, Frederick, 186, 233
Dracut, Massachusetts, 23
Draft riots, 139
Drury's Bluff, engagement at, 150
Dupasseur & Company, funds of, 126, 127
Dutch Gap Canal, 170, 173

Early, Jubal, raids District of Columbia, 154
Eastern Bay State Regiment, 91, 94, 278 (n. 19)
Eastern Shore, operations against, 82, 88, 90, 92
Edson School, Butler at, 19
Edson, Theodore, 24, 258 (n. 27)
Education, Butler's furtherance of, in Norfolk, 167
Eight Hour Day, Butler's interest in, 219, 239
Eighteenth Corps, 154, 297 (n. 64)
Eighth Regiment (Massachusetts), 66 ff.
Election Campaigns: 1840, 29-30; 1844, 31; 1848, 32-33; 1851, 35-37; 1852, 40; 1854, 42; 1855, 43; 1855, 43-45; 1857, 46; 1858, 47-48; 266 (n. 38); 1859, 49-50, 52-53, 266 (n. 52); 1860, 52-58; 1861, 88; 1862, 118-119, 130, 135; 1863,

# INDEX   351

139; 1864, 154, 158-165; 1866, 186-188, 305 (n. 59); 1868, 207-208; 1870, 221; 1871, 222-224; 1872, 224-225; 1873, 226-227; 1874, 230, 317 (n. 89); 1876, 232-233, 318 (n. 111); 1878, 239-241; 1879, 242-243; 1880, 243; 1882, 244-245; 1883, 249; 1884, 250-253; 1888, 254; 1892, 254
Electoral vote, count of, 1869, 213-214
Eliot, Charles W., 248
Emancipation Proclamation, 132
Enforcement Acts, 215
English Bill, Butler and, 47
Espionage, employment of Negroes for, 117; charges of, against Mrs. Phillips, 117; against Charles Heidsieck, 127; and Miss Van Lew, 146
Essex County, Massachusetts, candidacy in, 187; defeat in, 230; warnings from, 309 (n. 4)
Evarts, William M., represents Johnson, 199, 201; appointed by Hayes, 235; represents Beecher, 317 (n. 84)
Ewing, Thomas, and Johnson, 194
Exeter Academy, 18

Fabens, Joseph W., interests Butler in San Domingo, 210
Fanueil Hall, Jefferson Davis at, 47; Butler meeting in, 50, 136; Brown meeting in, 51, 90; Union meeting in, 89
Farewell Address, Butler's, in New Orleans, 133; to Army of the James, 174-175
Farnsworth, John, 217, 220
Farr, A. W., 27
Farragut, David G., and New Orleans expedition, 93, 98; description of, 99-100; difficulties of, 100; Butler's visits to, 100-101, 103; passes forts, 101-102; Butler and 103, 104; Butler as counsel for, 282 (n. 50); 320 (n. 38); captures New Orleans, 104 ff.; and Vicksburg expedition, 128-129

Fast Day, Proclamation for, 245, 246
Felton, S. M., and march to Washington, 66
Fessenden, William P., supports Pierpont, 168; votes for Johnson's acquittal, 203
Field, Walbridge A., Butler's opposition to, 237
Fifteenth Amendment, 214
Fifth Avenue Hotel, dinner at, 1864, 165
Fifth Regiment (Massachusetts), 72
Finance, Butler's views on, 46, 48, 187; 193-194, 218-219, 232, 235, 237, 313 (n. 3); Hayes' policies concerning, 235
First Regiment (North Carolina), 275 (n. 27)
Fish, Hamilton, Butler's support of, 211
Fisheries, Butler's interest in, 221, 314 (n. 27)
Flag, American, desecration of, in New Orleans, 105, 285 (n. 70); punishment for desecration of, 114
Flanders, B. F., elected to Congress, 132; supports Butler, 293 (n. 50)
Florida, electoral vote of, 234
Flour, speculation in, 122, 124
Floyd, John B., and secession crisis, 60
Force Bill, 1875, failure of, 317 (n. 93)
Foreign Affairs, Butler's views on, 221, 222, 254
Fort Clark, surrender of, 85
Fort Donelson, surrender of, 88
Fort Fisher, first expedition against, 170-174; 375 (n. 37); second expedition against, 173, 175, 303 (n. 72); mentioned, 241, 253
Fort Harrison, capture of, 156
Fort Hatteras, imprisonment of clergymen at, 300 (n. 6)
Fort Henry, surrender of, 88
Fort Jackson, plans for reduction of, 100, 101; passage of, 102; reduction of, 103, 282 (n. 39); controversy about, 103-104, 254; im-

prisonment of New Orleans citizens at, 113, 114, 125
Fort McHenry, 74
Fort Monroe, Butler's assignment to, 76 ff.; description of, 77-78; Butler's return to, 140; Ould at, 143; Grant at, 147; attempted banishment of Butler to, 153, 155, 297 (n. 57); interview with Cameron at, 159-160; mentioned, 72, 78, 81, 82, 91, 95, 158
Fort Moultrie, 60
Fort Powhatan, capture of, 294 (n. 14)
Fort St. Philip, description of, 100; passage of, 101-102; reduction of, 103
Fort Sumter, 60, 62, 77
Foster, Dwight, active on Andrew's behalf, 92
Fourteenth Amendment, 184, 185, 189, 215
Fowler, Josiah S., votes for Johnson's acquittal, 203
Fox, Gustavus V., education of, 19; Butler's visit to, 86; and New Orleans expedition, 93, 96, 280 (n. 65); and Fort Fisher, 302 (n. 37); mentioned, 103, 276 (n. 69)
France, visit of fleet of, 113; troubles of citizens of, 126, 127, 288 (n. 40); atrocities of, 133
Frankfurt, Germany, U. S. consul in, 212
Franklin, W. B., 294 (n. 4)
Frederick, Maryland, 71, 74
Fredericksburg, Battle of, 135
Freedmen's Bureau, Butler's ambition for headship of, 303 (n. 79)
Freedmen's Bureau Bill, Johnson's veto of, 184
Freeport Doctrine, 53
Free Soil party, 32, 35, 39, 41
Frémont, John C., and election of 1864, 160-161, 162; mentioned, 44
French, Jonas, disputed appointment of, 90 ff., 97; business ventures of, 220
Frying Pan Shoals, accident on, 98
Fugitive Slave Law, 39, 40, 45

Galveston, plans for capture of, 130
Gardner, Henry C., 42-43
Garfield, James G., on finance, 194; and Crédit Mobilier, 225; nomination of, 243; mentioned, 190, 312 (n. 73)
General Order Number 28, 11, 110-112, 116, 117, 158, 284 (n. 28)
George, Paul R., 99
Georgia, reconstruction of, 213-214, 221
Gettysburg, Battle of, 140
Gillmore, Quincy A., in Army of the James, 147, 148, 149, 151; departure of, 155; 295 (n. 36); and Hudson, 169
Gold, plot to raise price of, 164
Gordon, George H., attacks Butler, 207
Gore, Christopher, 246
Gosport Navy Yard, plans for recapture of, 73, 79-80, 82
Gould, Daniel, case of, 26
Gould, Jay, and Union Pacific Refunding Bill, 238-239, 319 (n. 27); contributes to Butler's election fund, 316 (n. 63)
Grand Army of the Republic, 255
Granite House, 231, 255
Grant, Ulysses S., takes Vicksburg, 129; and prisoner exchange, 143 ff.; strategy of, 293 (n. 54); 147 ff.; and Bermuda Hundred, 150; reduces Army of the James, 151, 295 (n. 33); attempts to remove Butler, 153 ff., 297 (n. 57, 58); and election of 1864, 162; and Fort Fisher, 171 ff.; removes Butler, 173, 174; Butler breaks with, 174-175, 176, 186, 193; final report of, 183, 295 (n. 18); and Johnson, 183, 190, 193, 194; and radicals, 193; nomination of, 205; Butler's reconciliation with, 205-209; and Dana, 207; relies on Butler, 208 ff.; Tenure of Office Act and, 208, 209; and San Domingo, 209-210; counting of votes for, 213-214; and reconstruction, 214 ff.; revolt against, 216, 274-

# INDEX

275; and reform, 219; failure of administration of, 222, 230; and salary grab, 225-226, 227; and Simmons appointment, 227-228; vetoes inflation bill, 229; and Gillmore, 295 (n. 36); popularity of, 309 (n. 4); Butler's remarks about, 310 (n. 32); avoids Johnson, 310 (n. 34); rumors of blackmailing of, 155, 310 (n. 37); quoted on Butler, 384 (n. 53); and eight-hour day, 313 (n. 9); renomination of, 315 (n. 50, 53); mentioned, 88, 304 (n. 33), 312 (n. 76), 313 (n. 16)

Great Britain, Butler's dislike for, 20, 221, 222; *Trent* affair and, 94; reaction to General Order No. 28 in, 111-113; troubles of subjects of, in New Orleans, 125, 127, 288 (n. 40); Butler's attacks on, 133; suggested as mediator, 271 (n. 18); possible war with, 320 (n. 49)

Greble, John T., at Big Bethel, 81

Greeley, Horace, and Butler, 1864, 160, 162; favors amnesty, 215-216; candidate for President, 224

Greely, A. W., reception of, 252

Green, John A., 164

Greenbacks, Butler's advocacy of, 193-194, 206, 218, 221, 232, 236-231, 242, 306 (n. 30); and campaign of 1876, 232; Hayes and, 235, 236-237; test case concerning, 319 (n. 16)

Greenback party, success of, 242; Butler and, 250, 252, 253, 321 (n. 4); mentioned, 237, 253

*Greyhound*, reporters on, 161; explosion of, 171

Grimes, James W., votes for Johnson's acquittal, 203

Groesbeck, William S., counsel for Johnson, 199, 201

Gulf, Department of the, creation of, 96; Butler's administration of, 107 ff.; rumors of corruption in, 122; military operations in, 128 ff.; Butler's removal from command of, 132 ff.; Butler attempts to return to, 135-139. *See also* New Orleans

Gurowski, Count Adam, 79, 81, 158-159

Guthrie, James, 57, 267 (n. 25)

Habeas Corpus, suspension of, 71

Haggerty, Peter, reconnoiters Baltimore, 73

Halleck, Henry W., at Corinth, 128-129; Butler's correspondence with, 132, 135; quoted on Butler, 146, 294 (n. 12); confuses Butler, 150; sends board of inquiry, 151; and Butler's intended removal, 153; correspondence with Grant of, 295 (n. 33)

Hallett, B. F., 40, 49, 56, 268 (n. 28)

Halstead, Murat, quoted on Butler, 56

Hamilton Corporation, 36

Hamilton Hall, ticket of, 316 (n. 64)

Hampton, Virginia, abandonment of, 82, burning of, 84

Hancock, Winfield S., at Petersburg, 152, 301 (n. 30); in 1880, 243

Harper's Ferry, John Brown's raid at, 9, 50; mentioned, 73, 74

*Harper's Weekly*, opposes Butler on inflation, 194; revelations concerning election of 1884 in, 252; attitude towards Butler of, 1862, 289 (n. 59)

Harrison, Benjamin, Butler's support of, 254

Harrison, William H., election of, 30

Harvard University, Butler's row with, 248-249

Hatteras Inlet, expedition against, 85, 86

Hawley, Joseph, and Butler, 223

Hay Market riot, 254

Hayes, Rutherford B., disputed election of, 234-235; Butler and, 235 ff.; labor policies of, 235, 236, 238; and Mrs. Mumford, 285 (n. 73)

Heidsieck, Charles, 127

Henderson, John B., votes against impeachment, 203, refuses subpoena, 308 (n. 76)
Henshaw, David, 260 (n. 26)
*Herald* (Boston), attack on Butler by, 222-223
*Herald* (New York), Stevens interview with, 305 (n. 42)
Herbert, J. K., 179
Hicks, Thomas H., troubles of, 67-68; Butler and, 68, 90, 91; and legislature of Maryland, 71-72; suggests mediation, 271 (n. 18)
Hildreth, Fisher, introduces Butler to Sarah, 24; buys paper, 31; patronage and, 41, 46-47; Butler confers with, 41; in legislature, 260 (n. 27)
Hildreth, Israel, 23
Hill, Daniel H., 80, 275 (n. 33)
Hill, Isaac, 20, 257 (n. 2)
Hillard, George, 39
Hincks, E. W., 149
Hiss, Joseph, 43
Hitchcock, Ethan A., and prisoner exchanges, 141 ff.; and Butler, 293 (n. 67)
Hoar, E. Rockwood, and Butler's libel suit, 37; resignation of, 211; nomination of, 232; Butler's letter against, 232; mentioned, 229
Hoar, George F., characterization of Butler by, 217; campaigns against Butler, 224, 226; and Simmons, 227; defeat of, 229; elected to Senate, 235; accuses Butler, 249; gives credit to Butler, 270 (n. 77), 274 (n. 18); and blackmailing of Grant, 315 (n. 37)
Homestead, strike at, and Butler, 325 (n. 69)
Howe, Frank, 280 (n. 68)
Holmes, Oliver Wendell, 136
Holt, Joseph, 60
Homans, Charles, 70
Hooker, Joseph, charges against Butler by, 229
Hope & Co., gold of, 125, 127
House of Representatives, Butler's unsuccessful candidacies for, 40, 44, 47; votes thanks to Butler, 136; Butler's election to, 188; Butler's first appearance in, 190; election of doorkeeper of, 237-238; demand for Butler's resignation from, 241; Butler's last session in, 242
Hudson, Henry, 169
Hunkers, in Massachusetts politics, 39 ff.; walk out of party, 56; Andrew's dislike for, 90; mentioned, 136, 264 (n. 43)
Hunter, David, and emancipation, 131
Huntington Hall (Lowell), accident at, 44-45; Butler's troubles in, 57-58; Butler's speech at, 1863, 136; 1865, 176

Impeachment of Johnson, articles of, 194-195; trial, 196-204; Butler's advocacy of, 305 (n. 50)
Incendiaries, Confederate, in New York, 163, 300 (n. 53)
Indianapolis, Greenback convention at, 250
Inflation, *see* finance
Inflation Bill of 1874, 218, 229
Irish population, in Lowell, 28; Butler's sympathy with, 38, 221, 222, 233, 247; gratitude of, 40, 42, 43, 48, 119, 239, 242; Cleveland and, 253

Jackson, Andrew, Butler's admiration for, 20; Massachusetts supporters of, 29; raises colored troops, 131
James, Army of the, campaigns of, 147-157; Butler's removal as commander of, 173-177
Jewell, Harvey, 224
Jews, Butler's dislike for, 286 (n. 93); Butler's insults to, 301 (n. 31)
Johnson, Andrew, cabinet of, 179; career of, 180; reconstruction policies of, 180 ff.; Butler's break with, 185 ff.; swing around the circle by, 186; in campaign of 1866; 186; Butler's attacks on,

189; radical measures against, 190; impeachment of, 186, 190, 192, 194-204; New Year's reception of, 208, 310 (n. 34); Alaska and, 210; charges concerning budget of, 211; mentioned, 236
Johnson, Reverdy, and seizure of Baltimore, 76; and corruption in New Orleans, 124; mission to New Orleans of, 126-127; mentioned, 268 (n. 33), 288 (n. 35)
*Journal* (Boston), Andrew's letter in, 91, attacks Butler, 222
Judiciary, reform of, 39, 48
Julian, George W., 179
*Julliard v. Greenman*, 319 (n. 16)

Kansas, troubles of, 43, 44, 46, 47
Kansas-Nebraska Act, 41, 42, 55
Karsner, George W., testifies in impeachment trial, 201
Kautz, August V., moves against Petersburg, 151
Kearney, Dennis, aids Butler, 240, 242
Keller, Fidel, arrest of, 117, 286 (n. 93)
Kelly, John, and election of 1884, 251
Kent, William H., 301 (n. 30)
Kentucky, Butler's prospects for command in, 153, 176
Key, David M., appointment to cabinet of, 235
Kilpatrick, Judson, and campaign of 1866, 207, 208
King, Preston, relation with Johnson of, 180
Know Nothings, Massachusetts victory of, 42-43
Ku Klux Klan, activities of, 213; legislation against, 215; mentioned, 233, 307 (n. 60)

Labor, condition of, in Lowell, 28; Butler's sympathy for, 19, 27, 28-29, 30, 32, 35-38, 187, 219, 222, 226, 239, 240, 243, 246, 247, 250, 251, 254; reduction of hours of, in Lowell, 38; in Massachusetts, 247; Hayes and, 235, 236, 239
Labor Reform party, 222
Labrador, Butler's trip to, 22
La Mountain, John, balloon ascents of, 275 (n. 40)
Land, confiscation of, Butler's advocacy of, in South, 165, 181
Larue, Ann, punishment of, 116, 117
Law, Butler's study of, 23; Butler's practice of, 24-27, 34, 52, 212, 231, 244, 254, 255, 260 (n. 12); contact with criminals through, 134
Lawrence, Amos, in election of 1860, 58
Leary, Stephen S., 261 (n. 46)
Lee, Henry, 92
Lee, Robert E., and Petersburg campaign, 147, 150, 152; surrender of, 178; Butler's demand for punishment of, 180, 181
Lee, Samuel B., 148
Lefferts, Marshall, refuses cooperation, 66, 69-70
Libby Prison, efforts to liberate prisoners of, 146; mentioned, 141
Liberal Republicans, 216, 224
Limburg, Roest van, protests of, 125, 126
Lincoln, Abraham, and election of 1860, 57, 58; inauguration of, 62; calls for troops, 62; correspondence of, with Hicks, 67, 68; and Maryland, 71; and seizure of Baltimore, 75-76; and sea power, 77; and emancipation, 78, 131, 132; reassigns Butler, 84; and Hatteras expedition, 86; and recruiting controversy, 90 ff., 92, 93, 95, 279 (n. 42); and New Orleans expedition, 92, 93-95; Porter and, 100; and foreign protests about Butler, 126 ff.; desires opening of Mississippi, 128; and Butler's removal, 132 ff., 135; considers new command for Butler, 136 ff.; and prisoner exchange, 137 ff.; and Butler's attempted removal, 1864, 154-155; re-election of, 158-165; considers Butler as running mate, 159-160;

sends Butler to New York, 163; and controversy with Pierpont, 167-169; and Fort Fisher, 170; removes Butler, 1865, 174; refuses to reassign Butler, 176; assassination of, 179, 191, 192, 198; sends Zacharie to New Orleans, 291 (n. 19); mentioned, 68, 80, 83, 276 (n. 60), 277 (n. 16), 280 (n. 75), 283 (n. 17), 291 (n. 11), 293 (n. 67), 300 (n. 6)

Locke, Joseph, 23, 26

Lodge, Henry C., 249

Logan, John A., clashes with Butler, 211, 217; mentioned, 89, 196, 225

Long, John D., defeats Butler, 243

Lord, Otis P., 38

Loring, George, helps Butler in 1886, 187; reputed deal with, 223; candidacy of, 224

Louisiana, prices in, 122; campaign in, 128-130; reconstruction plans for, 132; elections in, 132; electoral vote of, 234; withdrawal of troops from, 236

*Louisiana* (powderboat), 172

*Louisiana* (ram), 100, 104

Lovell, Mansfield, underestimates threat to New Orleans, 101; refuses to surrender, 105

Lowell, Massachusetts, description of, 18 ff.; Butler joins City Guard of, 28; changes in, 28-29; politics in, 30 ff., 46 ff.; working hours in, 38; in election of 1860, 57-58; Butler's return to, 1861, 86-88, 1863, 136; 1865, 176 ff.; Butler's house in, 28, 212; mentioned, 45, 48, 63, 91, 135, 175, 253

Lower California, Butler's interests in, 181

Lyceum, Butler's lecture at, 222

Lyman, Theodore, quoted on Butler, 155

Lynn, Massachusetts, 212

Lyons, J. H., 164

Lyons, Lord Richard, protests of, 112

McClellan, George B., and New Orleans expedition, 93, 94-97; Butler warns against, 138; in Peninsular campaign, 140; and election of 1864, 163; mentioned, 89, 117, 135, 279 (n. 54), 280 (n. 65, 75)

McClernand, John A., 89, 146

McClure, Alexander, corroborates Butler's account of rejection of offer to become Lincoln's running mate, 159, 298 (n. 10)

McCoy, Amasa, 291 (n. 11)

McDowell, Irvin, defeat of, 82

McLean, William, 8

McVeagh, Wayne, controversy of, with Butler, 236

Magruder, John B., defeats Butler, 80-82; mentioned, 275 (n. 73)

Maine, recruiting in, 90; Butler's address to legislature of, 306 (n. 3)

Mallory, Stephen Russell, 79

Manassas Junction, Butler's plans for operations against, 73; McClellan and, 95, 97. *See also* Bull Run

Manzereau, Adolphe, arrest of, 117

Marsh, Thomas, alleged mismanagement of, 247

Marcy, R. B., 279 (n. 54)

Maryland, Butler's campaign in, 65-75; safekeeping of Great Seal of, 272, (n. 46), 46

*Maryland* (ferry), 66, 67

Mason, James Y., sponsors Butler, 261 (n. 45)

Mason, Jeremiah, influence of, on Butler, 22-23, 25.

Massachusetts, Commonwealth of, politics of, 29 ff., 39 ff., 57 ff.; Constitutional Convention of, 38-39; militia of, 28, 42-43, 48, 49, 62, 63, 64, 186, 370 (n. 100); claims against United States of, 53; reforms in, advocated by Butler, 239 ff.

Massachusetts, Governor of, Butler's ambition for office of, 47, 49-50, 57-58, 222 ff., 226, 239-241, 242-243, 244-245; Butler's policies as, 245-249.

# INDEX

Massachusetts, Legislature of, limitation of child labor by, 28; Butler's candidacy for, 35-36, 37, 47; Butler's testimony to, 37; Butler's service in, 38, 48-49; adopts reforms, 241; hostility to Governor Butler of, 245 ff.; votes of thanks of, 291 (n. 7)

Meade, George M., Butler's attacks on, 175, 302 (n. 69); mentioned, 155, 162

Mechanics Hall, Worcester, seizure of, 240

Meigs, Montgomery, 151

Méjan, Count, Butler's troubles with, 125, 126, 127

Memphis, riots in, 186

Merrill, Joshua, 19

Merrimack Manufacturing Company, 18

Methuen, Massachusetts, postmastership of, 237

Mexican War, 31, 54, 261 (n. 48)

Michigan, election campaigns in, 253, 254

Middlesex County, Massachusetts, Butler's candidacy in, 231 ff.; sheriff of, 40

Middlesex Mills, Butler's purchase of interest in, 52; war contract of, 62; profits of, 85, 181; charges of underpayment of employees of, 241, 321 (n. 54)

Miller, Morris J., Butler's correspondence with, 68

Milligan Case, 184, 185

Mint, United States, in New Orleans, 105, 114

Mississippi River, planned opening of, 97, 128; defense of, 98, 100 ff.; Butler's prospective return to valley of, 136 ff., 139; Union control of, 146

Mississippi, State of, end of reconstruction in, 231

Missouri Compromise, repeal of, 42

Mobile, Alabama, plans for capture of, 130

Moieties, Butler's speech on, 228-229

Moore, Thomas O., and General Order No. 28, 111; and Negro troops, 131

Monroe, John T., and surrender of New Orleans, 105, 106, 107-109; arrest of, 113-114

Morgan, Edwin D., proposes Butler's removal in 1861, 276 (n. 60)

Morton, Levi P., attends Butler dinner, 165

Morton, Marcus, leads County Faction, 260 (n. 26)

Moulton, Francis T., retains Butler, 317 (n. 84)

Mugwumps, bolt of, 251, 252

Mumford, William, tears down American flag, 105; execution of, 114-115, 116, 117, 285 (n. 70, 71); Butler's treatment of widow of, 285 (n. 73)

*Myers v. United States,* 307 (n. 40)

National Home for Disabled Volunteer Soldiers, 220-221, 314 (n. 22)

National Hotel, food poisoning at, 45

Nativists, burning of convent by, 38; opposition to Butler of, 40; victory of, 42-43. *See also* Know Nothings.

Navy Department, Butler's relations with, 96; mentioned, 100

Navy, U. S., attacks Cape Hatteras, 85-86; plans capture of New Orleans, 93 ff.; 96; Butler's cooperation with, 100-101, 147; Butler's quarrels with, 129-130, 289 (n. 54), and prisoner exchanges, 144

Negroes, Butler's friendship for, 7-10, 184, 212-213; and Fugitive Slave Law, 45; and militia, 48, 50; arming of, 68, 130-131, 136, 137, 139; called "contrabands" by Butler, 78-79; problem of presence of, within Union lines, 82-83; emancipation of, 84, 130-131, 132; espionage by, 117; and prisoner exchange, 140 ff.; as soldiers, 152, 156-157, 212-213, 230,

297 (n. 54); Butler protects rights of, 167, 212-213, 214; Butler advocates cause of, 176, 177, 178, 181; suffrage for, 182, 183-185, 189; riots against, 186; Hayes and, 235-236; Butler's appointments of, 246, 247; progress of, and Butler, 256; scholarships for, 311 (n. 70)

Nelson, T. A. R., defends Johnson, 199, 201

Netherlands, troubles of New Orleans consul of, 125-127, 288 (n. 40)

New England, Butler's recruiting assignment in, 83, 86, 89 ff.; Department of, 90, 97

New Market Heights, charge at, 156-157, 212-213

New Orleans, plans for capture of, 93 ff., 96-97, 278 (n. 35), 280 (n. 75); capture of, 101, 103, 104-106; description of, 104-105, 107; spirit of, 107-108, 110; nature of Butler's regime in, 109, 110, 111 ff., 118; women of, 11, 111-114; disarmament of inhabitants of, 116; oath of allegiance in, 116; treatment of bankers in, 116-117; arrest of citizens in, 117 118; treatment of press in, 118-119; treatment of clergy in, 119; poor relief in, 119-120; sanitary measures in, 120-121; corruption in, 122-124; treatment of consuls in, 124-128; Butler's recall from, 122 ff., 132-136, 289 (n. 67); evaluation of Butler's administration of, 134; Butler's return from 135 ff.; Butler's efforts to return to, 136-140; proposed investigation of administration of, 158, 161; Zacharie mission to, 291 (n. 19); riots in, 186; anniversary of capture of, 1887, 254; mentioned, 17, 23, 68, 88, 157, 163, 212, 253

Newport News, occupation of, 80

Newspapers, capture of Baltimore and, 75, "contrabands" and, 79; Hatteras expedition and, 86; Southern, and Butler, 111-112; Butler's treatment of, in New Orleans, 118-119; criticize Butler on slavery question, 131; attacks of, on Butler, 1863, 139; and prisoner exchange, 141; and Butler's Presidential ambitions, 160; treatment of reporters of, 161

New York, Butler's 1860 trip to, 53; 1863 address in, 138-139; draft riots in, 139; Butler's occupation of, 1864, 163-165; 1865 address in, 179; 1866 election campaign in, 188; mentioned, 39, 65, 67, 122

Nineteenth Corps, 154, 297 (n. 64)

Norfolk, capture of, 140; Butler's administration of, 166 ff.; inquiry into Butler's conduct at, 176-177, 303 (n. 76); mentioned, 82, 99

North Carolina, coastal towns of, 140; reconstruction in, 181; mentioned, 98

Northern Virginia, Army of, 152, 153

Northern Pacific Railroad, 316 (n. 63)

Nottingham, New Hampshire, 17

Oath of allegiance, requirement of, 116, 285 (n. 77, 78)

Ohio, vote of thanks of legislature of, 291 (n. 7)

Opelousas Railroad, opening of, 109

Ord, Edward O. C., appointment of, 155; injuries of, 156; presides over Norfolk inquiry, 303 (n. 76)

Ould, Robert, negotiates with Butler, 142 ff.

Owen, Robert Dale, compromise plan of, 184

Packard, S. B., 236, 238

Palmerston, Lord, and General Order No. 28, 112

Panic of 1873, effects of, 226, 230

Parton, James, writes Butler's biography, 139, 158; mentioned, 283 (n. 12)

### INDEX

Pass Christian, Mississippi, expedition to, 100
Penal institutions, reorganization of, 241; Butler and, 248
Pendleton, George H., monetary theories of, 306 (n. 30)
People's Party, 253
Perkins claim, hinders purchase of Alaska, 210, 310 (n. 44)
Perryville, Maryland, 66, 73.
Petersburg, Virginia, battles at, 148 ff., 151, 152-153, 156, 295 (n. 18), 301, (n. 30)
Phelps, J. W., commands at Ship Island, 99; and slavery, 131
Phelps, Dodge & Company, attack on, 229
Philadelphia, radical convention in, 186; Johnson convention in, 186; Grant convention in, 315 (n. 53); mentioned, 65, 67
*Philadelphia* (steamer), 300 (n. 1)
Phillips, Eugenia, arrest of, 117-118, 286 (n. 92, 93)
Phillips, Wendell, supports Butler, 221-222, 223
Pierce, Ebenezer W., at Big Bethel, 81, 275 (n. 34, 38)
Pierce, Franklin, Butler's relations with, 40, 41, 42, 43, 44; mentioned, 45
Pierpont, Francis H., clashes with Butler, 167-169, 174
Pierrepont, Edwards, 286 (n. 85)
Pittsburgh, radical convention in, 186, 305 (n. 50)
Plymouth, North Carolina, loss of, 148
Plymouth, Noah, defeat of nomination of, 246; manages Butler's 1884 campaign, 251, 324 (n. 48)
Polk, James K., 31
Pollard, Edward, 145
Poll tax, Butler's attacks upon, 246, 247
Pomeroy, M. M., berates Butler, 207, 257 (n. 2), 259 (n. 3), 309 (n. 22)
Poor relief, in New Orleans, 109-110, 119-120, 133; in Norfolk, 167

Pope, John, 135
Popular Sovereignty, Douglas' advocacy of, 43, 46; Butler's attitude toward, 51, 52-53; Southern opposition to, 54 ff., mentioned, 32
Port Royal, South Carolina, 99, 283 (n. 17)
Porter, David D., and origin of New Orleans expedition, 93 ff., 278 (n. 35); and reduction of forts, 102-104; quarrels with Butler, 103-104, 254, 289 (n. 53); accuses Butler of corruption, 124, 130; and Vicksburg campaign, 129-130; and Fort Fisher expedition 170-173; and Grant, 254, 362 (n. 56)
Portsmouth, New Hampshire, Butler's meeting with Chandler in, 252
Portsmouth, Virginia, capture of, 82, 140
Potomac, Army of the, dislike for Butler of, 146; strategy of, 147, 150 ff.; crossing of James by, 152; siege of Petersburg by, 156
Potter Committee, Butler's service on, 238, 242
Powderboat, see *Louisiana*
Presidency, Butler's chances for, 138, 139, 158, 159, 160 ff., 165, 186, 249, 250 ff., 365 (n. 31), 314 (n. 32), 315 (n. 50)
*Princeton* (steamer), 300 (n. 1)
Prisoners of war, exchange of, 140-145; efforts to free, 146; Butler disclaims responsibility for suffering of, 175, 176, 193
Prohibition, party for, 222; advocacy of, 223; appearance of party for, in 1884, 253
Prussia, troubles of consul of, 127, 288 (n. 39, 40)
Pryor, Roger A., supports Butler, 322 (n. 47)
Publicity, Butler's flair for, 11, 32, 49, 140, 199, 221, 223, 230, 256; Butler's search for, 73, 139, 140, 146, 161
Public Credit Act, 1869, 218
Public lands, Butler's plans for, 239

*Punch,* quoted on General Order No. 28, 112

Quarantine, Butler at, 106; establishment of, in New Orleans, 120-121

Radical Republicans, Butler's relations with, 87, 92, 95, 130, 134, 137, 138, 154, 175, 176, 179, 186; and emancipation, 83; dislike for McClellan of, 95; and election of 1864, 158-167; assassination of Lincoln and, 178; opposition to Johnson of, 182 ff., 194 ff.; victory of, in 1866, 188-189; and reconstruction, 179 ff., 190; woo Grant, 193; impeach Johnson, 194 ff.; deplore rift between Butler and Grant, 205

Railroads, Butler and, 225; Butler's support of land grants to, 250

Randall, Samuel, and election of 1884, 251

Randolph, George W., at Big Bethel, 80

Rantoul, Robert, Sr., in constitutional convention, 38

Reconstruction, Butler's attitude toward, 138-139, 165, 178, 184, 212, 236, 303 (n. 78); Lincoln's attitude toward, 132; Butler's leadership in, 212-216, 221; Grant and, 214, 215-216; end of, 235-236; Joint Comittee on, 182, 183, 184, 185; House Committee on, 214

Reconstruction Acts, 189, 190, 193

Reeder, Andrew H., 43

Reform, Butler's advocacy of, 11, 38, 241; success of, 38, 256

Relay House, capture of, 73

Religion, Butler's attitude toward, 21, 24, 248-249

Republican party, and Negro rights, 7; formation of, 42; Butler campaigns for, 140; Butler asks for support of, 1864, 160; Butler joins, 182; financial policies of, 205, 229; Butler's power in, 208; efforts to establish in South, 212; Butler loses control of, 235; Butler's relations with leaders of, 236; adopts Butler's reforms, 241; repudiates Butler, 241. *See also* Election campaigns

*Republican* (Springfield), and 1871 campaign, 222-223; concedes Butler's usefulness, 241

Resumption, Butler's pledge of support of, 232; Butler's views on, 237

Rice, Alexander H., in 1871 campaign, 224; Butler's efforts to defeat candidacy of, 231

Richardson, W. A., 211, 316 (n. 60)

Richmond, Wistar's raid on, 146; plans for capture of, 147; siege of, 149 ff., 158; panic in, 156; capture of, 157; Dahlgren's raid on, 294 (n. 3); mentioned, 77, 80, 86, 88, 95, 101, 115, 124, 140, 142

Richmond, Dean, Butler's overtures to, 267 (n. 16)

Rivers and Harbors Bill, 1882, 244

Robinson, George D., defeats Butler, 249

Robinson, William S., Butler's fight with, 20; Butler's attack on, 223; campaigns against Butler, 224, 226; 1863 praise of, 291 (n. 10); dismissal of, 313 (n. 13)

Rockingham, New Hampshire, pro-Butler resolutions of Republicans of, 298 (n. 3)

Ross, Edmund G., votes against impeachment, 203-204

Russell, Lord John, attacks General Order No. 28, 112

Russell, William H., quoted on Hatteras expedition, 86

St. Charles Hotel, negotiations at, 108, 109; 283 (n. 12)

St. John, John, and election of 1884, 253

Salary Grab, 225-226

Salem, Massachusetts, Light Artillery, 94, 277 (n. 12), 279 (n. 47)

Sanborn, F. B., row with Butler of, 223

# INDEX

Sanborn, John D., supports Butler in 1863, 137; contracts of, 228-229
San Domingo, proposed annexation of, 209-210
Sanitation, Butler's interest in, in New Orleans, 120-121; 133
Schenck, Robert C., 221
Schofield, John M., 140
Schurz, Carl, 235
Schouler, William, Butler's fight with, 26, in Constitutional Convention, 38; as Adjutant General, 62 ff.; opposes Butler in 1866, 187-188; dismissal of, 189, 313 (n. 13)
Science, Butler's interest in, 21-22, 26
Scott, Dred, case of, 52-53, 199
Scott, Winfield S., and relief of Washington, 70-71; and seizure of Baltimore, 72-73, 74, 75, 273 (n. 63); and "contrabands," 79; instructions to Butler from, 79-80; relieves Butler, 1861, 84
Secession, spread of, 59 ff.; Butler's opinion of, 136; demand for punishment for, 138-139
Second Corps, at Petersburg, 152
Secret ballot, Butler's advocacy of, 30, 38, 246; passage of legislation for, 35, 247
Seddon, James, and prisoner exchanges, 143
Senate, coalition and, 35; function of, in impeachment trial, 199-200; Butler's 1868 fight with, 213; and Simmons appointment, 227-228; Massachusetts elections for, 229, 234-235
Sequestration, Butler's orders for, in Louisiana, 130
Seventh Regiment (New York), and relief of Washington, 66, 69, 70
Seward, William H., Butler's appeal for assistance to, 92; defends General Order No. 28, 112-113; and New Orleans consuls, 125 ff., 128; and radicals, 130; hostility to Butler of, 132; and Butler's recall from New Orleans, 132, 135; replies to Hicks, 271 (n. 18); Butler as suggested replacement for, 291 (n. 11)
Seymour, Horatio, and election of 1864, 164, 165; Butler's attacks on, 1866, 188; and election of 1860, 268 (n. 36)
Shaffer, J. Wilson, acts as Butler's agent, 137, 162; Lincoln's memorandum to, 159; distrusts Johnson, 180; appointed Governor of Utah, 212; death of, 314; and Butler's military abilities, 291 (n. 18)
Shaw, Lemuel, 28
Shepley, George F., and recruiting of volunteers, 90; accompanies Butler to Washington, 96; command of, 99; appointed Military Commandant of New Orleans, 114; appointed Military Governor of Louisiana, 126; sailing orders to, 280 (n. 65)
Sherman, John, and impeachment of Johnson, 199, 200
Sherman, Thomas W., 95
Sherman, William T., and election of 1864, 162; and Johnson, 194, 200; mentioned, 146, 147, 172, 173, 303 (n. 72)
Shields, James, supported by Butler, 238
Ship Island, Butler's assignment to, 92, 93, 94, 278 (n. 33), 279 (n. 54); description of, 99; troops at, 100; incarceration of secessionists at, 117; speculations at, 122
Sigel, Franz, 146, 147
Silver, alleged theft of, in New Orleans, 124; demand for free coinage of, 237
Simmons, William A., appointment of, 227-228, 235; negotiates for Butler, 232, 318 (n. 103); fails to secure reappointment, 237; supports Butler in 1879, 242-243
Sisters of Charity, 119
Sixth Regiment (Massachusetts), 72

Slavery, Butler's attitude toward, 10, 49, 50, 52-53, 57, 84, 135-136; Massachusetts Democratic party and, 29, 31, 32, 35, 39, 41, 42, 43; in territories, 32, 43, 46, 52-53; and Compromise of 1850, 39; and disruption of Democratic party, 54-57; and "contrabands," 79 ff.; Confiscation Acts and, 131

Slave trade, Butler's attack on, 56

Slave uprisings, Butler's offer of help against, 68, 72; fear of, in Louisiana, 130

Smith Brothers, gold of, 117, 176, 286 (n. 85)

Smith, Samuel F., at Waterbury College, 21

Smith, William, 23

Smith, William F., joins Army of the James, 147; in Petersburg campaign, 149, 151, 152, 153; characteristics of, 149; and Butler's attempted removal, 153-154, 155; suggests plan to Lincoln, 294 (n. 4); attacked by malaria, 301 (n. 50); accuses Butler of blackmail, 297 (n. 61); mentioned, 295 (n. 22, 33), 297 (n. 54)

Snead, Edward K., arrest of, 168

Soulé, Pierre, and surrender of New Orleans, 105; negotiates with Butler, 108, 109, 283 (n. 5); arrest of, 117, 118

South, Butler's attitude toward, 1859, 50-51; 1863, 138-139; feeling against Butler in, 111 ff; Republican party in, 212; electoral vote of, 234; withdrawal of troops from, 235

South Carolina, secession of, 59 ff.; commissioners of, 59-60, 269 (n. 57); electoral vote of, 234; withdrawal of troops from, 235

Spain, troubles of representatives of, in New Orleans, 127, 288 (n. 40)

Speculations, Butler's, in Louisiana, 122-123; Butler's interest in, 254

Spoons, alleged theft of, 124; in campaign of 1874, 230

Spottsylvania Court House, engagement at, 150

Springfield, Massachusetts, Butler's address in, 1871, 223; 1873 Republican convention in, 226-227; mentioned, 65

Stalwarts, and Hayes, 235, 236

Stanbery, Henry, defends Johnson, 199, 201

Standard Oil Trust, Butler's attack on, 250

Stanton, Edwin M., in Buchanan's cabinet, 60; and New Orleans expedition, 96, 280 (n. 65); relations of, with Butler, 126, 132, 135, 305 (n. 41); and prisoner exchange, 142 ff., 293 (n. 54); dismissal of, 193, 194, 199; applicability of Tenure of Office Act to, 198, 199, 200; and South Carolina commissioners, 269 (n. 57); mentioned, 106, 137, 163, 167, 180

Stanton, Elizabeth Cady, 313 (n. 11)

Statue, to Butler, controversy about, 256

Stevens, Thaddeus, relations of Butler with, 138, 176, 182-183, 185, 195; leads Congress, 182; views of, 185, 189; and impeachment of Johnson, 194 ff., 201; death of, 212; and Butler's recall from New Orleans, 289 (n. 67); *Herald* interview with, 305 (n. 42)

Stewart, William M., compromise plan of, 184

Storey, Moorfield, opposes Butler, 248, 249, 321 (n. 54)

Stowe, Harriet Beecher, 277 (n. 77)

Straw, Ezekiel A., at Lowell High School, 19-20

Strikes, Butler's attitude toward, 32, 219, 239; Hayes policy toward, 238-239; Butler's plans for settlement of, 251, 325 (n. 69)

Stringham, Silas M., and Hatteras expedition, 85, 86, 276 (n. 69)

Suffrage, Negro, Butler's views on, 183, 184-185, 187; radicals and, 189, 212

# INDEX

Sumner, Charles, and coalition, 35, 39; in Constitutional Convention, 38; joins Republican party, 42; Brooks' attack on, 47, 265 (n. 32); Andrew appeals to, 94, 279 (n. 42, 50); breaks with Grant, 209-210; and Civil Rights Bill, 7, 9-10, 215-216, 230-231; and campaign of 1871, 224; supports Greeley, 224; censured, 226, and Simmons appointment, 227; Butler wants help from, 303 (n. 79); mentioned, 63, 217, 221

Supreme Court, Butler's admission to, 31; and slavery, 52-53, 54

Surratt, Mary E., execution of, 191

Swann, Thomas, row with Butler of, 215

Swift Creek, engagement at, 149

Talbot, Thomas, defeats Butler, 241; endorses reforms advocated by Butler, 320 (n. 42); wages paid by, 321 (n. 54)

*Tallapoosa*, U.S.S., negotiations on, 252

Tammany Hall, Butler's attacks on, 188; in 1884, 251

Tarbox, John K., opposes Butler, 232-233; appointment of, 322 (n. 16)

Tariff, popularity of, in Lowell, 29; Butler's views on, 30, 48, 49, 251, 254, 324 (n. 57)

Tax reform, advocated by Butler, 244

Taylor, Zachary, 32

Temperance, advocates of, support Butler, 222; Butler's connection with, 267 (n. 1)

Ten-hour day, petition for, 1842, 30; Butler's ticket for, 1851, 35-37; Butler's advocacy of, 38, 40, 227; enforcement of, 241; for railroad workers, 246

Tenth Corps, 151

Tenure of Office Act, enactment of, 190; Johnson and, 194; and impeachment of Johnson, 195, 197, 198, 199, 200, 201; repeal of, 208, 209; constitutionality of, 200, 207 (n. 40)

Terry, Alfred H., and Fort Fisher expedition, 172, 175, 303 (n. 72)

Tewkesbury, Poorhouse in, 246, 247-248, 249

Thibodaux, Louisiana, capture of, 130

Third Regiment (Massachusetts), 72

Thirtieth Regiment (Massachusetts), 280 (n. 68)

Thirty-first Regiment (Massachusetts), 280 (n. 68)

Thomas, Lorenzo, and impeachment of Johnson, 194, 198, 200

Thomas, Stephen, and recruiting of volunteers, 90

Thompson, Charles P., defeats Butler in 1874, 230; Butler's endorsement of, 243

Tilden, Samuel, J., 233, 234

Tilton, Theodore, attends Butler dinner, 1864, 165; and Beecher trial, 317 (n. 84)

*Times* (London), 86, 112

*Times* (New York), quoted concerning Butler's loyalty, 60-61; and Big Bethel, 81

Tod, David, 56

*Transcript* (Boston), and Big Bethel, 81; attacks Butler, 223

Tremont Temple, Butler meeting at, 58; John Brown meeting at, 90

*Trent* affair, 94

*Tribune* (New York), and New Orleans, 118; and impeachment of Johnson, 202; and Big Bethel, 275 (n. 34); troubles of correspondent of, 301 (n. 30)

*True Delta* (New Orleans), seizure of, 109; editorial policy of, 118

Twenty-sixth Regiment (Massachusetts), 280 (n. 68)

Twenty-eighth Regiment (Massachusetts), 277 (n. 12), 280 (n. 68)

Twenty-ninth Regiment (Massachusetts), 278 (n. 32)

Twiggs, David, 124

Tyler, John, and Big Bethel, 275 (n. 33)

Unionists, position of, in New Orleans, 108; election of, in New Orleans, 132; services of, 286 (n. 87)
Union Pacific Railroad, and Crédit Mobilier, 225; funding of debts of, 238-239; Butler's services to, 313 (n. 17)
Usher, Roland G., 211, 242-243

Van Buren, Martin, 29-30, 31
Van Lew, Elizabeth, 146, 294 (n. 3)
Veterans, Butler's popularity with, 222; Butler advocates pensions for Confederate, 242
Vice-Presidency, Butler considered for, 158, 159-160, 298 (n. 3)
Vicksburg, campaign for, 128-130; capture of, 140
Virginia, Brown's invasion of, 50; House of Delegates of, and prisoner exchange, 143; reconstruction in, 312 (n. 76)
Virginia and North Carolina, Department of, Butler assumes command of, 140; Butler's recall from, 173; mentioned, 155
Virginia, S. E., Department of, 273 (n. 80)
Vox Populi (Lowell), 30

Wade, Benjamin F., relations of Butler with, 95, 162; and Lincoln, 162; dominates Joint Committee on Conduct of War, 175; confers about Johnson's cabinet, 179; opinions about Johnson of, 180; Presidential chances of, 198, 202; projected cabinet of, 202; mentioned, 213
Wade-Davis Bill, 297 (n. 56)
Wallace, Lew, 146
War Department, and Butler's speculations, 123; and Butler's military achievements, 128 ff.; Butler's hopes for, 161, 165, 291 (n. 11)
Warland, John, row of, with Butler, 36-37

Warren, Charles, 24
Warrington, see Robinson, W. S.
Washburn, William B., nomination of, 1871, 224; 1873, 226; elected U. S. Senator, 229; adopts reforms advocated by Butler, 318 (n. 112)
Washington, D. C., Southern atmosphere of, 59, 65; relief of, 1861, 64-71, 177; Early's threat to, 154; Butler's residences in, 212, 231, 255; Treaty of, 221; mentioned, 31, 45, 46-47, 53, 59, 73, 75, 76, 82, 83, 84, 86, 89, 91, 92, 94, 95, 98, 103, 117, 124, 126, 128, 130, 135, 136, 138, 140, 141, 142, 143, 154, 160, 174, 179, 213, 242
Waterville, Maine, College at, 21-22
Weaver, James B., Butler's support of, 254; mentioned, 253
Webster, Daniel, 23, 35
Webster, W. P., appointed consul in Frankfurt, 212
Weitzel, Godfrey, gives Farragut benefit of experience, 100-101; campaign of, in Western Louisiana, 130; at Fort Fisher, 171, 172; receives command of XIX Corps, 297 (n. 64)
Welles, Gideon, and origin of New Orleans expedition, 93, 278 (n. 35), 280 (n. 65); supports Pierpont, 168; sees Butler, 1867, 193; and Butler's assignment to New York, 292 (n. 48); skepticism of, 294 (n. 10), 302 (n. 37); and Johnson's 1869 New Years reception, 310 (n. 34)
Western Bay State Regiment, 91, 280 (n. 71)
West Point, Butler's rejection by, 20-21; Butler's dislike for, 20-21, 45, 174; appointment of Butler to Board of Visitors of, 45, 53; Butler's defense of cadets threatened with expulsion at, 211; Ben Israel Butler at, 242; appointment of Negro cadet to, 311 (n. 70); mentioned, 133, 149

# INDEX

Whig party, Butler's attitude toward, 20, 29, 30; power of, 29-30; coalition and, 34-35; and Secret Ballot Act, 38; Johnson's hostility to, 180; mentioned, 235, 262 (n. 24). See also Election campaigns
Whitney, James G., 49, 53, 58
Wilderness, Battle of the, 150
Wilkes, Charles, 94
Wilkes, George, urges reconciliation between Butler and Grant, 205-206
Williams, Thomas, manager in impeachment trial, 196
Williams, General Thomas, command of, 99; in Vicksburg campaign, 128-129; death of, 129
Williams College, confers degree upon Butler, 186; 1883 address at, 248-249
Williamsburg, Virginia, 140
Wilmington, North Carolina, efforts to close port of, 171, 172
Wilson, Henry, and coalition, 35; in Constitutional Convention, 38; joins Republican party, 42; Butler's warning against McClellan to, 138; and campaign of 1871, 224; in 1872, 224; mentioned, 63, 217, 225, 226, 262 (n. 8)
Wilson, James F., manager in impeachment trial, 196
Wilson's Wharf, occupation of, 294 (n. 14)
Winans, Ross, arrest of, 74; release of, 76, 126

Winthrop, Theodore, describes Butler's troops, 69; and "contrabands," 79; and Big Bethel, 80, 81; death of, 81; mentioned, 270 (n. 4), 274 (n. 19)
Wistar, Isaac, 146, 294 (n. 2)
Woman order, see General Order No. 28
Woman Suffrage, Butler's sympathy for, 219, 223, 246, 256, 313 (n. 11)
Wood, Fernando, 158
Woodbury, Levi, Butler's support of, 32
Woodhull, Victoria, 219, 313 (n. 11)
Wool, John E., supersedes Butler, 84, 276 (n. 60); mentioned, 86, 273 (n. 80)
Woolley, Charles, and impeachment vote, 203, 308 (n. 75)
Worcester, Massachusetts, 1871 Republican convention in, 224; 1878 Democratic convention in, 240-241; 1880 Democratic convention in, 243; mentioned, 47
*World* (New York), attack on Butler by, 164

Yellow fever, John Butler's death from, 17; in New Orleans, 120-121, 132; in Norfolk, 166-167
Yorktown, Virginia, 80
Young, John R., and impeachment of Johnson, 202; mentioned, 211

Zacharie, Isachar, mission to New Orleans of, 291 (n. 19)